*Also by Variorum:*

**Ed. MALCOLM BARBER**
The Military Orders: Fighting for the Faith and
Caring for the Sick

**Ed. BENJAMIN Z. KEDAR**
The Horns of Hattin

**BERNARD HAMILTON**
The Latin Church in the Crusader States:
The Secular Church

*In the Collected Studies Series:*

**HANS EBERHARD MAYER**
Kings and Lords in the Latin Kingdom of Jerusalem

**ALAN FOREY**
Military Orders and Crusades

**JEAN RICHARD**
Croisades et Etats latins d'Orients

**JAMES A. BRUNDAGE**
The Crusades, Holy War and Canon Law

**ANTHONY LUTTRELL**
The Hospitallers in Cyprus, Rhodes,
Greece and the West (1291–1440)

**BENJAMIN Z. KEDAR**
The Franks in the Levant, 11th to 14th Centuries

**MICHEL BALARD**
La Mer Noire et la Romanie génoise, XIIIe–XVe siècles

**W.H. RUDT de COLLENBERG**
Familles de l'Orient latin, XIIe–XIV siècles

**BERNARD HAMILTON**
Monastic Reform, Catharism and the Crusades (900 1300)

**GILES CONSTABLE**
Monks, Hermits and Crusaders in Medieval Europe

**DAVID ABULAFIA**
Italy, Sicily and the Mediterranean, 1100–1500

VARIORUM COLLECTED STUDIES SERIES

# Crusaders and Heretics, 12th–14th Centuries

Dr Malcolm Barber

Malcolm Barber

# Crusaders and Heretics
# 12th–14th Centuries

ASHGATE
VARIORUM

**Published in the Variorum Collected Studies Series by**

Ashgate Publishing Limited
Wey Court East
Union Road
Farnham
Surrey, GU9 7PT
England

Ashgate Publishing Company
110 Cherry Street
Suite 3-1
Burlington
VT 05401-3818
USA

Ashgate website: http://www.ashgate.com

Reprinted 2003

ISBN 0-86078-476-2

**British Library CIP Data**
Barber, Malcolm
Crusaders and Heretics, 12th–14th Centuries
(Variorum Collected Studies Series; CS 498)
I. Title II. Series
940.18

**US Library of Congress CIP Data**
Barber, Malcolm
Crusaders and Heretics, 12th–14th Centuries / Malcolm Barber.
p. cm. — (Collected Studies Series: CS498)
I. Europe—Church history—600–1500. 2. Europe—History—
476–1492. 3. Crusades. 4, Heresies, Christian—History—Middle
Ages, 600–1500. I. Title. II. Series: Collected Studies: CS498.
BR270.B37   1995                              95–15733
270.5—dc20                                    CIP

Transferred to Digital Printing in 2014

MIX
Paper from
responsible sources
FSC
www.fsc.org   FSC® C004959

Printed and bound in Great Britain
by Printondemand-worldwide.com

VARIORUM COLLECTED STUDIES SERIES CS498

# CONTENTS

This volume contains x + 289 pages

# INTRODUCTION

The central theme of these articles is the study of a society which believed itself to be threatened. Often the threat was much more limited than contemporaries thought, or in reality came from quite a different source. Indeed, sometimes it did not exist at all, but the attitudes displayed are no less interesting because of these misapprehensions. In the twelfth and thirteenth centuries two organised institutions were created to combat these threats: the military orders against external enemies, the Muslims, and later the 'pagans' of eastern Europe; and the Inquisition, against internal subversion, epitomised for many by the Cathars. In the cases of the trial of the Templars between 1307 and 1314, and the alleged plot to overthrow Christendom in 1321, the beliefs in external and internal threats coalesced, with explosive results.

The institutions which these fears produced left valuable evidence of their activities (even though the main Templar archive in the east was probably destroyed by the Ottomans in 1571), and this documentation forms much of the raw material for their study. However, such evidence need not only be used in the most obvious ways, as Emmanuel Le Roy Ladurie showed in his sociological study of the early fourteenth-century peasant community of Montaillou in the Pyrenees, a book which is based on inquisitorial records, but is about neither heresy nor the Inquisition. Inquisitorial depositions are valuable material for the social historian (III), just as the government propaganda pumped out to convince a sceptical audience of the guilt of the Templars can also offer insights into the contemporary world view (VII). Nevertheless, reaction to supposed threats was not always through these specialist structures, since sometimes the threat arose with insufficient warning or was too temporary to be encompassed by them. Thus the 'peasant crusades' of 1251 and 1320 succeeded in generating a powerful internal impetus before they were eventually dispersed by governmental and municipal forces (V and IX). Their destruction was accompanied by much strident condemnation from the uncomprehending clerical literary caste which wrote up their activities (IX), and in these cases the chronicle sources are often more valuable as witnesses to the attitudes of the ruling classes than they are as observers of the real nature of the peasant unrest. The two earliest pieces arose from a series of short biographies of the Grand Masters of the Temple, which formed the subject of a Ph.D. thesis submitted to the University of Nottingham in 1968 (I and II). Three further articles represent attempts to show the interaction of the Templars and the crusades with their environment. 'The Social Context of the Templars' (VIII) and 'Supplying the Crusader States' (XII) are intended to illustrate how events in the east could have profound effects on the western base of the Order of the Temple. There seems little doubt that, as Giles Constable argued, the crusades were a major promoter of the fundamental socio-economic changes taking place in western Christendom in the twelfth and thirteenth centuries. Attitudes to the Latin conquest of large parts of the Byzantine Empire after 1204 (X) demonstrate another aspect of the complex relationship between western society and the crusades, suggesting that however the canonists might view the spiritual benefits accruing to the crusader, many contemporaries nevertheless maintained a fairly clear hierarchy of crusading priorities in their minds. Papal propaganda in the thirteenth century did little to undermine this scale of values.

Research on the last Grand Master of the Temple, James of Molay, leads naturally to the trial of the Templars as a whole which, thanks to the diligent notaries employed by the Inquisition, produced a large body of depositions from individuals who might otherwise have left no historical record, although for most of them, their brief fame was bought at a heavy price of squalid imprisonment, torture and sometimes death by burning. Such a sensational end gave rise to many myths about the survival of members of the Order in secret, together with some of their treasured possessions. These myths were given a new lease of life by the masonic organisations of the late eighteenth century and they still have considerable mileage left in them now. The piece on the Turin Shroud (VI) was intended to emphasise that in cases like this scientific evidence is not sufficient on its own for, without a convincing historical provenance, the whole shaky edifice will fall down. The Templars' trial did, however, induce one quite substantial aftershock. In 1321 the lepers of France were arrested and tortured, having been accused of poisoning the wells at the behest of the two elements which medieval Christians had been taught to hate and distrust - the Jews and the Muslims. This was, in some ways, the culmination of the fears raised in the trial, although, in the end, the panic rose to too high a pitch to be sustained (IV). For the Jews, nevertheless, it was simply an intensification of the insecurity in which they always lived; only the previous year the Pastoureax, frustrated in their attempts to reach the Holy Land, had turned upon the Jewish communities of Languedoc and northern Spain (V).

During the crusader era, indeed, the Jews were the perennial victims, but the attack on the lepers was a new phenomenon, for attitudes towards lepers in Latin Christendom were deeply ambiguous. In the crusader east the Order of Saint Lazarus had a leper as Master and a mixed membership of lepers and healthy brothers; by the 1220s it had developed into a military organisation as well (XIII). While the knights of Saint Lazarus were not the most honoured members of crusader society, they nevertheless retained their dignity and fulfilled distinct functional roles, in sharp contrast to the persecution of 1321.

The trial of the Templars was of course a distortion of the original aims of the Inquisition, which had come into being in the 1230s largely to combat the Cathars. The depositions of the Cathars are the foundation of two further articles, neither of which is concerned with the Inquisition as such, but rather represent attempts to reconstruct the social milieu of Languedoc in which Catharism flourished (III and XI). The study of the geographical and social patterns of heresy in the twelfth and thirteenth centuries is as interesting to the medievalist as the efforts to find explanations for the spread of the Reformation or the distribution of witchcraft are to the early modern historian.

MALCOLM BARBER

*University of Reading*
*February 1995*

*PUBLISHER'S NOTE: The articles in this volume, as in all others in the Collected Studies Series, have not been given a new, continuous pagination. In order to avoid confusion, and to facilitate their use where these same studies have been referred to elsewhere, the original pagination has been maintained wherever possible.*

*Each article has been given a Roman number in order of appearance, as listed in the Contents. This number is repeated on each page and quoted in the index entries.*

*References to corrections made in Corrigenda at the end of articles I & II are indicated by an asterisk in the margin by the line to be altered.*

## ACKNOWLEDGEMENTS

Grateful acknowledgement is made to the following persons, institutions, and publishers for kindly permitting the reproduction of the studies included in this volume: the editors of *Studia Monastica*, Abadia de Montserrat, Barcelona (I, II); the editors of *Reading Medieval Studies*, Graduate Centre for Medieval Studies, University of Reading (III); The Historical Association, London (IV); the editors of *The Journal of Ecclesiastical History* and Cambridge University Press (V); Rev. Mgr. Robert Trisco, editor of *The Catholic Historical Review*, Washington, D.C. (VI, XIII); Dr David Abulafia, editor of *The Journal of Medieval History* and Elsevier Science, Amsterdam (VII); The Royal Historical Society, London (VIII); Professor Norman Ravitch, editor of the *Proceedings of the Western Society for French History*, University of California, Riverside (IX); the editors of *Latins and Greeks in the Eastern Mediterranean after 1204*, London, 1989, and Frank Cass and Co., London (X); Professor Christopher Harper-Bill and Dr Ruth Harvey, editors of *The Ideals and Practice of Knighthood*, vol.3, Woodbridge, Suffolk, 1990, and Boydell and Brewer Ltd. (XI); and Yad Izhak Ben-Zvi, Jerusalem (XII).

# I

# THE ORIGINS OF THE ORDER OF THE TEMPLE

The armies of the First Crusade finally captured the city of Jerusalem on 15th July, 1099, after a siege lasting more than five weeks. In retrospect it can be seen that the crusaders had succeeded against heavy odds. But, once the excitement evoked by the capture of the Holy City had passed, they found themselves faced with new problems. They held a narrow strip of land clinging to the coast, stretching from Antioch in the north, through Tripoli and Jerusalem, to the region of Ascalon in the south. In parts their control was tenuous. The only appreciable progress inland had been made by Baldwin of Boulogne in Edessa. None of these territories was easily defensible. Aleppo, Hama, Homs, Baalbek and Damascus remained uncaptured on the eastern flank. The Franks had few men to defend and control these territories. Many had been lost during the crusade itself; many others now returned to the west, their vows fulfilled. Dr. Smail has shown that they were never able to muster sufficient trained men for both a large field army and an adequate garrison for their castles.[1] Although the position improved at certain periods, the problem of manpower continued to plague the crusader states throughout the two hundred years of the Frankish occupation. King Thoros of Armenia visited the kingdom of Jerusalem in the 1160's, and was shocked by this situation. He proposed sending 30,000 Armenians to defend and colonize the country. Although the project fell through because the Armenians were unwilling to pay the tithes demanded by the Latin clergy, it is nevertheless a striking comment on the manpower situation even at this date.[2]

However, even though the numbers of those who settled permanently were never great, the capture of Jerusalem inevitably encouraged pilgrimages from the west. A conscientious pilgrim would expect to

---

[1] R. C., SMAIL, *Crusading Warfare. 1097-1193*, Cambridge, 1956, chap. 5.
[2] See J. PRAWER, *Colonization Activities in the Latin Kingdom of Jerusalem*, in *Revue Belge de philologie et d'histoire*, 29 (1951), 1086.

I

visit, apart from Jerusalem itself, Nazareth, Mount Sion, the Mount of Olives, Bethlehem, Hebron, Bethany, the River Jordan, and Tiberias.[3] But, in the early twelfth century, men could seldom be spared to patrol these pilgrim routes, nor to escort new arrivals from the ports. In 1102-3, the Norse pilgrim, Saewulf, was horrified by the journey from the port of Jaffa to Jerusalem. Saracen robbers roamed the rocky mountains, waiting for bands of pilgrims. Stragglers were picked off and robbed and killed. Saewulf saw members of other parties lying unburied along the route, the corpses gnawed by wild animals. The ground was often hard and unyielding with little, if any, topsoil. Men did not linger to undertake the difficult task of burying the pilgrims in conditions such as these. Instead, they passed on rapidly for fear of being attacked themselves. Little provision seems to have been made along the route to supply the pilgrim with food, and above all, water, and those who survived the journey seem to have arrived at Jerusalem in a severely distressed condition. The brigands made sure that the pilgrims had no access to the natural water that was available.[4]

Three years later the Russian Abbot Daniel spoke of frequent raids by Egyptian soldiers from the city of Ascalon on the Church of St. George, about seven miles from Jaffa. There was a considerable number of springs in the region which apparently made it a convenient place for an overnight stop. Moreover, St. George had been martyred there and the zealous pilgrim was anxious not to miss any place of interest. Such camps were easy targets for raiding parties. The roads around Jerusalem itself were also extremely hazardous. Pilgrims visiting the Jordan were often ambushed, or if they escaped the brigands, sometimes died from sunstroke or from thirst. It was unwise to travel to Bethlehem and Hebron without a large escort. But such an escort was not always available. Daniel shows that the prudent traveller would have to wait until a company had gathered. He counted himself fortunate that he was always able to find such a company. When he visited the Sea of Galilee he attached himself to King Baldwin's campaign army. The abbot took the advice of his guides and did not visit Mount Lebanon because of the danger of being attacked. He had to content himself with a description from

[3] *Guide-Book to Palestine*, trans. J. H. BERNARD, *Palestine Pilgrims' Text Society*, VI, London, 1894. This is an anonymous work, written circa 1350, which gives a comprehensive guide to the principal centres for pilgrims.
[4] *An Account of the Pilgrimage of Saewulf to Jerusalem and the Holy Land in the years 1102 and 1103*, trans. W. R. B. BROWNLOW, Bishop of Clifton, London, 1892, P.P.T.S., IV, pp. 8-9.

a distance. Lesser perils included lions and other wild animals which lived in the Jordan valley.[5] The situation had not improved when Ekkehard, the Abbot of Aura, made a pilgrimage, sometime between 1110 and 1115. He too speaks of ambushes and pillaging along the pilgrim routes.[6] It was as a response to the conditions prevailing along these routes that, in 1119, a group of knights, led by Hugh of Payens and Godfrey of St. Omer, dedicated themselves to protect pilgrims visiting the Holy Places.

\* \* \*

The village of Payens or Payns is situated in the département of the Aube, on the left bank of the Seine, about eight miles north of Troyes. In about 1100, Hugh, Count of Champagne, renounced the rights he held over the village of Rouilly-Saint-Loup. Among the witnesses was a *'Hugo de Paeniciis'*.[7] A grant of lands to the abbey of Montièramey by the same count on 21st October, 1100, also shows *'Hugo de Peanz'* as a witness.[8] It seems likely that this is the man who later became the first Grand Master of the Temple, although of course it is possible that the Hugh of Payens mentioned here was a relative, perhaps his father or an uncle. The Abbé Petel points out that in this document he is found in quite exalted company. Miles, Count of Bar-sur-Seine, Andrew, Count of Ramerupt, Guy of Vignory, Hilduin of Villemar, Gobert of Châtillon, and Ponce of Pont-sur-Seine, were all men of standing in the county.[9] This serves to show that if Hugh was not related to the count of Champagne as some authorities have thought,[10] then he may well have been one of his officers at some period.[11] Certainly, he was more than a minor knight. Roserot, in his dictionary of Champagne, says that the family had possessions in the chatellanies of Isles, Pont-sur-Seine, and Troyes at Estissac, Fontvannes, Montigny, Onjon, and in the wood of St. Mary, near Cérilly

---

[5] *The Pilgrimage of the Russian Abbot Daniel in the Holy Land, 1106-7 A.D.*, trans. C. W. Wilson, London, 1888, P.P.T.S., IV, pp. 9, 26, 42-3, 48-50, 56-7, 59, 61, 65-6, 72.

[6] *Ekkehardi Hierosolymita*, ed. H. Hagenmeyer, Tübingen, 1877, p. 309.

[7] Ch. Lalore, *Collection des principaux cartulaires du diocèse de Troyes*, I, Cartulaire de l'Abbaye de Saint-Loup, Paris, 1875, no. 3, pp. 11-14.

[8] *Ibid.*, VII, Cartulaire de l'Abbaye de Montièramey, Paris, 1890, no. 18, pp. 23-5.

[9] Abbé A. Petel, *La Commanderie de Payns et ses dépendances à Lavières, à Saint-Masmin et au Pavillon (Bar-sur-Aube)*, extract from *La Revue champenoise et bourguignonne*, 1904, p. ix.

[10] J. Richard, *Le Royaume Latin de Jérusalem*, Paris, 1953, p. 105.

[11] E. Mannier, *Ordre de Malte. Les Commanderies du Grand-Prieuré de France*, Paris, 1872, p. xiii; T. Boutiot, *Histoire de la ville de Troyes et de la Champagne meridionale*, I, Troyes-Paris, 1870, p. 195.

(Yonne),[12] although he supplies no evidence for this. However, one '*Hugo de Pedano Montiniaco dominus*' appears in the *Cartulaire de Molesme* as a witness to grants in 1085-90, 1100, and 1102.[13]

The names *Péanz, Paens, Paence, Paenz, Paains, Paiens, Payens* and *Paienz*, in French, and *Peancium, Peancia, Peantium, Paencium, Paganus* and *Pagani*, in Latin, are all medieval variants on the name of Payns.[14] It is less clear whether Pedano or Pedans qualifies. Theories that he came from Haute-Provence,[15] or was of Neapolitan origin,[16] can therefore reasonably be dismissed.

Almost nothing is known about his family. It can be assumed that he was married, for he had a son, Theobald, who became abbot of St. Colombe-de-Sens in 1139 and died in 1148.[17] The '*Guido de Peantio*' mentioned in a document made sometime between 1131 and 1140, could have been another relative, perhaps a brother or another son.[18] Quite possibly Hugh took the Cross after the death of his wife.

Hugh does not appear again until 1113. Here once again he is witness to a donation of Count Hugh to the abbey of Montièramey and he is shown as '*dominus de Peanz*'.[19] There is no mention of him in the cartularies collected by Petel[20] and this author believes that he spent the intervening years in the east on crusade with Hugh of Champagne, who left for the Holy Land in 1104. Several friends, vassals, and knights of Champagne accompanied him on this voyage, and Hugh could well have been one of them. The count returned the following year, but Petel thinks that the absence of Hugh of Payens from the charters of Champagne of this period indicates that he stayed in the east, possibly until 1113.[21] However he does not appear in the charters of the east either in this period, so this theory is far from conclusive. Other writers have thought that he took part in the First Crusade,[22] which is possible, although he was obviously in Cham-

[12] A. ROSEROT, *Dictionnaire historique de la Champagne méridionale (Aube) des origines à 1790*, II, Langres, 1945, p. 1096.
[13] J. LAURENT, *Cartulaires de l'Abbaye de Molesme, 916-1250*, II, Paris, 1911, no. 138, pp. 134-6; no. 230, pp. 214-15; no. 254, p. 237.
[14] E. SOCARD and T. BOUTIOT, *Dictionnaire topographique de l'Aube*, Paris, 1874, pp. 118-19.
[15] L. NIEPCE, *Le Grand-Prieuré d'Auvergne*, Lyons, 1883, pp. 77-8n.
[16] B. L. PAGAN, *Divers ouvrages de Monsieur le comte de Pagan trouvés dans ses Écrits après sa mort*, Paris, 1669, pp. 73-4.
[17] *Gallia Christiana*, 1770, XII, ed. D. DE SAINT-MARTHE, p. 149.
[18] LALORE, *op. cit.*, IV, *Cartulaire de l'Abbaye de la Chapelle-aux-Planches*, Paris, 1878, no. 145, p. 247.
[19] *Ibid.*, VII, no. 18, pp. 30-1.
[20] PETEL, *op. cit.*, *Templiers et Hospitaliers dans le diocèse de Troyes*, 1910, extract from *Mémoires de la Société académique de l'Aube*, 1909-10, LXXIII and LXXIV.
[21] PETEL, *La Commanderie de Payns*, p. x.
[22] J. CHARPENTIER, *L'Ordre des Templiers*, Paris, 1944, pp. 16-17.

I

pagne in October, 1100. Richard does not think that he left until 1116.[23] In 1114 the Count of Champagne returned to the east in an attempt to escape his wife Elisabeth. The escape was consolidated by joining the Order of St. John.[24] This seems to be Hugh's most likely date of departure, although, of course, it does not preclude the possibility that this was the second time that he had taken the Cross, or even the third.

Hugh of Champagne did not stay long in the east, for he was forced to return to his wife by the intervention of the canonist, Ivo of Chartres.[25] But, in 1125, he once more threw over the traces, ceded his lands to his nephew, Theobald, Count of Blois, and sailed east. There he joined the nascent Order of the Temple.[26] This is further evidence of the connection of Hugh of Payens with the count and of his origin in Champagne. The order was relatively unknown in Europe at this time; in 1128 its members totalled only nine.[27] The count's preference for this new Order may well have been because it was led by a compatriot, perhaps a former officer of his house.

Further circumstantial evidence of Hugh's origins is provided by the Council that recognised the new Order and gave it a Rule. This council was held in 1128 at Troyes, and attended by Theobald of Blois and Andrew of Baudement, the most important lords of Champagne, and most of the bishops and abbots of the region.[28] It seems too great a coincidence that the Council should have been held in the nearest large town to the village of Payens, that it was held primarily to recognise the Order of the Temple, and that the leader of that Order should be surnamed 'de Payens'. Petel shows that Theobald of Payens was closely connected with the region. For instance, when he left for crusade in 1147, he deposited some of the precious property of the abbey of St. Colombe-de-Sens with the Jews at Troyes, in order to raise money.[29] Finally, Payens later became a

---

[23] RICHARD, loc. cit., says that he arrived in 1116 with 30 others, but does not give his source for this statement.

[24] See H. DE ARBOIS DE JUBAINVILLE, Histoire des Ducs et des Comtes de Champagne, II, Paris-Troyes, 1860, pp. 110-14.

[25] See Epistoles Ivonis Carnotensis Episcopi, in M. BOUQUET, Recueil des Historiens des Gaules et de la France, XV, Paris, 1808, no. CXL, pp. 162-3. The editor wrongly states that the Count had joined the Temple.

[26] Chronica Albrici Monachi Trium Fontium, ed. SCHEFFER-BOICHORST, in Monumenta Germaniae Historica, XXIII, p. 826.

[27] WILLIAM OF TYRE, XII, 7, p. 521. References to William's history are from the edition of the Académie des Inscriptions et Belles-Lettres, Recueil des Historiens des Croisades, Historiens Occidentaux, I (i), Paris, 1844.

[28] G. SCHNÜRER, Die ursprüngliche Templeregel, Freiburg, 1903, Prefatio, II, III, pp. 130-2; H. DE CURZON, La Règle du Temple, Paris, 1886, para. 6, pp. 16-18.

[29] Ex Chronico Senonensi S. Colombae, in R.H.G., XII, Paris, 1781, p. 288.

I

224

Commanderie of the Temple, although it was relatively unimportant, having only four or five hundred arpents of land attached to it. When the Hospital took over after the dissolution of the Temple, it was joined to the Commanderie of Troyes.[30] Petel must be right in thinking that it carried this status in memory of the birthplace of the founder of the Order.[31]

\* \* \*

At Easter, 1119, a group of pilgrims set out from Jerusalem for the Jordan. They had reached a lonely place in the mountains near the castles of Cushet and Burgevins when they were attacked by Saracens from Tyre and Ascalon. Unarmed and tired by the journey, they were easy victims. According to Albert of Aix, three hundred were killed and sixty were captured. The event, says Albert, afflicted the king and the Patriarch Gormond with great sorrow.[32] The figures are probably too high, and certainly too neat, but the incident once more drew attention to the appalling risks taken by unarmed pilgrims.

Later in the year, a group of knights took vows of poverty, chastity, and obedience before the Patriarch of Jerusalem. They vowed to live as regular canons. The two most distinguished members of the group were Hugh of Payens and Godfrey of St. Omer.[33] Presumably these two can be regarded as of higher social rank than the others. Godfrey was a brother of William, the chatelain of St. Omer, and a vassal of the Count of Boulogne.[34] The date has usually been given as 1118, after William of Tyre, but the archbishop contradicts himself when he states that at the Council of Troyes the Templars were in the ninth year of their existence.[35] According to Jean Michel, the secretary, the Council was held 'in sollempnitate sancti Hylarii, anno M°C°XX°VIII° ab incarnato Dei Filio, ab inchoatione predictae mili-

---

[30] MANNIER, op. cit., p. 309.
[31] PETEL, op. cit., pp. xii-xiii.
[32] Alberti Aquensis Historia Hierosolymitana, in Recueil des Historiens des Croisades, Historiens Occidentaux, IV, Paris, 1879, Bk. XII, Chap. XXXIII, pp. 712-13. Albert dates this incident, 'in anno secundo regni Baldewini secundi, in Sabbato sancto ejusdem Resurrectionis...' Baldwin II was crowned on Easter Sunday, 1118, Fulcheri Carnotensis Historia Hierosolymitana 1095-1127, ed. H. HAGENMEYER, Heidelberg, 1890, pp. 615-16. Since Easter Sunday fell on 14th April in 1118 and on 30th March in 1119 it would seem that the massacre took place in 1120. However, Easter in 1120 fell on the 18th April, which was the third year of Baldwin's reign. It seems reasonable to assume therefore that Albert means the second Easter of the king's reign, which would be in 1119.
[33] WILLIAM OF TYRE, XII, 7, p. 520.
[34] J. MALBRANCQ, De Morinis et Morinorum rebus, III, Tournai, 1654, p. 150, where he is given as 'consanguineus' of William of St. Omer.
[35] WILLIAM OF TYRE, loc. cit.

*ciae nono'*.[36] It is likely therefore that William is mistaken about the first date.[37]

The new group received two small grants. Temporary accommodation was made over to them by the king on the north side of the Temple of Solomon, and they received a square in the same area belonging to the canons of the Temple. In addition, the king, the patriarch, and various individuals supplied them with a number of benefices sufficient to feed and clothe them.[38] They probably excited little attention at the time. Fulcher of Chartres, for instance, does not seem to have been aware of them.

It is by no means clear who had the idea of using this group for the protection of the pilgrim routes. William of Tyre says that the patriarch and the other bishops enjoined on them that 'as far as their strength permitted, they should keep the roads and highways safe from the menace of robbers and highwaymen, with especial regard for the protection of pilgrims'.[39] This is as would be expected since they had taken their vows at the hands of the patriarch. The idea may have been that of the king or of the patriarch. They were both aware of the dangers to pilgrims as the massacre described by Albert of Aix shows. It has sometimes been assumed that Hugh and Godfrey took the vows for this express purpose and the idea may have been theirs alone. William of Tyre however, does not say this. They took their vows because they were pious and Godfearing.[40]

There is little evidence to suggest that interest in the group increased very much after 1119. As shown, William of Tyre reckons their number at only nine in 1128, although there may have been a few more. However, significantly for the future, they did attract the attention of Fulk V, the Count of Anjou, who made a pilgrimage to

---

[36] SCHNÜRER, *op. cit.*, *Prefatio*, II, p. 130; CURZON, *op. cit.*, para. 3, pp. 13-14.
[37] V. CARRIÈRE, *Les Débuts de l'Ordre du Temple en France*, in *Le Moyen Age*, 18 (1914), 309, has tried to date the foundation more closely than this. There is a charter of Theobald of Champagne, granting a house to the Temple on All Saints' Day, 'anno octavo ab institutione prenominatorum conmilitorum Christi', MARQUIS D'ALBON, *Cartulaire général de l'Ordre du Temple. 1119?-1150*, Paris 1913, no. IX, p. 6. Carrière argues that if this is in 1126 then the foundation was on or before 31st October, 1119, but if in 1127, it was after that date. If the evidence of Jean Michel and William of Tyre is accepted, then the eighth year finished at the latest on 12th January, 1128. Therefore the charter of Theobald appears to be in 1127, and the Temple was founded between 1st November, 1119 and 12th January, 1120. This seems to be a circular argument. By the same token, the ninth year began at the earliest on 14th January, 1127, and therefore the Temple could have been founded before 31st October, 1119. As will be seen, the probability is that Theobald's charter can be placed in 1127, but this is by no means certain.
[38] WILLIAM OF TYRE, *loc. cit.* The translated extract is from a *History of Deeds done beyond the sea, by William, Archbishop of Tyre*, ed. and trans. by E. M. BABCOCK and A. C. KREY, New York, 1943, pp. 324-5.
[39] WILLIAM OF TYRE, *loc. cit.*
[40] *Ibid.*

Jerusalem in 1120-1. During his stay he lodged at the Temple and, according to Orderic Vitalis, he joined the new group. It is clear from the later course of his life that he did not take vows in the same way as Hugh and Godfrey, but instead seems to have become some kind of lay associate, a form which became common in the course of the twelfth century. Such men would usually make a donation to the Templars, and by this means hope to acquire the spiritual benefits that such piety might bring. Fulk himself granted the Templars an annual subsidy of 30 livres angevins from his lands in Anjou. Orderic Vitalis says that many other French lords followed his example, although the documentary evidence for this has not survived.[41]

But, apart from this grant, there is little record of the Templars in the east in the period up to 1128. Röhricht cites only three documents in which the name of Hugh of Payens appears, and in all cases he is just one signatory among many, on documents of no direct relevance to the Temple. Hugh was present when, on December 30th, 1120, Baldwin II confirmed the privileges granted by his predecessor to the Hospital of Jerusalem (20th June, 1112),[42] and five years later, on May 2nd, at Acre, he attached his seal to the grant of privileges which Gormond, the Patriarch, had made to the Venetians.[43] The latter document gives Hugh the title of 'magister Templi' and therefore indicates that he had been accepted as leader by this date. The third document is a confirmation of a grant of a parcel of rights and lands by the same patriarch to the abbey of St. Mary of the valley of Josaphat.[44] Hugh then was present in the kingdom of Jerusalem in the period 1120 to 1125.

There is one further document in this period which could be of considerable importance. This is a letter purporting to be from King Baldwin II to Bernard of Clairvaux commending to him two knights of the Temple, Andrew and Gondemar, and asking him to obtain approval of the Order from the Pope. D'Albon dates this letter between 28th June, 1119, and 15th October, 1126.[45] Its potential importance can be seen once it is taken into account that it was St. Bernard who drew up the Rule for the newly-constituted Order in 1128,

[41] *Orderici Vitalis Historia Ecclesiastica*, ed. A. Le Prevost and L. Delisle, IV, Paris, 1854, p. 423.
[42] R. Röhricht, *Regesta Regni Hierosolymitani*, II, Innsbruck, 1904, no. 90 (a), p. 6.
[43] *Ibid.*, I, Innsbruck, 1893, no. 105, p. 25.
[44] *Ibid.*, no. 101, p. 23.
[45] D'Albon, *op. cit.*, no. I, p. 1.

and it was St. Bernard who produced the tract «*De Laude Novae Militiae ad Milites Templi*». St. Bernard's widespread moral influence and unrivalled ability as a propagandist were therefore brought to bear in support of the tiny Order. D'Albon cites two documents before 1126 recording donations to the Temple. The first is an annual rent of grain on the church of La Motte-Palayson by William the Poitevin, given on 1st July, 1124,[46] and the second is a grant by one Baldwin Brochet of all his property at Planque in Flanders and is dated by D'Albon circa 1125.[47] The latter is even suspect in its dating since it says, concerning the Temple, '*quorum gloriosa fama, ubique terrarum patenter diffusa.*'[48] The only other grant, apart from the initial donations made by the king and patriarch in 1119, is that of Fulk of Anjou, already mentioned. Yet, in the period after 1126 until Hugh's death ten years later, D'Albon has found 104 documents recording one or more donations, 7 exchanges between the Temple and another party, and 5 sales to the Order. This may not be complete, but it probably gives a rough indication of the proportions before and after 1126. The period after the Council of Troyes sees the beginning of a sustained and rapid expansion which lifted the Temple from obscurity to international fame and power. St. Bernard was instrumental in this rapid rise. The initiator of any move to gain the support of the single most powerful churchman in western Europe at this period therefore made a decisive contribution to the growth of the Order and, as will be seen, may even have saved it from extinction.

King Baldwin was certainly amicably disposed towards the Order as is shown by his encouragement in 1119, but it is unlikely that he was so interested in its development as to have taken the initiative alone. If Hugh of Payens was responsible, it says much for his foresight and ability as a leader. Another possibility is Count Hugh of Champagne. The Count had been generous to religious houses and may have originally given St. Bernard the site for Clairvaux.[49] After he had joined the Temple, Bernard wrote and congratulated him for

---

[46] *Ibid.*, no. II, pp. 1-2.
[47] *Ibid.*, no. IV, pp. 2-3.
[48] See CARRIÈRE, *op. cit.*, pp. 312-3.
[49] See E. VACANDARD, *Vie de St. Bernard, Abbé de Clairvaux*, I, Paris, 1895, p. 61. Hugh had helped the growth of the Cistercian Order, but it is not certain that he provided the original site for Clairvaux; see also H. BLEIS, *La Place prise par l'Abbaye de Clairvaux au temps de Saint Bernard, dans la Rivalité entre le Comte de Champagne et le Duc de Bourgogne*, in *Mélanges S. Bernard*, Dijon, 1953, pp. 28-31, who argues that the contribution of the Count of Champagne to Clairvaux had been little more than pious words.

giving himself to the service of God. He refers to him as 'carrissimus meus Hugo'. There is however a reproachful note when Bernard says how disappointed he is that Hugh had not joined the Cistercians.[50] But there is no real evidence to indicate that Hugh was on bad terms with St. Bernard. Possibly he felt that Jerusalem was farther away from his wife Elisabeth than Clairvaux. Hugh of Champagne was therefore in a position to influence Bernard and to recommend the Templars to his attention. He may have persuaded the king to put the request in official form. But this is only a possibility, for the letter could have been written before 1125. Indeed, the only time it could not have been written was between April, 1123, and August, 1124, when Baldwin was a prisoner of the Moslems.[51]

To add to these doubts, the letter has been dated 1139. Manrique cites a Portuguese translation which attributes it to King Fulk in that year.[52] If so, it might have been the prelude to the far-reaching privileges in favour of the Temple contained in the bull «Omne Datum Optimum» of March, 1139.[53] If the Andrew mentioned is Andrew of Montbard, a later Grand Master, then this date is more logical, because he did not enter the Order until 1129 at the earliest.[54] But this is a large assumption. Gondemar, a knight apparently of Spanish origin, is not mentioned elsewhere, and the Andrew who accompanied him may be equally obscure. The text of the letter favours the view that it was written by Baldwin II. He is titled 'princeps Antiochae' and was in fact regent of Antioch from the death of Roger of Antioch in June, 1119, until the arrival in the east of the heir to the principality, Bohemond II, in October, 1126.[55] These are the dating limits set by D'Albon. Fulk was neither prince nor regent in 1139. Moreover, the letter contains the phrase 'Fratres Templarii apostolicam confirmationem obtinere et certam vite normam desiderent',[56] which could

[50] Sancti Bernardi Abbatis Clarae-Vallensis Epistolae, in MIGNE, P.L., 182, no. XXXI, col. 135-6.
[51] FULCHER OF CHARTRES, pp. 658-9, 749-51; WILLIAM OF TYRE, XII, 17, pp. 536-7; XIII, 15, p. 576.
[52] A. MANRIQUE, Annales Cistercienses, I, Lyons, 1642, p. 375.
[53] See D'ALBON, op. cit., Bullaire, no. V, pp. 375-9, for the provisions of this bull. By means of this bull the Order and its houses were taken under direct papal protection.
[54] In 1129, as a layman, Andrew of Montbard appeared on a document of Bernard II of Montbard, Abbé J. B. JOBIN, Saint Bernard et sa Famille, Paris, 1891, Pièces Justificatives, no. XV, pp. 574-5. However, he is mentioned as a member of the Order in the east in a letter of St. Bernard to the Patriarch of Jerusalem, William of Messines. This letter was probably written between the beginning of 1130 and 21st August, 1131, see D'ALBON, op. cit., no. XXXV, p. 27.
[55] FULCHER OF CHARTRES, pp. 620-4, 819-22; WILLIAM OF TYRE, XII, 10, pp. 525-6; XIII, 21, pp. 588-9.
[56] See P. COUSIN, Les débuts de l'ordre des Templiers et saint Bernard, in Mélanges S. Bernard, p. 50.

only have been written before the Council of Troyes. It is of course possible that the letter is not genuine, and Mme. Melville states that D'Albon regarded the letter as spurious,[57] but he has printed it without comment. In summary, therefore, it would be dangerous to draw any definite conclusions from the letter concerning its authorship, its inspiration, or indeed its authenticity. If Hugh of Payens prompted it, then he made a decisive contribution towards the growth of the Order, but it must be concluded that Hugh of Champagne is the more likely contender.

*  *  *

The Council of Troyes opened in January, 1128. It was presided over by the Papal Legate, the Cardinal Matthew of Albano. He had been sent to France at the end of 1127 in order to negotiate with Louis VI, who could sometimes be difficult over ecclesiastical matters.[58] The Council then was called not only to consider the claims of the Temple for recognition (although this seems to have been its primary purpose), but also to consider French domestic matters. Most of the important clergy and laymen of the region attended. These included Hugh of Montaigu, the bishop of Auxerre, and Stephen Harding, the abbot of Cîteaux. With them were ten bishops and seven abbots, and the archbishops of Sens and Reims. The two leading laymen of the area, Theobald, Count of Blois and Champagne, and Andrew of Baudement, Count of Nevers, were also present. The attendance of the prominent ecclesiastics must have been the work of St. Bernard, who despite the onset of fever, was at Troyes to take part in the proceedings.[59] Most of these men came from in and around Champagne, but the Cardinal's duties were wider, thus John II, the bishop of Orleans, came to represent Louis VI.[60] The Council was supposed to give a ruling on the quarrel between Louis VI and Stephen, the bishop of Paris.[61]

---

[57] M. MELVILLE, La Vie des Templiers, Paris, 1951, pp. 18-9.
[58] See A. LUCHAIRE, Louis VI le Gros, Paris, 1890, p. cxxix, and Dom BERLIÈRE, Le Cardinal Mathieu d'Albano, in Revue bénédictine, 18 (1901), 125.
[59] SCHNÜRER, op. cit., Prefatio, III, p. 131; CURZON, op. cit., para. 6, pp. 16-18; WILLIAM OF TYRE, XII, 7, pp. 520-1. These sources indicate St. Bernard was present. Sancti Bernardi Epistolae, op. cit., no. XXI, col. 123, is a letter from St. Bernard to Matthew of Albano written shortly before the Council, which speaks of the abbot's serious fever.
[60] SCHNÜRER, op. cit., Prefatio, III, p. 131; CURZON, op. cit., para. 6, p. 16.
[61] C. J. HEFELE, Histoire des Conciles, trans. and ed. H. LECLERCQ, vol. 5, part I, Paris, 1912, p. 668.

Hugh of Payens had the task of putting his case before the Council. With him were five brothers, Godfrey of St. Omer, Roland, Geoffrey Bisol, Payen of Montdidier, and Archambaud of Saint Amand.[62] Hugh was at Acre in May, 1125, and at the Council by January 14th, 1128. His movements between these two dates are not known. He must have been in the west by mid-1127, since he would almost certainly have been involved in the preparations for the Council in Champagne. It has been suggested that he had been to Rome where he met the Pope and Matthew of Albano and plans for the Council were begun.[63] The expenses for the journey probably came from the royal treasury at Jerusalem, for part of his task while in the west was to recruit men for Baldwin II, who was planning an attack on Damascus.[64] The fact that Baldwin seems to have sent Hugh to the west for this purpose tends to support the view that the letter attributed to the king is genuine.

At the Council Hugh told of the humble beginnings of the Order and narrated its history. The Council then deliberated upon its constitution.[65] Valous has shown that certain aspects of this oral tradition were incorporated into the written Rule. The Rule states where changes have been made.[66] In this way therefore Hugh of Payens had considerable influence. The Order was under the jurisdiction of the clerical authorities, but apart from this reservation the Master had the right of obedience from the knights. He took decisions concerning the whole Order, after having consulted the community.[67] Like the regular clergy in Jerusalem, the Templars participated in the usual offices of the choir, which they were not allowed to miss. Before 1128 they were expected to attend the entire office, but this was modified by the Rule. A knight on outside service could replace Matins with a recitation of thirteen Pater Noster, those of other hours with seven, and Vespers with nine.[68] Even at this time they had a small number of servants and horses. Each knight had been allowed one horse, but this was extended to a maximum of three.[69] They took meals in com-

---

[62] SCHNÜRER, op. cit., Prefatio, III, p. 131; CURZON, op. cit., para. 7, pp. 19-20.
[63] CARRIÈRE, op. cit., pp. 311 12.
[64] WILLIAM OF TYRE, XIII, 26, pp. 595-6.
[65] SCHNÜRER, op. cit., Prefatio, II, pp. 130-1; CURZON, op. cit., para. 3, pp. 13-14.
[66] G. DE VALOUS, Quelques observations sur la toute primitive observance des Templiers et la Regula pauperum commilitorum Christi Templi Solomonici, rédigée par saint Bernard au concile de Troyes (1128), in Mélanges S. Bernard, pp. 32-7.
[67] SCHNÜRER, op. cit., para. 33, p. 143; para. 47, pp. 146-7; para. 57, p. 149.
[68] Ibid., para. 2, p. 135; para. 7, pp. 136-7; para. 18, pp. 139-40.
[69] Ibid., para. 30, p. 142.

I

mon in a room of the palace, and meat was authorised three times a week, except for Christmas week, Easter, and the Feasts of the Virgin and the Apostles. They were allowed only one meal on Fridays between All Saints' Day and Easter. What was left of meals was given to the servants and the poor.[70] The colour of their clothes was not fixed, except that it should be uniform, and the clothes of plain material. Lamb's wool was allowed in winter. Arms and harnesses should not be ornamented with gold and silver, or any precious material or be brightly coloured. Their hair and beard were kept short.[71] They were allowed no contact with women, not even relatives.[72] The founders of the Order therefore lived a strict and simple life under Hugh of Payens. Valous believes that the main outline of the Rule was formulated along these lines before 1128, and that that St. Bernard's part has been exaggerated.[73] However, it was essential to have a man of his stature and ability to draft and clarify it, rejecting those parts which were not appropriate. Hugh and his companions lacked the expertise for such an operation.

In broad outline the Rule, systematised and moulded by St. Bernard was as follows. Firstly, the division of the Order into four categories namely knights, sergeants, priests and clerks for religious services, and servants and artisans; secondly, the right of a white cassock; thirdly, the right of possessing and governing estates and vassals; and fourthly, the right of taking tithes for charity. Regulations were set down in considerable detail governing their way of life.[74]

The Council of Troyes was a personal triumph for Hugh of Payens. It represented a great step forward at a time when the Order seems to have been in considerable difficulty. Dom Jean Leclercq has drawn attention to a letter of Hugh of Payens, probably written from the west at the time of Troyes, which throws light on the situation.[75] The letter has been attributed to Hugh of St. Victor, whose name appears in the prologue,[76] but Leclercq argues convincingly in favour of Hugh of Payens. The letter is to be found in the

[70] *Ibid.*, para. 8, p. 137; para. 10, p. 137; para. 11, p. 138; para. 13, p. 138; para. 14, p. 138. para. 14, p. 138.
[71] *Ibid.*, para. 20, pp. 140-1; para. 24, p. 141; para. 28, p. 142; para. 35, p. 144.
[72] *Ibid.*, para. 70, p. 153.
[73] VALOUS, *op. cit.*, pp. 37-8.
[74] SCHNÜRER, *op. cit.*, and CURZON, *op. cit.*
[75] J. LECLERCQ, *Un document sur les débuts des Templiers*, in *Revue d'Histoire Ecclésiastique*, 52 (1967), 81-91.
[76] C. SCLAFERT, *Lettre inédite de Hugues de Saint-Victor aux Chevaliers du Temple*, in *Revue d'ascétique et de mystique*, 34 (1958), 275.

Bibliothèque municipale de Nîmes, between an edition of the Rule and St. Bernard's «*De Laude*». It has been rejected by historians as the work of Hugh of St. Victor. Leclercq therefore argues that the prologue does not belong to the letter. Moreover, the prologue talks of a sermon to follow, yet the text is in letter form. The ideas are those which would be applicable to the Templars and are written by one who knew their thoughts and temptations well. The Latin is unpretentious, as would be expected from a man not trained as a clerk, and one of the Biblical quotations is incorrect. In the second paragraph, the author, speaking of the efforts of the devil, 'to corrupt our intentions in good works' refers to a passage in Scripture which says, '*Fac bonum bene*'. This quotation does not appear in Holy Scripture.[77] In short, the letter has the marks of having been written by a layman, but a layman closely associated with clerics.

Hugh was absent from Palestine in the years 1127-30. It is possible that he heard of an internal crisis among the Templars left in the east during this period. He must, at any rate, have had a good idea of their general state of mind. The letter was written to stiffen morale. They lived in real poverty without any distinctive habit; recruitment had been minimal. The task which they had undertaken may have been overwhelming for such small numbers. Some seem to have been afflicted by doubts about the nature of their calling. The association of the bearing of arms with the monastic life was a completely new concept; their lack of striking success may well have introduced doubts about God's approval.

The general theme of the letter is aimed at strengthening their will to go on with their task despite the temptations of the devil. It begins with a general exhortation backed by Scriptural quotations intended to overcome their doubts. Hugh continues by saying that all have their part to play in the Christian community, 'if all the members of the body performed only one function, the body itself could not entirely subsist'. The devil works in a subtle way to corrupt their motives. He does not tell them to envy, to fornicate, to dispute, to deny. Instead, he suggests hatred and fury when they are engaged in killing, greed when the spoils are gathered. But it is not the man they hate but the iniquity, and the spoils are justly taken for 'the labourer is worthy of his hire'. The devil then cannot deny that they are doing good. He therefore tries to persuade them to leave this lesser good for a greater one, not in order that they might do the

---

[77] LECLERCQ, *op. cit.*, p. 86.

latter, but that they might fail to do the former. He will promise anything to tempt them away from their task, 'he makes majesty glisten to remove humility'. But the exterior is nothing in the eyes of God. It might be objected that the occupation of the Templars deals with exterior care and thus hinders interior progress, but to be seated with Christ they must not refuse to work. Even hermits in the desert have to feed and clothe themselves. 'If there were not those who laboured, those who sowed, those who reaped, and those who prepared, what would be brought to those who contemplated?' The devil, on the pretence of piety, is trying to lead them into error. But if this fails, the devil will try to stir up discontent because their fervour is not recognised and appreciated by their superiors. He will tell them to retire from such a society where they are ignored. However, they all know virtue to be more secure when hidden. None can be in doubt that they will be recompensed. Once more the tempter is made foolish.

The style and sentiments accord with what is known of Hugh's career. He was a pious knight, probably not highly educated, but on the other hand not illiterate, like many of the nobility of this period. The views expressed are unoriginal, representing a fairly conventional idea of society in the twelfth century, although the method of expression is often striking. Each was born to perform his allotted task, and those who failed to do so were the victims of the temptations of the devil. All should be satisfied with their position on earth; God will reward them in the next world. The letter clearly indicates a flagging spirit within the Order, and Hugh may have done well to keep them going to this point. Possibly one motive for his journey to the west was a fear that without greater support and recognition the Order might fail. Of course, the responsibility for this state of affairs may have lain with Hugh himself, but this does not accord with the other information available about his character — the foundation of the Order, the praise from William of Tyre, 'pious and God-fearing', 'devoted to the Lord', the energetic and successful efforts to gather troops after the Council of Troyes, and the letter itself, which displays certain qualities of leadership.

* * *

After the Council Hugh and the other Templars set about the task of recruiting men and founding commanderies in Europe. They dispersed to their homelands for this effort. In Flanders, the Count William granted the Order the right of relief on his lands, probably soon after the Council, and Osto of St. Omer, Godfrey's nephew, was witness.[78] On September 15th, 1128, William, the chatellan of St. Omer, conceded the right of relief on the chatellanie of Warrêton-Bas.[79] These grants presumably testify to the activity of Godfrey of St. Omer. The existence of a commanderie at Fontaine, near Montdidier, in Picardy, indicates that Payen of Montdidier was similarly engaged.[80] To begin with, Hugh concentrated on Champagne. Doubtless here he had the support of Count Theobald, the nephew of Hugh of Champagne. Theobald had reason to be grateful to his uncle, for Hugh's wife, Elisabeth, had a son, Odo of Champenois. But Hugh's dislike of his wife had caused him to disinherit Odo, claiming that he was not his son.[81] It was in Champagne that the Order would have received the most initial publicity because of the Council. Theobald's grant at Provins in October, probably the previous year, of a house at Barbonne, had been an important example. The charter mentions that several of the count's vassals had previously made grants to the Temple.[82] Hugh of Payens himself of course gave his lands to the Order, and Joscelin, one of the fathers at Troyes, later speaks of this donation.[83] In the month of the Council Hugh and Godfrey were present when Raoul the Fat and his wife left all their possessions near Troyes to the Order, to be received after their death.[84]

Hugh then appears to have left for Anjou. This was probably to meet Count Fulk, the designated successor of King Baldwin II. The Count was at this time making preparations for his departure to the east. Hugh was at Le Mans on Ascension Day, 1128, when Fulk took the Cross at the hands of the Archbishop of Tours. William of Bures, leader of the embassy sent by Baldwin II to bring back his successor was also present. Hugh made some contribution towards the settlement of Fulk's affairs at this time when he acted as arbitrator between Hugh of Amboise and the monks of Marmoutier. Hugh persuaded the lord of Amboise to accept his culpability and to make apology to the monks for the wrongs done to them.[85] On the same day, 31st May, the Grand Master received two grants from Peter, lord

---

[78] D'ALBON, op. cit., no. VII, p. 5.
[79] Ibid., no. XVII, pp. 11-12.
[80] MANNIER, op. cit., pp. xiii, 592.
[81] See ARBOIS DE JUBAINVILLE, op. cit., vol. II, pp. 135-6.
[82] D'ALBON, op. cit., no. IX, p. 6.
[83] Ibid., no. LIX, pp. 42-3.
[84] Ibid., no. XXII, p.16, The document is undated, but D'Albon places it circa January, 1129. The year before seems more likely.
[85] Ibid., no. XII, pp. 8-10; J. CHARTROU, L'Anjou de 1009 à 1151, Paris, 1928, Pièces Justi-ficatives, no. 39, pp. 369-72.

I

of the Garnache, who gave the Temple two marks annually derived from the rent on the revenues of the port of Beauvoir,[86] and one from a certain Olifand, who gave a marsh and the salt produced from it.[87] Sometime between 3rd April, 1127, and 22nd April 1128, Fulk recalled a gift he had made to two hermits, Renaud and Geoffrey, of a portion of the forest of Bréchenay, situated between Cormery and Azay-sur-Cher. This gift was confirmed and the hermits were exempted from all customary seigneurial rights. Hugh of Payens was present at this concession.[88] Since mention is made of Fulk's previous expedition to the east, it is reasonable to place this document in the spring of 1128, and it can be assumed that Hugh stayed in Anjou for at least two months.

The Anglo-Saxon Chronicle says that Hugh of the Temple from Jerusalem visited Normandy, England, and Scotland in 1128. Although the months are not given it is both chronologically and geographically likely that this journey took place after the visit to Anjou. Fulk's eldest son, Geoffrey, was married to Matilda, the heiress of Henry I, at Le Mans on 17th June.[89] Probably Hugh had been present at tne ceremony and perhaps he received an invitation at this time. In Normandy Henry gave the Grand Master gifts of gold and silver and Hugh then crossed the Channel. He was equally well-received in England and Scotland, where he conducted a successful recruiting campaign. According to the Anglo-Saxon Chronicle, he collected more men for the east than at any other time since the First Crusade. It appears though that a number later returned to Europe when they discovered that war was not raging on the scale that they had imagined. The Anglo-Saxon Chronicle considers that they had been tricked.[90] Also, no grants to the Order seem to have been made at this time, so the visit cannot be counted a complete success. It was not until the reign of Stephen that the Order began to make appreciable progress in England.

Hugh then returned to the continent, probably to Flanders. The Temple was by now well-known in the area. At Cassel, Thierry, the new count of Flanders, conceded to the Order a number of reliefs on various fiefs in the county (13th September, 1128), in the presence of Hugh of Payens and Godfrey of St. Omer. This was granted in

[86] D'ALBON, op. cit., no. XIII, p. 10; no. XIV, p. 10.
[87] Ibid., no. XV, p. 10.
[88] CHARTROU, op. cit., Pièces Justificatives, no. 38, pp. 367-9.
[89] See CHARTROU, op. cit., pp. 22-3, n. 4, on the date of this marriage.
[90] The Anglo-Saxon Chronicle, ed. D. WHITELOCK, London, 1961, year 1128, pp. 194-5.

I

the Church of St. Peter at Cassel, and it is probable that the Order received a number of recruits on this occasion.[91] Hugh was back in the Kingdom of Jerusalem by 1130.[92] In that year he was signatory to a grant made to the Venetians by Baldwin II at Acre.[93] He does not appear to have arrived in time to take part in Baldwin's unsuccessful attack on Damascus which began in November, 1129, although probably a number of the men he had recruited were present.[94] He may have travelled back via the Rhone valley and Marseilles, for on January 29th, 1130, Lauger, the bishop of Avignon, granted to him the Church of John the Baptist at Avignon.[95] Although he is mentioned by name it is not certain that he was personally present. What is clear is that the trip had been a great success. French response had been so large that Hugh appointed Payen of Montdidier to take care of the province.[96]

European expansion continued rapidly after the Grand Master's departure. In these early years the predominant interest was north French, but the Order also gained ground in Spain, Portugal, and Provence. The possibilities were soon grasped in Portugal, for the Temple received a grant there as early as March, 1128,[97] and sometime
* between 1128 and 1130 Queen Theresa donated various properties.[98] D'Albon prints 32 transactions in Spain and 6 in Portugal involving the Temple in the period up to 1136, out of a total of 104. These included the extremely active efforts of Raymond-Berengar III, Count of Barcelona and Provence, who joined the Temple as an associate member on 14th July, 1130, when he ceded the fortress of Grayana to the Order,[99] and the extraordinary will of Alphonso, king of Aragon and Navarre, who in 1131, divided his kingdom between the Temple, the Hospital, and the Holy Sepulchre.[100] Alphonso was killed on 7th September, 1134, but the matter took until 1143 to settle.[101]

---

[91] D'Albon, op. cit., no. XVI, pp. 10-11.
[92] William of Tyre, XIII, 26, p. 595.
[93] G. A. Quarti, I Cavalieri del Santo Sepolcro di Gerusalemme, Milan, 1939, pp. 480-2.
[94] The Damascus Chronicle of Crusades, extracted and translated from the Chronicle of Ibn Al-Qalanisi, ed. H. A. R. Gibb, London, 1932, pp. 187-99; William of Tyre, XIII, 26, pp. 595-6, who places the campaign in the next year.
[95] D'Albon, op. cit., no. XXX, p. 23.
[96] Ibid., no. XXXI, pp. 23-4.
[97] Ibid., no. X, p. 7.
[98] Ibid., no. XIX, pp. 12-13.
[99] D'Albon, op. cit., no. XXXIII, pp. 25-6.
[100] Ibid., no. XL, pp. 30-1, in October at the siege of Bayonne.
[101] The chaos caused by this will was slowly reduced to order by Raymond-Berengar, the Count of Barcelona, who emerged in 1140 from the general war as king of Aragon. He could not accept the terms of the will but he did grant the Order extensive privileges in the region. See J. Piquet, Des Banquiers au Moyen Age: Les Templiers, Paris, 1939, pp. 233-4.

Carrière has provided a survey of Templar expansion in France during these early years.[102] The Order had the active support of the Church. At a synod held in Reims on 19th October, 1131, the bishops of the region, led by Renaud of Reims, granted to the Temple the offerings made at the chapel of Obstat, at Ypres, during the three days of the Rogations and the five days following.[103] With the early donations the Templars became established as important landlords. They began to organise and cultivate their estates. A new function was therefore appearing even within the lifetime of the founder, that of the exploitation of land. At a time when large areas of previously uncultivated land were being taken up in Europe and agriculture and trade were feeling the benefits of increased monetary circulation, the new Order found itself the recipient of a large number of gifts of land. These were not negligible factors in the rapid growth of the Temple after Troyes.

St. Bernard's wholehearted support and encouragement were, of course, invaluable. In 1131 he wrote to William, the Patriarch of Jerusalem, asking him to give full support to the Temple, to the men who were prepared to lay down their lives for their brethren.[104] In 1135 he attended the Council of Pisa, convened primarily to deal with erring clergy. A number were excommunicated and deposed. The size of the Council was considerable; 113 bishops and 13 abbots attended. St. Bernard took this opportunity to gain pecuniary help from the assembly for the Temple. The Pope promised a mark of gold annually, his chancellor Aimery, two ounces of gold, and the other bishops and prelates a mark of silver each.[105]

But St. Bernard's most important contribution was the production of the tract «*De Laude Novae Militiae ad Milites Templi*». The date of its composition is not known, but it must have been after 1128 and before Hugh's death in 1136. The Grand Master had been pressing for such a tract. He wanted a justification from a man whose word carried so much weight. In the Prologue, St. Bernard states, 'Once, twice, three times, dearest Hugh, you have asked me to write a work of exhortation to yourself and your fellow knights'.[106] Basically this was a justification of the fighting monk as opposed to the feudal knight,

---

[102] CARRIÈRE, *op. cit.*, pp. 323-35.
[103] D'ALBON, *op. cit.*, no. XLI, p. 31.
[104] *Sancti Bernardi Epistolae, op. cit.*, no. CLXXV, col. 336-7; D'ALBON, *op. cit.*, no. XXXV, p. 27.
[105] HEFELE, *op. cit.*, pp. 706-13, for the Council of Pisa.
[106] *S. Bernardi Abbatis De Laude Novae Militiae ad Milites Templi Liber*, in *P.L.*, 182, col. 921.

and in this way it was an important contribution towards the attempts to enforce the truce of God which had been prevalent since the late tenth century.[107] On a wider plane, it was a justification of the whole idea of the Crusade. The immediate aim was to «exhort» the knights of the Temple themselves. These new knights saw death as desirable and therefore they went into combat with the Infidel without fear. If they survived they would be covered in glory; if not, they were happy martyrs. If the cause of the warriors was good, then the end could not be evil, but if one fought in a bad cause, one was murdering. St. Bernard describes the worldly knights, covetous for riches, their wars products of bad temper, vanity and greed. The secular knights of the time were servants of the devil. In contrast the fighting monk need fear neither death nor the giving of death. Death given for Christ was not a criminal act; it was a title to glory. The reason for killing the pagans was so that the sinners did not menace the just. Bernard compares the zeal of the Templars with the zeal of Christ when he chased the money-lenders from the Temple. He concludes that here is a miracle. Bernard encourages sinners to join the Temple, for by this means they will be saved and engage no more in the works of the devil.[108] The tract is not very original except in the fact that its ideas were applied to the new monks. Most of its concepts had been expressed at the time of the First Crusade.[109] However, it was important in publicising the Temple and indeed in strengthening its own members. It must have appeared very convincing in the context of European society in the 1130's. It bears certain similarities to the letter written by Hugh of Payens, and perhaps marks Hugh's recognition of the need for propaganda as well as conviction. Hugh was well aware that St. Bernard's capacity to sway the Christian world was infinitely greater than his own.

During the years 1130 to 1136 there is little evidence concerning Hugh's activities in the east. He seems to have avoided any conflicts with the major powers in the kingdom, although his reaction to the additions and alterations in the Rule made by the Patriarch of Jerusalem, Stephen of La Ferté, in 1130, is not known. Stephen added 24 new chapters out of 72 and modified 12. This seems to have been an aspect of his attempts to extend his authority, attempts which

---

[107] See M. BLOCH, *La Société Féodale*, II, Paris, 1940, pp. 201-14 for peace movements initiated by the Church, which attempted to curb feudal warfare.

[108] *De Laude, op. cit.*, col. 921-40.

[109] See P. ROUSSET, *Les Origines et les Caractères de la Première Croisade*, Neuchatel, 1945, pp. 159-67.

had often led him into conflict with the king.[110] The Temple had only begun to attain political and military importance during Hugh's Mastership. Hugh himself was a pious, rather conventional knight. His letter indicates that a number of his companions were more interested in the monastic life than in fighting or political activity. Inevitably this would change as the Military Orders became aware of their unique position, and as outside powers sought to control them.

The Mastership of Hugh of Payens therefore saw dramatic changes in the position of the Order of the Temple. It had begun as a group of individuals who had wished to lead a better life. But when Hugh died on May 24th, 1136,[111] the basis of a huge corporation had been formed. It was to be a corporation for fighting, for politics, for banking, for landowning. It would not be long before this organisation lost any resemblance to the original band. In 1172, the pilgrim Theoderich described the stables belonging to this organisation at Jerusalem. 'They have below them stables for horses built by King Solomon himself in the days of old, adjoining the palace, a wondrous and intricate building resting on piers and containing an endless complication of arches and vaults, which stable we declare, according to our reckoning, could take in ten thousand horses with their grooms. No man could send an arrow from one end of their building to the other, either lengthways or crossways, at one shot with a Balearic bow'.[112] The strength of character of Hugh of Payens in founding and nuturing the early band therefore eventually produced a rich and powerful Order of which he could not have conceived in the 1120's.

After the Council of Troyes the Order had begun to gather momentum. The economic circumstances were propitious, St. Bernard approved enthusiastically, the king of France, the pope, and the French clergy all gave full support. Prevailing social conditions favoured recruitment, for the Templars presented a dual attraction to the upper classes of Frankish society. The feudal warrior lived by arms, but even the most worldly wanted to be saved. The Order of

---

[110] VALOUS, *op. cit.*, pp. 38-9.
[111] E. DE BARTHÉLEMY, *Obituaire de la Commanderie du Temple de Reims*, in *Collection des documents inédits. Mélanges historiques*, IV, Paris, 1882, p. 321, for the day and the month; D'ALBON, *op. cit.*, no. CXXVIII, pp. 89-90, dated 3rd October, 1136, and showing Robert of Craon as Grand Master. Hugh is last mentioned in a document which cannot be dated later than 14th April, 1134; D'ALBON, *op. cit.*, no. LIX, pp. 42-3. He may therefore have died earlier than 1136.
[112] *Theoderich's Description of the Holy Places (circa 1172)*, trans. and ed. A. STEWART, *P.P.T.S.*, V, London, 1891, pp. 30-2.

the Temple offered the potent combination of more or less constant warfare and the pursuit of the religious life. For these reasons the foundation of the Order can be seen as a logical development within the context of the crusading movement. Indeed, in the twelfth century, while the crusade remained popular, the continued growth of the Order was assured.

**Corrigenda**
p. 229, l. 22, for: Andrew of Baudement; read: William II.
p. 236, l. 20, for: Queen Theresa; read: Countess Theresa.

# II

## JAMES OF MOLAY, THE LAST GRAND MASTER OF THE ORDER OF THE TEMPLE

On Thursday, October 12th, 1307, the Grand Master of the Temple, James of Molay, attended the funeral of Catherine, the wife of Charles of Valois, brother of King Philip the Fair of France. James had a place of honour at the ceremony, for he held one of the cords of the pall. Early the next morning he was suddenly arrested by the king's officials. Simultaneously, all the members of the Order in French territory were taken into custody.[1] This well-planned operation was the first move in Philip's determined and ultimately successful attempt to destroy the Order. It ended with the execution of the Grand Master in 1314.

\* \* \*

James of Molay entered the Temple in 1265 at Beaune in the diocese of Autun. He was received by Humbert of Pairaud, the Master in England, and Aimery of La Roche, the Master in France.[2] He was therefore probably Burgundian and his most likely place of origin was the village of Molay in Franche-Comté, which is about 31 miles from Beaune. Beyond this, it is difficult to find any information about his background.[3] It seems unlikely that he was any older than twenty-one at the time of his entry. Even this would mean that he was in his middle sixties during the trial and seventy at the time of his execution. It is of course possible that he was younger than twenty-

---

[1] *Chronique Latine de Guillaume de Nangis de 1113 à 1300 avec les continuations de cette chronique de 1300 à 1368*, ed. H. GERAUD, vol. I, Paris, 1843, p. 360.
[2] G. LIZERAND, *Le Dossier de l'Affaire des Templiers*, Paris, 1923, pp. 32-5.
[3] There are a number of theories concerning his origins, but none are entirely convincing. Most authors believe that he came from Franche-Comté. See G.-J. PERRECIOT, *Quels sont les princes et seigneurs de Franche-Comté qui se sont distingués pendant les croisades*, in *Mémoires et documents inédits pour servir à l'histoire de Franche-Comté*, vol. IV, 1867, p. 364; *L'Art de vérifier les dates*, vol. V, Paris, 1818, p. 356; N.-A. LABBEY DE BILLY, *Histoire de l'Université du Comté de Bourgogne et des différens sujets qui l'ont honorée*, vol. II, Besançon, 1815, pp. 145-6; V. THOMASSIN, *Jacques de Molay, dernier Grand Maître de l'Ordre du Temple*, Paris, 1912, p. 11; C. LAVIROTTE, *Mémoire statistique sur les Établissements des templiers et des hospitaliers en Bourgogne*, Paris, 1853, pp. 55-7; E. BESSON, *Étude sur Jacques de Molay, dernier Grand Maître des Templiers*, in *Mémoires de la société d'émulation du Doubs*, series V, vol. I, 1876, p. 485.

one in 1265, for there were several Templars at the trial who had been admitted when in their teens.[4] There was no fixed age for entry, but new members were expected to be able to bear arms in combat.[5] Probably then, James was born in 1243 or 1244.

James himself speaks of being in Outremer at the time of the Mastership of William of Beaujeu, who ruled the Order from 1273 until he was killed when Acre, the last Latin city on the mainland, fell to the Moslems in 1291. James may well have arrived in the east in 1275 after the Council of Lyons, at which William of Beaujeu had taken a leading role. Almost inevitably, the younger knights, including James, came into conflict with William of Beaujeu's policy of co-existence with the Moslems. They objected to the ten-year truce which had been made with the Moslems by the government at Acre in 1272.[6] This fixes 1282 as the latest possible date for James's arrival in the east. Of course, William of Beaujeu would not break the truce because he knew the weakness of the crusader states. But James and the others wanted to prove themselves with feats of arms and it took them some time to adjust to the pattern of life led by the native Franks. Preconceived ideas about the crusade were not easy to shift. However, according to James, they eventually realised the sense of their Grand Master's policy. It was indeed the only policy if the crusader states were to survive.[7] James of Molay probably remained in the crusader states; the Order could ill-afford to lose men to the west. At the trial, a preceptor from a house in France remembered having seen him at Nicosia in 1291. The occasion was a chapter-general of the Order, attended by 400 brothers. James made a speech, which probably explains why the perceptor remembered his presence.[8] This may indicate that James had escaped from Acre when the city fell, but he could equally well have arrived from France. The witness to his presence had probably come from the west. The number of brothers who had either extricated themselves from Acre, or who had remained in Cyprus at the time, must have been very much less than four hundred.

William of Beaujeu was succeeded by Theobald Gaudin, who appears to have been the most senior of the surviving leaders of the

[4] J. MICHELET, Le Procès des Templiers, vol. I, Paris, 1841, pp. 242, 412; vol. II, pp. 295, 298, 354, 359, 382.
[5] H. DE CURZON, La Règle du Temple, Paris, 1886, para. 14, pp. 25-6.
[6] L'Estoire de Eracles Empereur et la Conqueste de la Terre d'Outremer, in Recueil des Historiens des Croisades, Historiens Occidentaux, vol. II, Paris, 1859, pp. 461-2.
[7] Lizerand, op. cit., pp. 168-71.
[8] Procès, II, p. 139.

Order.[9] He was elected Grand Master in Cyprus which, after the fall of Acre to the Moslems, now became the main Latin base in the east. His reign was short. James was Grand Master at the earliest by late April, 1292, and at the latest, by 8 December, 1293. On the latter date, Edward I of England acquitted Guy of Foresta, the Master of the Order in England, of various amercements made on the previous Master, Robert of Turville, and other Templars. The acquittal was at the request of James of Molay, Master of the Military Order of the Temple of Solomon.[10] It has been suggested that James was Master in England at about this period.[11] In fact Guy of Foresta held this post from 1291 to 1294,[12] and Robert of Turville during the preceding period, 1276 to 1290.[13] There is no documentary evidence to suggest that James was Master in England before 1276, nor indeed that he held any subordinate position in the hierarchy, although he probably served in at least one senior post before becoming Grand Master.

If a Templar called Hugh of Faure from the diocese of Limoges is to be believed, James only gained the leadership of the Order by intrigue. At the trial, Hugh of Faure claimed that the electors were divided between James of Molay and Hugh of Pairaud, the Visitor of the Temple, and nephew of the man who had received James into the Order. Since the majority, which consisted mainly of the men who came from Limousin and Auvergne, wanted Hugh of Pairaud, James's position was weak and, realising this, he declared to Odo of Grandisson and other leading knights of the Order that he did not wish to become Grand Master and would vote for Hugh of Pairaud. On the strength of this promise James was made Grand Prior, a post which carried the duty of governing the Order until a new Grand Master was elected. According to Hugh of Faure, James then used this position to push his own candidature and succeeded in forcing the assembly to elect him Grand Master.[14] A disputed election was of course possible and in times of stress such disputes are likely to be made public. The Grand Prior was a key position, and he could

---

9 *Procès*, I, p. 646; II, pp. 238, 313.
10 *Calendar of the Close Rolls*, Edward I, 1288-96, London, 1904, 22 Ed. I 1293, p. 339.
11 See T. W. PARKER, *The Knights Templars in England*, Tucson, Arizona, 1963, p. 125.
12 *Cal. of the Patent Rolls*, Ed. I, 1281-92, London, 1893, pp. 446, 508; *Cal. of the Patent Rolls*, Ed. I, 1292-1301, London, 1895, pp. 22, 41, 75; *The Rolls and Register of Bishop Oliver Sutton, 1280-99*, ed. R.M.T. HILL, vol. I, Hereford, 1948, pp. 189, 208; Bibliothèque Nationale de Paris, *Nouvelles Acquisitions Latines*, 61, fol. 189.
13 *Cal. of the Close Rolls*, Ed. I, 1272-9, London, 1900, pp. 331; *Cal. of the Patent Rolls*, Ed. I, 1272-81, London, 1900, p. 331; *Cal. of the Patent Rolls*, Ed. I, 1272-81, London, 1901, pp. 208, 252, 371, 436, 444, 445, 450; *Cal. of the Patent Rolls*, Ed. I, 1281-92, pp. 19, 20, 77, 251, 293, 296, 399.
14 *Procès*, II, pp. 223-4.

have manipulated the choice of electors even though it be against the general will. However, there is no evidence to corroborate Hugh of Faure's allegation and statements made at the trial are inevitably suspect. He may have blamed the Grand Master for the Order's plight and therefore have tried to show that the majority of the knights did not approve of him, or simply have desired a leader from his own native region.

The new Master almost at once began to repair the Order after the shattering effects of the expulsion of the Latins from the Holy Land in 1291. In 1293, at Venice, the Templars equipped six galleys with men and arms for the protection of Cyprus.[15] By the last months of 1294, the Grand Master himself was in Italy, visiting Pope Boniface VIII. On 23rd January, 1295, King James II of Aragon wrote around to Barcelona and the other cities of the region telling them that he had received news from James of Molay, the Grand Master of the Temple, who was at that time in Rome. The Grand Master had told him that Pope Celestine V had abdicated and on 24th December last the Cardinal Benedict had been elected pope, taking the name of Boniface VIII.[16] Two days before King James had sent out this letter, the Grand Master had written to Peter of St. Just, the preceptor of Graynane, informing him that he was staying at the Papal Curia, and that he had crossed the sea for the benefit of the Christian community and for the Order. He intended to leave Rome on 24th June and requested the help of the preceptor in his mission.[17] The implication is clear. James had come to Europe to try to make up the losses of the Order sustained at Acre, and perhaps, to stimulate enthusiasm in the west for a new crusade. He must have had discussions with the pope about the future of the crusade, and the question of a possible fusion of the Military Orders, which had been discussed at least since the Council of Lyons in 1274, was doubtless examined. According to James, Boniface rejected any scheme of union.[18]

The tangible results of James's visit were two bulls issued on July 21st. One was of a general nature and granted the Order the same privileges in Cyprus as in the Holy Land.[19] The other was addressed to Edward I and asked him to allow the Master and brothers

---

[15] *Jacobi Auriae Annales Genuenses*, in MURATORI, *Rerum Italicarum Scriptores*, vol. 6, Milan, 1725, bk. X, col. 606.

[16] H. FINKE, *Acta Aragonensia*, vol. I, Berlin, 1923, no. 17, pp. 26-7.

[17] *Ibid.*, vol. III, no. 18, pp. 31-2.

[18] LIZERAND, *op. cit.*, pp. 4-5.

[19] *Les Registres de Boniface VIII*, ed. G. DIGARD, and others, fasc. I, Paris, 1884, no. 487, col. 169-70.

II

of the Temple to export, without hindrance, supplies needed for the sustenance of Cyprus.[20] It seems that while he was in Rome, James took the opportunity to request that the Order be excused from voluntary gifts because of its great expenses overseas, although the obligatory gifts would still be made.[21] It may have been because of this request that the chronicler known as the Templar of Tyre, who had been secretary to William of Beaujeu, believed that the Grand Master was a mean and avaricious man. He says that *«frère Jaque de Molay, maistre dou Temple quant il ful outremer, se porta mout escharsement vers le pape et les cardenaus, car il s'estoit mout eschars hors de rayson...»*[22]

James also made contact with Charles II, the king of Naples. Charles still had a claim to the kingdom of Jerusalem and was naturally interested in its recovery. His own idea was a commercial war against Egypt, which he hoped would produce a boycott on Egyptian goods. Similarly, certain Christians should be prevented from supplying Egypt with essential materials like iron and wood. To make this effective, Charles proposed a union of the Military Orders, led by a chief of undisputed authority, who would be promised the throne of Jerusalem.[23] In the meantime he co-operated with the Grand Master's plans for the provision of the island of Cyprus. On 12th January, 1295, and again on 25th, he ordered his officers to allow James of Molay, *«dilecti amici nostri»*, to export up to 2,000 *salmae* of wheat, 3,000 of barley, and 500 of vegetables, produced on the estates of the Templars and destined for Cyprus, without the levy of any taxes.[24] Exports were still continuing in 1299, for in May of that year, a shipment of grain for the Temple and the Hospital, purchased by the Bardi and other companies, was sent out through Manfredonia.[25]

During this period, James travelled to England and France. He held chapter meetings with Hugh of Pairaud in both countries.[26] It is not clear whether he visited these countries before or after his stay in Rome. A priest of the Order, named John of Stoke, remembered seeing him in England in 1294,[27] but Peter of St. Just, the commander

---

[20] *Ibid.*, no. 489, col. 170.
[21] *Procès*, I, p. 629.
[22] *Gestes des Chiprois*, ed. G. RAYNAUD, Geneva, 1887, p. 329.
[23] See J. DELAVILLE LE ROULX, *La France en Orient au XIV⁰ siècle*, Paris, 1886, pp. 16-18.
[24] L. DE MAS LATRIE, *Histoire de l'Ile de Chypre*, vol. II, pt. I, Paris, 1852, pp. 91-2; *Rapport sur le recueil des archives de Venise intitulé «Libri pactorum» ou «Patti»*, in *Archives des missions scientifiques*, series I, vol. II, Paris, 1851, p. 365.
[25] MAS-LATRIE, *Chypre, op. cit.*, pp. 97-8.
[26] K. SCHOTTMÜLLER, *Der Untergang des Templeordens*, vol. II, Berlin, 1887, p. 192; *Procès*, I, p. 475.
[27] D. WILKINS, *Concilia Magnae Britanniae et Hiberniae*, vol. II, London, 1737, pp. 387-8.

of the Temple at Correus (in Picardy) testified that James and Hugh of Pairaud had received him into the Order at Paris in 1297.[28] If the latter is the same man to whom the Grand Master wrote in 1295, his memory is obviously at fault. Probably James had left England by 1296. Two orders from Edward I at Berwick, dated April 24th, 1296, seem to testify to the Grand Master's activity. Both were addressed to Stephen of Pencestre, the constable of Dover Castle. The first told him to allow Guy of Foresta, the former Master in England, to leave the country in the train of the bishop of Albano. Guy was taking with him three horses and a quantity of worsted cloth to be used as robes for the brethren in Cyprus.[29] The second was to allow Brian of Jay, the current Master in England, to travel in the same party so that he could confer with the Grand Master and take with him his contribution.[30] Presumably this meant money collected on the Templar estates in England.

This European tour bears certain similarities to that made by the first Grand Master of the Order, Hugh of Payens, in 1128-30, when he gathered together large numbers of men and considerable property for the cause of the Holy War. However, by the end of the thirteenth century it was an uphill task for, despite the work of propagandists like Ramon Lull, contemporary literature shows that the west had little real interest in a new crusade.[31] It was to become evident that James did not fully realise the extent of the changes which had taken place since the days of Hugh of Payens. The «open» and expansionist Europe of the early twelfth-century had been replaced by a more stable society, in which men had more to gain by staying at home. A combination of economic prosperity and stronger government had made the dangerous and largely unprofitable expeditions to the east seem much less attractive. The constant failure of the crusades had only strengthened the belief that there was little point in undertaking such ventures. Monarchs paid lip-service to the idea, but had no intention of actually embarking for the east. Even Boniface VIII was more interested in European affairs. In a letter to Gregory, the patriarch of Armenia, in 1298, he wrote that, once affairs in Europe had been settled and in particular the question of Sicily, a new crusade could be launched. Meanwhile the Armenians should remember

---

[28] *Procès*, I, pp. 474-5.
[29] *Cal. of the Close Rolls*, 24 Ed. I 1296, p. 511.
[30] *Idem.*
[31] See P.A. THROOP, *Criticism of the Crusades*, Amsterdam, 1940, *passim*.

that the Lord was always with those in tribulation.[32] Soon Boniface was to be involved in the conflict with Philip of France which was to end in the pope's death. Inevitably, eastern affairs came a poor second in his order of priorities. There was an attempt to enforce the blockade against Egypt and decrees against the sale of arms were renewed in 1299, but Boniface did not go beyond this.[33] James of Molay was doing his best in difficult circumstances.

*    *    *

In December, 1293, al-Asraf Khalil, the conqueror of Acre, was murdered by his emirs.[34] At this time the Christians in Cyprus were too weak to take advantage of the situation. However, by 1300 circumstances had changed. They had obtained a limited amount of help from the west, at least partly due to James of Molay's efforts, and more important, they hoped for an alliance with the Mongols against Egypt. Ghazan, the Mongol Khan, arrived in Syria in 1299 with a large force. He twice sent invitations to the Cypriots to join him, but the Christians were not able to react. They were paralysed, not so much by their weakness, but as so often in the crusader states, by internal dissension. The reigning king of Cyprus, Henry II, failed to agree on a plan with the Masters of the Hospital and the Temple, with the result that Ghazan met and defeated the Egyptian forces nears Homs, on 23rd December, 1299, without Christian aid.[35] At long range Pope Boniface tried to placate the factions in Cyprus. In 1298 he wrote to King Henry asking him to treat the Orders with favour, for they had rendered great services to his kingdom.[36] On 20th March, 1299, he told James of Molay to make peace with Henry. The king, he said, had received the Order after the expulsion of the Christians from Syria. If the Temple and the king continued to quarrel it was likely that the island would suffer from Saracen attacks.[37] The pope had set himself a difficult task. To satisfy the king he had forbidden the Orders to acquire extra estates in Cyprus without the permission of both king and pope. But, in June, 1299, he wrote to say that

[32]  Reg. de Boniface VIII, op. cit., fasc. 5, Paris, 1890, no. 2663, col. 180-1.
[33]  Ibid., no. 3421, col. 597-8; MAS LATRIE, Chypre, op. cit., pp. 92-3.
[34]  HAYTON, La Flor des Estoires de la Terre d'Orient, in R.H.C., Documents Arméniens, vol. II, Paris, 1906, pp. 229-31; FLORIO BUSTRONE, Chronique de l'île de Chypre, ed. R. DE MAS LATRIE (Collection des documents inédits sur l'histoire de France, 5), Paris, 1886, p. 128.
[35]  HAYTON, pp. 291-8; Chroniques d'Amadi et de Strambaldi, ed. R. DE MAS LATRIE, Paris, 1891, pp. 234-5.
[36]  Reg. de Boniface VIII, op. cit., fasc. 5, no. 2439, col. 38-9.
[37]  Ibid., no. 2438, col. 37-8.

this had been interpreted too strictly. The Orders were to be allowed small-scale additions to their property.[38] Boniface seems to have had temporary success. The Christians were able to mount a number of campaigns in 1300 in which James of Molay and the Templars took part. The first of these campaigns was against Egypt itself but included a raid on the Palestinian coast. It was a feeble affair. Sixteen galleys were equipped, together with a number of smaller vessels, and the king, the Temple and the Hospital, all supplied troops and money. They left Famagusta on 20th July, and managed to inflict some damage on Rosetta, Alexandria, Acre, and Tortosa. This was the full extent of their success. When a Hospitaller attack on Maraclea was beaten off, they gave up and returned to base.[39] But the Mongol Khan was not discouraged, for he once more sent an envoy to Cyprus asking that the Christians wait for him in Armenia, ready for a new campaign in the winter. This time Amaury of Lusignan, the titular constable of Jerusalem and brother of King Henry, set sail with the two Orders, including James of Molay. They reached the island of Ruad, off Tortosa, and from there they ventured to Tortosa itself. However, the gathering of an enemy force led to a rapid decampment. Ghazan had failed to appear and it was not until Febraury, 1301, that one of his emirs arrived in the region. Accompanied by the king of Armenia, the Mongols conducted a brief campaign, but by this time Amaury's force had returned to Cyprus.[40]

Meanwhile James of Molay had tried to make some more positive moves. He attempted to organise Ruad as a base for attacks on the Saracens. A predominantly Templar garrison was left there under the command of Bartholomew, the marshal of the Order. It consisted of 120 knights, 500 archers, and 400 servants. In reality the garrison occupied a hopeless position. In 1302, the Sultan of Egypt sent one of his emirs, with a fleet of 20 galleys, to Tripoli. The Templars had no galleys to oppose them. The Egyptian force marched 'to Tortosa and landed at Ruad. The Christians were not strong enough to prevent this and retreated to a tower that they had built. They then tried the only course available to them, which was to negotiate. Brother Hugh of Dampierre was sent to parley with the enemy, and managed

[38] *Ibid.*, nos. 3060-2, col. 411-12.
[39] AMADI, pp. 236-7; *Gestes des Chiprois*, pp. 303-5; BUSTRON, pp. 131-2.
[40] AMADI, pp. 237-8; *Gestes des Chiprois*, pp. 305-6; MARINO SANUDO, *Liber Secretorum Fidelium Crucis super Terrae Sanctae*, in BONGARS, *Gesta Dei per Francos*, II, Hanover, 1611, p. 242; BUSTRON, p. 132.

to obtain a safe-conduct for the departure of the garrison, but when they emerged the promise was broken and most of then were killed or taken into captivity.[41] The Moslems could act this way with impunity, for they knew there was little danger from Cyprus. According to Amadi, the king and the Masters of the Orders had contemplated sending a relief expedition and had assembled ships at Famagusta, but they were too late. The Moslems had already seized the island.[42] In retrospect, the idea of using Ruad as a base seems foolish. Even if James of Molay had not actually planned it, he had certainly sanctioned it and therefore bears the responsibility. However, it must be said that he alone had attempted something beyond isolated and ineffectual raids by sea, for by this time the futility of such raids must have been obvious to all. It seems that the Grand Master was genuinely interested in the recovery of the Holy Land, although it is clear that he lacked the ability and the resources to make a success of it.

After the events of 1300 to 1302, there was little chance of launching a new offensive. Indeed, from time to time, the island of Cyprus itself was raided by Saracen pirates. One such attack took place in March, 1302, when, operating from their base in Rhodes, pirates landed in the region of Limassol. They broke into the castle of Guy of Ibelin, the titular count of Jaffa, and seized him, his wife, Maria, and a son and daughter. James of Molay obtained their release, but only after payment of a ransom of 45,000 silver pieces. [43] The position was therefore extremely discouraging, if even pirates could make such damaging sorties. But despite this the Grand Master stayed in the island at least until the summer of 1306, and then left only at the request of the pope. In depositions made at the trial, the Grand Master is mentioned as being resident in Cyprus between 1302 and 1304. He was present at receptions held at Limassol, Famagusta, and Nicosia.[44] Efforts seem to have been made to ensure that the Order maintained a reasonable number of serving knights on the island. An Italian Templar called Antonio testified that there were 120 brothers or more assembled when he was received by James of Molay at Limassol in 1304.[45]

During this time James was in contact with western rulers. On May 13th, 1304, Edward I of England wrote to him from Stirling.

[41] AMADI, pp. 238-9; BUSTRON, p. 133.
[42] AMADI, p. 239.
[43] Ibid., p. 238; BUSTRON, p. 134.
[44] Procès, II, pp. 289-90, 294-5.
[45] Ibid., I, p. 562.

William of La More, the Master in England, had been ordered to Cyprus by James of Molay, and Edward willingly gave his permission for William to make the journey. The king recommended William to James's favour, but would be grateful if the Master in England was allowed to return as soon as possible because his services were so valuable. At the end of the letter Edward sounded a hopeful note. He had been involved in many wars, but when he was free he would fulfil his vow to undertake a new crusade. For this reason he asked the Grand Master to give William of La More all the information relevant to such an expedition. William would then be able to help the king with his plans.[46] There was of course little chance that Edward would ever be able to travel to the east again, but the letter is significant because it shows the continued interest of James of Molay in the recovery of the Holy Land.

Relations with the French monarchy were more equivocal. The Order was largely French in membership and it had been closely associated with the Capetian monarchy at least since the time of the Second Crusade. The Templars had performed valuable financial services for Louis IX, and in 1258 the king had confirmed them in all their possessions.[47] Signs of strain had appeared during the reign of Philip III, who had tried to stop them acquiring property in *main-morte*,[48] but the prohibition had not been effective. Philip the Fair had tried to enforce it by confiscating all the property that the Order had acquired since 1258, but this move also failed.[49] Since 1294 the Templars had been relieved of control of the French finances after more than a century of complete dominance. This had not been the result of a coup, but of a progressive change-over, much of which had been the work of the treasurer of the Temple in Paris, John of Tour. During the next year a group of Florentine bankers took charge, but after that royal agents took over. The Templars and the Florentines were both used in various capacities after this date however, and there does not seem to have been any ill-will. Some of the royal treasure was kept at the Louvre, but the Templars still retained the guard of a portion of it. The change was part of a general re-organisation of the royal finances which, with the growth of the royal domain and the increase in Philip's financial needs, was inevi-

[46] *Cal. of the Close Rolls*, Ed. I, 1302-7, London, 1908, 32 Ed. I 1304, p. 208.
[47] H. PRUTZ, *Entwicklung und Untergang des Tempelherrenordens*, Berlin, 1888 no. 3, p. 297.
[48] A. BAUDOUIN, *Lettres Inédites de Philippe Le Bel*, in *Mémoires de l'Académie des Sciences, Inscriptions et Belles Lettres de Toulouse*, 8th series, vol. 8, Toulouse, 1886, no. 184, pp. 211-13. This is a confirmation by Philip IV of his predecessor's prohibition.
[49] PRUTZ, *op. cit.*, nos. 10-13, pp. 302-3.

II

table at some date. However, the re-organisation does seem to have been a little premature, for by 1303 the Templars were back in control, probably in order to help the king finance his Flemish wars.[50] During the early years of the Mastership of James of Molay, the Order retained its property and privileges within France. Prutz has set out a number of royal confirmations made between January, 1293, and March, 1295.[51] Therefore, up to the year 1303, there is no real evidence to indicate that Philip the Fair intended to make a determined attack upon the position of the Order. The Capetian monarchy had been extending its authority within the kingdom for two centuries, and these sporadic attempts to limit the independence of the Order of the Temple cannot be seen in isolation from the general policy of the Capetians. James of Molay would have had no reason to see Philip's policy as ominous, or even unusual.

The period after 1303 is full of rumour and legend, eagerly supplied by those who wrote with knowledge of the aftermath. According to the *Gestes des Chiprois*, Bustron, and 'Amadi', the treasurer of the Temple in Paris had, in the early years of the fourteenth-century, made a loan of 400,000 florins to the king. The loan was against the wishes of James of Molay and the man had been expelled from the Order. All Philip's efforts failed to gain his reinstatement. As a result, the king determined to revenge himself on the Order.[52] A modern writer has suggested that when the king's minister, William of Nogaret, returned from his inglorious action against Boniface VIII at Anagni in the autumn of 1303, he might have brought with him information from the Colonna family which indicated that the Templars had been secretly financing Boniface VIII.[53] The Order did make contributions to the Holy See at various times. In February, 1297, the Grand Master had authorised a payment to be made to papal legates,[54] but this cannot be regarded as very significant. In fact, on June 13th-15th, 1303, Hugh of Pairaud was among those who promised to give support to the king against Boniface VIII.[55] In June, 1304, the king made a general confirmation of Templar property in France.[56]

---

[50] BAUDOUIN, *op. cit.*, no. 148, pp. 163-4, shows that Hugh of Pairaud was entrusted with the collection of the war subsidy of 1303.
[51] PRUTZ, *op. cit.*, nos. 14-18, pp. 303-5.
[52] *Gestes des Chiprois*, pp. 329-30; BUSTRON, p. 163; AMADI, pp. 280-1.
[53] J. SHALLOW, *Conjectures on the Templar Procès*, London, 1918, p. 6.
[54] *Reg. de Boniface VIII*, *op. cit.*, fasc. 1, no. 2323, col. 914.
[55] G. PICOT, *Documents relatifs aux États Généraux et Assemblées réunis sous Philippe Le Bel*, Paris, 1901, no. XIV, p. 50, no. XV, p. 53.
[56] PRUTZ, *op. cit.*, no. 21, pp. 307-8.

Even if Hugh of Pairaud really had been a rival to James of Molay in the election of a Grand Master, this agreement could hardly have been accomplished without James's approval. In short, whatever may have been in the mind of the king of France, it cannot be said that James of Molay regarded himself as an enemy of Philip. As for the king, in 1303 he needed allies. He had suffered defeat in Flanders, he had quarrelled with the Papacy, he had been forced to debase the coinage. At this time it was expedient to ensure the continued support of the Templars.

In Cyprus the position was somewhat different. Here, King Henry clearly regarded James of Molay as his opponent. Sometime before 1306, the king had made a formal complaint to the Pope about the Grand Master, claiming that the hostility of the Templars towards his predecessor, Hugh III, had been transferred to him after Hugh's death.[57] But James of Molay was not alone. Others had come into conflict with the king. At the centre of the opposition was Amaury of Lusignan, the king's brother, who had become increasingly discontented with Henry's government. On 26th April, 1306, Amaury took action. Supported by a number of powerful lords, including Hamerin, the Constable, and Baldwin, titular prince of Galilee, he summoned to Nicosia all the royal vassals who were available.[58] According to Makhairas, James of Molay was not in Nicosia at the time, but on receiving a message from Amaury, he joined him in the city.[59] The lords who were present swore an oath to protect Amaury against any man except the king, although not all did so willingly. A charter was issued electing Amaury governor of Cyprus and deposing Henry.[60] The Grand Master's name does not appear on this, but Bustron claims that, together with Peter of Erlant, the bishop of Limassol, James of Molay was responsible for drafting it.[61] On the same day Amaury presented a declaration detailing his complaints against the king. It said that the country was badly defended, that there was poverty and famine, that there had been practically no diplomatic activity, and that justice had not been fairly administered. The Hospital, the Temple, and the clergy, were among those who were supposed to have

---

[57] MAS LATRIE, Chypre, op. cit., vol. II. pt. I, pp. 108-9, who has dated it pre-April, 1306, on the grounds that it contains no mention of the coup of Amaury of Lusignan of that date.
[58] LEONTIOS MAKHARIAS, Recital concerning the Sweet Land of Cyprus entitled «Chronicle», ed. and trans. R.M. DAWKINS, vol. I, Oxford, 1932, pp. 42-51; Gestes des Chiprois, pp. 317-18; BUSTRON, pp. 137-8; AMADI, p. 248.
[59] MAKHAIRAS, pp. 46-7.
[60] C. KOHLER, Documents chypriotes du début du XIV⁺ siècle, in Revue de l'Orient Latin, II, 1905-8, pp. 244-52; MAKHAIRAS, pp. 44-5; BUSTRON, p. 138; AMADI, loc. cit.
[61] BUSTRON, loc. cit.

suffered as a result. James of Molay was in the list of signatories to this charter.[62] According to 'Amadi' and Bustron, James acted as a mediator in the negotiations that followed,[63] but there is no doubt that his sympathies lay with Amaury of Lusignan. His allegiance may have been strengthened by the fact that Amaury owed the Order 40,000 white besants.[64] After twenty days of negotiations it was decided that the king and his household were to retain the revenue necessary for their expenses, but the rest was to be left to the governor.[65]

Although James of Molay may not have helped to plan the coup, he was a willing supporter. There does seem to have been some justification for discontent on his part. The Saracen pirate raid against the Ibelin castle in 1302, for instance, shows how vulnerable was the island. James had made efforts to rectify food shortages by supplying Cyprus from the west. Moreover, he still believed in the possible recovery of the Holy Land. It appears that a sick king was not offering the kind of leadership which could solve the island's problems, nor did he seem interested in the crusade. But the Grand Master had little opportunity to see if the new government was able to improve on Henry's record. Soon after the coup, he was summoned to the west by Pope Clement V. King Henry was eventually restored in 1310,[66] but by that time graver events had overtaken James of Molay.

\* \* \*

Clement V was crowned on November 14th, 1305. From the outset he determined upon a more systematic approach towards the crusade than that of his immediate predecessors. His method was similar to that of Gregory X. On 6th June, 1306, he summoned the Grand Masters of the Hospital and the Temple to meet him at Poitiers so that they could advise him on a project for sending aid to the kings of Armenia and Cyprus.[67] James of Molay produced two written memoirs, one on the organisation of a crusade, the other on a possible union of the Military Orders.

[62] L. DE MAS LATRIE, Allocution au Roi Henri II de Lusignan, in Revue des Questions historiques, XLIII, 1888, pp. 524-41.
[63] AMADI, p. 251; BUSTRON, p. 139.
[64] MAKHAIRAS, pp. 46-7; AMADI, p. 248, says 50,000.
[65] MAKHAIRAS, pp. 46-7; AMADI, pp. 251-3; BUSTRON, pp. 139-40.
[66] AMADI, p. 379.
[67] Regestum Clementis Papae V ... cura et studio Monachorum Ordinis S. Benedicti, ann. I, Rome, 1885, no. 1033, col. 190-1. The order to James of Molay has not survived, but the one addressed to the Master of the Hospital is still in existence. It can be assumed that the order to James was sent out at the same time.

The Grand Master was very much in favour of a general crusade. Since they had no bases to work from, isolated groups would be useless. Obviously, he had learned from his experience at Ruad. Professor Atiya points out that the idea of a *passagium parvum* was being canvassed at this time in Europe. Writers like Marino Sanudo thought that this could precede a *passagium generale*.[68] James was anxious to show that this was an illusion. The landing-place for this general crusade, he felt, should not be Armenia, even though it was Christian. He though that the climatic conditions would be very wearing to westerners, that the Armenian style of fighting was not compatible with that of the Franks, and that in any case the local inhabitants were of doubtful loyalty. If a general crusade were organised, it would have to be in sufficient force to repel the Egyptian army without any help. The number needed would be 15,000 knights and 5,000 foot. This was based on a statement supposed to have been made by the Sultan Baibars, who had once said that he could fight 30,000 Tartars, but would have to give way to half that number of Franks. James wanted to see the support of the kings of France, England, Germany, Sicily, Aragon, and Castile, and to have the Italian cities supply transport. All these combined should be able to raise the forces required. The vessels used should be larger than galleys for this would be more economical, but if galleys were to be employed then ten would be wanted to sail ahead and clear the eastern Mediterranean. Then they should institute a blockade on the Egyptian coast. The commander
* of the fleet should be Roger of Loria, whose reputation was such that his leadership could not be challenged. Venice and Genoa might
* object to either of the Military Orders being in charge. Roger of Loria would be impartial because at this time he regarded most powers with equal hostility, certainly the courts of Aragon, Naples, and Palermo. Rather than go to Armenia, the main crusade should land in Cyprus in order to recuperate before making the final offensive.[69] The memoir is an honest, if not particularly original, attempt to persuade the pope to preach a general crusade. Schemes for blockade and limited military action might have achieved temporary and local results, but James was undoubtedly correct in his emphasis on a general passage if there was to be any serious attempt to recover the Holy Land. The memoir takes little account of European political

---

[68] Sanudo, pp. 262-81; see A.S. Atiya, *The Crusade in the Later Middle Ages*, London, 1938, p. 55.
[69] E. Baluze, *Vitae Paparum Avenionensium*, ed. G. Mollat, vol. III, Paris, 1921, pp. 145-9,

II

and social realities, but then neither did the premise from which the Grand Master was required to work.

A connected problem was the position of the Military Orders. Proposals that they should be fused into one had been put forward since the time of St. Louis and had been seriously considered at the Council of Lyons in 1274. James himself had discussed the matter with Boniface VIII. However, the Grand Master's memoir on this subject was much weaker than his discussion of the crusade. This was perhaps a more emotional subject and, in consequence, James's arguments are far from strong. To begin with, he outlined the historical background. The idea had been abandoned in 1274, he said, because the Spanish kings objected. They did not want the three specifically Spanish Orders of Calatrava, Alcantara, and St. James of the Sword, to be involved in such a union. It had been taken up again by Pope Nicolas IV in 1291 mainly, claimed James, because he wished to convince Europe that he was sincere when he talked of the recovery of the Holy Land. It was a method of deflecting current criticism that he had not done enough for the crusader states before the fall of Acre. Finally, Boniface VIII had toyed with the idea but had abandoned it. James then went on to discuss the advantages and disadvantages of such a scheme. At least this appears to have been his intention, but in fact the rest of the memoir is largely taken up with a rather muddled attack upon the idea of union. He did not think it was honourable, for rarely did good come of innovation. It would imperil the souls of men who had freely chosen one Order, but who were now forced to join another. It might well cause quarrels leading to armed fights between former Templars and Hospitallers who felt that they were better off before the union. It would reduce the amount of charity dispensed separately by the Orders. It would cause disputes between local houses since the house of one Order would inevitably have to be subordinate to the other. There would be rivalry between the various officers who held equal rank in their respective Orders. The rivalry which was now said to exist between the separate Orders was, far from being a disadvantage, a positive benefit, for it stimulated the Orders to do great deeds against the Saracens and to make great efforts to bring supplies to the Holy Land. This also holds true for the priests of the Orders, who made greater efforts in their preaching and in celebrating the divine offices as a result of this rivalry. A union would affect military tactics, for the two Orders always formed the rear-guard and the advance-guard of any army in the Holy Land. This was because the Orders were

experienced in fighting the Saracens. Anybody who had disregarded
this had regretted it. If the two Orders were united, this formation
would not be possible, and other forces would have to take up these
positions. Moreover, pilgrims had always found aid and comfort with
one or other of the Orders. He knew of two advantages of union.
A unified Order would be stronger and better able to resist those
who sought to damage it and deprive it of its property. Also the
expense of the duplication of preceptories would be spared. Only
one house would be needed in each area instead of two. He concluded by saying that the proven men of the Order were always ready
to advise the pope when needed. They were the best people to guard
the Holy Land, for knights in the Order cost less to keep and were
more obedient than otherwise would be the case. Finally, if the pope
intended to assign revenues, the Grand Master would be grateful if
they were given separately to the Orders otherwise, as was only
human, one or other would try to take more than its due.[70]

The document is full of trivial and irrelevant points. It does not
compare with the work of men like Pierre Dubois and Ramon Lull.
But then James of Molay had not been trained in this way. He had
spent all his adult life within this Order and therefore it was almost
certain that he would be resistant to change. Similarly, it was not
a contemplative Order; he would not have had the opportunity (or
perhaps the inclination) to have read deeply and thus acquired a
greater literary sophistication. The memoir has an air of bewilder-
ment, since James did not really understand the implications behind
the idea of union. The crusading advice, while not an intellectual tour
de force, reads much better because here the Grand Master was dealing with matters with which he had been familiar all his life. The
world of political pamphleteering was alien to him. Lizerand calls
the document, «mesquines, intéressés, egoïstes»,[71] and it does contain
an element of self-seeking. But it must be regarded as natural enough
for him to have pride in an Order that he had served for so many
years and for him to wish to retain his position at the head of that
Order. The memoir is yet another indication that James did not
really grasp the political circumstances in the west. The only glimmer
can be seen when he talks of the greater strength of a combined
Order in resisting hostile forces, although here he was probably thinking of the secular clergy rather than any lay power. Even this does

---

[70] LIZERAND, op. cit., pp. 2-15.
[71] Ibid, p. II.

not tackle the problem of where the ultimate control of this united Order would lie. There is here a failure to understand fundamental realities; a tendency to take situations at their face value.

*  *  *

Philip the Fair had two overriding and connected problems: the maintenance and extension of his power within the state and the need to finance this policy. The arrest and trial of the Templars was a facet, and at first probably not a very important facet, of these wider problems. Since the bull «Omne Datum Optimum» of 1139, the Order of the Temple had been theoretically free of all authority except that of the pope.[72] In the east it had a record of defiance of lay power. It possessed considerable wealth, both in land and moveables. The much-quoted estimate of Matthew Paris, who reckoned they possessed 9,000 manors, was made in the mid-thirteenth century.[73] Other Orders were more wealthy, notably the Cistercians, as well as the Hospital,[74] but the Temple was more vulnerable at this point in time. For several years rumours had been circulating about immorality within the Order,[75] and despite the efforts of the Grand Master, the Temple itself had found no real employment since 1291. In contrast the Hospitallers had begun the conquest of the island of Rhodes in September, 1306, a task which they completed in August, 1308, and from here they were able to perform some useful function against pirates in the eastern Mediterranean.[76]

Mme. Melville has suggested that Philip was hostile to the Templars because they were an enclave of the papacy,[77] and although this is equally true of the Hospitallers, again the Templars could more easily be attacked. However, this could not have been a serious consideration on the part of the French monarchy. The Templars were willing enough to oppose Boniface VIII in 1303. It is difficult to say how far the Order represented a danger to the state. Calculations by Lea and Finke have concluded that they probably numbered fewer than 2,000 in France, and that these were scattered throughout

[72] See MARQUIS D'ALBON, *Cartulaire général de l'Ordre du Temple, 1119?-1150*, Paris, 1913, *Bullaire*, no. V, pp. 375-9.
[73] MATTHEW PARIS, *Chronica Majora*, ed. H.R. LUARD, vol. IV, Rolls Series, London, 1878, p. 291.
[74] See H.C. LEA, *A History of the Inquisition of the Middle Ages*, vol. III, New York, 1889, pp. 250-1.
[75] The best-know is the denunciation made by Esquieu of Floyran of Lerida. See FINKE, *Papsttum und Untergang des Templeordens*, 2 vols., Münster, 1907, vol. I, pp. 111-12, vol. II, no. 57, pp. 83-5.
[76] *Gestes des Chiprois*, pp. 319-23; AMADI, pp. 254-9.
[77] M. MELVILLE, *La Vie des Templiers*, Paris, 1951, p. 249.

the country.[78] In this case they would not have presented any real danger to the French monarchy. It is perhaps more difficult to say how far they represented a danger in Philip's mind or in the minds of his advisers. The truth seems to be that the opportunity arose for Philip to alleviate some of his financial problems, and he grasped that opportunity. To the king the matter of guilt or innocence was a side-issue. He probably thought that the affair could be quickly settled, as it had been when he had seized the property of the Lombards in 1291 and that of the Jews in 1306.[79] In 1303, he had used the expedient of a double subsidy on all usurers.[80] As Professor Mollat points out, once the Templars had been arrested Philip began to assign the rents on their property.[81] Delisle gives an example of this take-over. Before the arrest the Templars paid a rent to one Othon of Granson. This amounted to 2,000 livres tournois payable at Paris and Lyon. In 1308, Philip the Fair was assigning this rent to Othon on property belonging to the Templars in the dioceses of Langres, Sens, and Troyes.[82]

To a large extent therefore, James of Molay was caught in a situation over which he had little control. In the eyes of Europe he may have appeared as the leader of a redundant Order, but since his election he had tried hard to revive the crusade. His visit to France in 1307 was part of this policy. It has been suggested that he could have transferred the efforts of the Order to Spain,[83] but this is to view the matter with hindsight. He believed that a new crusade could recapture the Holy Land and that it was his duty to work towards this end. It is unlikely that the idea of turning to Spain would have occurred to him. The Spanish kings had their own Orders. The task in Spain was almost complete; the task in the east needed to be restarted.

The Grand Master arrived in France in late 1306 or early 1307. He may have gone first to the pontifical court, but he had certainly reached Paris by June, 1307. Two witnesses at the trial stated he

[78] LEA, op. cit., p. 250; FINKE, op. cit., I, pp. 72-3.
[79] See C.V. LANGLOIS, Saint Louis, Philippe le Bel, Les derniers Capétiens directs (1226-1328), in E. LAVISSE, Histoire de France, vol. III, pt. II, Paris, 1901, pp. 222-30.
[80] E. BOUTARIC, Documents inédits rélatifs à l'histoire de France sous Philippe Le Bel, in Notices et extraits des Manuscrits de la Bibliothèque Impériale et autres Bibliothèques, vol. XX, Paris, 1862, pt. II, no. XX, p. 154.
[81] MOLLAT, The Popes at Avignon, 1305-1378, trans. J. LOVE, Edinburgh, 1963, p. 232.
[82] Reg. Clem. V., op. cit., ann. 3, no. 4404, col. 213-16; see L. DELISLE, Mémoires sur les Operations financières des Templiers, in Mémoires de l'Institut national de France: Académie des Inscriptions et Belles-Lettres, vol. 33, Paris, 1889, p. 92.
[83] MELVILLE, op. cit., pp. 246-7.

II

held a chapter-meeting in the city on either 24th or 29th.[84] Lea has shown that he had not come to take up permanent residence in France.[85] The main administrators of the Temple had remained in Cyprus. When orders for the arrest of the Templars reached the island in May, 1308, the marshal, the treasurer, the turcopolier, and the draper, were among those still present.[86] Only Raimbaut of Craon, the preceptor in Cyprus, had travelled with the Grand Master.[87] The bulk of the cash reserves had been left in Cyprus.[88]

James's primary purpose was the organisation of a new crusade, but once in France he was faced with a more immediate problem. The stories of immorality and heresy within the Order needed to be scotched, and it is possible that the June chapter-meeting was held in order to discuss this. Probably James then had a meeting with the pope. On 24th August, Clement wrote to King Philip telling him that he proposed to begin an inquiry into the accusations being made against the Temple. This inquiry had been specifically requested by James of Molay and various preceptors of the Order.[89] An approach may also have been made to King Philip, for about this time the Grand Master made a defence of the Order in front of the king. William of Plaisians, a minister of the king, brought this matter up in May, 1308, in a public consistory at Poitiers. Apparently in the course of this defence, James had admitted that he had heard confession and had given absolution in chapter, a practice for which he theoretically did not have the power.[90] Such an action could be interpreted as heresy and of course the king's minister had mentioned it for this reason, but by no means all theological opinion would have accepted it as such.[91]

James of Molay therefore did take steps to forestall possible trouble. A few Templars took more positive action and fled the country.[92] They may have known something of Philip's plans, or they may have had reason to be apprehensive of the results of the papal inquiry. The Grand Master stayed in Paris, his confidence boosted by Philip's apparent friendship. In the early autumn of 1307 it pro-

---

[84] *Procès*, I, p. 475, II, p. 279.
[85] LEA, *op. cit.*, pp. 248-9.
[86] BALUZE, *op. cit.*, vol. III, p. 85.
[87] *Procès*, II, p. 374.
[88] See SCHOTTMÜLLER, *op. cit.*, pp. 66-9.
[89] BALUZE, *op. cit.*, p. 60.
[90] FINKE, *op. cit.*, II, no. 88, p. 143.
[91] See LIZERAND, *Les Dépositions du Grand Maître Jacques de Molay au procès des Templiers, 1307-14*, in *Le Moyen Age*, XXVI (1913), pp. 82-3.
[92] FINKE, *op. cit.*, II, no. 50, pp. 74-5.

110

bably did not seem to the Grand Master that he needed to take any drastic action. He would wait for the completion of the inquiry. But Philip was becoming impatient with the inactivity of the Papacy. He had been bringing pressure to bear on Clement V since April,[93] and could wait no longer. He therefore instituted the mass arrests of October 13th.

The charges are well-known. It was alleged that, on reception, knights were required to deny Christ three times and to spit on the crucifix; that they worshipped idols; that they practised sodomy; and that priests left out the words of consecration during the Mass. Other minor charges were piled up, as was the custom in such cases.[94] James of Molay's conduct during the trial was that of a confused and frightened man, advanced in years and worn down by the pressure of the king's officers. He was out of his depth in the circumstances of the trial. He was brought before the Inquisitor, William of Paris, on 24th October, 1307. He told of his reception at Beaune 42 years before and said that at this reception he first of all made several promises with regard to the statutes and observances of the Order. Then they placed a mantle around his neck, and a large bronze cross was brought before him. He was told to deny Christ in front of this cross, and he obeyed. Next, he was to spit on the cross. In fact, he spat on the floor and this only once. He categorically denied engaging in homosexual practices, or that he was ever told to do so. He believed that other Templars were received in the same way, although he usually left this to an assistant. Finally, the interrogators asked him if he had told any lie through fear, either of prison or torture, but the Grand Master replied that he had told the pure truth for the safety of his soul.[95]

The king rapidly made use of this confession. The next day various people were assembled at the Temple in Paris — canons, religious and secular masters, bachelors and scholars from the University of Paris. James of Molay and other leading Templars — Geoffrey of Charney, the preceptor in Normandy, Gerard of Gauche, Guy Dauphin, and Walter of Liancourt, were presented to them. In their name and his own, the Grand Master confirmed his confession. Those who had been received into the Order had denied Christ, had spat on the cross presented to them, and had committed several other enormities. He

[93] Boutaric, *Clément V, Philippe le Bel et les Templiers*, in *Revue des Questions historiques*, X, 1871, pp. 321-6.
[94] Cont. Nangis, I, pp. 261-2.
[95] Lizerand, *Dossier, op. cit.*, pp. 32-7.

had not wished to reveal these things because he knew that it would bring the downfall of the Temple, but they had been brought to light by the intervention of King Philip. In conclusion, James requested the gathering to intercede with the king in order that he might obtain the grace and mercy of the latter.[96] The Grand Master followed this up by writing an open letter to the Templars telling them of his confession and ordering them to do the same in virtue of the holy obedience which they owed to him. They should do this because for a long time they had been deluded by error.[97]

This confession fitted in very neatly — too neatly to be accepted at its face value — with Philip's plans. The public statement in front of the theologians and university men and the letter to the members of the Order should have been enough to crush the Templars. It would certainly have tended to demoralise those members who might have been thinking of denying the charges, and it must have caused sufficient scandal to shatter any hope of recovery on the part of the Temple. It was a show confession and it is possible that the king's officials had led James to believe that if co-operation were forthcoming then no further action would be taken against the persons of the Templars. It is perhaps significant that, in 1309, in front of the papal representatives, James said that it appeared fantastic to him that the Roman Church should suddenly wish to proceed with the destruction of the Temple when the sentence of deposition on the Emperor Frederick II had been postponed for thirty-two years.[98] It could have been implied that a similar delay would be employed in the case of the Templars. Eleven days passed from the day of James's arrest to his first appearance before the Inquisitor. This was ample time for the king's officials to have arranged for the confession and for the Grand Master's resolve to resist (if any such had existed) to have been broken down.

The affair therefore might well have been over by Christmas, 1307, for the Templar revenues were within Philip's grasp. But the pope interfered. Clement was affronted by Philip's action, not because he wished to save the Templars, but because his authority had been

---

[96]  FINKE, op. cit., II, no. 149, pp. 307-9.
[97]  CONT. NANCIS, I, p. 362; Excerpta e Memoriali Historiarum Auctore Johanne Parisiensi, Sancti Victoris Pariensis Canonico Regulari, in Recueil des Historiens des Gaules et de la France, vol. 21, Paris, 1855, p. 651. In the latter source the letter is dated 25th May, 1308. This seems unlikely, since both chronicles give the impression that the letter was circulated directly after the Grand Master's confession in front of the masters of the University of Paris which took place on 25th October, 1307.
[98]  LIZERAND, op. cit., pp. 148-9.

undermined. Philip had more than once tried to force the pope to bring the Templars to trial before the October arrests. But Clement had taken no positive action beyond beginning the inquiry asked for by James of Molay. Philip had thus acted for him. Strictly speaking, the arrests were legal,[99] but the king had shown a fine disregard for Clement's opinions. In a letter to Philip on 27th October, Clement showed his anger, «... we had indicated to Your Highness in our letters that we had taken this matter in hand and that we wished to search carefully for the truth. In the same letter we asked you to be

\* careful to comunicate to us anything which you had discovered on this subject, promising to send you anything which we ourselves found out. Despite this, you perpetrated these outrages on the persons and the property of people who are immediately responsible to us and the Roman Church.» It was «an insulting scorn of us and the Roman Church». The pope therefore demanded that the Templars be sent to him for examination.[100] It was clear that the pope could not reverse Philip's action, so in order to emphasise his own higher authority in the matter, on 22nd November, Clement ordered all Christian rulers to arrest the Templars in their lands and to take over the Order's property in his name.[101] This shows once more that he was more concerned about his own position than about the fate of the Templars.

Since he had extracted the Grand Master's confession, the memory of which, as later events proved, no amount of protestation could remove, Philip was quite prepared to conciliate the pope. He handed over the Templars to the papal representatives, Berengar Fredol and Stephen of Suisey James of Molay appeared before the cardinals on 24th December, 1307. Philip had made a tactical error, for the Grand Master revoked his confession. It had been made because he feared torture.[102] Indeed, he may have gone farther than this, for a Templar called John of Folliaco later testified that wax tablets from the Grand Master had been circulated at this time. The tablets said that the king and the cardinals were coming to the buildings in which the Templars were imprisoned. Some brothers had retracted their confessions, and now the others were to do the same.[103]

---

[99] BOUTARIC, op. cit., pp. 327-31. Philip claimed that it was his sacred duty to act on behalf of the Church to protect it from heresy. His action had the approval of the Inquisitor in France, William of Paris.
[100] Ibid., pp. 332-5.
[101] P. DUPUY, Histoire de la condamnation des Templiers, Brussels, 1751, pp. 221-3.
[102] FINKE, op. cit., II, no. 69, p. 102.
[103] SCHOTTMÜLLER, op. cit., II, p. 37.

There is a dramatic account of the revocation of James of Molay, given by a Catalan living in France. In a letter to a correspondent in Majorca, he tells how the Grand Master asked for a large assembly of people that they might hear him confess an error much greater than those of the previous October. When the crowd had gathered, James was shown to a platform from which he could declaim. He admitted that he and other Templars had confessed, but cried out that they had been made to say what was wanted. He tore his clothing to reveal that his arms were cut and burnt, and that the flesh on his legs, back, and stomach, was scorched. The cardinals were so overcome that they wept at the sight. The king's councillors then told the cardinals to give the sentence that the pope had commanded, but they answered that they could not do so, in the sight of God, against men who were not guilty.[104]

There does not seem to be any truth in this account. All the evidence suggests that James was not tortured. Finke has printed a memoir, by an anonymous jurist, which says that the Grand Master confessed in front of witnesses and then to members of the University of Paris. He kept to the confession for two months before retracting. Then he said that he wanted to be tortured so that the other brothers would not think that he had destroyed the Temple without being forced.[105] A letter to James II of Aragon, sent by one of his envoys in France, and dated at Poitiers on 30th May, 1308, describes how the king's men were putting pressure on the pope to destroy the Templars, but mentions also a statement by William of Plaisians that James of Molay had confessed without the use of torture.[106] The chronicle of John of St. Victor denies torture in the Grand Master's case.[107] Finally, according to the Florentine chronicler, Villani, James himself had said that he had confessed, «per paura di tormento, e per lusinghe del Papa, e del re di Francia».[108] There are two other points. Firstly, although some of this evidence comes from supporters of the king, it is not necessarily a fabrication. In the circumstances of a heresy trial, torture could be justified. In 1252 Innocent IV had authorised the use of torture by the secular authorities in such proceedings.[109] If then the Grand Master had been tortured, there was

---

[104] FINKE, op. cit., II, no. 75, pp. 116-17.
[105] Ibid., II, no. 69, p. 102.
[106] Ibid., II, no. 88, p. 143.
[107] JOHN OF ST. VICTOR, p. 658.
[108] Johannis Villani Florentini Historia Universalis, in MURATORI, R.I.S., vol. XIII, Milan, 1728, bk. 8, chap. XCII, col. 430.
[109] See LEA, op. cit., I, pp. 421-4.

no reason to hide the fact. Secondly, the cardinals had not come to give a judgement at this hearing, as the Catalan states.[110] This mistake further indicates that his whole account is fictious.

The reason for the Grand Master's retraction can only be conjectured. Perhaps he thought that he had been tricked, that the proceedings were not to be rapidly concluded as he had been led to believe. If this was so, it must have appeared to him that Philip was determined to destroy him and that his only chance was to revoke his confession in front of the cardinals. James must have known that as a relapsed heretic his position would be even more precarious than before. He could therefore have concluded that the risk involved in co-operating with the French authorities was greater than the one he ran as a possible relapsed heretic. Thus the effect of Clement's intervention was to prolong the trial, turning it into a conflict between king and pope, with James of Molay and the Templars becoming merely the means by which this battle was being fought. The failure of James of Molay to understand the underlying forces operating in contemporary European politics meant that he never really grasped this fundamental fact.

The consequence of the cardinals' hearing was to sharpen this conflict. In February, 1308, Clement announced that he would deal with the matter himself.[111] Philip reacted by refusing to hand over the Templars as he had originally intended, and by beginning a campaign of pamphlet warfare against the pope.[112] In May, probably between 11th and 17th, he invoked an Assembly of Notables at Tours. Here, the Estates approved the king's policy and declared that the Templars should be sentenced to death.[113] Philip then went to Poitiers in an attempt to bully the pope by threats and propaganda.[114] But Clement refused to be moved, and the king decided to change his tactics. On 27th June he released a number of Templars into papal custody. However, James of Molay and the other leaders of the Order were kept under royal control at Chinon. The Grand Master could not come, it was explained, because he was ill.[115] This may have been an excuse, but is was also probably true. The Grand Master was

---

[110] The Pope had here only instituted a preliminary examination. See LIZERAND, *Dépositions*, op. cit., p. 89.

[111] See LIZERAND, *Clément V et Philippe IV le Bel*, Paris, 1910, pp. 108-10.

[112] DOUTARIC, *Docs. inédits*, op. cit., pp. 166-86. The pamphlets seem to have been written by Pierre Dubois.

[113] JOHN OF ST. VICTOR, pp. 650-1. Philip was at Tours between 11th and 17th May, 1308, see *Philippe Quarti Itinera*, in *R.H.G.*, vol. 21, Paris, 1855, p. 449.

[114] Philip arrived at Poitiers on 26th May, FINKE, op. cit., II, no. 86, pp, 134-5.

[115] LIZERAND, *Clément V*, op. cit., *Appendice*, no. 10, pp. 440-1; *Reg. Clem. V*, op. cit. ann. 3, no. 3402, col. 284-7.

not young, and he had been kept in captivity since October. Nor was it the relatively comfortable captivity so often afforded to important enemies taken in battle, for he was confined in prison.[116] The Templars that Clement did received were hand-picked. It was expected that they would repeat their confessions without difficulty,[117] and that the pope would then be satisfied that his authority had been upheld. It seems that Clement was impressed, but he was not prepared to drop the matter so quickly. He now set up two inquiries — an episcopal inquiry in each diocese against the persons of the Templars, and a papal inquiry against the Order itself. A council, to be held at Vienne, on October 1st, 1310, would, in the light of the evidence collected, then make judgement.[118] These inquiries were another attempt to set the pope's authority above that of King Philip and to preserve the idea of papal independence. The practical effect of these measures on James of Molay was that several times more, he would be brought before various interrogators and bombarded with questions. Confused and ill, he would be able to contribute nothing to his own defence or to that of his Order.

Three cardinals — Berengar Fredol, Stephen of Suisey, and Landolf Brancacci — were sent to Chinon to see the Grand Master and the other leaders. The interrogation of the leaders lasted for four days, from 17th to 20th August. James was questioned on the last day. It appears that he returned to his original confession. He also asked that the commission listen to a serving brother, who added his own confession. He then genuflected and, clasping his hands together in a gesture of humility, requested absolution. This was granted to all the leaders after they had abjured their heresy. In a letter to the king the cardinals asked that he pardon these dignitaries. There is no verbal transcription of this interrogation, but it is recorded in a letter addressed by the three cardinals to the king, and by a letter of Philip to the king of Aragon.[119] It is also dealt with in two papal bulls — *«Faciens misericordiam»* and *«Regnans in coelis»*.[120] These bulls are dated 12th August, thus pre-dating the interrogation. The most plausible explanation is that offered by Finke, Lizerand, and Viollet, that this inconsistency is the result of a scribe's error. A large number

---

[116] JOHN OF ST. VICTOR, pp. 649, 650; CONT. NANGIS, I, p. 360.
[117] *Livre de Guillaume Le Maire*, ed. C. PORT, in *Mélanges historiques*, vol. II, *Collection de Documents Inédits sur l'histoire de France*, p. 420, in which the Pope speaks of those Templars who confessed in front of him (5th July, 1308).
[118] FINKE, *op. cit.*, no. 90, pp. 152-3; CONT. NANGIS, I, p. 366.
[119] BALUZE, *op. cit.*, III, pp. 98-100; FINKE, *op. cit.*, II, no. 95, pp. 171-2, no. 154, p. 328.
[120] *Reg. Clem.* V, *op. cit.*, ann. 3, no. 3402, col. 284-7, no. 3626, col. 386-91.

II

of these bulls were sent out and they would have taken a long time
to copy. In addition, there are a considerable number of papal documents unconnected with this matter which have been given the
same date. A scribe, working through them some days later, may
have made a guess and dated them en bloc.[121]

A greater problem connected with this interrogation is the reason
for this new confession by the Grand Master. He had retracted in
December, 1307, and in November, 1309, when the papal commission
officially begun its inquiries, he was to give a very equivocal answer.
Yet between these dates there is a new confession. Viollet believes
that James made no new confession at Chinon, that it was invented
by the cardinal Berengar Fredol, who based it on the original statements made in October, 1307. The cardinal knew that James's fate
would be death if he were condemned as a relapsed heretic, and this
was an attempt to save the Grand Master's life. To Viollet, this is
the explanation for James's curious outburst at the inquiry of November, 1309, when during the reading of the bull «*Faciens misericordiam*», the Grand Master expressed astonishment and anger, apparently over its record of the proceedings at Chinon.[122]

Lizerand has shown this to be unlikely.[123] The confession at Chinon
has certain differences from that of the previous October. At Chinon
James said that he knew nothing of idols or illicit kisses, neither of
which he mentioned at Paris. Previously he had talked about the
methods of receiving brothers, but did not include this at Chinon.
Moreover, Berengar Fredol and his fellow commissioners were making
a large assumption if they thought that retraction automatically meant
death. In 1310, nineteen masters of the faculty of theology at Paris,
declared that a retraction did not constitute a relapse into heresy.
Only three supported the opposite view.[124] Finally, it would have been
impossible for Berengar Fredol or the other cardinals to have acted
independently in the way suggested by Viollet. The cardinals' letter
shows that the interrogation was secret only in so far as it was not
held in public. The king's men, in the persons of William of Nogaret,
William of Plaisians and John of Janville, were present in force.[125]

[121] FINKE, *op. cit.*, I, pp. 229-30; LIZERAND, *Dépositions, op. cit.*, pp. 96-7; P. VIOLLET, *Les Interrogatoires de Jacques de Molai, Grand Maître du Temple, Conjectures,* in *Mémoires de l'Académie des Inscriptions et Belles-Lettres*, Paris, 1911, pp. 127-8. There are a large number of bulls dated 12th August, 1308, Poitiers, see *Reg. Clem. V*, op. cit., ann. 3.
[122] LIZERAND, *Dossier, op. cit.*, pp. 150-3; see VIOLLET, *op. cit.*, p. 132.
[123] LIZERAND, *Dépositions, op. cit.*, p. 100.
[124] See N. VALOIS, *Deux nouveaux témoignages sur le procès du Temple* in *Académie des Inscriptions et Belles-Lettres, Comptes-rendus des séances*, 1910, p. 232.
[125] BALUZE, *loc. cit.*

II

Perhaps the explanation is simpler than that offered by Viollet. James of Molay, perplexed and frightened, did confess again at Chinon, and perhaps changed his mind several times during the year, never knowing whom to trust, never sure of the course which would save his life.

It was not until Wednesday, 26th November, 1309, that the Grand Master was brought before the papal commission investigating the charges against the Order as a whole. Philip the Fair's fears concerning the slowness of papal action, fears which had prompted the original arrest, were well-justified. Clement by now was obviously interested in employing all the delaying tactics at his command. The commission, which met at the monastery of Sainte-Geneviève in Paris, was not composed in the same way as that of August, 1308, for most of its members were prelates who supported the king.[126] Moreover, it is clear that the king's ministers were allowed to enter freely, contradicting the commissioners' duty to respect the secrecy of the depositions put before them. Once more James of Molay was the victim of the conflict between king and pope.

The Grand Master was asked if he wished to defend the Order. In reply, he said that the Order had been confirmed and given privileges by the Apostolic See and that it was unbelievable that the Roman Church should now wish to destroy it. At this point he made mention of the postponement of the sentence on the Emperor Frederick. He said that he was prepared to defend the Order, although he was not confident of his ability to accomplish this. However, it would be dishonourable if he failed to do this for his brothers. He thought it would be difficult because he had no money.

The commission would allow him a delay to prepare his defence, although he could not have counsel as this was not the practice in heresy cases. He was told to bear in mind that he had already made a confession both on his own behalf and that of the Order. James was then given the apostolic letters relating to the case and asked to read and translate them to ensure that he understood the situation fully. It was when he came to the documents relating to the Chinon confession that the Grand Master made his dramatic outburst. He became very agitated and crossed himself twice. He appeared to be amazed at what was in the confession and said that if those commissioners were present then he would have something else to say. Not unnaturally the existing commissioners were affronted by his

---

[126] *Procès*, I, p. 1; see LIZERAND, *Clément V, op. cit.*, p. 148.

manner and answered coldly that they had not come to receive a battle challenge. James replied that he did not mean such a challenge, but that the methods of the Saracens and Tartars should be used against such wickedness (presumably meaning that of the commissioners at Chinon). The Saracens and Tartars cut off the hands of the wicked and cleft their bodies down the middle. But the commissioners were not moved by this, only replying, rather ominously, that the Church judged the heretics whom she knew as heretics and that she sent the obstinate to the secular courts.

James's outburst therefore availed him nothing and seems to have affected him more than anyone else, for he turned to William of Plaisians for help. William had entered the hall uninvited, presumably to keep a watch on the proceedings. He now spoke up on behalf of the Grand Master, saying that they were both knights and that James of Molay was his friend. He warned James not to compromise himself without cause. The effect of this advice was probably what William of Plaisians had intended, which was to confuse the Grand Master still further and perhaps to implant doubts in his mind about the wisdom of undertaking the defence of the Order. James then asked for a delay until Friday. This was granted and he was offered a longer period if he needed it. At the end of the session, the commissioners asked, as was usual, if anyone wished to defend the Order, but there was no response. It was stated that the commission would wait until Thursday for a reply.[127]

It had not been a very intelligent or dignified performance by the Grand Master, but then he had been in prison for two years. His state of mind can perhaps be gauged by the fact that, of all people, it was to William of Plaisians that he turned for advice. A great deal of attention has been paid to his outburst against the Chinon commissioners. Labbey de la Roque has suggested that this was because he had been cheated. He had confessed at Chinon after being promised that the confession would not be used in the procedure nor placed in front of the pope.[128] Lizerand's view runs along the same lines. A promise to James that if he kept to his confession, the commissioners would see no damage was done to the Order.[129] Neither of these theories seems very likely in the context of the situation prevailing in the summer of 1308. There was no real reason for the papal

---

[127] LIZERAND, *Dossier, op. cit.*, pp. 146-55.
[128] M. LABBEY DE LA ROQUE, *Essai sur Jacques de Molay, dernier Grand Maître de l'Ordre du Temple*, in *Mémoires de l'Académie de Caen*, vol. I, 1825, pp. 21-2.
[129] LIZERAND, *Dépositions, op. cit.*, pp. 105-6.

commissioners to have acted in this highly irregular fashion, particularly so soon after the establishment of the inquiries by Clement V. Any view is necessarily conjectural, but perhaps too much significance has been attached to this incident. In the circumstances, James would naturally have been anxious to erase the impression, at least in the minds of members of his Order, that it was he who was responsible for the current position of the Order. A man about to embark upon its defence would want to minimise the effect of previous confessions. Viollet and Lizerand have assumed that the outburst was against some genuine or imagined wrong; it may have been simulated. This was not an overly subtle method, but the depositions of the Grand Master do not indicate that he was capable of anything more.

The commission reconvened on Friday, the 28th, in order to hear James's defence. He does not seem to have prepared any coherent statement, but instead he made an attempt to avoid committing himself to anything. He said that he was unlettered and poor, and that he had gathered from an apostolic letter he had read the previous Wednesday that the pope himself was to give judgement in his own case and in those of the other leaders.[130] He therefore would not say anything concerning the defence of the Order, but asked the commission to make known to Clement his wish to appear before him. He would not interfere with the commission's proceedings against the Order in general. Beyond this, «in order to relieve his conscience», he had three things to say about the Order. Firstly, only in cathedral churches was the service better celebrated and he did not know of any other Order that had such beautiful chapels, churches, and ornaments. Secondly, he knew of no other Order that had distributed more charitable gifts. Thirdly, to his knowledge, no other Order has shed its blood more readily. It was because of this that the Count of Artois had wanted the Templars to be the advance-guard of his army. Even though the Grand Master of the time advised against the count's plan of attack, he did not abandon him and, as a result, died in the action.[131]

In the circumstances these were hardly telling points, and the commissioners were quick to draw James's attention to the fact. All this was of no value, they said, if the Catholic faith was lacking. James replied that he knew this to be true and that he himself was a good

---

[130] LIZERAND, Dossier, op. cit., pp. 162-5.
[131] This is a reference to an incident at Mansourah in the Nile Delta during the first crusade of Louis IX in 1250. The reigning Grand Master, William of Sonnac, apparently tried to restrain the king's brother, Robert of Artois, from making a reckless attack upon the city.

believer in one God and a trinity of persons and «*in aliis pertinenciis ad catholicam fidem*». There was one God only, one faith only, one baptism only and one Church only. When the soul was separated from the body, one would see who was good and who was bad and then all would know the truth of the things at present in question.

William of Nogaret however was not prepared to let these statements pass unchallenged. Their very unsophistication might have seemed convincing. Most heretics were more subtle and knowledgeable. William unearthed a story, supposedly from the chronicles of St. Denis,[132] which told of a Grand Master and other leaders of the Temple who had paid homage to Saladin. The result was that the Templars had suffered a great disaster which the Grand Master publicly attributed to the vice of sodomy practised among the Templars and to their failure to observe their faith and law. James of Molay professed never to have heard this story, and in this he was probably not alone. However, James had a story of his own to contribute. This was the description of his early years in Outremer under William of Beaujeu, when he and other younger men were anxious to fight, although they later realised that truce was the only sensible policy. Finally, James asked to be allowed to hear Mass and the other divine offices and to have his chapel and chaplains. The commissioners and William of Nogaret praised the devotion that he showed and made provision for his request to be granted.[133]

The commission was still in being in March, 1310, and on the 2nd, James was required once more to appear for interrogation. Again he was asked if he wished to defend the Order. This was clearly another move in the papal strategy and cannot, by this time, have been remotely connected with any interest in the Grand Master's answer. He had already shown himself incapable of defending the Order. James stated that he would not undertake the defence, but that he would appear before the pope. The lord pope, he said, was reserving his case. The commissioners reminded him that they were proceeding against the Order and not against individuals, but added that they would communicate his wishes to the pope.[134] Since learning that the pope was prepared to judge his case, the Grand Master seems to have placed his faith in this to the exclusion of all else. He had at first tentatively agreed to defend the Order, but now he appears to have been ready to abandon it to whatever fate might befall it.

---

[132] The source for this story is not now extant, if it ever existed.
[133] LIZERAND, *op. cit.*, pp. 166-71.
[134] *Ibid.*, pp. 174-6.

II

The events which followed did not directly concern James of Molay. King Philip was rapidly tiring of the affair. A number of Templars had retracted their confessions since 1307, partly as a result of the intervention of the papal commissioners, whom they may have thought to be more sympathetic, and partly because of the Grand Master's example in December, 1307. Unlike their leader, many of them had kept a steady course since then. On May 11th, 1310, a provincial council at Sens condemned, as relapsed heretics, 54 such Templars. The following day they were burnt at the stake. Four days later nine more were burnt.[135] By this action Philip silenced the defenders of the Temple who remained. This at least set a time limit on the papal commission, and on June 5th, 1311, Clement was at last forced to bring it to an end.[136] He could find little use for it now. But there still remained the General Council. On October 16th, at Vienne, Clement opened the council that he had promised to consider the case.[137] There was little that the pope could do but suppress the Order, achieving this end with the help of a secret consistory and an order of silence on the council during the second session on 3rd April, 1312.[138] It had been a long and bitter battle, but Clement struck the final blow. The property of the Templars was to be handed over to the Order of the Hospital. However, Philip did receive compensation from the Hospital to the extent of 200,000 livres tournois.[139]

On Monday, 18th March, 1314, the cardinals Nicolas of Freauville, Arnold of Auch, and Arnold Nouvel, passed sentence on the leaders of the Order. They were to be condemned to life imprisonment. Hugh of Pairaud and Geoffrey of Gonneville took this in silence, but James of Molay and Geoffrey of Charney would not accept it. The Grand Master knew now that there was no hope left. For once he could see the issue clearly. The heresies and sins attributed to them, said the two leaders, were not true. The Order was pure and holy. They had basely betrayed the Order to save their own lives. The cardinals seem to have been taken aback, and handed the two men over to the Provost of Paris. They would decide what to do the next day. But Philip the Fair came to a more rapid decision. They were to be burnt as relapsed heretics. A fire was built up on the Ile

---

[135] Cont. Nangis, I, p. 378.
[136] Procès, II, pp. 269-73.
[137] Cont. Nangis, I, p. 388.
[138] Ibid., I, pp. 389-92; for the council, see Lizerand, Clément V, op. cit., pp. 250-340, and Finke, op. cit., I, pp. 345-69.
[139] Reg. Clem. V, op. cit., ann. 7, no. 7885, col. 65-71; see L.L. Borrelli de Serres, Recherches sur divers services publics du XIIIe au XVIIIe siècle, vol. III, Paris, 1909, pp. 35-7.

II

122

des Javiaux and at dusk the two leaders were taken to the stake, still protesting their innocence. James of Molay looked towards Notre-Dame, the sanctuary of the Virgin, and called the vengeance of Heaven upon his persecutors.[140]

\* \* \*

It is unlikely that the Order as a whole was guilty of the crimes alleged by the French monarchy. Mollat has shown that, despite an extensive search, no physical evidence has been found, either then or since. The case therefore rests on the depositions of individual Templars, depositions which are widely contradictory. Moreover, not one of the Templars was prepared to die for the heresies with which he had been charged.[141] However, this does not rule out the possibility that there was an element of truth in some of the charges in certain cases. The initial rumours provided the pretext for the attack and it is unlikely that every story told against the Temple could be traced back to the French monarchy. It would be unfair to place the entire blame for the presence of these rumours on James of Molay. He had inherited a legacy of unpopularity caused by the arrogance of certain Templars, particularly in Europe, over much of the preceding period. Furthermore, at almost any time, in almost any Order, there were certain to be individuals who broke one or more of their vows, or who held unconventional, even heretical opinions.

The evidence concerning the Grand Master himself is inconclusive. There was an undercurrent of dislike for James of Molay and some of the other leaders which makes the evidence given in depositions even more difficult to assess than would otherwise be the case. One William of Giaco, who was received as a serving brother in 1303 and was a personal attendant to the Grand Master, stated that «*major Magister dicti Templi habuit rem cum eo carnaliter ter in una nocte, in Cipro*».[142] Another brother attached to the Grand Master's staff was Peter of Saphet, originally from Acre, who had been received at Nicosia in 1302 or 1303. He also maintained that the Grand Master had had homosexual relations with him.[143] Hugh of Narsac, the commander of Epannes in Saintonge, said that it was well-known that James of Molay had a scandalous relationship with his favourite valet-

---

[140] CONT. NANGIS, I, p. 402; JOHN OF ST. VICTOR, p. 658; VILLANI, bk. 8, chap. XCII, col. 430; *Chronique rimée attribuée à Geoffroi de Paris*, in *R.H.G.*, vol. 22, Paris, 1865, p. 145.
[141] MOLLAT, *Popes at Avignon, op. cit.*, pp. 242-6.
[142] *Procès*, II, pp. 289-90.
[143] *Ibid.*, II, p. 294.

de-chambre, a man named George.[144] However, two other members of the Order, Aimon of Barbonne and Pons of Bonoeuvre who, at various periods, had guarded the Grand Master's bedchamber, reported nothing amiss.[145] In fact, despite his vacillations, James himself never admitted that he had been involved in homosexual activity.

In England, a priest of the Order called John of Stoke claimed that he had met James of Molay when the Master had visited the kingdom in 1294. This was about a year after his reception. The meeting with James took place at the preceptory of Garwy in Herefordshire, where the Master was accompanied by two foreign knights. The priest was commanded to sit on the end of a bed, a crucifix was brought, and he was asked whose image it bore. He had replied that it was the image of Christ, who had suffered for the redemption of the world. But the Grand Master said this was not so, for he was the son of a woman and was crucified for calling himself the son of God. James told the priest to renounce Christ, but he refused. He only gave in after threats with drawn swords. He was assured that it was a custom of the Order, so he had renounced Christ, but only in words.[146] A certain brother Rainier of Larchant claimed that members of the Order in the chapter at Paris worshipped and kissed an idol with a beard. Under pressure, he said that he thought that the Grand Master had custody of this idol.[147]

It is impossible to draw any conclusions from such depositions. Some witnesses may have borne a grudge against the Grand Master. This is particularly likely among certain of his personal attendants. Others may have been tortured into saying these things, or they may have thought that if they testified against the leader of the Order they themselves would receive better treatment, or perhaps even release. As James himself feared, some may have blamed him for their predicament and thus sought revenge. To men accustomed to obey without question, the disillusion was great when the leadership failed. It is almost certain that James had no coherent set of heretical beliefs, whatever else passed through his mind. His depositions at the trial testify to his unintellectual approach towards theology. As Langlois points out, it is unlikely that there was any strong spiritual life in the Temple,[148] but this was almost inevitable in the very nature

---

[144] *Ibid.*, II, pp. 207-8.
[145] *Ibid.*, I, pp. 40, 538.
[146] WILKINS, *Concilia, op. cit.*, II, pp. 387-8.
[147] *Procès*, II, p. 279.
[148] LANGLOIS, *Le Procès des Templiers d'après des documents nouveaux*, in *Revue des deux mondes*, CIII, 1891, p. 414.

of the Order. It really implied that they thought very little about such matters. It is possible that at certain receptions there was some horseplay and even blasphemy, which some men at this period would regard as humorous. James might have been involved in some such receptions.

James of Molay was an unsubtle man. Even if the unlikely story about his election is accepted, it does little to change this picture, for the method employed was hardly very complicated. The Grand Master's plea that he was «unlettered and poor» may have been mere rhetoric, but the fact remains that he did not have the mental resources to deal with the situation produced by the trial. He was little more than a pawn in the elaborate manoeuvres of the king of France and the pope. He was caught in circumstances he did not understand, in a world in which he had not been trained to operate. He understood the position in the east as well as any of the other leaders in Cyprus and he reacted to it in much the same way. But in the west the crusades no longer formed an important part of life. Nor increasingly, did the universal papacy as conceived by Gregory VII and interpreted by Innocent III. The Capetian patrimony and fiefs were beginning to take on the characteristics of a coherent state. Probably few were consciously aware of these changes, but many were responsive to them. James of Molay was not. He thought the matter at stake was the Order of the Temple, but the issues were much wider. In crude terms, the trial was an aspect of the conflict between the universal papacy and the incipient national monarchy. James of Molay and his Order were the victims, as the papacy itself was later to be. When the situation was clear to him, the Grand Master could act decisively. He did so in the years after 1291 when he tried to revive crusading plans, and he did so in 1314 when he chose to die rather than suffer imprisonment. But the conditions prevailing during the trial frightened and confused him. They paralysed his will. Thus he failed to make any contribution towards the defence of the Order. He never realised that he and his Order had become anachronisms in a changing world.

**Corrigenda**

p. 99, ll. 31–4, for: An Italian Templar ... at Limassol in 1304; read: A Templar serving brother, Humbert of Germilla, testified that there were 120 brothers or more assembled at Limassol in 1304.[45]

p. 104, ll. 25 & 27, for: Roger of Loria; read: Rogeron of Loria.

p. 112, l. 10, for: comunicate; read: communicate.

# III

## WOMEN AND CATHARISM

Participation of women in sustaining and spreading the dualist heresy known as Catharism in Languedoc in the first half of the thirteenth century was greater than the passive role generally assigned to them in medieval society. The records of the Inquisition (which survive in France from the 1230s) bear witness to this, for these carefully recorded depositions and sentences contain many examples of women who became perfectae, or ministers of the Cathar faith, and many more who were credentes, the believers of the faith who provided economic support and shelter for the 'perfect'. So commonplace was the participation of women in Cathar society that there is a case of a female spy having been used by the Inquisition. In the mid-1230s Marquèse, the wife of Bertrand de Prouille, three times sent information to a Master Raoul of Narbonne (an official of the Inquisition) concerning gatherings of heretics to which she was freely admitted, for she came from a family of heretics. On each occasion Master Raoul came in response to her information, but she was not apparently a very efficient spy - since he caught only one heretic. Nevertheless, he thought it worthwhile to supply Marquèse with money ostensibly to help the heretics, for whom she bought food. [1] This method could hardly have been employed had not the Cathars accepted women as members of the sect and placed confidence in female supporters. The aim of this essay is twofold: first, to describe the role of women in Catharism during the first half of the thirteenth century by means of examples taken largely from inquisitorial records (in particular from the Collection Doat in the Bibliothèque Nationale), and secondly, to try to offer some explanation for this role which contrasts so markedly with the usual 'right order' of things in medieval society.

In essentials the Cathar Church was divided into two classes: the perfecti and the credentes. The perfecti were a small minority who had received the consolamentum in a special ceremony, vowing to live lives of absolute purity, pacific, chaste, without property, eating and drinking only what was strictly prescribed. Their lives were devoted to preaching, conversion and contemplation. The credentes did not take vows of this kind, but outwardly at least, integrated with the society around them, participating in economic life, marrying and bringing up families and engaging in warfare when the occasion arose. Generally they received the consolamentum from the perfecti when on the point of death.

In the Catholic Church the ministry was of course exclusively male. No such distinction was made among the Cathars. Women became perfectae, indeed were sometimes brought up with this specific purpose in mind, rather as Catholic children were sometimes vowed to the Church from an early age.

A striking example of this kind is recorded in the deposition of Arnaude de Lamothe, from Montauban, who appeared before the Inquisitor Friar Ferrier in 1244. She recalled that in 1209 (when she was still a girl) she and her sister Péronne had been handed over by their mother, who was a believer, to heretics, who took them to the house of a perfecta called Poncia at Villemur. This was a kind of convent for female heretics. Here they stayed for about four months until they were taken to the house of Raymond Aymeric, the deacon of the heretics at Villemur. In the presence of a large gathering of Cathars they received the consolamentum, thus entering the ranks of the per- fect. Austorgue, the mother, had evidently selected these two girls to be- come perfectae from her seven children mentioned in the deposition. Bernard de Lamothe, who was probably an older brother, eventually became the Cathar bishop of Toulouse, and the other four (two girls and two boys) were believers in the sect.

Arnaude and Péronne lived at Poncia's house for another year after 'ordination' until the arrival of the Albigensian Crusade in the vicinity forced them and their companions to flee. This marked the beginning of a life spent 'on the run', during which Péronne died, and which finally ended with the arrest of Arnaude by the Inquisition. The sisters were taken from house to house and farm to farm, or they lived in cabins or huts built in the woods, sometimes staying overnight or for a few days, at other times remain- ing for as long as a year (and on one occasion for three years) when they lived in a cattle-shed. Food was brought to them by believers, who guided them from place to place and provided shelter. At one point, about two years after the flight from Villemur, frightened by persecution, they returned to Montauban and 'put aside the sect of the heretics and ate meat and they were reconciled by the bishop of Carcassonne'. Although remaining in con- tact with the heretics, they did not resume the life of perfectae for eight years, when they entered a convent of female heretics at Linars and received the consolamentum once more, this time together with their mother.

Péronne eventually died in 1234, while they were hiding in a cabin in a wood – 'underground in a certain cell', says Arnaude's deposition – and there she was buried. Since the perfecti and perfectae invariably travelled in pairs, a new companion called Jordana was found for Arnaude de Lamothe, and she continued her itinerant life, but now staying more frequently in out- of-doors clandestine places rather than in the houses of believers, presumably because of the pressure being brought to bear by the Inquisition (active in the region since at least 1235). Once they appeared before the Inquisition at Linars where, presumably, they received some kind of penance, but what- ever the sentence it remained unfulfilled, for they at once returned to the society of the Cathars. This existence was finally brought to an end when, in 1243, the two perfectae were captured while living in a tent in a wood

near Lanta. They were taken to Toulouse where they appeared before Friar
Ferrier. [2]

   The case of Arnaude de Lamothe suggests the importance of the early
family environment in the making of a perfecta. The deposition of the
elderly Hélis, the wife of Arnaud de Mazerolles, in 1243, shows the importance of women in the wider family links upon which Catharism depended.
Hélis de Mazerolles told the inquisitors that she had been a Cathar believer
since her youth. She had been brought up in the notorious heretical village
of Fanjeaux, where her grandmother, Guillelme de Tonneins, her mother,
Aude de Fanjeaux, and her sister, Braida, were all perfectae. In the 1190s
her grandmother had openly held a house of female heretics at Fanjeaux, and
Hélis recalled that when she was a girl she had visited the house many times
and had been given bread, wine, nuts and fruit by her grandmother. Hélis
remembered too that her sister-in-law, Fabrissa, had held a house of heretics
at Montréal early in the century, before being forced to evacuate the castle
in the face of the crusaders and take shelter at Gaja-la-Selve. [3] Montréal
was one of the possessions of the lords of Laurac, another heretical family
with whom Hélis de Mazerolles had close contact. Bernard Oth, the lord
of Niort, testified in 1242, that more than forty years before, both his grandmother, Blanche de Laurac, and his aunt, Mabille, had been what he called
'garbed heretics', meaning perfectae, and for four or five years prior to
adolescence he had been brought up by his grandmother. [4] His mother was
another of Blanche's daughters, Esclarmonde, who had married Guillaume de
Niort. Among Esclarmonde's brothers and sisters were Aimery de Montréal
and Guiraude de Lavaur, both killed by the crusaders after the fall of Lavaur
in 1211, and Navarre de Servian, who also became a perfecta. [5]

   The families of Mazerolles, Laurac and Niort were part of a tightly-
connected group, bound to each other by frequent marriages. For instance,
Marquèse, an aunt of Hélis de Mazerolles, was married into the family of
Mirepoix, which also made her the aunt of Alazais, the wife of a knight
called Alzeu de Massabrac. Alazais was the sister of Raymond de Péreille,
the lord of the famous Cathar stronghold at Montségur, and she testified
before the Inquisition in 1244. When she was a child, Fournière, her mother,
had secretly taken her away from Mirepoix, which was the castle of Guillaume-
Roger, her father, to Lavelanet. In 1208, Fournière (with persumably complete control over her daughter) led her 'through her words and preaching to
receive the consolamentum from the heretics'. Alazais led the life of a
perfecta for three and a half years before leaving the sect and marrying Alzeu
de Massabrac. Although this was apparently something of a rebellion
against her mother's wishes, she remained a believer, and when in the early
1240s the royal seneschal, Humbert de Beaujeu, arrived in the south, she
fled to Montségur. A year and a half later, in March 1244, the castle surrendered to the royal forces and she was captured. She admitted to the

III

inquisitors that two or three weeks before Montségur fell, while the castle was still under siege, she and other noble women there had made a pact that they would receive the consolamentum should they be near to death, even if they had lost the power of speech. [6]

These depositions show clearly that the Cathars gained many female recruits when they were relatively young. Indeed, some - such as Jeanne, the daughter of Isarn del Pas, of Barheiras - were little more than children. In her deposition of August 1244, she is described as 'a girl of fifteen years'. During the previous two years, together with her friend, Bonansias, who was herself later hereticated, she had stayed with female heretics in cabins in the woods, accompanying them when they gathered crops in the fields. She received the consolamentum and for a few weeks lived the nomadic life of a perfecta until, in late May 1244, she was captured and taken to Toulouse. [7]

Equally, however, there were other women who received the consolamentum at a more mature age, rather as many Catholic women entered nunneries in their later years. For example, in the early 1230s, Meline, châtelaine of the castle of Prades, received the consolamentum during an illness, presumably in anticipation of death, but she recovered, and for three or four years went to live with a group of female heretics in a number of cabins which she had had built in a wood. [8] Dias, the wife of Pons, co-seigneur of Saint-Germier and Caraman, is a similar case. She was consoled by Bertrand Marty, the Cathar bishop of Toulouse, at Montségur in 1240. She lived in a cabin in a wood for a year, but was forced to flee, 'since some [persons] knew that this witness and other female heretics were in the aforesaid wood'. But this only delayed her capture, for soon after she was reported to the authorities, apparently by some children who had been looking after cattle and had seen her hiding in the wood. [9]

Finally, there is the case of perhaps the best known perfecta, Esclarmonde, the daughter of Roger-Bernard I, the Count of Foix, who has retrospectively become a heroine of the Cathar movement among some of its more romantic present-day supporters in Languedoc. Relatively little is known about her, except that after the death of her husband, Jourdain II de l'Isle, in 1204, she was hereticated in a ceremony at Fanjeaux, together with three other noble women, one of whom was Aude de Fanjeaux, mother of Hélis de Mazerolles, mentioned above. A large assembly of the local nobility was present, including the Count of Foix, her brother. [10] In the following years, Esclarmonde presided over a house of heretics at Pamiers where, according to Pierre des Vaux-de-Cernay, the highly partisan chronicler of the Albigensian Crusade, she worked with other women 'to seduce the hearts of the simple'. [11]

These and other examples give no indication that any distinction was made between the perfecti and the perfectae by the heretics who supported

48

them: a perfecta could provide the same spiritual services and was entitled to the same respect and support as a perfectus. Perfectae received the allegiance of believers in the greeting known as the melioramentum, which the Inquisition chose to call an 'adoration'. The believer genuflected before the perfect and received a blessing and a prayer that he or she would receive the consolamentum before death. There are frequent references to this ceremony in depositions concerning the perfectae, [12] and, less frequently, references to the preaching of perfectae [13] and to their ability to administer the consolamentum. [14]

The perfectae were also involved in more secular activities. The evidence of inquisitorial sentences and depositions strongly suggests that a rigid separation from the material elements of the world, which represented their ultimate goal, was not fully achieved by many of the perfect, male or female, and that the necessities of everyday life led them to participate in economic activity to an extent not entirely compatible with their professed views on the nature of evil. Perfectae either gave or sold a variety of goods to their supporters, including bread, fish, wine, clothing, bags, linen, cloth, shoes and wax. [15] They undoubtedly handled money, for they sometimes paid for food and accommodation provided for them and sometimes made monetary gifts or loans to believers. [16] In 1241, for instance, a Pierre Guitart was sentenced to go on a number of pilgrimages for receiving the very considerable sum of 100 solidi as a loan from a perfecta. [17] On a smaller scale, in 1243, Rubea, the wife of a Bernard de Ceteraiz from Minerve, received a loan from two perfectae of 6 solidi and 4 denarii tholosanis, for which she gave some linen cloth as security. The cloth was held for the perfectae by another believer. [18] It seems likely that the small communities of female heretics, so frequently mentioned in the depositions, maintained themselves by involvement in economic life, often as spinners and weavers. [19] Some perfectae seem also to have acquired medical knowledge, for a certain Pierre Étienne, sentenced in 1241, had 'consulted a female heretic many times for his illness', [20] while Arnaude de Lamothe treated believers for their ailments. [21]

It may perhaps have been a consequence of this close involvement with the community that produced a certain failure rate among the perfectae. Even the stoical Arnaude de Lamothe wavered in her devotion and left the ranks for eight years, while others made a more permanent break. In 1243, Berbeigueira (wife of Lobenx, a knight from Puylaurens) testified that her sister, Poma, had, before the time of the crusaders, left the sect of the heretics and returned to her husband and was with him for a long time. [22] According to the deposition of Saix de Montesquieu, also from Puylaurens, in 1243, his sister had been a perfecta and had stayed at his house for a year in 1217, but 'afterwards Bérengère put aside the sect of the heretics and was reconciled and received a husband'. [23] Barcelone, the wife of Guillaume de Brugairolles from Villepinte, was brought up in a heretical family, in which her uncle was a perfectus and her family were believers. Her mother seems to have expected her sister, Teziada, to devote herself to the life of a perfecta but, although she held to the sect until about 1218, 'afterwards she was converted to the Catholic faith and received a husband'. [24] Bernarde Targuier, a perfecta for three and a half years, was a similar case; in the early 1220s she was reconciled by Fulk, the bishop of Toulouse, and was married, claiming in the deposition that 'afterwards she did not see heretics', except to reclaim a sum of money owed her by Bernard de Lamothe. [25]

The prominence of women among the perfect was more than matched by their role among the believers, for female believers occupied a key position in the social and economic structure upon which Catharism was based. The career of Arnaude de Lamothe shows to what a high degree the Cathar perfecti were dependent upon the hospitality which the believers could provide. Both the inquisitorial sentences and the depositions offer numerous examples of the provision of accommodation, sometimes as a temporary hiding place, sometimes as a semi-permanent residence, for long periods. [26] Austorgue, the wife of Pierre de Resenguas, who lived in Toulouse, was typical of such believers. She had probably known and accepted the existence of the Cathars from her childhood; in her deposition she describes two female heretics in Toulouse as neighbours (vicinae). She was evidently accustomed to helping them when the need arose. One night in 1227, Asalmars, a perfecta whom she knew, left another perfecta, previously unknown to Austorgue, inside the gate of her house. Austorgue went out and found her and hid her for two days, even seeking out her companion and bringing her from another house in Toulouse, since the perfecta 'did not wish to eat without her companion'. The heretics were eventually taken to another hiding place by another believer. The network was evidently extensive, for Austorgue was told by Guillaume Salamon, a deacon of the heretics at Toulouse, of a certain female weaver in Toulouse, who would show her where heretics could stay, and, indeed, when Austorgue visited the weaver's house, she was taken through the building to another house in which a perfectus was hiding. [27]

Food and drink were also readily provided by the female believers: bread, fish (especially eels), vegetables (cabbages, lettuce and onions are particularly mentioned), grain, fruit, oil, cakes, wine and cider, are among items given. [28] When food was not donated, the heretics arranged for its purchase. A Raimonde Salinera said that she often sold her bread to certain female heretics, and that she had many times brought fish and other necessities for them, 'at their request and with their money'.[29] Clothing, bedding, linen, woollen thread, bags, dishes, and gifts of money (or in one case a pound of pepper, presumably to be used as currency) were among non-food items donated or bequeathed by female believers.[30] Female believers provided essential support in other ways too: Bernarde Targuier lent money to Bernard de Lamothe, the bishop of the heretics, [31] Humberge Paline, 'received goods given to them', [32] Berbeigueira, the wife of Lobenx from Puylaurens, looked after items of value for the heretics, including a book, 60 solidi in money and a piece of wax, [33] Bérengère, the wife of Assalit de Monts, 'handed over the legacy of a certain perfected heretic to the heretics', [34] and Maria, the widow of a certain Hughes, went out to buy clothes in which a certain dead heretic was buried. [35] Although the task was more frequently done by men, some women were also responsible for acting as guides to heretics, taking them to safe houses in country in which they were unfamiliar, or giving them advice on where to stay. [36]

The acceptance of women in a position of equality among the spiritual elite of the Cathar Church was not, however, confined to female believers. Male believers helped perfecti and perfectae apparently without discrimination: one took two heretics to the leper colony at Cortinals and also delivered half a cart of chestnuts to a certain person, both actions being at the request of perfectae, [37] another sought food for perfectae, received them in his house, listened to their preaching and, in inquisitorial parlance,'adored' them; [38] another took his sister, a perfecta, from Toulouse to Montauban, found her and her companions shelter on a farm, paid 50 solidi for accommodation for them, and made his sister a tunic and a cap, [39] while a fourth man brought timber and repaired a cabin in which perfectae were living. [40]

These examples clearly show that the role of women in Catharism was active and central, both as perfectae and as believers. The foundation of a Catholic women's convent at Prouille, near Fanjeaux, by St. Dominic in 1206, shows his recognition of the need for a counter-attraction for pious women in this region, as well as giving an indication of a contemporary's view of the extent of Cathar recruitment of women. The relative importance of women within the Cathar Church is more difficult to assess. By concentrating on examples of female participation in the heresy (as we have argued here) it would be easy to exaggerate their role. In fact, it is evident from the records which are extant that many more men than women were cited before the Inquisition, and that many more men than women were named by witnesses as being involved both as perfecti and credentes. Moreover, despite the admission of women to the Cathar ministry, there are no examples of women among the leaders of the sect, i.e., as bishops or deacons in the Cathar hierarchy. The nearest estimate which can be made at present is that about a third of the perfect were women, based upon the figures of Professor Duvernoy who has traced the names of 1,015 perfecti up to 1245, of whom 342 were women, [41] but these figures, even if they were complete, would be a very crude way of measuring relative importance.

Granted these reservations, the evidence shows female participation and support for the Cathar heresy on a large scale. The reasons are difficult to establish with complete certainty, but three distinct factors are worthy of consideration. These are: (i) the nature of Occitan society; (ii) the precocious development of the urban economy of Languedoc; (iii) the implications of Cathar belief itself.

Languedocian society in the first half of the thirteenth century displayed certain differences from that of northern France. By 1200 the north region had experienced the consolidation of a series of princely regimes which had subordinated the former allodial land-holders under their feudal control, a process which opened the way for the extension of monarchical power in the thirteenth century. A recognisable hierarchy was forming, based upon male primogeniture, reaching its theoretical apex in the person of the king, and sanctified by clerical support. The south presented a more diversified picture in which the word fief had a much less precise meaning than in the north, and where the allod was a far more common survival. [42] Primogeniture tended to be confined to the great comital families. The community of interest between the aristocracy and the upper clergy, which, despite their quarrels tended to characterise northern society, was to a great extent lacking. Although there does seem to have been an attempt to attach more positive obligations to the fief in Languedoc in the course of the twelfth century, it seems that the practical results of this were small, although the absence of modern local studies makes generalisation difficult. Dognon, writing in the 1880s, believed that in the early thirteenth century about half the lands remained allodial, and that the power of the Count of Toulouse rested not in military service owed, but in his large allodial estates. [43]

The typical southern nobility therefore tended to exist on divided lands or within a collective lordship, in which male and female heirs might hold jointly, and in which there was little loyalty to the Count of Toulouse, the nominal overlord. Because the connection between tenure and military service had not been effectively made, there was consequently a much weaker attachment to primogeniture and male inheritance; in the early middle ages the accession of a woman to all or some of the family property was not therefore uncommon. While the twelfth century pressures brought some changes in this, in that women were more often dowried in money than in land, and in that female inheritance was forbidden in some lordships except in default of male heirs, [44] nevertheless the role of women as land-holders remained important and consequently their social influence was considerable. In this kind of social structure it is not difficult to imagine the influence of the matriarchal figure, presiding over the co-heirs and maintaining a strong grip upon family ties and attitudes. An implicit recognition of the importance of this structure in southern society is contained in article 46 of the Statutes of Pamiers, imposed upon Languedoc by the victorious Simon de Montfort in 1212, which forbade noble women to marry an indigenous person during a period of ten years without the consent of the count, a position which Montfort held de facto at that time. [45]

    This southern aristocracy felt no community of interest with the local clergy. Petty seigneurs, confined to their share of the co-seigneury, found a display of anti-clericalism a convenient pretext for the usurpation of church lands, an attitude which perhaps reflected the policies of leaders like the Counts of Toulouse and the Counts of Foix. [46] Pierre des Vaux-de-Cernay describes in detail the atrocities committed by Raymond-Roger, the Count of Foix, among which was a murderous attack upon the canons of St. Antonin of Pamiers, when they objected to the establishment of the count's aunt, a perfected heretic, as head of a Cathar house in the town. [47] While these attitudes can be exaggerated - the crusading tradition was strong in the south and the Military Orders were well-established there - nevertheless, it does seem that such a society presented no united authoritarian front to deviation and heresy. Catharism and Waldensianism flourished in the south, because the crust of repression, so much thicker and more uniform in the north, was thin and brittle in the south. According to another crusade chronicler, Guillaume de Puylaurens, the knights of Languedoc rarely vowed their children to the priesthood, apparently because they saw Catharism as a better alternative, more suited to their needs and attitudes. [48] Jordan of Saxony, the second master-general of the Dominican Order, maintained that the perfectae were assured of a steady supply of girls from the noble families of the Lauragais 'by reason of poverty', a reference to the practice of holding through co-seigneurs. [49]

    Catharism and the problem of the existence of evil was not peculiar to Languedoc; it was simply that this fundamental religious and philosophical problem was more able to find expression within the riven social structure of the south. Such a society gave women greater opportunities for self-expression, both through heresy and through the patronisation of the troubadours. Consequently, the habit of tolerating heresy became ingrained. Pons Magrefort, a knight of St.-Michel-de-Lanes, who appeared before the Inquisition in 1243, recalled that he had seen many heretics conducting themselves quite openly at Mas-Saintes-Puelles and Laurac and in many other castles and towns, because 'nobody was on their guard before the first arrival of the crusaders'. [50] Similarly, feudal and clerical theories concerning the divine ordering of society in which women were definitely subordinate, were less convincing in the southern environment. The fundamental difference in the attitude of the Catholic hierarchy and the perfectae is encapsulated in the famous rebuke delivered by Brother Etienne de Nîmes to Esclarmonde de Foix when she tried to make her own contribution to a disputation between Cathars on one side and the bishop of Osma and Dominic Guzman on the other, held in Pamiers in 1207. She was brusquely told, 'Go Madame, tend your distaff, it does not appertain to you to speak in debates of this kind'. [51] The kind of social structure which existed in the south and the social attitudes which it engendered seem therefore to offer some explanation for the existence of heresy and the prominence of women in it.

The importance of the matriarchical figure has already been suggested: Arnaude de Lamothe, Hélis de Mazerolles, Bernard Oth of Niort, and Alazais de Massabrac, all recalled that either grandmothers or mothers or both had been hereticated. A closer look at one particular family shows the relationship between social structure, heresy and the position of women in less general terms. This is the family which held the Cathar stronghold of Montségur. Raymond de Péreille, the lord of the castle, had heard heretics preach since he was a boy and, in the early thirteenth century, had been persuaded by certain perfecti to rebuild the castle. Until its fall in 1244 Montségur was both a haven for refugees and a centre for worship, and many families from the surrounding region came there to stay. Raymond was married to Corba, the daughter of Marquèse de Lanta, a perfected heretic; in later years Corba herself received the consolamentum. The children of this marriage - Alpais, Philippa, Esclarmonde and Jourdain - were all believers. Alpais married Guillaume de Rabat from another heretical family, and Philippa married Pierre-Roger de Mirepoix, to whom Raymond granted the partial lordship of Montségur. Philippa testified that she, her mother and sisters had frequently eaten at the house of her grandmother, while Alpais remembered her grandmother's heretication by Bertrand Marty, later a Cathar bishop of Toulouse. [52] In such circumstances the importance of female influence within the family structure is hardly to be doubted.

The lords of Mirepoix into whom Philippa married are a good example of the kind of family which seems to be associated with heresy. Although the integrity of the lands was maintained and there was always a recognised head of the family, there were large numbers of co-seigneurs: 11 in 1159, 35 in 1207, and 14 in 1223, [53] among whom was Arnold-Roger, one of Raymond de Péreille's brothers, whose marriage connected them to two other heretical families, those of Montserver and Mas-Saintes-Puelles. The tightness of the structure is emphasised by the fact that Raymond de Péreille and Pierre-Roger were first cousins. Most of the nobility of the Lauraguais were interlinked in this way. Among others, there were joined the families of Mirepoix, Niort, Mazerolles, Fanjeaux, Laurac, Cabaret, Massabrac, Robat, Montserver and Mas-Saintes-Puelles, all of whom included important perfectae.

Equally, a social structure which permitted strong feminine influence also offers examples of determined women who were prepared to defy their families, either by joining the Cathars, or by refusing to participate in heretical practices. Berbeigueira, the wife of Lobenx de Puylaurens, testified in 1243 that she had been a believer for thirty years, yet when her husband was gravely ill in 1226, he refused the attentions of the _perfecti_, whom he ordered to be expelled from the house. [54] In the case of Bernard Faber de Caragodos the heretic was not his wife, but his daughter, Guillelme, who, against her father's wishes, had become a _perfecta_. In 1240, he arranged a meeting with her, taking with him a number of other persons sympathetic to heresy, whom he hoped might convince her to return home, but she did not wish to hear. Two other attempts to persuade her to change her mind also failed, for she said 'absolutely she would never do that'. [55] Feminine determination could also operate in the opposite direction. Faber de Podio Hermer said in 1243 that he had often inveighed against his wife, 'because she did not wish to esteem the heretics', [56] while Raymond de Miravel from Hautpoul saw, in 1228, when his father was dying 'that his mother absolved the said ill husband his heresy before he received the consolamentum from the heretics'. [57]

The second relevant factor concerns the relatively advanced urban development of Languedoc. The prevalence of heresy in the region has often been so ascribed for this was supposed to promote the free movement of traders and their goods, and with them, heretical ideas, possibly derived from the eastern lands in which the Manichaean heresy found its origins, and to which many western merchants travelled. There is certainly some truth in this explanation, for the most urbanised regions of western Christendom - Languedoc, northern Italy, Flanders, Champagne, and the Rhineland - do seem to have been most prone to outbreaks of heresy, but perhaps it might be better to change the emphasis and suggest that the existence of the urban environment was more important in encouraging the appearance of ideas and beliefs already in existence, rather than simply as a means of importing ideas and beliefs from outside. Certainly the latter helped ignite the former, but dualism was latent in Languedoc in the first place. This may help to explain the prominence of women, for women played a proportionately greater part in the industry and commerce of most towns than they did in the militaristic society of the feudal nobility. Moreover, the major industry of the towns of Languedoc, that of textile manufacture, was by no means exclusive to men, as the examples cited above illustrate.

Research into the guild records of Toulouse shows that in the statutes on cloth-making of 1227, which are the earliest known for the city, women were admitted both as masters and as artisans, apparently on an equal basis with men, while spinning may well have been an exclusively feminine occupation. [58] Later guild records of the city, between 1279 and 1322, show that

five crafts specifically allowed the membership of women, but Sister Mulholland, who did the fundamental research on this, thinks that women 'shared
in the industrial life of the city wherever the work of the craft was appropriate and possible' and that therefore other guilds must have admitted women
too. [59] The legislation of 1227 clearly favours the dominus or domina of the
crafts, for they controlled both the raw materials and the outlet for the
finished products, so perhaps Catharism gave the artisans an opportunity to
escape the economic subjugation which their work involved, enabling them
to gather together in the houses so frequently mentioned in the depositions,
rather like the beguinages which became increasingly common in northern
Europe during the thirteenth and fourteenth centuries. Although beguinages
in their northern manifestation were sometimes seen as bastions against heresy -
Fulk, the bishop of Toulouse, was an enthusiastic supporter for this reason -
it is clear that their adherence to the cult of virginity and voluntary poverty
reflected aspirations similar to those of the Cathars and Waldensians of the
Midi, and that they fulfilled similar religious needs for women, especially
those from the urban classes. [60] On the other hand, the Toulouse statutes
of 1227 do not create a monopoly, despite their bias in favour of the masters,
for, theoretically at least, they allow freedom for any qualified person to
enter the textile crafts, [61] thus offering no barrier to those who set themselves up in houses of the kind used by heretics and engaged in textile manufacture.

The third and final point concerns the nature of the Cathar religion
itself. The Cathars believed that the way to salvation was to be found
through the release of the soul from the material prison of the body, so that
the soul might rejoin its guardian spirit. It followed logically that the
Cathars should reject a society which they saw as being based upon material-
ism, including the Catholic Church, which, to quote one perfect, had instituted the mass 'for love of the great oblations', [62] and the feudal way of
life which glorified warfare. Theoretically, each new body born into this
environment represented another victory for Satan, another soul trapped in
the material body. Matrimony and procreation were therefore to be condemned for perpetuating the lordship of Satan. Women believers sometimes
expressed what they had heard about this in their depositions: one heard that
matrimony and baptism were of no profit, [63] another that she could not make
the greeting of the melioramentum while she was pregnant, [64] and a third
that if she died pregnant she could not be saved. [65]

Catharism was then in theory subversive of the whole social order of
medieval Christendom. The interpenetration of church and feudality which
characterised the north, and which ensured the subordination of women, was
rejected by Catharism for its materialist base. Aquinas's human family with
its hierarchy of the wise ensuring good order was of no relevance if one

believed in a transmigration of souls in which the sex and social class of the bodies concerned were of no consequence. The weakness of the feudal hierarchy and the corruption of the Church in the south left a vacuum which could be filled by heretical ideas, and it is not difficult to see the attraction to women accustomed to being taught that they were by nature inferior, fit only to be pawns in the political chess-board of feudal land-holding and as slow-witted receptacles for the lord and master's male heir, an heir who would perpetuate the whole system. It would not be an exaggeration to interpret the attraction of Catharism for some women at least as an expression of discontent against masculine domination. While it would be facile to offer this as a general explanation for the prevalence of Catharism in the south, it would be equally wrong to dismiss the ideology of the heresy as being of no relevance to its adherents. The long, bitter persecution of Catharism by the Catholic Church needs to be seen in the light of the threat it seemed to present to the social order, a threat clearly recognised by the Catholic Church. The extremity of the measures reflects the extremity of the threat. On the other side of the coin, it would be stretching credibility indeed to deny that at least some of the Cathars, including women, recognised their religion as a means of escaping the established order of things, an order which they saw as essentially a Satanic creation.

These explanations are partial and tentative. It is evident that the reasons which led people to become followers of the Cathar religion are often complex and contradictory. One woman may have become a perfecta because her family expected it of her, while another may have taken up this way of life as a form of rebellion against the family as an institution. To take the third point concerning the nature of the Cathar religion: it is clear that the theoretical views of the Cathars did not always accord with the compromises forced upon them by daily life. Although the perfecti and perfectae were widely admired for their way of life - even Catholic writers give grudging recognition of this - some of the evidence already cited indicates that they did not always adhere to the strict rules of poverty, while the apparent double-standards of many of the believers have often been the subject of discussion and attack. In the same way, despite the strictures on matrimony, it was the family structure of Languedoc which provided Catharism with its most trustworthy foundation. Moreover, it cannot be relied upon that all the supporters of Catharism rigorously examined the full implications of their religion or indeed were even interested in doing so. If there is any truth in the assertion that Christianity was not fully absorbed by all its adherents, then equal doubts can be expressed about Catharism given the wide range of support which it attracted in Languedoc. Market-place gossip sometimes surfaces in the depositions, and lends support to the idea of incomprehension and superstition. [66]

Generalisation is therefore hazardous; the explanations for the evident connection between women and Catharism may be as varied as the women
who were attracted by the heresy.    On balance, however, it seems safer to
give more weight to the nature of the medieval social and legal structure of
Languedoc in encouraging the prominence of women in heresy, rather than to
the social implications of Cathar belief as such.

NOTES

1.   Bibliothèque Nationale, Collection Doat, vol.23, f.98-99.

2.   ibid., 23, f.3-50.

3.   ibid., 23, f.162-180.

4.   ibid., 24, f.83v-84v.   See also Wakefield, W.L., 'The Family of Niort in the Albigensian Crusade and before the Inquisition,' in Names. The Journal of the American Name Society, 18, 1970.

5.   See Roquebert, M., L'Epopée Cathare, 1198-1212: l'invasion, Toulouse, 1970, p.114, for this family.

6.   Doat, op.cit., 24, f.204-207v.

7.   ibid., 23, f.274-291v.

8.   ibid., 23, f.127-127v.

9.   ibid., 23, f.57v-62v.

10.  Devic, C. and Vaissete, J., Histoire Générale de Languedoc, vol.8, Toulouse, 1879, no.373, pp.1150-1151; see Vidal, J.-M., 'Esclarmonde de Foix dans l'histoire et le roman,' in Revue de Gasgogne, 11, 1911.

11.  Vaux-de-Cernay, Pierre des  Histoire Albigeoise, ed. and trans. Guébin, P. and Maisonneuve, H., Paris, 1951, p.82.

12.  E.g., Doat, op.cit., 21, f.205v-206; 22, f.2v, 263v; 23, f.8-9, 11, 17-17v, 20-21v, 34-35, 47v-48, 59, 182, 239v, 277.

13.  E.g., ibid., 21, f.230v-231; 23, f.10.

14.  E.g., ibid., 23, f.234v, 300.

15.  ibid., 21, f.230v-231, 259; 23, f.182v-182 bis, 237v, 259-259v.

16.  E.g., ibid., 21, f.231, 266v-267, 289-289v.

17.  ibid., 21, f.239.

18.  ibid., 23, f.183v-184v.

19.  E.g., Bigordana, a believer, was sentenced to go on pilgrimage in 1241, for, among other things, providing two female heretics with thread (filum), from which they made head-bands (vittae), ibid., 21, f.311v.   See also Duvernoy, J., 'Les Albigeois dans la vie sociale et économique de leur temps,' in Annales de l'Institut d'Etudes occitanes, Actes du colloque de Toulouse, années 1962-3, Toulouse, 1964, pp.67-8.

20. Doat, op.cit., 21, f.297v-298.

21. ibid., 23, f.46v-47, 72-72v.

22. ibid., 24, f.136.

23. ibid., 24, f.126-126v.

24. ibid., 23, f.121-4.

25. ibid., 22, f.2v.

26. E.g., ibid., 21, f.189v, 200v-201, 201v, 213-213v, 307-307v, 312-312v; 23, f.33-33v, 250, 254, 309v-310v.

27. ibid., 24, f.1v-7v. Austorgue was eventually sentenced to perpetual prison (Toulouse, 17 March 1245), Guiraud, J., Histoire de l'Inquisition au Moyen Age, vol.2, Paris, 1938, p.146, appendix to ch. 5.

28. E.g., ibid., 21, f.190v, 213-213v, 216, 217-217v, 271, 293, 300, 301, 306v, 307-307v, 311v; 22, f.57v; 23, f.182-182v, 246v-247, 259-259v; 24, f.1v-7v, 140-140v, 199v-200; Documents pour servir à l'histoire de l'Inquisition dans le Languedoc, ed. A. Douais, vol.2, Paris, 1900, nos.X-XIV, pp.252-7.

29. Doat, op.cit., 21, f.240-240v.

30. ibid., 21, f.190v, 216, 290-290v, 293, 301, 303, 306, 307-307v, 311v; 23, f.46v-47, 170v, 173, 182v, 300v; 24, f.1v, 140-140v.

31. ibid., 22, f.2v.

32. ibid., 21, f.213-213v.

33. ibid., 24, f.140-140v.

34. Douais, op.cit., vol.2, no.XVIII, p.44; she received a sentence of perpetual prison (18 August 1247), Guiraud, op.cit., p.148.

35. Douais, op.cit., vol.2, p.45.

36. E.g., Doat, op.cit., 21, f.209v-210, 216, 303; 23, f.49-49v.

37. ibid., 21, f.266v-267.

38. ibid., 21, f.205v-206.

39. ibid., 21, f.242-3.

40. ibid., 23, f.62.

41. Duvernoy, 'La Liturgie et l'église cathares,' in Cahiers d'Etudes Cathares, 18, 1967, p.25.

42. See, for instance, Dossat, Y., 'La Société méridionale à la veille de la croisade albigeoise,' in Revue du Languedoc, 1944.

III

43. Dognon, P., Les Institutions Politiques et Administratives du Pays de Languedoc du XIIIe siècle aux guerres de religion, Toulouse, 1888, pp.16-19.

44. Molinier, A., 'Etude sur l'administration féodale dans le Languedoc,' in HGL, vol.7, Toulouse, 1879, pp.152-4.

45. Timbal, P., Un Conflit d'Annexion au Moyen Age. L'Application de la Coutume de Paris au pays d'Albigeois, Toulouse, 1950, p.183 (text of the statutes).

46. See Dossat, 'Le Clergé méridional de la veille de la croisade albigeoise,' in Revue du Languedoc, 1944, pp.276-8.

47. Pierre des Vaux-de-Cernay, op.cit., p.82.

48. Guillaume de Puylaurens, Historia Albigensium in RHG, vol.XIX, Prologue.

49. Jordan of Saxony, in Acta Sanctorum, vol.35, Paris and Rome, 1867, col.544.

50. Doat, op.cit., 23, f.86v.

51. Guillaume de Puylaurens, op.cit., c.VIII, p.200.

52. Doat, op.cit., 22, f.201-214, 259-264; 24, f.198-202.

53. Pasquier, F., Cartulaire de Mirepoix, Paris, 1921, vol.1, introd., p.15, and pièces just, no.IV, pp.24-6; vol.2, no.I, pp.1-6.

54. Doat, op.cit., 24, f.143, 140v.

55. ibid., 23, f.67-69.

56. ibid., 22, f.5.

57. ibid., 23, f.235. See also similar but more suspect cases, 23, f.96, and 24, f.10-10v. Both these cases may have been an attempt to minimise involvement in heresy before the inquisitors.

58. Mulholland, M., 'Statutes on Clothmaking, Toulouse, 1227,' in Essays in Medieval Life and Thought presented in honour of A.P. Evans, ed. J.H. Mundy, New York, 1955, arts. IV and II, p.173.

59. Mulholland, Early Gild Records of Toulouse, New York, 1941, p.xxiv.

60. See especially McDonnell, E.W., The Beguines and Beghards in Medieval Culture, New York, 1969, pp.3-7, 436.

61. Mulholland, 'Statutes', op.cit., e.g. art. XII, p.175.

62. Doat, op.cit., 22, f.31v.

III

63.  ibid., 22, f.65v-66.
64.  ibid., 21, f.296-296v.
65.  ibid., 22, f.57.
66.  ibid., 22, f.32.  See also, for example, 22, f.26-26v.

# LEPERS, JEWS AND MOSLEMS: THE PLOT TO OVERTHROW CHRISTENDOM IN 1321

'In 1321', says Bernard Gui, Inquisitor at Toulouse between 1307 and 1324, 'there was detected and prevented an evil plan of the lepers against the healthy persons in the kingdom of France. Indeed, plotting against the safety of the people, these persons, unhealthy in body and insane in mind, had arranged to infect the waters of the rivers and fountains and wells everywhere, by placing poison and infected matter in them and by mixing (into the water) prepared powders, so that healthy men drinking from them or using the water thus infected, would become lepers, or die, or almost die, and thus the numbers of the lepers would be increased and the healthy decreased. And what seems incredible to say, they aspired to the lordship of towns and castles, and had already divided among themselves the lordship of places, and given themselves the name of potentate, count or baron in various lands, if what they planned should come about.'[1] In this way, Bernard Gui begins his description of the hysteria which gripped a large part of France during the spring and summer of 1321 and which swelled into a tide of panic which engulfed the king and the court as well. For a short period, it was seen as the ultimate threat to the faith as conceived by the orthodox: a plan by subversive elements, both inside and outside society, to overthrow the whole structure of Christendom.

In June 1321, King Philip V was staying at Poitiers, where he intended to hold an assembly of representatives of the towns of southern and central France.[2] According to the anonymous monk who continued the chronicle of Guillaume de Nangis, it was there that, about the time of the Feast of St. John the Baptist (24 June), rumour reached him that many lepers in Upper Aquitaine had been arrested and burnt to death because they had confessed to infecting the fountains and wells with poison, with the purpose of either killing or making leprous all the Christians of France and Germany.[3]

---

[1] Bernard Gui, *Vita Joannis XXII* (excerpta ex chronicis quae nuncupantur *Flores chronicorum seu Cathalogus pontificum romanorum*), in E. Baluze, *Vitae Paparum Avenionensium*, ed. G. Mollat, vol. 1 (Paris, 1914), pp. 163–4. Bernard Gui did not set out to write an original work, but says that he extracted material from other works which he believed the most authentic. His history down to 1311, for instance, is heavily dependent upon Ptolemy of Lucca. However, he had a good knowledge of the Midi, in which he spent all his life, and his information on local events in the Toulousain seems to come from direct knowledge. He certainly obtained some information on the 'plot' through his presence at the interrogations of lepers who had been arrested. For an analysis of his work see Mollat, *Étude critique sur les Vitae Paparum Avenionensium d'Étienne Baluze* (Paris, 1917), pp. 22–9.

[2] See C. H. Taylor, 'French Assemblies and Subsidy in 1321', *Speculum*, XLIII, 1968, pp. 217–44.

[3] *Chronique Latine de Guillaume de Nangis de 1113 à 1300 avec les Continuations de cette chronique de 1300 à 1368* (Société de l'Histoire de France), ed. H. Géraud, vol. 2 (Paris, 1843), p. 31. This is the most detailed narrative source for the episode. Nangis and his

## 2      LEPERS, JEWS AND MOSLEMS

A French historian, G. Lavergne, has shown from a study of local archives that the lepers in and around Périgueux had been accused of this plot in the spring of 1321, and, on 16 April, a systematic arrest of the lepers of the neighbourhood ' ?d been ordered by the mayor of Périgueux. By May, many had been tortured into confession and condemned to death by burning. The news may therefore have been brought to the king by the representatives of Périgueux who had been sent to attend the meeting of the towns at Poitiers on 14 June.[4]

The chroniclers Jean de Saint-Victor and the Nangis continuator report that 'about this time', further details arrived from another source: that of the lord of Parthenay (just to the west of Poitiers), who is conveniently not named.[5] 'It is said', relates the continuator of Nangis with the customary caveat, that this lord sent the king a sealed letter containing the confession of an important leper who had been captured in his lands. The letter broadened the implications of the plot considerably, for the leper had confessed that he had been led to take part in the poisoning by 'a certain rich Jew', who had given him the poisonous potions together with 10 *livres*, promising a large amount of money if he would corrupt the other lepers. The Jew had told him that the potion consisted of a mixture of human blood and urine, three unnamed herbs, and a consecrated host, all of which were mixed into a powder, placed in bags, tied with a weight, and thrown into the wells and fountains.[6] The Nangis continuator claimed that he himself had seen at Poitiers the potions made by a certain female leper, which were intended for the town, but which she had thrown away in a panic, still in their bag, as she feared capture. 'There was found in the bag

continuators were monks of St. Denis; their aim seems to have been to provide the abbey with a body of authentic annals written in Latin (Géraud, I p. xvi). This continuator wrote the section covering the period 1317 to 1340. Géraud believes that he was in Poitou in 1321 and was an eye-witness of some of the events of the leper conspiracy (I, p. xviii). Jean de Saint-Victor, *Vitae Joannis XXII*, in Baluze, *op. cit.*, I, 132–4, provides a more concise version, which does not differ in essentials from the *Cont. Nangis*. Nothing certain is known about the author. His chronicle has much detail about the region of Paris and it must be assumed that he lived there, but there is no evidence that he was a canon of St. Victor. He probably wrote his chronicle c.1326. Before 1316 he is dependent upon other works, but for some events after this date he seems to be writing from his own observation. His description of the leper conspiracy comes into this category. He was not well-informed about activity in governmental circles, but in Mollat's view is valuable as a reflection of public opinion in the first quarter of the fourteenth century, Mollat, *Étude, op. cit.*, pp. 86–101. Substantially the same story can be found in *Chronique de Saint-Denis depuis 1285 jusqu'en 1328*, in *Recueil des Historiens des Gaules*, vol. 20, pp. 703–5; *Chronicon Girardi de Francheto et Anonyma Ejusdem Operis Continuatio*, in *R.H.G.*, vol. 21, pp. 55–7; and *Les Grandes Chroniques de France* (Société de l'Histoire de France), ed. J. Viard, vol. 8 (Paris, 1934), pp. 357–60.

[4] G. Lavergne, 'La persecution et la spoliation des lépreux à Périguex en 1321', in *Recueil de Travaux offerts à M. Clovis Brunel* (Paris, 1955), vol. 2, pp. 107–12, for a detailed account of events in Périgueux based upon Archives communales de Périgueux, cotés CC 42, 43,44 (Arch. dep. de la Dordogne). See also I.-I. Escande, *Histoire de Périgord* (Cahors, 1934), vol. 1, pp. 138–9. For the attendance of the representatives of Périgueux at Poitiers see Taylor, *op. cit.*, p. 231.

[5] The anonymity of the lord of Parthenay is in keeping with the suspicious nature of the 'sealed letters', so typical of stories based on rumour. The lord of Parthenay at this time was in fact Jean Larchevêque, who had succeeded his brother, Hugues, in 1318: see P. Guérin, *Recueil des documents concernant le Poitou contenus dans les registres de la Chancellerie de France*, vol. 2, in *Archives historiques de Poitou*, XIII (Poitiers, 1883), pp. 99–100, n. 1.

[6] *Cont. Nangis*, pp. 31–2; Jean de Saint-Victor, p. 132.

the head of a snake, the feet of a toad and hairs as of a woman, having been mixed with a certain black and fetid liquid, so it was not only horrible to feel, but also to see.' The strength of the poison was revealed when this bag was thrown on a fire, for the contents would not burn.[7]

Philip V, himself a man of deeply superstitious nature,[8] seems to have been prepared to believe the reports and, on 21 June, issued an ordinance from Poitiers to his *baillis* to effect a general arrest of the lepers. The ordinance states that 'public knowledge and the course of experience' have shown that the lepers have attempted to kill Christians by throwing poisonous potions into the waters, not only in France, but 'in all kingdoms subject to the faith of Christ'. For this reason the king had caused them to be arrested and some had confessed and been burnt for the crime. However, others remained unpunished, so, with the advice of his council, the king had decided upon the following measures: (i) lepers who have confessed or who confess in the future are to be burnt alive; (ii) if they will not confess 'spontaneously' then torture should be applied 'so that the truth can be extracted'; (iii) female lepers should be treated in the same way, except those who were pregnant, who should be imprisoned until their infants are of sufficient age 'to live and feed without their help', and then these women should be burnt; (iv) lepers who confess nothing, those who will be born in the future, and leper youths, both male and female, who were less than 14 years old, should be imprisoned in their places of origin; (v) lepers who have reached their majority, which was 14 years of age, and who confessed in the way set out above, were to be burnt. According to the ordinance, the crime of the lepers was one of *lèse-majesté* and therefore all the goods of the lepers 'should be placed and held in our hand'. The imprisoned lepers should be provided for from there, as should the brothers and sisters who had taken care of them and who had lived from the revenues of the leper property. The ordinance stressed that the nature of the crime meant that the administration of justice in this case appertained to the royal power only and not to any temporal lords.[9]

However, unlike the arrest of the Templars in October 1307, which had been instituted by Philip IV and kept secret until a predetermined day, many lords had already executed lepers and confiscated their goods. The provisions of the ordinance notwithstanding, therefore, Philip V was unable to take advantage of the situation and reserve the goods entirely for himself. Although the *baillis* acted upon the royal orders[10], the king nevertheless found it politic to issue another ordinance on 16 August. This declared that, at the request of several prelates, barons, nobles, communities and others who said that from ancient times they possessed the right to administer the *léproseries* and to appoint their governors, he had

[7] *Cont. Nangis*, pp. 32–3.
[8] See P Lehugeur, *Histoire de Philippe de Long, Roi de France (1316–22)* (Paris, 1897), esp. pp. 462–3.
[9] H. Duplès-Agier, 'Ordonnance de Philippe de Long contre les lépreux (21 juin 1312)' *Bibliothèque de l'École des Chartes*, XVIII (1857) pp. 270–2. This example is addressed to the *bailli* of Vermandois.
[10] A. Thierry, *Recueil des Monuments Inédits de l'Histoire de Tiers État* (Paris, 1850), vol. 1, pp. 386–7, for the death sentence on lepers by the *bailli* of Amiens, as a case of administration of justice on behalf of the crown (1 August 1321).

4                          LEPERS, JEWS AND MOSLEMS

restored the goods which he had seized, without prejudice to his own rights and without creating any new right.[11] The king had already been forced to acknowledge local rights over *léproseries* in particular cases. In Narbonne the *sénéchal* had taken over the goods of the lepers in the king's name, but the *consuls* of Carcassonne had protested that they had been accustomed to administer the goods for pious ends, a protest accepted by the king who, on 4 August, ordered the *sénéchal* to release the goods.[12] The king found it equally difficult to control local action against the lepers themselves. The Bishop of Albi and his justiciars, for instance, were among those who had taken the law into their own hands and arrested the lepers. Some had been condemned to death while the rest were imprisoned. Since the king had said that the crime was one of *lèse-majesté*, he had levied a fine on the bishop. However, by 18 August, he had been obliged to remit the fine and to order his *sénéchaux* at Carcassonne and Toulouse to accept the episcopal jurisdiction over the lepers' case on the grounds that there was some doubt whether the crime could be regarded as *lèse-majesté*. In a matter such as this, he said, which required immediate action, the delays caused while it was being resolved would be too great.[13]

Local authorities were perhaps themselves carried along by popular fervour. According to the anonymous continuator of the chronicle of Rouen, the lepers were burnt 'more by the people than by secular justice'.[14] Bernard Gui confirms this. 'In many places, in detestation of the horrible act, the lepers, both men and women, were shut up in their homes with all their things, (and) fire having been applied, they were burnt by the people without any judgement.'[15] Flanders seems to have been an exception for, according to the *Genealogia Comitum Flandriae*, although they were arrested, they were afterwards freed, which 'displeased not a few people'.[16]

[11] *Ordonnances des Rois de France de la Troisième Race*, ed. E. de Laurière, (Paris, 1723), vol. I, pp. 814–15.
[12] L. Le Grand, 'Les Maisons-Dieu et les léproseries du diocèse de Paris au milieu du XIVe siècle', in *Mémoires de la Société de l'Histoire de Paris* (Paris, 1898), vol. XXV, p. 141, n. 3, where the text is given.
[13] *Ordonnances*, XI, Paris, 1769, pp. 481–2. Perhaps the king's indulgence towards the bishop stemmed from ecclesiastical claims to jurisdiction over *léproseries*: see H.-M. Fay, *Lépreux et Cagots du Sud-Ouest* (Paris, 1910), pp. 209–10. However, the king granted the same privilege to the baronage of the *sénéchaussée* of Carcassonne, as is shown in an order to his *sénéchal*, Hugues Giraud, also of 18 August: Bibliothèque Nationale, Collection Doat, vol. 152, ff. 154–6.
[14] *E Chronici Rotomagensis Continuationes*, in *R.H.G.*, vol. 23, p. 349.
[15] Bernard Gui, p. 164. An indication of the extent of popular hysteria can be gleaned from a papal letter of October 1331, in which John XXII granted absolution to a friar, Gaufrid de Dimegny, for an incident which had occurred in his youth at the time when 'it was generally said that the lepers and certain Jews should be burnt by secular justice'. Gaufrid had accused a customer at his father's tavern of hiding an evil potion in his sack. The man was arrested and tortured, and confessed that he had used the potion to put people to sleep so that they could be easily robbed. He was therefore executed. Gaufrid felt responsible for the man's death, presumably because by 1331 he realized that he had been a victim of the panic of the time. See S. Grayzel, 'References to the Jews in the Correspondence of John XXII', in *Hebrew Union College Annual*, XXIII, part II, 1950–1, no. xxxix, pp. 79–80.
[16] *Genealogia Comitum Flandriae*, in E. Martene and V. Durand, *Thesaurus novus anecdotorum*, III, Paris, 1717, col. 414. Nevertheless, Flemish sources confirm the general tendency for people to take the law into their own hands: see *Istore et Chroniques de Flandres*, in *Collection de Chroniques Belges inédites*, ed. Kervyn de Lettenhove (Brussels, 1879), vol. I, p. 325.

The extent of popular involvement in the affair is shown by the pogrom against the Jews which accompanied the attacks upon the lepers. The royal ordinances make no mention of the involvement of the Jews, but their part in the well-poisoning was nevertheless readily believed, both by the chroniclers and by the populace. The anonymous *Chronique Parisienne*, for instance, asserts that 'this devilry was done by the encouragement and the incitement of the Jews'.[17] According to the Nangis continuator, 'the Jews in some parts were burnt indiscriminately and especially in Aquitaine'. They seem to have received little protection from the authorities. At the royal castle of Chinon in the *bailliage* of Tours, for instance, the continuator of Nangis reports that 160 Jews were burnt to death in a large pit. Many women, widowed by the executions, were said to have thrown their own sons onto the fire to prevent them being baptized 'by the Christians and the nobles present there'.[18] It seems unlikely that this could have taken place without the connivance of the *bailli* of Tours. Indeed, the chroniclers claim that attacks also took place against the Jews in Paris from which the king gained direct financial benefit. Those found guilty were burnt, while others were condemned to perpetual exile. Some of the richest were kept until their debts were known, and their incomes and goods were absorbed into the royal fisc. The king was said to have had 150,000 *livres* from them.[19]

The chroniclers have one more dramatic example of the fate of the Jews. At Vitry 40 Jews held in the royal prison, despairing of survival, decided to commit suicide. Their most aged and venerable member was chosen to cut their throats, a task which he was not prepared to perform without the assistance of a younger man. The two men did as the community wished, but when they were the only ones left, they were faced with the problem of who should kill the other. At length the old man prevailed in his wish to be killed first, and the younger man was left the sole survivor. However, instead of killing himself, he took whatever could be found from the bodies in the way of gold and silver, made a rope from clothes and climbed down from the tower in which they had been imprisoned. Unfortunately, the rope was shorter than he needed and this fact, together with the weight of the gold and silver, caused him to fall and break his leg, thus making his recapture possible. He, too, was then executed.[20] Lehugeur, in his study of the reign of Philip V, believes this to be merely a fable, 'for the edification of the reader',[21] and he is probably correct to be sceptical, since the story of the mass suicide among Jews in the face of adversity was well-established by 1321.[22] Moreover, certain details, such as the possession of gold and

[17]*Chronique Parisienne Anonyme de 1316 à 1339*, ed. A. Hellot, in *Mémoires de la Société de l'Histoire de Paris et de l'Île-de-France*, vol. XI, Paris, 1885, pp. 57–9, for the lepers' plot. The author was probably a judicial official in Paris. He was in touch with the attitudes of *le menu peuple* and sometimes provides additional details not found in other contemporary accounts. However, he has no significant extra information on the leper conspiracy.

[18] *Cont. Nangis*, p. 35.

[19] *Idem*; Jean de Saint-Victor, pp. 133–4.

[20] *Cont. Nangis*, p. 36; *Chroniques de Saint-Denis*, p.704; *Chronicon Girardi de Fracheto*, p. 57.

[21] Lehugeur, *op. cit*., p. 433.

[22] For discussion of this issue see R. B. Dobson, *The Jews of Medieval York and the Massacre of March 1190* (York, 1974), p. 27.

## 6      LEPERS, JEWS AND MOSLEMS

silver by the imprisoned Jews, strike a false note. Nevertheless, because of the extent of popular fury not only in 1321, but also in the rising of the Pastoureaux of the previous year, the possibility of some further outrage at Vitry cannot be discounted.

Local jurisdictional claims and mob action therefore considerably diminished the control which the king sought through his ordinance of 21 June; nevertheless, he had ordered a general arrest and interrogation of the lepers. A number of depositions must undoubtedly have been produced by this action and, indeed, a royal order of 8 February 1322 commands that the *baillis* of Tours, Chaumont and Vitry send to *Parlement* 'the confessions of the lepers and the Jews' relating to the poisoning of the waters and other crimes.[23] Such depositions have not apparently survived, but they may well have been extensive, for the affair was widely known throughout France. Contemporary references to it occur in the provinces of Flanders, Vermandois, Anjou, Touraine and Aquitaine, and in the specific towns of Paris, Amiens, Rouen, Caen, Avranches and Coutances in the north, Chaumont, Vitry and Mâcon in the east, Tours, Ouches, Limoges, Poitiers and Périgueux in the centre, and Toulouse, Carcassonne, Albi, Narbonne, Pamiers and Lyons in the south.[24] However, the diligence of Jacques Fournier, Bishop of Pamiers between 1318 and 1325, makes it possible to examine a deposition of the kind which might have been produced by royal inquiries. The contents of this document suggest that it was through this and other depositions that tortured lepers greatly broadened the implications of the conspiracy to include not only lepers and Jews but also outside Moslem powers as well. The chroniclers, writing after the event, were then able to incorporate this additional strand within their narratives.

Guillaume Agasse, head of the leper colony at Estang in Pamiers, appeared before Marc Rivel, Fournier's deputy, on 2 June 1321, nearly three weeks before Philip V issued orders for the general arrest.[25] In the story told by Agasse, two lepers from Estang, Guillaume Normand and Fertand Espanol, as long ago as the previous Feast of St. Catherine (25 November 1320) had gone to Toulouse to seek some poisons, staying overnight on the way back with a leper called Gaulaube, commander of the house of Auterive. On their return to Estang, they told the witness that they had done good work, for they had brought poisons which would be put into the waters of Pamiers and which would make everybody into

---

[23] E. Boutaric, *Actes du Parlement de Paris*, vol. 2, 1299–1328, *Inventaires et Documents* (Paris, 1867) no. 6661, p. 420. This, however, is the only such reference in the *Actes*, while there is only one mention of this process in accounts of Charles IV, which is for the *bailliage* of Coutances, *Les Journaux du Trésor de Charles IV le Bel*, ed. J. Viard, *Collection de Documents Inédits sur l'Histoire de France* (Paris, 1917), no. 4848, p. 807.

[24] In addition to the sources already cited, see in *R.H.G.*, vol. 23. E *Chronico Sanctae Cutherinae de Monte Rotomagi*, pp. 409–10; *Ex Uticensis Monasterii Annalibus et Necrologio*, p. 483; *Ex Chronico Sancti Stephani Cadomensis*, p. 993; and E *Chronico Abricensi*, p. 569. Also *Chronicon Turonense Abbreviatum*, in *Recueil de Chroniques de Touraine*, ed. A. Salmon (Tours, 1854), p. 198, and G. Guigue, 'Fragment d'une chronique Lyonnaise. Treizième et Quatorzième Siècle', *Revue Lyonnaise*, III (1882) p. 296. Chronicle references do not, however, enable the directional spread of the rumour to be traced in any detail.

[25] *Le Registre d'Inquisition de Jacques Fournier, 1318–25*, ed. J. Duvernoy, vol. III (Toulouse, 1965), pp. 135–47.

lepers. They then proceeded to poison the water of the fountain of Tourong, among other water-sources in Pamiers. Gaulaube at Auterive had been given poisons for the same purpose, while Etienne de Valès, a leper in Cahors, had poisoned the waters there too. At Estang the witness claimed that when the bank of the ditch of a local spring was opened up, he had seen a great ball of dung sunk into it, and that he had also seen, about a year ago, a certain leper coming away from that place. When asked if he had tried to prevent the poisoning, he replied that, on the contrary, it pleased him.

Guillaume Agasse appeared again on 9 June before Bernard Fassier, the official of Pamiers, and this time implicated himself more directly. In May 1320, a certain youth, whom he did not know, brought him some letters in which the preceptor of the lepers of Porte Arnaud Bernard of Toulouse asked him to come at once on the following Sunday to his house 'to conduct and order certain things which would result to his advantage and honour'. He set out, stopping overnight at the leper colony in Saverdun, where he discovered that Raimond, the commander of that house, had received a similar letter, and so, the next morning, they travelled to Toulouse together. On the Saturday night, they stayed at the house at Toulouse 'with many other lepers, ministers and preceptors'. On Sunday, 11 May 1320, about 40 lepers assembled in the main hall (*aula*) of the house and were addressed by the commander: 'You see and hear how other healthy Christians hold us who are ill in shame and disrespect, and how they throw us from their meetings and gatherings and that they hold us in derision and censure and disrespect.' Because of this, it was decided that all healthy Christians in the world should be poisoned so that they too became lepers, and then the present lepers would take 'their administration and governance'. 'And to obtain and cause this, the preceptor said and announced that it had been decided and ordained among the leaders that they would have the King of Granada in their aid and defence, which king, . . . had already announced to other leaders of the *malades* that he was prepared to give his advice, help and aid in the matter . . .' The plot would be achieved by placing powders in the waters, and to this end 'with the advice of doctors' many powders had been made, a portion of which each of those present would receive in a leather bag. The meeting broke up on the Tuesday, the witness and Raimond de Saverdun returning to their respective houses each with a full bag of powder. About a month after, Guillaume Agasse, 'wishing to keep the oath which he had sworn at Toulouse', carefully distributed the powder in various fountains and wells in Pamiers, finally throwing what he had left into the River Ariège. Agasse knew that the commanders of the houses of Saverdun, Mazères, Unzent and Pujols had been present at the assembly at Toulouse, but had not recognized any of the others. They had done it because they had been promised the lordship of the various places where they lived. He repeated his story about the journey made to Toulouse by Guillaume Normand and Fertand Espanol, but this time confessed that he had helped Guillaume Normand place a bag of poison in the local fountain of Rive, which they had pegged down among the stones and tiles.

Guillaume Agasse made a third appearance on 6 July, before Jacques Fournier himself, stating that he had been tortured on the day that he had

IV

made his first confession, but not since. He still maintained, however, that his confessions were true. He then repeated his story of 9 June concerning the delivering of the letters and the journey to Toulouse, but appreciably enlarged his account of what had happened there. This time the number present had risen to 50 or 60 and he specified that they came from the Toulousain, the Quercy, the Limousin, and from Gascony and the Agenais. The commander of the house of Porte Arnaud Bernard was named as Jourdain, and he made them all swear an oath 'on a certain book' from the chapel of the house not to reveal anything that occurred there, and to agree to do all the things which they were ordered to do. The assembly itself took place in the main hall of the house and there 'on one side next to the door stood a certain man, tall and black, wearing a sword, having a helmet on his head, as it seemed, (and) holding a halberd in his hands.' When one of the lepers asked what this r.n was doing there, Jourdain replied, that he was there 'on account of those things which they ought to do there', adding that there were many others in the house who would come if it was necessary. Jourdain then explained that the plot to poison the Christians was supported by 'the King of Granada and the Sultan of Babylon', who, in return for obedience to their orders, promised the leper commanders 'great riches and honours' and the lordship of the places where they lived. The messenger from the two rulers was the commander of the leper house of Bordeaux. The Moslem rulers demanded that the lepers 'deny the faith of Christ and his Law', and that they should receive the poison which the kings had ordered to be made. This was a mixture of the powdered remains of a consecrated host, 'which the Christians call the body of Christ', and a concoction made from snakes, toads, lizards and bats, together with human excrement. If any of the commanders resisted these orders, then the man with the halberd would at once decapitate him.

When the lepers present had denied Christ, Jourdain told them that in the near future there would be another chapter-meeting in which all the leper commanders of the Christian world would be present, where they would meet the King of Granada and the Sultan of Babylon. There, the commanders would again deny Christ and 'spit on the cross of Christ and upon his body, and also that the body of the Lord and his cross should be trampled underfoot'. This had been promised by the commander of Bordeaux and without this denial the two Moslem rulers 'would not come to them nor confide in them'. All the commanders present promised to do all this when the King and the Sultan came and to obey their orders. Indeed, there were said to be present at the time representatives of the two kings, who would report what had happened. Jourdain told them that these things 'were done to the end that the Sultan of Babylon and the King of Granada would be lords of the whole land, which was now held by the Christians, the Christians having been killed or made lepers'.

Jourdain and another commander, whom Guillaume Agasse thought was the commander of Bordeaux, then briefly left the room before returning with the deadly powders. Jourdain carried a large pot and the commander a large basin, which were placed in their midst. Jourdain told them that the pot contained the powdered host, and then proceeded to mix this with the powder in the basin, before distributing a portion contained in the leather bag to each of the commanders present. Guillaume Agasse received about half a pound. This was the powder which would infect the waters; care should be taken to put it in linen bags held under the water by a stone so that the poison did not dissipate too quickly, and should have the maximum effect. This was the end of the assembly and that day they ate together before returning to their homes. Ten or twelve days later (*i.e.* 24 or 26 May), he began to put poison in the wells and fountains of Pamiers and into the Ariège, as he had explained before.

Finally, at the end of his deposition, Guillaume Agasse denied that the evidence which he had given against his fellow lepers, Guillaume Normand and Fertand Espanol, was true. It was he who had done these things and it was he who had remained for three months in the belief that the Christian faith was of no value. He had told no one nor given any poison to other lepers to place in the waters. He had also given false testimony against Raimond de Saverdun (who had already been burnt to death) and Pierre de Mazères. He confessed this 'without any torture applied or threatened to him, freely and spontaneously, wishing to save his soul and repentant that he had committed the aforesaid'. A year later, on 5 July 1322, Guillaume Agasse abjured his crime and received sentence of perpetual prison from Jacques Fournier. Bernard Gui was among those present.[26]

Between Agasse's second and third depositions, two further pieces of evidence appeared which apparently lent support to stories such as those told by him involving Moslem powers in the plot. These are two letters allegedly written by the Moslem kings of Granada and Tunis, which suggest that they were actively providing financial support for the plot and indeed sending actual poison. The letter of the King of Granada is addressed to Sanson, son of Helias the Jew, and speaks of a plot already in being in which the king had provided money for the Jews, so that they could persuade the lepers to distribute poison in the cisterns, wells and fountains, poison sent by the king himself. One hundred and fifteen lepers had taken an oath that they would participate. The king was sending a special poison to be put into the water drunk by Philip V. No effort was to be spared to gain success. The letter of the King of Tunis is addressed generally 'to his brethren and their children' and promises them sufficient money for their expenses. If they should wish to send their children to him he would guard them like his heart. The agreement between the king, the Jews and the lepers had been made the previous Easter. An oath was sworn which involved 75 Jews and lepers. The letters are in French, having been translated from Arabic by Pierre d'Aura, a physician. The date given is 2 July. Unlike Agasse's deposition, however, they do not seem to have emanated from Languedoc, but from Mâcon, since Francon d'Avinières, the royal *bailli* of Mâcon, Pierre Maiorelli, a royal clerk, and two clerics, Bartholomew de Go, an archdeacon, and Guiot de l'Aubépin, a canon of Mâcon, together with 4 royal notaries and Pierre de Leugny, a leading citizen of the commune of Mâcon and keeper of its seal, attested their presence. The letters give no indication of the location of the originals or of

[26] P. van Limborch, *Liber Sententiarum Inquisitionis Tholosanae* (Amsterdam, 1692), pp. 295, 296–7.

## 10    LEPERS, JEWS AND MOSLEMS

how and where they entered France, but there seems little likelihood that they are genuine.[27] Their content strongly suggests that whoever created them based his information upon confessions extorted from lepers similar to that made by Guillaume Agasse, following the ordinance of 21 June. Some of the chroniclers also believed in Moslem perfidy.[28] The Nangis continuator claimed 'it was generally said' that the King of Granada, wishing to take revenge for his defeats at the hands of the Christians, especially by Peter, uncle of the King of Castile, had plotted this evil in concert with the lepers. He had promised the Jews 'an infinite amount of money' if they would carry it out, but they refused to do so themselves because, 'as they said, they were suspect to the Christians'. The Jews, however, were 'susceptible to evil' and, instead, arranged for the actual poisoning to be done by the lepers, 'who continually mix with the Christians'.[29] The leaders of the lepers convoked four general councils, attended by representatives from all except for two English *léproseries*, and persuaded them that if everyone in the world became a leper then they would no longer be despised. As a further incentive, the offices of power were divided among the lepers in anticipation of their future victory. The Nangis continuator knew of a leper burnt at Tours who had called himself the Abbot of Marmoutier. Not all chroniclers, however, mention the Moslem connexion. The author of the *Chronique Parisienne* is apparently unaware of this dimension to the conspiracy,[30] while Bernard Gui, who knew of the content of confessions such as that of Guillaume Agasse, nevertheless omits the accusation against the King of Granada,[31] which suggests a certain scepticism on his part about this aspect of the affair.

Just like the Pastoureaux of the previous year, the disturbances seem to have spent themselves within a few months. The following summer, on 31 July 1322, at Paris, Charles IV issued an ordinance which permanently imprisoned the lepers within walls, their subsistence to be provided from their goods. In parishes where no proper endowments existed, the lepers were to be maintained at parish expense.[32] Bernard Gui records this decision with approval, for although he believed in the existence of a plot, he clearly deplored action without due legal process as had characterized the pogroms of 1321. 'At length more mature advice and consultation having been taken, the rest, all and individually, who had remained alive and were not found guilty, circumspectly providing for the future, were enclosed in

[27] For the text of the letters see J.-M. Vidal, 'La poursuite des lépreux en 1321', *Mélanges de littérature et d'histoire religieuses publiés à l'occasion du jubilé episcopal de Monseigneur de Cabrières évêque de Montpellier, 1874-99*, vol. I, 1899, pp. 512-4, from Archives Nationales, J 427, no. 18. See also H. Chrétien, *La prétendu complot des juifs et les lépreux en 1321* (Châteauroux, 1887), pp. 15-16.
[28] *Cont. Nangis*, pp. 33-4; *Jean de Saint-Victor*, pp. 133-4, *Chroniques de Saint-Denis*, p. 705; *Chronicon Girardi de Fracheto*, p. 56.
[29] 'qui continue cum christianis conversantur'.
[30] *Chronique Parisienne*, p. 58, sees the Jews as the prime movers in the affair.
[31] Bernard Gui, p. 164, mentions leper assemblies or 'chapters', but says nothing about Moslem influence.
[32] *Ordonnances*, XI, pp. 483-4. The ordonnance printed here is addressed to the *sénéchal* of Carcassonne and reprimands him for failing to execute a similar order on the same subject made previously.

places from which they could never come out, but wither away and langu-
ish in perpetuity, so that they would not do harm or multiply, men being
completely separated from women.'³³ As for the Jews, the accusations
seem to have provided yet another excuse for monarchical financial extor-
tion and, in 1322, for another 'expulsion in perpetuity'.³⁴

The delusion that a conspiracy between the lepers, the Jews and the
Moors actually existed in 1321, is a revealing instance of medieval mental
attitudes under the strains created by the economic and social problems of
the fourteenth century. Neither singly nor in combination did the elements
in the supposed plot present any threat to society nor, as the anonymous
chronicler of Tours admitted, did any Christian die or suffer ill from the
poisoning of the water-supplies,³⁵ yet the accusations were widely believed
through the whole spectrum of the social order from the king downwards.
They were believed because the nature of the accusations accorded with
the contemporary mental climate during a period of stress in which a
scapegoat for society's ills seems to have been sought. The prosecutions of
the previous twenty years had accustomed people to expect to find anti-
social conspirators, ready to overturn society by whatever means came to
hand. Most shocking of these plotters had been the Templars who, during
their trial between 1307 and 1312, had confessed to the denial of Christ,
spitting, trampling and urinating on a crucifix, the worship of monstrous
idols, the encouragement of sodomy, and the abuse of the sacraments,
especially by the omission of the words of consecration during the mass.
These had been perpetrated in secret chapters and reception ceremonies
which excluded outsiders.³⁶ Other signs of stress had been present for some

³³ Bernard Gui, p. 164.
³⁴ Jean de Saint-Victor, p. 134. See J. Parkes, *The Jew in the Medieval Community* (London, 1938), pp. 170–4, for the position of the Jews in relation to the French monarchy
between 1315 and 1322.
³⁵ *Chronicon Turonense*, p. 198. Lehugeur, *op. cit.*, p. 424, speculates that there may have
been some deaths from contaminated water, typhoid or other disease in Aquitaine at this
time, which may have started the panic. On this see E. Wickersheimer, 'Les Accusations
d'empoisonnement portées pendant la première moitié du XIVe siècle contre les lépreux et
les Juifs; leur relations avec les epidémies de peste', in *4e Congrès International d'Histoire de
la Médicine (1922), Communications* (Antwerp, 1927), p. 82. It is also possible that once the
panic had begun this in itself induced symptoms like diarrhoea which might be interpreted as a
consequence of poisoning. On panic and disease, see A. M. Meerloo, *Patterns of Panic* (New
York, 1950), p. 63. Only a late source, published about 1553, that of the Portuguese Jew,
Samuel Usque, in his *Consolation for the Tribulations of Israel*, tr. M. A. Cohen, *Judaica.
Texts and Translations*, 2nd ser., no. 1 (Philadelphia, 1965), p. 191, mentions 'a mysterious
plague which showed no symptoms in any part of the body', but both the lateness of the
source and the didactic purpose of the writer make this very unreliable evidence. Usque
wished to show that the tribulations which the Lord had imposed upon his people for their
apostasy were coming to an end, and his work is geared to this objective. Thus the accusations
of well-poisoning in alliance with the lepers and its awful consequences for the Jews 'is the
incurable leprosy mentioned by Moses: "The Lord will smite you with the boil and the scab,
whereof you cannot be healed" (Deut. 28.27)'.
³⁶ See, for instance, in addition to the trial of the Templars, the trials of Boniface VIII,
Guichard of Troyes, Enguerrand de Marigny, Mahaut d'Artois, Jeanne de Latilly, Hugues
Géraud, Huguenin de Bosy, among others. The trial of Hugues Géraud, Bishop of Cahors, in
1317, is an illustration of attempted murder by magic and poison. He was executed by burning
for trying to murder the pope and certain cardinals by means of wax images and incantations,
as well as by actual poison, such as *realgar*. A Jew, Bernard Jourdain of Toulouse, was alleged
to have manufactured the wax images of the proposed victims for 5 *sous toulousains*: see E.
Albe, *Autour de Jean XXII. Hugues Géraud, Évêque de Cahors* (Cahors and Toulouse, 1904),
p. 58 *et passim*.

IV

years. The famines between 1315 and 1317 in northern Europe had clearly
been more prolonged and more serious in their impact than the frequent
local shortages which were inseparable from the medieval agrarian system.[37] However, local disasters also occurred, for in some regions affected
by the leper conspiracy such events are recorded under the same year. In
Flanders, for instance, extensive flooding from the sea is reported, destroying houses and drowning men and animals, while at the opposite end of the
kingdom, at Lyons, there was a shortage of fruit, a lack of sun, famine and
disease.[38] At Tours, the chronicler was more cosmic in his observations. 'In
this year, on the Feast of the Consecration of the Body of Christ (18 June),
the halo (radius) of the sun was red in colour for the whole day, as if it were
blood.'[39] This is not, however, to argue that there is a direct causal connexion between the famines of 1315–17 and the accusations against the lepers,
or indeed to imply that the chroniclers make any link between the leper
conspiracy and the natural and supernatural phenomena which they report,
beyond the close juxtaposition of the events. It is rather to suggest that the
existence of the widespread belief in such a plot is itself evidence of a
society under stress and should be added to other such indications noted by
historians.[40]

These are, however, generalizations. Two specific questions arise from
this affair: why did these particular groups become scapegoats and why
were these particular allegations made? The Jews were of course the traditional victims of medieval prejudice, especially during the crusading era.
They had suffered severely the previous year when the Pastoureaux or
Shepherds' Crusade, frustrated in the attempt to reach Outremer, turned
its fury upon the Jews more conveniently near at hand than the Moslems.
The shepherds' movement had begun in the spring of 1320. Initially, they
had concentrated upon Paris, but having failed to rouse the king to begin
his long-awaited crusade, set off towards Languedoc. Here, during the
summer, they attacked the Jews wherever they could find them: towns
specifically named include Saintes, Verdun, Grenade, Castelsarrasin,
Toulouse, Cahors, Lézat, Albi, Auch, Rabastens and Gaillac. Royal
enquiries after the event stress the excesses committed against the Jews in
the sénéchaussées of Toulouse, Périgord and Carcassonne. Property was
plundered, documentary evidence of debts burnt and whole communities

[17] See H. S. Lucas, 'The Great European Famine of 1315–17', *Speculum*, V (1930)
[38] *Genealogia Comitum Flandriae, loc. cit.;* Guigue, 'Fragment', *loc. cit.*
[39] *Chronicon Turonense, loc. cit.*
[40] On links between outbursts such as this and social strains, see N. J. Smelser, *Theory of
Collective Behaviour* (London, 1962), esp. chapters 1 and 8, and A. M. Meerloo, *Total war
and the Human Mind* (London, 1944), pp. 21, 34, 37–8, 51 *et passim*. An interesting comparison may be made with G. Lefebvre, *The Great Fear of 1789: rural panic in revolutionary
France* (London, 1973). Belief in the accusations was not confined to the fourteenth century.
Vidal, the first historian to take into account the deposition of Guillaume Agasse in a study of
these events, was inclined to accept the idea of a localized plot involving Agasse, although
even he rejected the idea of a national or international conspiracy. For him the abundance of
detail in Agasse's deposition, together with the leper's sincerity, make a convincing picture.
The effects of torture, he thought, could be discounted, for he had only been tortured once at
the beginning of his testimony, when his confession was rather vague, whereas later, when it
was claimed that torture had not been applied, he presented a specific story backed by dates
and circumstantial detail. Vidal, *op. cit.,* pp. 498–510.

of Jews massacred or forcibly baptized, usually with the complicity of the local inhabitants.[41] The return of the Jews in 1315 after the expulsion of 1306 and the energetic pursuit of their debts by royal agents had made a major contribution to the diversion of these would-be crusaders against the Jews.[42] Quite possibly, increased small-scale debts owed to the Jews incurred during the hardships of 1315–17 underlay some of the animosity. However, although the Pastoureaux had been crushed by royal military force, the fundamental reasons for anti-Semitism in medieval society—religious, cultural and economic—had been left untouched.

The association of the Jews with the lepers is more difficult to identify. It may have been the revival of an old prejudice which finds its written origins as long ago as the third century B.C., in which the Jews were chased out of Egypt as impure and leprous, a story which thereafter established itself in the mentality of the ancient Mediterranean world,[43] or it may stem from a contrary idea based on the belief that the Jews rarely contracted leprosy, and could therefore have plotted with the lepers without fear of infection. Henri de Mondeville, physician to Philip the Fair and Louis X, listed as one of the causes of leprosy, sexual intercourse during menstruation, but explained that since Jews rarely have sexual intercourse during this time, few Jews are lepers.[44]

The lepers themselves were new victims, but their circumstances made them vulnerable. Like the Jews, they formed distinctive and definable communities, and they could be recognized by their dress and sometimes by their disfigurement. The Church had contributed to their separation from society by applying the Levitical precepts of ritual defilement to leprosy, so that they were, in theory, to be regarded as unclean people to be kept apart from the rest of the community.[45] A standard church service

[41] See, for instance, the inquiries at Lézat, B.N. Collection Doat, vol. 102, pp. 266–79, and at Albi, C. Compayré, *Études historiques et documents inédits sur l'Albigeois, le Castrais, et l'Ancien Diocèse de Lavaur* (Albi, 1841), pp. 252–5.

[42] For the vicissitudes of Capetian policy towards the Jews in the late thirteenth and early fourteenth centuries, see R. Chazan, *Medieval Jewry in Northern France: a political and social history* (Baltimore and London, 1973), chapters V and VI.

[43] See J. Parkes, *The Conflict of the Church and the Synagogue: a study in the origins of antisemitism* (London, 1934), pp. 14–16; T. Reinach, *Textes d'auteurs grecs et romains relatifs au Judaïsme* (Paris, 1895), no. 11, pp. 27–34.

[44] *Die Chirurgie des Heinrich von Mondeville*, ed. J. L. Pagel, *Leben, Lehre und Leistungen des Heinrich von Mondeville* (Berlin, 1892), vol. I, p. 422.

[45] See P. Richards, *The Medieval Leper and his Northern Heirs* (London, 1977), p. 9, for a discussion of this point. The isolation of the lepers can be exaggerated. The comment of the continuator of Nangis, p. 33, that the lepers continually mixed with Christians should be taken into account, as should the deposition of Guillaume Agasse which assumes considerable freedom of movement among lepers. In the thirteenth century there was provision in the rules of leper houses for outside journeys, e.g. the Rule of the house of Grand-Beaulieu de Chartres, in L. Le Grand, *Statuts d'Hôtels-Dieu et de Léproseries. Recueil de textes de XIIe au XIVe siècle* (Paris, 1901), pp. 214–23, and more ambitiously, there were leper pilgrims, E Chronico Alberici Monachi Trium Fontium, in R.H.G., vol. 21, p. 604. Alberic is describing the diocese of Lodi in Lombardy in 1231. This degree of social participation, together with the absence of emotional foci for attacks upon them (in contrast to the Jews, who were always in danger during the calling of a crusade) might partially explain why the vulnerability of the lepers had not been exploited before.

14    LEPERS, JEWS AND MOSLEMS

laid down detailed regulations for the separation of lepers and their conduct in relation to the rest of the community,[46] and some of these are
reiterated in the rules of leper houses.[47] Ecclesiastical regulations, however, may simply have been formalizing an existing separation created by
local communities rather than making new conditions. Canon 23 of the
Third Lateran Council of 1179 established separate churches and
cemeteries for lepers, but the reasoning behind the canon was that lepers
had not been able to live with the healthy and attend their churches and
therefore no proper religious provision was being made for them.[48]
    Perhaps most pertinent to the question of popular attitudes towards
leprosy is the fact that it was the community which usually had to decide if
a person had contracted the disease, for medical advice was frequently
unavailable. Leprosy, therefore, gained an accusatory aspect not dissimilar
to heresy or witchcraft.[49] Fear of infection, or simply repulsion at the
appearance of those in the more advanced stages of the disease, must have
powerfully reinforced the Church's precepts. The Nangis continuator portrays the leper leaders at their four great assemblies describing themselves
and their fellow lepers as 'the most vile and abject persons among the
Christians',[50] while the king demanded, in the ordinance of 18 August
1321, that the land be cleansed of the 'putridity' of the 'fetid lepers'.[51]
Popular stories expressed this instinctive repulsion. The story from the
Gesta Romanorum, for instance, 'On the Evils of Leprosy', which must
have had wide circulation in oral versions even though the stories were not
collected together and written down until c.1340, taken literally, perpetu-
ates the idea that leprosy could be sexually transmitted and this was in itself
a means of ridding oneself of the disease and passing it on to another. At
the same time, the moral interpretation of the story takes leprosy as a
synonym for wickedness and describes the Fall as a process by which 'man
was spiritually made a leper'.[52] Even the Cathars, themselves outcasts and
fugitives by 1321, viewed the lepers as the lowest among humanity. Guillaume Bélibaste, the last of the Cathar perfecti, is reported as describing
the arrest of Christ in the following way: 'And on these words the pharisees

[46] Richards, op. cit., p. 50, and doc. no. 1, pp. 123–4. See also R. M. Clay, The Medieval
Hospitals of England (London, 1909), pp. 273–6, appendix A, under the heading, 'The
manner of casting out or separating those who are sick with leprosy from the whole'.
[47] e.g. statutes of Grand-Beaulieu de Chartres, op. cit., cl. 11–18, 23, 24, pp. 216, 218–9.
[48] C.-J. Hefele, Histoire des Conciles, tr. H. Leclercq, vol. 5, pt. 2 (Paris 1913), p. 1104.
[49] Indeed, comparison between heresy and disease was 'a comprehensive and systematic
model' of ancient origin and not 'just a casual metaphor', see R. I. Moore, 'Heresy as Disease'
in The Concept of Heresy in the Middle Ages, eds. W. Lourdaux and D. Verhelst (Louvain,
1976), and the same author's The Origins of European Dissent (London, 1977), pp. 246–50.
Perhaps the identification of heresy with leprosy actually had some basis in fact, for inquisitorial depositions do reveal scattered references to the Cathars taking refuge in or even living in
leper houses: B.N., Collection Doat, vol. 21, ff. 266v–267, vol. 24, ff. 115.
[50] Cont. Nangis, p. 34.
[51] Ordonnances, XI, p. 482.
[52] Gesta Romanorum, ed. H. Oesterley (Hildesheim, 1963 facs. reprint of 1872 ed.),
chapter 151, pp. 507–9. A lady who had contracted leprosy is forced by her husband to solicit
like a prostitute in order to free herself from the disease '. . . go to the city and make yourself
available to all comers and whoever takes you first will contract the infirmity and you will be
cured from all infirmity'. On the idea that leprosy could be sexually transmitted, see Henri de
Mondeville, Die Chirurgie, op. cit., p. 422.

and their servants with them, sons of the devil, came, and they took him, and all the injuries and opprobrium which they could bring to him, the pharisees and ministers brought to the Son of God, to such an extent that a certain leper spat at him in the face . . .'[53] Contemporary medical opinion did nothing to dispel this popular image. Henri de Mondeville apparently believed that the physical deterioration was accompanied by a disintegration of the leper's character, presumably because of a growing imbalance in the bodily humours. When the blood of a leper is washed through a cloth, he said, black stains will remain, which are the evil elements.[54] Perhaps this is what the chronicler Jean de Saint-Victor meant when he presents the Jews as saying that the lepers would consent to the plot, 'having been easily debased (*dejecti*) by them (i.e. the Jews)'.[55] Until this time, however, the lepers were less likely objects of antagonism than the Jews, since they were at least co-religionists and were seen as worthwhile objects of charity during the fashion for the endowment of hospitals in the twelfth and thirteenth centuries.[56] Indeed, while both Biblical precepts and popular fears continued to influence the treatment of lepers throughout the High Middle Ages, the harsher effects of these attitudes had been mitigated by the greatly increased provision of leper hospitals. Ironically, in the long term, this contributed to the lepers' vulnerability, for it helped to make them an identifiable minority, collected in a distinct place, just like the Jews.[57]

The second question which arises concerns the nature of the allegations. The essence of the allegations centres upon the magical use of poison which would either kill or make leprous. The ingredients of the poison have no apparent relationship to the alleged effects in the sense that they are not herbal or chemical poisons. The preference for a magical form of poison is further evidence of the panic which gripped society for, despite limited scientific knowledge, it is clear that more specific methods of poisoning, without the use of magic, were known even at a popular level. To take another contemporary example from the depositions of the Cathars: when the group of exiles in Catalonia centred upon Guillaume Bélibaste wished to poison a suspected traitress, an attempt was first made with 'a herb called *vulaire*' placed in her food, and when this failed they tried to purchase *realgar* or red arsenic from the local apothecary for the same purpose, making the excuse that they wanted it to cure ailments among their animals. The necessity for making an excuse does itself suggest that the poisonous properties of the substance were well-known.[58] The lepers' plot therefore was essentially based on magic in the sense that it is

---

[53] *Reg. Fournier*, II, p. 47: Deposition of Arnaud Sicre.

[54] *Die Chirurgie, op. cit.*, p. 423.

[55] Jean de Saint-Victor, p. 133.

[56] Le Grand, *Statuts d'Hôtels-Dieu, op. cit.*, pp. xxvi–xxvii, suggests that in the twelfth and thirteenth centuries Christians had sometimes regarded leprosy as a mark of religious predestination. See Clay, *op. cit.*, pp. 66–8, on the lepers as 'beloved of God'.

[57] For a wide-ranging analysis of attitudes towards leprosy in the Middle Ages, see S. C. Mesmin, *The Leper Hospital of Saint Gilles of Pont-Audemer: an edition of its cartulary and an examination of the problem of leprosy in the twelfth and thirteenth centuries*, unpublished Ph.D. diss., University of Reading, 1978, pp. 1–74.

[58] *Reg. Fournier*, II, p. 56–7, Deposition of Arnaud Sicre. See also II, p. 485, where another potential victim of *realgar*, suspecting an attempt to poison him, first tested his food on a dog in an experiment which was far from magical.

## 16    LEPERS, JEWS AND MOSLEMS

defined by Professor Thorndike: 'Magic appears . . . as a way of looking at the world which is reflected in a human art or group of arts employing varied materials in varied rites, often fantastic, to work a great variety of marvelous results, which offer man a release from his physical, social and intellectual limitations . . . The *sine qua non* seems to be a human operator, materials, rites, and an aim that borders on the impossible, either in itself or in relation to the apparently inadequate means employed.'[59]

The poison itself was a mixture, although the proportions of the elements included are not given and were indeed regarded as unknowable.[60] According to the reported letter of the lord of Parthenay it included human blood and urine, three unnamed herbs and a consecrated host; in the continuator of Nangis it is made up of a head of a snake, the feet of a toad and the hairs of a woman, all of which was mixed with a black and fetid liquid; and Guillaume Agasse claimed that it contained the powdered remains of a consecrated host mixed with a concoction made from snakes, toads, lizards and bats together with human excrement. However, despite the irrelevance of the constituents to leprosy, they did at least have harmful associations. The reptiles named were those thought to be born in corruption or earth, like worms, rather than from seed, and they were believed in themselves to be poisonous. The popular view of these creatures was expressed by Guillaume Bélibaste, even though the Cathar outlook on the created world differed radically from that of the orthodox. He explained that Cathar *perfecti* could not kill anything that had blood, whether it walked on the ground or flew in the air, except for a group which he called 'impure', which included mice, snakes, toads, frogs and lizards.[61] Human waste, which might be seen by some as the poisonous part of the elements being expelled from the body, was the corruption in which the 'impure' beings flourished and was therefore associated with them, while the desecrated host linked the whole mixture with anti-Christian and heretical groups such as the Jews, who had been frequently accused of desecrating the host during the thirteenth century.

Finally, in the most detailed account of how the plot was supposedly organized—that of Guillaume Agasse—the 'heretical' element emerges most markedly, which is not surprising in view of the inquisitorial nature of the hearing. In Agasse's deposition there are secret chapters, an oath sworn to preserve secrecy, the denial of Christ, spitting and trampling on the cross, and a sinister armed man or devil figure. Agasse's confession suggests not only that both he and his inquisitors had been directly

---

[59] L. Thorndike, *History of Magic and Experimental Science* (New York, 1929), vol. 2, p. 974.

[60] According to Peter of Abano (1250-c.1318), 'We do not know and we never shall know the quantities and the weights of the elements in the compounds', Thorndike, *op. cit.*, II, p. 906. Even if one is disposed to challenge the idea of well-poisoning by this method, no physician would have been able to disprove it, see S. Guerchberg, 'The Controversy over the Alleged Sowers of the Black Death in the Contemporary Treatises on the Plague', in *Change in Medieval Society*, ed. S. L. Thrupp (New York, 1964), p. 215 (originally in *Revue des Études Juives*, vol. 108, 1948).

[61] *Reg. Fournier*, II, p. 481. Deposition of Jean Maury. Ironically in view of Bélibaste's ideas, the toad in particular had previously been associated in the public mind with heretical orgies as portrayed in orthodox propaganda.

influenced by the accusations made against the Templars in their recent trial, but also that their ideas could still pass muster as a means of establishing who were the enemies of society.

The attacks upon the lepers and the Jews were symptoms of pressures with which society could not cope. The previous year they had taken the form of a pseudo-crusade; in 1321 they expressed themselves as a belief in a phantom plot to overturn society. The need to protect society from enemies both external and internal had been a fundamental tenet of the twelfth and thirteenth centuries. But, despite massive efforts, it seemed that the threats remained, for the Mameluks had pushed the Christians into the sea in 1291, and the inquisitors continued to insist upon eternal vigilance against the enemy within. Even the idea that Moslem agents were sometimes sent to poison the Christian population had already had some currency, for Matthew Paris alleged that there had been found in the baggage of one of the leaders of the Pastoureaux movement of 1251 a large sum of money, some documents in Arabic and Chaldean and various poisonous powders. The documents were found to be letters from the Sultan, exhorting the leader to act in return for a promise of a great reward. Apparently, it was intended that innumerable Christians would be handed over to the Sultan.[62] In 1321 this idea caught the imagination of a large section of the French population, although then the agents took the form of the lepers and the Jews. It can be seen as a prelude to the much more widespread pogroms which accompanied the Black Death, and perhaps helps to explain the nature of the society which was struck by the plague and therefore society's view of the causes of that disaster.

[62] Matthew Paris, Chronica Majora, ed. H. R. Luard (Rolls Series) vol. V, A.D 1248–56, R.S. 57 (London, 1880), p. 252.

# The Pastoureaux of 1320

The rising in France in 1320 known as the *Pastoureaux*, or Shepherds' Crusade, receives little attention in most histories,[1] and it is, indeed, a relatively small-scale event for which there are limited sources. Nevertheless, it has wider implications than have been generally recognised. The purpose of this paper is therefore twofold: to describe these events through the available sources and to offer some ideas concerning their historical importance.

There are three main categories of sources. Firstly, there are the chronicles, in particular those of north French contemporaries like Jean de Saint-Victor, the anonymous monastic continuator of the chronicles of Guillaume de Nangis, and the author of a chronicle of events in and around Paris who was probably a judicial official;[2] those of observers of the Languedocian scene like Bernard Gui, the papal inquisitor in the Toulousain, and Amalric Auger, prior of Aspiran near Béziers;[3] and two later works, the early fifteenth-century compilation know as the *Chronographia Regum Francorum* and the account of Samuel Usque, a sixteenth-century Portuguese Jew.[4] These can be supplemented

---

[1] For previous accounts see C. Devic and J. Vaissete, *Histoire générale de Languedoc*, ed. A. Molinier, Toulouse 1885, ix. 402–6; P. Lehugeur, *Histoire de Philippe le Long, roi de France (1316–22)*, Paris 1897, 416–22; P. Alphandéry and A. Dupront, *La Chrétienté et l'idée de croisade*, Paris 1959, ii, 257–64; N. Cohn, *The Pursuit of the Millenium*, rev. ed., London 1970, 102–4. I have been unable to obtain J.-M. Vidal, 'L'Émeute des Pastoureaux en 1320' in *Annales de Saint-Louis des Français*, iii (1899).

[2] Jean de Saint-Victor, *Prima Vita Joannis XXII*, in E. Baluze, *Vitae Paparum Avenionensium*, ed. G. Mollat, Paris 1914, i. 128–30; *Chronique latine de Guillaume de Nangis de 1113 à 1300 avec les continuations de cette chronique de 1300 à 1368*, ii, ed. H. Geraud, *Société de l'histoire de France*, Paris 1843, 25–8; *Chronique parisienne anonyme de 1316 à 1339 précédée d'additions à la chronique française dite de Guillaume de Nangis (1206–1316)*, in *Mémoires de la Société de l'Histoire de Paris et de l'Ile-de-France*, xi (1884), Paris 1885, 46–8.

[3] Bernard Gui, *Tertia Vita Joannis XXII* (*excerpta ex chronicis quae nuncupantur Flores chronicorum seu Cathologus Pontificum Romanorum*), in Baluze, op. cit., i. 161–3; Amalric Auger, *Septima Vita Joannis XXII* (*excerpta ex chronicis quae dicuntur Actus Romanorum Pontificum*), in Baluze. op. cit., i, 191–3.

[4] *Chronographia Regum Francorum*, i, ed. H. Moranville, *Société de l'histoire de France*, Paris 1891, 250–2; Samuel Usque, *Consolation for the Tribulations of Israel*, trans. M. A. Cohen, Philadelphia 1965, 186–90.

© 1981 Cambridge University Press

by slighter references in other accounts. Secondly, there is a long and
detailed inquisitorial deposition by a Jew from Toulouse called Baruch,
made before Jacques Fournier, bishop of Pamiers, in 1320.[5] Thirdly,
there are the official responses, including papal letters,[6] the records of
inquiries instituted after the event by the government in an attempt to
find out the extent to which the populace had co-operated with the
Pastoureaux,[7] and, less important, some scattered references in royal
financial documents, some of which were the consequence of the royal
inquiries,[8] and in acts of the Parlement.[9]

The chronicle accounts enable a rough framework of events to be
constructed, although it is inevitably sketchy since the chroniclers are
both unsympathetic and uncomprehending and the participants were no
more able to record their own impressions than were the adherents of the
People's Crusade in 1095–6. The beginnings of the movement are
described in most detail by the northern chroniclers, Jean de Saint-Victor
and the continuator of Nangis, in obviously related accounts, although
each had his own personal comments to make, and by the author of the
*Chronique Parisienne*, which from late 1316 is an original and important
source for events in Paris. Writers with knowledge of Languedoc, such as
Bernard Gui, are more valuable for the later stages of the movement,
passing over events in the north and in Paris in particular in very general
terms. 'About the beginning' of 1320, says Jean de Saint-Victor, bands of
'shepherds and simple men' began to gather, proclaiming their wish to
fight the enemies of the faith and in this way repossess the Holy Land for
the Christians. The *Chronique Parisienne* says more specifically that the
movement of the *'simples'* began in Normandy in May, and that they
pretended that they had been inspired by a vision of angels, commanding
them to help the Holy Land.[10] They had leaders—men who had

---

[5] *Le Registre de l'inquisition de Jacques Fournier, 1318–25*, ed. J. Duvernoy, Toulouse 1965,
i. 177–90. I have been unable to obtain an analysis of this by J.-M. Vidal, *Déposition du juif
Baruc devant l'inquisition de Pamiers*, Rome 1898. See also S. Grayzel, 'The Confession of a
Medieval Jewish Convert', in *Historia Judaïca*, xvii (1955), 89–120, which is particularly
concerned with the validity of forced conversion.
[6] A. Coulon, ed., *Jean XXII (1316–34). Lettres secrètes et curiales relatives à la France*, 2 vols.,
Paris 1906.
[7] Bibliothèque Nationale, *Collection Doat*, cii. 266–79, for Lézat; C. Compayré, *Etudes
historiques et documents inédits sur l'Albigeois, le Castrais et l'ancien diocèse de Lavaur*, Albi 1841,
252–5, for Albi.
[8] J. Viard, ed., *Les Journaux du trésor de Charles IV le Bel*, (*Collection de documents inédits*),
Paris 1917, nos. 36, 1047, 1048, 3667, 3668, 4953, 5155, 9615.
[9] E. Boutaric, ed., *Actes du parlement de Paris*, ii, *1299–1328*, *Inventaires et documents*, Paris
1867, nos. 6220, 6782, 6835, 6856, 6857, 6904.
[10] In an account by Samuel Usque, a Portuguese Jew whose *Consolation for the Tribulations
of Israel* was published about 1553, the inspiration is a dove which alights on the shoulders
and head of a 17-year-old Spanish boy. He apparently believed that he had been visited by
the Holy Ghost. Miracles followed: a beautiful maiden appeared and made him 'a
shepherd on earth', whose task was to fight the Moors, and then an account of these
experiences, mysteriously written on his arm, confirmed these events. Another man at the

144

V

instigated the movement according to Jean de Saint-Victor—in particular
a priest stripped of his orders 'because of his wickedness' and an apostate
Benedictine monk. Among their followers youth was much in evidence,
boys as young as fourteen being present. In the words of the continuator
of Nangis: 'These two (i.e. the leaders) had made mad these simple
persons, so that there also hastened after them boys of sixteen years of
age, against their parents' will, with only a bag and a staff, without
money, abandoning the pigs and sheep in the fields, flowing after them
like herds, to such an extent that there was a great multitude of men.' The
southern chroniclers, Bernard Gui and Amalric Auger, however, saw
them as leaderless and stressed the lack of preparation for any serious
attempt on the Holy Land. They had no ships, or even victuals, 'except to
the extent that they were administered to them by the Christian faithful
for the love of God', says Amalric Auger. Their numbers were augmented
by the usual opportunists. Bernard Gui: 'There were added to them the
destitute and other wandering men and women seeking concealment for
freedom of evil-doing... under the appearance of piety, begging artfully
and generally, and victuals were given to them in abundance.' Amalric
Auger believed that 'they visited all the ecclesiastical leaders, asking for a
subsidy to be given to them under the pretext of piety and poverty.' More
sympathetically, the author of the *Chronique Parisienne* describes them as
hanging out purses for contributions, but that 'they demanded nothing'.
Despite the hand-to-mouth existence however it seems likely that, as the
northern chroniclers indicate, they did have some form of leadership and
even rudimentary organisation. Amalric Auger himself describes how,
when their numbers had greatly increased, they were divided into groups
and marched two by two in procession, preceded by the banner of the
cross, 'without a word', he adds. According to the *Chronique Parisienne* they
carried banners and pennants portraying the Crucifixion and depicting
the arms of Louis of Clermont.

The silence claimed by Amalric Auger does not seem to have endured,
for very soon they began to conflict with the authorities. Either because
officials were nervous of such a large assembly or because the Pastoureaux began to provoke disorders, some of their number were
imprisoned, only to be forcibly freed by others. Their first objective seems
to have been Paris, which confirms the north French origin of the

---

same time claimed that the boy had discovered a cross on his shoulder. The public
reaction was to treat the boy as a saint and a large crowd gathered ready to fight the
Moors. However, when a Jew made a scornful remark about the miracle, the wrath of the
mob was turned away from Granada and directed against the Jews. Usque's account of the
Pastoureaux is interesting and detailed, but of very limited value, for three reasons: (i) its
late date; (ii) the probability that his chief source was written no earlier than the late
fifteenth century (see appendix B, pp. 269–84); and (iii) the purpose of the writer, which
was to convey to his people the message that the Jews had been punished by God for their
apostasy, but that now that era was ending and the millenium was at hand (see pp. 19–28).
He therefore 'uncritically accepted any source that furthered his thesis' (Cohen, p. 19).

movement,[11] but here too their arrival provoked disorder. Some were imprisoned in the priory of Saint-Martin-des-Champs by Gilles Haquin, *prévôt* of Paris, on royal orders, according to the *Chronique Parisienne*, but again others broke down the gates and released them. The *Chronique Parisienne* dates this 3 May. By this time their number had swelled to thousands; 'like an army', says the *Chronique Parisienne*. According to a later source, the *Chronographia Regum Francorum*, about 10,000 Pastoureaux entered Paris and, approaching the royal palace, 'shouted in a loud voice that the king should lead them with his army against the infidels to the Christian name, to revenge the injuries to Christ, and that angels had announced (this) to them on behalf of God, whence many were amazed, since they believed them to be speaking the truth'. The king did not, however, meet them, and, according to Jean de Saint-Victor and the Nangis continuator, they proceeded to the Châtelet, which was the seat of the *prévôté* of Paris and also a prison,[12] broke in and freed some of their supporters imprisoned there and seriously injured the *prévôt*, who had tried to oppose them, by pushing him down the stairs. The *Chronique Parisienne* describes this conflict as taking place in the rue Saint-Germain-l'Avenchoiz. Perhaps fighting took place in both places for they then assembled on the Field of Saint-Germain (the Field of the Clerks),[13] apparently believing that the *miles vigilum*, or the knight of the watch, as Jean de Saint-Victor calls him, intended to lead a large force against them. He did not, however, appear; 'I do not know by whose advice prevented', comments Jean de Saint-Victor with obvious disapproval. So the Pastoureaux left Paris unharmed and unhindered, and turned south towards Aquitaine, seemingly with the intention of reaching the Mediterranean ports en route to the Holy Land. The author of the *Chronique Parisienne* believed that some were aiming for Marseilles, others for Brindisi, while others intended to meet the pope at Avignon.

Perhaps emboldened by the spiritless response of the Parisian authorities, they now began to kill any Jews they could find and to seize their goods, incited, says the *Chronique Parisienne*, by some of the debtors of the Jews. Jean de Saint-Victor says specifically that this began after they had left 'France' and entered Aquitaine. The chronicle of Saint-Martial of Limoges remarks briefly that they passed through the city,[14] although

[11] Walsingham says that some came from England and other parts of the world, Thomas Walsingham, *Quondam monachi S. Albani Historia Anglicana*, ed. T. H. Riley, Rolls Series, xxviii. 1, London 1863, 157. Usque, op. cit., 186–7, describes only the Spanish and south French manifestations.

[12] The Châtelet, situated on the right bank next to the Ile-de-la-Cité, was originally built to defend Paris in the ninth century, but with the growth of the city became obsolete for this function and, instead, became the seat of the *prévôté* of Paris: see J. Hillairet, *Évocation du vieux Paris*, i, *Moyen âge et renaissance*, Paris 1951, 157–60.

[13] The Field of St Germain was probably to the south-west of the walls of Philip II's era, beyond the Porte St Germain. See also the maps at the end of H. Géraud, *Paris sous Philippe-le-Bel* (*Collection de documents inédits sur l'histoire de France*), Paris 1837.

[14] *Anonymum S. Martialis Chronicon ab anno M°CC°VII° ad M°CCC°XX°*, in *Chroniques de*

their direction is not clear since acts of the Parlement in 1322 show that they burned a royal tower at Saintes in which the Jews had taken refuge and massacred them, probably with the help of some of the local inhabitants.[15] It is, of course, possible that by this time there was more than one group on the move. The Jews fled before them, many taking shelter in a royal fortress, identified by Bernard Gui as Verdun on the Garonne. Here a major confrontation took place. The governor of the fortress had put the Jews in a high tower and when the Pastoureaux attacked they defended themselves fiercely, hurling wood and stone at the besiegers, and even throwing their own children at them, report the chroniclers, getting carried away by the drama of the event. Finally the attackers piled wood against the tower and, setting fire to it, 'gravely afflicted the Jews within by smoke and flame'. Rather than fall into the hands of the uncircumcised, as Jean de Saint-Victor puts it, the Jews are said to have agreed to a suicide pact, in which one of their number was chosen to cut the throats of the others with a sword. But when he had killed about fifty of them he surrendered to the Pastoureaux, taking with him some Jewish children. He told the Pastoureaux what had happened and then offered to be baptised with the children, but it was to no avail. The Pastoureaux replied that he had been a traitor to his own people and, in the words of the continuator of Nangis, tore him to pieces 'limb from limb'. The children were, nevertheless, spared and taken to be baptised.

The Pastoureaux then moved southwards again towards Toulouse and Carcassonne, massacring Jews in the dioceses of Toulouse, Cahors and Albi, and, in Bernard Gui's words, 'in the city of Toulouse itself exercising their madness, by the general connivance and favour'. But the movement does not seem to have been aimed exclusively at the Jews, for Amalric Auger claims that they robbed churches, and Bernard Gui says that 'they struck terror and dread of their name in the communities of the towns and the castles, and in the rectors and leaders of them, and among the princes and the prelates and rich persons'. He also alleged that 'there was afterwards found through some of them that they had arranged to rise up against the clergy and monks having riches and to seize their goods'. Moreover, they had been proceeding to Avignon, where the pope and the cardinals had been waiting in terror for their arrival; indeed, one anonymous chronicle source asserts that the papal chamberlain ordered the clergy to preach against them.[16] The pope was certainly alarmed about the movement. On 19 June he wrote to a number of leading prelates and royal officials in Languedoc about disorderly assemblies of rustics, calling themselves Pastoureaux, which, he had learned, included

*Saint-Martial de Limoges*, ed. H. Duplès-Agier, Paris 1874, 147.

[15] Boutaric, *Actes*, no. 6220, p. 338; no. 6835, p. 458; no. 6856, pp. 460–1; no. 6857, p. 461.

[16] *Ex Historia Satirica Regum, Regnorum et Summorum Pontificum ab anonymo auctore ante annum M.CCC.XXVIII, scripta*, in *RHG*, xxii, 15.

women and youths, who had set out without provisions or leadership to cross the sea to aid the Holy Land. They were savagely killing both clergy and laity as well as the Jews and seizing their goods. 'By their improper acts these persons show themselves bereft of devotion ... weak in strength and sense.' The passage to the Holy Land was a matter close to his heart, said the pope, and King Philip V had himself laboured hard towards the same end, but the Pastoureaux were acting against the will of God and must be stopped both by ecclesiastical censure and by temporal justice.[17]

Both the chroniclers and the later inquiry, however, make it clear that the temporary success of the Pastoureaux was achieved because they often received the support of the populace and even the town governments. Bernard Gui talks of them being 'favoured by weighty persons', despite his stress on upper class fear of the movement. But, like so many popular movements, they could not survive when professional military skill was mobilised against them. Aymery de Cros, sénéchal of Carcassonne, was not prepared to permit disorders like those at Toulouse to occur in his sénéchaussée, for he ordered 'under pain of death that no one should in the least extend any favour to the Pastoureaux', says the Nangis continuator. The Jews should be defended from the Pastoureaux since, as Jean de Saint-Victor describes them, they were 'serfs of the king'. On 29 June Aymery de Cros wrote to the consuls of Narbonne warning them that many of the Pastoureaux had fled towards Narbonne, fearing their capture at the hands of the sénéchal. Unlike many urban authorities in Languedoc the consuls seem to have been prepared to co-operate, for they claimed that they would keep a day and night vigilance both in and around the city.[18] Many others, though, did not obey him saying, according to the continuator of Nangis, that 'it was not just that they should defend the infidel Jews and enemies of the Christian faith against faithful and Catholic people'. Nevertheless, despite popular antagonism, the sénéchal was able to assemble an army and, again according to the Nangis continuator, the Pastoureaux 'were reduced to nothing in a very short time'. The attack seems to have broken up the main body, for thereafter many were captured in relatively small groups and were hung in tens, twenties and thirties from gibbets and trees wherever they were found.[19] Bernard Gui places these events at harvest time in 1320.

Dispersion seems to have ended the movement as such, but bands of Pastoureaux remained. Some crossed the Pyrenees near Jaca and entered

[17] Coulon, Jean XXII, ii. no. 1104, pp. 936–8, letter to the archbishop of Narbonne. See also no. 1105, p. 938, no. 1107, p. 939, no. 1111, p. 941, no. 1113, p. 942, no. 1114, pp. 942–4, no. 1115, pp. 944–5, no. 1116, pp. 945–6. Other recipients were the archbishops of Toulouse and Arles, the sénéchaux of Beaucaire and Toulouse, and Gaucelin, cardinal-deacon, the papal legate. For the papal view see also G. Tabacco, La Casa di Francia nell'azione politica di Papa Giovanni XXII, Rome 1953, 238–9.

[18] B.N., Coll. Doat, lii. 67–9.

[19] Some must have been captured and held for trial, for proceedings were taken against 'those calling themselves Pastoureaux' in Toulouse by an order of April 1322, Boutaric, Actes, no. 6782, p. 444.

# V

Aragon, apparently drawn by the wealth of the Jewish communities of Navarre, especially Tudela and Pamplona. There the French pattern was repeated, for, in the course of their journey, they massacred a large part of the prosperous Jewish community of Montclus at the foot of the Pyrenees in the province of Sobrarbe and sold the booty to willing Christian buyers. The local *alcade* seems to have been implicated, for soon afterwards he fled to avoid the wrath of King James II of Aragon under whose protection the Jews of Montclus had lived. The damage to the Jewish community was extensive, for the Aragonese kings were obliged to issue a stream of immunities to them in order to help them restore their position. Even so, in 1335, it was still necessary to extend the term of the immunities, specific mention being made of the effects of the damage caused by the Pastoureaux of 1320. After attacking Tudela, the Pastoureaux were eventually overtaken by the forces of Alfonso, son of James II of Aragon, and destroyed.[20]

A single late source, the *Chronographia Regum Francorum*, adds a curious footnote, not found in contemporary writers, on the fate of some of the Pastoureaux. According to this compilation, the expedition mounted by Philippe de Valois, cousin of Philip V, at the behest of the pope, to relieve King Robert of Sicily under siege in Genoa by the Visconti and the Ghibellines in 1320, was accompanied by some remnants of the Pastoureaux who had been led to believe that by this means, they could go beyond the sea to combat the Saracens. A secondary element in the expedition seems, therefore, to have been to divert these violent but naïve crusaders away from France, for the Pastoureaux, dressed in tight linen clothes called *sarros* and marked with crosses and carrying wallets and staffs, were held in derision by the rest of the army. Once the battle had begun the Pastoureaux were thrown in at once and 'with a great shout' they rushed against the Ghibellines whom they had been told were 'infidels and enemies of the cross of Christ'. They killed many with their staffs, but at length they were overcome and no more is heard of them on this expedition.

The accounts of the chroniclers furnish the general outlines of the movement, but the striking testimony of Baruch l'Allemand, a Jew who was one of the victims of the Pastoureaux, gives a very different perspective, more detailed but concerned only with a small part of the larger movement. Baruch had been forcibly baptised by the Pastoureaux in Toulouse and, on 13 July 1320, then found himself brought before the

[20] See J. Miret y Sans, 'Le Massacre des juifs de Montclus en 1320. Episode de l'entrée des Pastoureaux dans l'Aragon, in *Revue des Études Juives*, liii (1907), 255–66, for an account of this, including large extracts from the documents. Usque (*Consolation*, 187) claims that the Jews of Tudela were massacred by a mob of 30,000. He describes similar massacres at Lérida and Jaca before the son of the king of Aragon cleansed the region of 'their venom' (p. 118). Usque has details, such as the repression of the Pastoureaux by the son of the king of Aragon, which accord with contemporary sources, but the chronology and the geography are often confused.

vigilant Jacques Fournier, bishop of Pamiers, to answer for having afterwards returned to Judaism. As a Jew who had supposedly apostatised, even though converted to Christianity through fear, he was considered to be under the jurisdiction of the Inquisition in the same way as any heretic.[21]

Baruch first gave an account of the experiences of two friends of his, Salamon de Vudas and Heliazer, his *scriptor*, who were in the town of Grenade-sur-Garonne, up-river from Verdun, when it was heard that the Pastoureaux were approaching. At first the local *bayle* assured them of his protection, but when, on Thursday 12 June, 'a great multitude of the Pastoureaux' had come, his confidence evaporated and he advised Salamon and Heliazer to sail down to Verdun, 'which was a strong fortification of the king'. But they never reached it, for the Pastoureaux heard of their escape (perhaps from local anti-Semites), sailed after them and brought them back to Grenade.[22] Offered baptism or death, they chose the former, although the *bayle* bravely challenged the Pastoureaux to kill him as well if they killed Salamon. Baruch learned this story when his friends arrived in Toulouse the next day to ask his advice as to whether the baptism was valid. Consultation with Raimond de Jumac, the representative of the Inquisition in Toulouse, and Master Jacques, his notary, seemed to suggest that it was not and Baruch returned to Salamon and Heliazer and told them 'they should boldly revert to Judaism'. He heard afterwards that Salamon 'had placed himself in the prison of the *sénéchal* of Toulouse, until the *sénéchal* had certified through the Roman Curia if such a baptism was a baptism'.

Baruch himself was attacked by the Pastoureaux in Toulouse, a city to which they first came as prisoners. Baruch does not claim to be an eyewitness, but his account of their arrival was based on what was 'generally told in Toulouse' at that time. According to Baruch, the Pastoureaux were brought into Toulouse on the following Sunday (15 June), prisoners of Alodet, *sous-viguier* of Toulouse, who had captured them 'on account of the killing which they had done of 152 Jews at Castelsarrasin and places in the vicinity'. From this evidence the movements of the Pastoureaux prior to their capture are not absolutely clear. Baruch's deposition seems to suggest that they attacked Grenade, Verdun and Castelsarrasin in that order, that is, they turned north-west and followed the river Garonne downstream before being rounded up by the *sous-viguier* of Toulouse and brought south. It is, however, entirely possible that Baruch's friends, Salamon and Heliazer, fled from Grenade

[21] See, for instance, the bull of Nicolas III, 7 May 1278, B.N., *Coll. Doat*, xxxvii. 191–2, and A. Pales-Gobilliard, 'L'Inquisition et les juifs: le cas de Jacques Fournier', in *Cahiers de Fanjeaux*, xii (1977), 97–114, in which she analyses the issues raised by this deposition, concerning the jurisdiction of the Inquisition over Jews.
[22] The *consuls* and inhabitants of Grenade were later accused of complicity with the Pastoureaux, and on 22 September 1322, the *sénéchal* of Toulouse was ordered to take proceedings against them, Boutaric, *Actes*, no. 6904, p. 473.

only to meet at least some of the Pastoureaux coming upstream from Verdun, having already captured the fortress. Given the general southerly drive of the movement this would seem the more logical direction, and, indeed, the continuator of Nangis says that they proceeded from Verdun 'towards Carcassonne'. Baruch's statement that the *sous-viguier* captured them after the massacre of Jews at Castelsarrasin and places nearby is not sufficiently precise to exclude either possibility.

The *sous-viguier* had loaded his prisoners into 24 carts and had managed to move 20 of them into the Château Narbonnais, when the occupants of the last carts began to shout for help to the large crowd which had assembled, saying that they were about to be imprisoned because 'they wished to avenge the death of Christ'. This seems to have incited the mob, some of whom began to cut the bonds by which the Pastoureaux were tied, and Pastoureaux and people began to shout together that all the Jews must be killed.[23] From this point Baruch became personally involved. He was standing in his study when the mob reached his street and they shouted at him that he must accept baptism or be killed. 'Seeing the fury of the people and seeing that they were killing other Jews who said that they did not wish to be baptised', he agreed, and they dragged him off to the church of Saint-Etienne. The scene at the church was terrifying. He was met by two Christian clerics who urged upon him the need for baptism because otherwise he would be killed, a point underlined by the bodies of Jews already lying there, and Baruch says that he was 'lightly struck' by those standing around him, which suggests that he was jostled by the mob. Baruch did not panic but attempted to talk his way out by expressing a fervent wish to be baptised, although asking that a certain Dominican, Jean l'Allemand, be his godfather, for, as he told Jacques Fournier, the Dominican was his 'great friend' and he had hoped that once in his hands 'he could be saved from death without being baptised'. However, as the two clerics took him from the church with the intention of going to the Dominican's house, Baruch saw two Jews killed in front of him, one of whom, Asser, from Tarascon de Provence, he knew by name. Moreover, the clerics were challenged as to whether Baruch had been baptised and, despite his plea that they should pretend that he had been, the clerics refused to help. Someone in the crowd then struck him a heavy blow to the head, which caused a swelling and his eyes to dance, and the clerics told him that it was futile to try to

---

[23] Usque (*Consolation*, 187) speaks of 10 wagon-loads of Pastoureaux who had been captured, but he has them released by monks who rise at midnight for this task. The release of the shepherds is seen as a miracle, which inflamed the mob to attack and kill 200 Jews. Apart from Baruch's deposition, no contemporary source mentions the captured Pastoureaux in the wagons, which, together with certain other details (see above note 20), does suggest that Usque's source must ultimately have had some connection with a lost contemporary account. There is another sixteenth-century account by Solomon ibn Verga, *Sefer Shevet Yehudah*, which, like Usque, is too late in date to be of more than limited value in this context, see Grayzel, 'Medieval Jewish Convert', 97.

reach Jean l'Allemand's house because he would be killed before he reached half-way. On the advice of the clerics, they retreated inside the church where once more Baruch attempted delaying tactics, first asking them to wait to see if his sons had come and then, when they did not appear, asking for the *sous-viguier* to come to be his godfather, hoping that Pierre de Saverdun, one of the *viguier's sergents*, and a friend of the witness, might come and protect him. But word came that the *sous-viguier* was too tired after his efforts against the Pastoureaux earlier in the day, and Baruch was left with no alternative but to undergo the ceremony in which he was forced to express sentiments of sincerity. He was baptised 'Jean'.

Baruch was now worried about his house and property and asked the clerics to escort him back there. They were not apparently very keen on the task, for they excused themselves on the grounds that they were 'tired and sweating'. They did, however, take him to their own house where they gave him some wine, and afterwards they set out for Baruch's house, presumably when the mob had had some time to thin out. His home had, of course, been pillaged, for his books were in pieces and his money stolen. The only items of value which were left were seven pieces of cloth, including a silk coverlet, which were either pledged to him or owned by him, and he was fortunately able to use these as a bribe to one of the *capitouls* of Toulouse, who had supposedly been designated to guard the Jews and was near his house at the time. The *capitoul* then handed him over to a *sergent* with instructions to protect him on behalf of the *Capitole*, the *sous-viguier* and the *sénéchal* of Toulouse.

The *sergent* led Baruch by the hand and took him near to the *Capitole*. When challenged the *sergent* said that he was a converted Jew and, in this way, Baruch survived until finally the killing and depredation of the Jews in Toulouse spent itself, at about vespers of that day. At this time Baruch persuaded the *sergent* to take him to the *sous-viguier's* house, so that he could ask him if his baptism, made under the threat of death, was valid. After supper, the *sous-viguier*, having consulted with Baruch's friend, Pierre de Saverdun, said that he had no wish to baptise anyone by force, from which Baruch had assumed that he was not validly baptised. In the meantime, Pierre de Saverdun warned Baruch that to stay at the Château Narbonnais was too dangerous and arranged for him to leave Toulouse, supplying him with money and taking him to the head of the road which led to Montgiscard, to the south-east of Toulouse. He should go quickly and speak German on the way. But Baruch did not make good his escape for a band of Pastoureaux challenged him on the road and, although at first he denied that he was a Jew, he eventually admitted it, and was taken by them and imprisoned with other Jews overnight, apparently with the complicity of Bernard Loup, the local *bayle*. On the following night he was taken under guard of the *bayle's* men to Mazères and thence to Pamiers. It was his presence in Pamiers that led him to be brought before Jacques Fournier.

152

# V

After his description of his experiences at the hands of the Pastoureaux, Baruch was then asked a series of questions by Fournier designed to discover his attitude to the baptism. Baruch's replies are not directly relevant to the history of the Pastoureaux, although he does mention that he thought 115 Jews had been killed at Toulouse on that Sunday. In the end Fournier professed to be convinced that Baruch's baptism was not 'by force or absolute coercion' and warned him that if he remained 'obstinate in Judaism, he would proceed against him as a heretic'. Baruch replied that he would put aside Judaism if the bishop could prove the articles of the Christian faith to him and there followed a massive disputation which seems to have lasted over six weeks and in which, according to the notarial record, Baruch was completely vanquished. The hearings eventually ended on 3 December 1320.

While Baruch's deposition furnishes considerable detail about the activities of the Pastoureaux in Toulouse, the royal inquiries initiated to find out the truth concerning the attacks upon the Jews, the theft of their goods and 'the many great excesses done by those saying that they were Pastoureaux, generally in the *sénéchaussées* of Toulouse, Périgord and Carcassonne', are especially valuable for events in other towns. Detailed reports on Lézat and Albi illustrate the complicity of the local population, including the urban consulates, which Bernard Gui describes. Charles IV issued commissions on 15 November 1322,[24] and the records of the activities of his representatives Pierre Tilbert and Jean de Moras, royal castellan of Monreale, appeared two years later, on 2 August for Lézat and on 10 November for Albi.

The story which emerged at Lézat was that, on or about the Feast of St John the Baptist (24 June) 1320, the Pastoureaux had been openly and publicly allowed into the town for a period of several days and nights. They carried prohibited arms, namely swords, large knives, lances, spears, shields and helmets, among other weapons, but, far from opposing them, the *consuls*, supposedly the responsible authority, favoured them and, together with the rest of the populace, provided them with victuals. Indeed, more than twenty inhabitants actually took up arms and joined them, again with the full knowledge of the *consuls*. The Pastoureaux broke into the house of Atan, a Jew of Lézat, even though he and his goods were under the special protection of the king, and seized cloth, money and documents (*instrumenta*). They then demanded that Master Mathieu Ermengaud, a local notary, hand over recognisances of debts to the Jews, so that they could burn them as had been done in Toulouse and in Cahors. The notary's appeal to the *consuls* to defend him, since the Jews, their goods and documents were exclusively for the king's use, fell on deaf ears, for the *consuls* and many of the inhabitants of Lézat owed a considerable amount of money to Atan and wanted to see the documents destroyed. For their failure to stop the Pastoureaux, despite having the

24 B.N., *Coll. Doat*, cix. 73.

powers to do so, the inhabitants of Lézat were initially sentenced to lose their consulate and be deprived of all jurisdictional powers and privileges. However, at length a settlement was worked out which protected the urban privileges at the cost of a payment of 400 *livres tournois* to be paid in annual instalments of 50 *l.t.* each Christmas.

Albi was a town of greater size and importance. Here again the commissioners alleged that despite being elected with full financial control and power over criminal jurisdiction, the twelve *consuls* failed to prevent armed Pastoureaux from entering the town on several different days at about the time of the Feast of St John the Baptist 1320. Indeed, they abdicated their responsibility by allowing them in 'openly and publicly . . . without any resistance', by not closing the gates to them, and by not chasing them away or capturing them and subjecting what are called 'mortal enemies of the royal majesty' to 'rightful punishment'. According to the report, similar incidents had occurred at Auch, Verdun, Castelsarrasin, Toulouse, Rabastens and Gaillac, among other places, as was generally known in Albi at this time. The Pastoureaux had killed the Jews and stolen their goods which were 'in the safe and special guard of the king', they had attacked royal castles, and everyday had committed further crimes, 'not only to the injury and damage of the royal majesty but also to the whole public weal'. Yet, despite this, at Albi, Pastoureaux of both sexes and all ages had been allowed in freely over a number of days, in groups of 60, 80 or 100, and received 'with joyful expression', being provided with bread, wine and other food, as well as accommodation. They were permitted to search the town for the Jews in order to kill them and to break open the houses in which their goods were kept and to steal gold and silver ornaments, precious stones and jewellery and other movable goods to the value of 1,000 *livres tournois*. The inhabitants seem also to have seized the opportunity to loot the storehouses once they had been broken open. The goods were then quite openly sold in the town's main square.

The *consuls* defended themselves by arguing that they by no means possessed the sweeping powers that the royal agents claimed, having ceased to have 'the recognition of civil and criminal causes and the power of judgement', that the carrying of arms was prohibited in Albi, a fact which they had publicly proclaimed, that the Jews no longer lived in Albi despite attempts by them to gain the right to live there by offering a sum of money to the bishop, and that since no Jews lived in the city they did not know that the Pastoureaux had come there to attack them. They admitted that the Pastoureaux had come to Albi, but claimed that their arrival had been so sudden that they had had no advance warning of it. When they had realised what was happening—that the Pastoureaux were armed and were committing 'various evil acts and thefts'—they gathered armed resistance through the bishop, 'since otherwise they would not have dared', and attempted to guard the city gates. They further claimed that if some goods of the Jews had been stolen by the Pastoureaux, then the buyers had revealed the matter to the royal court and the goods had been restored to their owners, and that no Jew had been killed or even wounded in Albi. In any case the Pastoureaux could not have been stopped by closing the gates since Albi was not entirely encircled by walls. Finally, they said that the Pastoureaux had initially been received in good faith because 'they publicly asserted that they had assumed the cause of God against the enemies of the faith'.

The defence of the *consuls*, although full of inconsistencies which suggest that the Pastoureaux did indeed attack the Jews of Albi and seize their goods, nevertheless did have some justification, for on 26 June the secular judge of Albi, on behalf of the bishop and various *consuls*, had indeed asked for help against the Pastoureaux from royal officials and he had made sure that this was recorded.[25] The fact was that the Pastoureaux could not easily be stopped by the *consuls* of a particular town once they had gained public sympathy which, for a period in the summer of 1320, seems to have been relatively easy to obtain. In the end, since the matter was considered doubtful, the *consuls* settled for a fine of 800 *livres tournois* to be granted to help the king's war in Gascony.

Acts of the Parlement show, in less detail, that there had been a reckoning, too, at Saintes. In May and June 1322, the *sénéchal* of Saintes and Angoulême was ordered to find out who had been responsible for allowing the tower at Saintes to be taken and burned. Guillaume de la Mole, a royal sergeant, had originally been accused by the *sénéchal* of removing the guard on the tower, having put a number of Jews and Jewesses in the tower for their supposed safety and then of having stolen their goods by putting them on a boat on the river Charente. He had, however, been cleared and suspicion transferred to a certain Itier 'Pictavini', whose fate is not recorded. As for the Pastoureaux themselves, some had taken refuge in the castle of Saintes which appertained to the king of England, and his officials refused to hand them over.[26]

A limited number of references in *Les Journaux du Trésor* of Charles IV between February 1322 and January 1326 confirm that royal displeasure at the disturbances must have been tempered by the extent of the incomes gained from the aftermath. The entries, while clearly by no means giving a complete picture of the financial consequences of the uprising, do give some indication that the crown was able to profit from it. There are fines upon the Pastoureaux themselves totalling 273*l.* 10*s.* 8*d.t.*,[27] and a gift to Hugues de Bouville, the royal chamberlain, of 1,000 *l.t.* to be taken upon forfeitures of the Pastoureaux,[28] which indicate that

[25] Compayré, *Études historiques*, no. lxx. 251–2. In 1297 Cathar heretics had been able to enter Albi at night without apparent difficulty, so it is possible that there was some truth in the consuls' assertion that the city was not secure: G. W. Davis, *The Inquisition at Albi, 1299–1300*, New York 1948, 166.

[26] Boutaric, *Actes.*, no. 6835, p. 458, no. 6856, pp. 460–1, no. 6857, p. 461, no. 6220, p. 338.

[27] Viard, *Les Journaux du trésor du Charles IV*, no. 36, 10–11.

[28] Ibid., no. 9615, p. 1543.

at least some of the would-be crusaders had some capacity to pay, a sum of 2,225 *l.* 17 *s.t.* gathered from the property of the Jews who had been killed by the Pastoureaux,[29] and fines, apparently imposed for offences similar to those of the citizens of Lézat and Albi, of 2,098*l.* 15*s.* 4*d.t.*.[30] In relation to these sums a single entry recording that Gencien Tristan together with 24 men and 8 servants had been sent to Corbeil to arrest some of the Pastoureaux at the cost of 8 *l.p.* plus 20 *s.p.* for the services of a boatman, seems a minor expenditure.[31]

The uprising of the Pastoureaux lasted for only a few months in the spring and summer of 1320. It provides one of those brief and tantalising glimpses of peasant feeling which apparently subsided as abruptly as it arose. There are no peasant witnesses to the episode and, since the chroniclers are describing events involving the peasants, about whom they knew little, and the Jews, who were so often portrayed as stereotypes in the Middle Ages, the accounts need to be treated with more than the usual caution. For example, the account of the suicide of the Jews at York in 1190 by cutting each other's throats while besieged in the castle keep and the massacre by the mob of the few survivors who emerged is not dissimilar to the description of the Verdun episode, while both stories probably owe something to the portrayal of the fall of Masada in Josephus, *The Jewish War*. At both Verdun and Masada the suicide was provoked by the enemy setting fire to the defences and in both cases a few children survived, together with an adult who tells the story, who, however, in the case of Masada, was an old woman.[32] On the other hand, the Jews at Verdun might have been aware of past Hebrew traditions in such circumstances, so that such accounts should not necessarily be expected to differ greatly.[33] In addition, the chroniclers are socially conservative and therefore uniformly hostile; indeed, Bernard Gui claimed only to be recounting the story so that posterity could avoid similar dangers. He saw the Pastoureaux as essentially fraudulent, only 'pretending' to have zeal for the faith and attacking the Jews 'in order that their favour might increase more among the populace', and he uses the word 'madness' (*vesania*) to describe their actions. Jean de Saint-Victor and the continuator of Nangis see them as simple-minded youths led astray by evil and renegade clerics. 'Since it was not healthy at the outset', says the Nangis continuator, 'it scarcely recovered in the course of time.'

---

[29] Ibid., nos. 3667, 3668, pp. 633–4.

[30] Ibid., no. 4953, p. 822, no. 5155, p. 857.

[31] Ibid., nos. 1047, 1048, pp. 206–7.

[32] See R. B. Dobson, *The Jews of Medieval York and the Massacre of March, 1190*, York 1974, esp. 26–8; Josephus, *The Jewish War*, trans. G. A. Williamson, London 1959, 385–90.

[33] Cf. the mass suicides of the Jews of the Rhineland during the First Crusade: *The Jews and the Crusaders. The Hebrew Chroniclers of the First and Second Crusades*, trans. and ed. J. Eidelberg, Madison, Wisconsin 1977, especially the chronicle of Solomon bar Simson, 23, 31–6, 51–5, 57–8, 60.

V

Amalric Auger calls the movement 'a terrible plague', while the anonymous monk who continued the chronicle of Rouen calls the participants 'wanton and foolish'.[34] Even the author of the *Chronique Parisienne*, who is less condemnatory than the others, nevertheless sees them as in contempt of royal justice and describes their activities in the south as 'taking up their error more ardently than before'. As for the official documents, they reflect the concern of the authorities for public order and tell a story of punitive military action, fines and confiscations, stressing that the Pastoureaux were mortal enemies of both the king and the public weal.

Can any conclusions be deduced from the episode therefore? The only explanation offered by the sources is that they intended to travel to the Holy Land and to defeat the Saracens in Christ's name. Bernard Gui describes how the simple believed that the movement was 'a thing made by God'. Their behaviour is consistent with this, for they first went to Paris, which may be seen as an attempt to rouse the king, and then turned south, presumably heading for the Mediterranean ports and Aigues-Mortes in particular. Their anti-Semitic behaviour is similarly consistent with the attitudes of crusaders from the time of the People's Crusade onwards. Their appearance confirms this; they carried the traditional badges of the pilgrim, the staff and the scrip, they wore crosses on their clothing and carried banners bearing the sign of the cross. According to the *Chronique Parisienne* and the *Chronographia*, they believed that they were inspired by visions of angels, just like the shepherds who had hurried to the Bethlehem stable. It seems to have been largely a movement of the poor, although the fines suggest some participation of other social groups (perhaps some lesser nobles if past movements are any indication), and to have included not only boy shepherds but all ages and both sexes. By the time they reached Paris, some were certainly armed. The timing of the movement suggests that at least initially the religious element was strong, for Easter and the preceding period of Lent seem to have been particularly associated with both popular crusading fervour and anti-Semitic riots in the past.[35] Easter fell on 30 March in 1320, so that 'at the beginning' of the year as suggested by Jean de Saint-Victor could well have meant the Lent/Easter period, especially as the year in France sometimes ran from Easter to Easter.[36] The *Chronique Parisienne* dates their arrival in Paris as 3 May, so that the impetus for the movement may well have been generated around Easter time.

Several of these features had appeared during the crusading era in the past: in the People's Crusade of 1095–6, during the crusade preaching of

[34] *E Chronici Rotomagensis Continuatione*, in *RHG*, xxiii, 349.
[35] See Dobson, op. cit., 25.
[36] Pedantically, it could also be described as 'about the end' of the previous year, but this seems an unlikely approach for a chronicler about to describe events extending into the summer and autumn.

Fulk of Neuilly and his followers between 1198 and 1202, in the Children's Crusade of 1212,[57] among those other Pastoureaux marching to rescue St Louis in 1251 and, most recently, in an abortive popular crusade of 1309. The movement of 1309 was within easy memory in 1320 and may have played a part in stimulating the Pastoureaux. It found its origins in Flanders, Germany and England. The stimulus seems to have been papal propaganda in favour of the Hospitallers who had recently conquered Rhodes. As the crusaders marched from Germany and Flanders into France, many Jews were massacred, although those who took refuge in the castle of Genappe, held by Jean II, Duke of Brabant, were saved by the duke's forces which killed or dispersed many of the would-be crusaders. The remainder moved south, first to Paris, and then to Avignon and Marseilles. There, a combination of papal dissuasion and lack of shipping seems to have discouraged them and the movement fizzled out.[58] The movement of 1320 may, therefore, be seen in the tradition of emotional and irrational action by the inarticulate and, in the eyes of the upper classes, animal-like masses. Indeed, most of the chroniclers see the movement as a kind of natural phenomenon which occurred from time to time, unexplained and inexplicable: Jean de Saint-Victor called it 'a certain commotion, the course of which is utterly unknown'; 'like a whirlwind', says the continuator of Nangis; and Bernard Gui says of their end that 'like smoke they disappeared'. Bernard Gui and the author of the *Chronique Parisienne* do, however, draw a parallel with the movement of 1251; Bernard Gui had read about it in the chronicles, although he takes his analysis no further than that. For the upper classes, therefore, the peasants were part of an environment which, like an earth tremor or a flood, occasionally became disruptive.

[57] See Alphandéry and Dupront, *La Chrétienté*, ii. esp. 71, 119. The celestial letters of 1095, 1199 and 1212 may be seen as the equivalent to the vision of angels of 1320, while the children who took to the roads in 1212 abandoned their flocks and forsook their parents without permission just like the youth of 1320. Mass following for charismatic and often heretical leaders may also be related to this, for, among their traits, the Pastoureaux exhibit definite anti-clerical tendencies.

[58] See J. Stengers, *Les Juifs dans les Pays-Bas au moyen âge*, Brussels 1950, 15–17, 102–8, for an account of the 1309 'crusade' together with detailed source references, and R. Röhricht, 'Études sur les derniers temps du royaume de Jérusalem', in *Revue de l'Orient Latin*, i (1881). 650–1. The *Chronique Parisienne* has a brief account mentioning that they came to Paris, but placing the events in 1308. Ptolemy of Lucca, *Secunda Vita Clementis V* (*excerpta ex Historia ecclesiastica*), in Baluze, *Vitae Paparum*, i. 34, claims that 30,000 of them reached Avignon in August 1309, but the Hospitallers did not want them, 'saying that they had sufficient people'. Bernard Gui, *Tertia Vita*, 67, and Amalric Auger, *Septima Vita*, 98, (Baluze, op. cit.) mention that there was talk of preparations for a general passage in 1309, but bad weather stopped the project at Brindisi. This may have combined with the crisis in wheat supplies of the same year, which began in south and west Germany and spread to the rest of Western Europe, to provoke popular disturbances. On this see G. Duby, *Rural Economy and Country Life in the Medieval West*, trans. C. Postan, London 1968, 295.

But the peasants were human and their feelings could be exploited by those who knew how, and it is therefore necessary to look for specific causes of the 1320 movement rather than simply explaining it away in terms of past disturbances. The environment created by the upper classes, king, nobles and higher clergy, provided the opportunity for this exploitation. The impossible dream of liberating the Holy Land stemmed from the failure of contemporary social leaders to achieve this themselves and, in particular, from their failure to crusade in the East since the days of St Louis, despite promises to do so and despite tax-collections to pay for those unfulfilled journeys.[39] A conspicuous example was the tenth granted to Philip IV for six years at the Council of Vienne in March 1312, which was based on his promise that at the end of that time he would go personally to the Holy Land.[40] He and his sons, including the future Philip V, took the cross in June 1313, and afterwards, according to the continuator of Nangis, a multitude of common people, having heard the crusade preached, 'hastened to do the same from devotion'.[41] This was hardly surprising for great publicity was given to the venture. The Dominican bishop, Ptolemy of Lucca, describes the taking of the cross at a great feast in Paris on 3 June, where the king knighted his three sons. Edward of England and Isabella, his queen and Philip IV's daughter, attended, and 'about a thousand' nobles were present. When Philip took the cross at the hands of the papal legate, so too did the king of England and Philip's three sons and 'almost all the baronage'.[42] Bernard Gui stresses that after this assembly, the crusade was preached publicly[43] and Amalric Auger described the taking of the cross as being 'in the presence of a copious multitude of the faithful'.[44]

Neither Philip IV nor Louis X lived to fulfil this vow, but in 1316 it again seemed as if the government was prepared to take the project seriously, for Robert of Clermont and his sons, Louis and Jean, took the cross before a great assembly at Paris on 23 July. The assembly had been moved by Pierre de Courpalay, the titular patriarch of Jerusalem, who had preached passionately about the pitiable state of Outremer. The count of Poitiers, the regent and future King Philip V, ordered that all those who had taken the cross both previously (at the assembly of 1313) and at this time should make preparations for departure at Pentecost, the following

[39] See Alphandéry and Dupront, op. cit., 257-8. The Children's Crusade was also at least partly the consequence of the failure of the upper classes to liberate the Holy Land, although the economic, social and political context of this failure is different (p. 120).

[40] Walter of Hemingborough, *Chronicon, De Gestis Regum Angliae*, ed H. C. Hamilton, London 1868, ii. 291. See C.-J. Hefele, *Histoire des conciles*, trans. and ed. H. Leclercq, Paris 1915, vi (2). 658-9.

[41] *Cont. Nangis*, i. 396.

[42] Ptolemy of Lucca, *Secunda Vita*, 50.

[43] Bernard Gui, *Tertia Vita*, 75.

[44] Amalric Auger, *Septima Vita*, 103-4.

year.[45] According to the *Chronique Parisienne*, popular enthusiasm was again high, for 'a great multitude of people' swore to aid the Holy Land at this time.[46] But in 1317 the enthusiasts were again disappointed for no systematic preparations were made, despite another public display of intention by Louis of Clermont in Paris on the Feast of the Exaltation of the Holy Cross (14 September), when he ostentatiously formed 'the confraternity of the Holy Sepulchre of our Lord' at a great feast and then held a service in the Church of the Holy Cross, a church which had been founded by St Louis.[47] Two years later the Pastoureaux carried banners showing the arms of Louis of Clermont.[48]

Philip v continued to maintain his ardent desire to go on crusade personally, and on 13 September 1318, at Longchamp-en-Lions, he officially designated Louis of Clermont captain-general of crusading forces which were to be sent to the Holy Land as a preliminary to the general expedition in which Philip himself would take part.[49] In practice, however, Flemish affairs were more pressing and, as the pope became increasingly aware, the royal interest was mainly confined to the collection of crusading tenths. Arnald de Cumbis, a correspondent of the Aragonese king, James II, describes how Philip v and his brother Charles had pressed the pope for clerical tenths even at the time of his coronation on 5 September 1316, asking for, among other things, a double tenth for five years for the passage to Outremer. Arnald claimed that the pope was kept at Lyons 'against his will' because of the royal importuning. On 16 September 1316, 'the cross was solemnly preached by a certain cardinal in the presence of the pope and other cardinals and a copious multitude of people. And it was announced that Louis of Clermont, who was present, and many other nobles of France, who were said to be beyond 5,000, had taken the cross with the intention of going at their own expense in March in two years' time. Then there ought to be a general passage which, as the cardinal said, is to be deferred for the good of the Church.' Arnald adds however that 'concerning these things there ought not to be belief, except what it seems ...'[50].

Like others among King James's ambassadors and correspondents at the papal court, Arnald proved to be a perceptive observer. In March

---

[45] *Cont. Nangis*, i. 427–8; *Chronique Parisienne*, 25–6. See C. H. Taylor, 'French assemblies and subsidy in 1321' in *Speculum*, xliii (1968), 220–44; Lehugeur, *Philippe le Long*, 194–8; and A. de Boislisle, 'Project de croisade du premier duc de Bourbon (1316–33)', in *Annuaire-Bulletin de la Société de l'Histoire de France*, ix (1872), 230–2, for the background to these projects.

[46] *Chronique Parisienne*, 26.

[47] Ibid., 29–30.

[48] Ibid., 47.

[49] J. A. Huillard-Bréholles, *Titres de la maison ducale de Bourbon*, Paris 1867, i, no. 1509, p. 259.

[50] H. Finke, *Acta Aragonensia*, Berlin and Leipzig 1908, i, no. 145, pp. 223–4.

# V

1318, the pope granted the king two-tenths for three years, supposedly for the preparations for the general passage to Outremer,[51] but in fact to alleviate heavy royal debts.[52] Henri de Sully, the royal butler, seems to have been the chief agent in obtaining this money, apparently by determined harassment of the pope.[53] Nevertheless, emphasis was still given to the idea of a crusade, for 100,000 florins were to be retained 'for a certain particular passage',[54] and the following year the king called a conference at Paris at Christmas to deliberate upon the projected crusade. In the convocations for the assembly Philip stressed that to make the passage to Outremer was more important 'than all the other needs which we have at heart'.[55] A further meeting, specially composed of venerable crusading veterans, took place on 17 February 1320, where the king apparently garnered their collective wisdom extending back to the days of St Louis.[56] These meetings were as abortive as their predecessors, but by the spring, the 'shepherds' had taken matters in their own hands.

Hardly a year had passed since 1312, therefore, when there had not been some attempt to incite enthusiasm for the crusade, but the chief consequence for most people had been an increase in financial burdens, not the joyous liberation of Outremer. The clergy had not suffered alone, for, in a request made in June 1321 to the pope by the king for further subsidies, Philip asks that the Church first declare what she intends to grant, so that he can then calculate what he needs from his lay subjects.[57] It seems reasonable to assume that this was normal practice during this era. The danger that some people, especially those less worldly-wise than Arnald de Cumbis, would take the call for a crusade seriously, became a reality with the rising of the French rustics in 1320. Royal and papal attitudes towards the crusade after 1320 are a tacit acknowledgement of this, for, although the king continued his attempts to raise money, in 1321 in France itself he did not link this with the idea of a new crusade,[58] while Pope John, in replying to King Charles IV on the matter of the crusade in 1323, warned that if definite plans for it were fixed, then

[51] Coulon, *Jean XXII*, i, no. 512, pp. 433-4.

[52] Ibid., no. 513, pp. 435-6.

[53] Ibid., no. 505, p. 425.

[54] Ibid., no. 515, pp. 438-40.

[55] *Chronique Parisienne*, 43; P. Guérin, *Recueil des documents concernant le Poitou contentus dans les registres de la chancellerie de France*, ii (*Archives Historiques de Poitou*, XIII), Poitiers 1883, no. CCXXVI, 67-8, convocation of the knight Guy de Bauçay. Other letters were addressed to the duke of Burgundy, Charles of Valois, Charles, count of La Marche, the count of Evreux, Louis of Clermont and 30 other persons.

[56] Guérin, op. cit., no. CCXXVII, pp. 68-9. On these assemblies, see C. H. Taylor, 'The composition of baronial assemblies in France, 1315-20' in *Speculum*, xxix (1954), 448-50.

[57] Coulon, *Jean XXII*, ii, no. 1262. p. 12.

[58] See Taylor, 'French assemblies', 223, for a discussion of Philip's reticence on the subject of the crusade of France in 1321.

popular disturbances could be provoked 'in grave prejudice of the affair'.[59]

Crusade plans under Philip v seem, therefore, little more than a means of raising revenue, just as they had been under his father. Yet the later Capetians had frequently emphasised their special role as 'the most Christian kings', ruling over an elect people.[60] Philip IV had constantly stressed the importance of his descent from St Louis, claiming that he had inherited the characteristics of his predecessors who had given so much to the Church, and it was indeed true that the three Capetians who preceded Philip IV had all died when on some form of crusade. What could be more natural than for the peasantry, with their limited experience of the wider world, to ignore practical problems and concentrate upon the image of the innocent and the lowly succeeding where the corrupt and the high-born had failed? The young shepherds especially may have seen themselves as the elect, who could succeed against the Saracens with only the pilgrim's staff. Medieval drama may have reinforced the shepherds' conviction of their own importance for, by this period, their role in the Christmas story as performed in church was a prominent one, in which priests representing shepherds approached the crib and adored the child, and afterwards 'ruled the choir' during the remainder of the service.[61] The dramatic representation of the Christmas story had, in turn, itself developed from the account in St Luke's Gospel. Perhaps the mental horizons of the simple men, described by the *Chronique Parisienne* as pretending that they had been inspired by an angelic vision, were partly determined both by such drama and by the familiar Christmas story. The upper classes may, therefore, have seen the movement of the Pastoureaux as a plague and a madness, but they had created the circumstances which made it possible and as such the movement of 1320 is a good indication of the moral bankruptcy which came increasingly to afflict the social leaders of the fourteenth century and which is a significant element in what some historians have seen as 'the fourteenth-century crisis'.

But moral crises often have their roots in material problems, the signs of which had already become evident by 1320, most strikingly in the prolonged famine of 1315–17, which afflicted France north of the Alps. The famine provoked popular religious demonstrations. The Nangis continuator describes processions of clergy and people at the church of the Holy Martyrs in Paris, in which the bodies of saints and other relics

[59] Coulon, op. cit., ii, no. 1848, p. 405. The pope had already been reluctant to proceed with crusade plans in 1319–20, for in an undated letter between 21 September 1319 and 4 September 1320 he had put up a series of difficulties probably intended to frustrate Philip's continued financial demands, ibid., ii, no. 1227, pp. 1018–20.

[60] See J. R. Strayer, 'France: The Holy Land, the Chosen People and the Most Christian King', in *Medieval Statecraft and the Perspectives of History: Essays by Joseph R. Strayer*, ed. J. F. Benton and T. H. Bisson, Princeton, N. J. 1971, 300–14.

[61] See E. K. Chambers, *The Medieval Stage*, ii, Oxford 1903, 41–9, and K. Young, *The Drama of the Medieval Church*, ii, Oxford 1933, 3–28.

V

were carried, which took place at the height of the famine in the summer of 1315. Some people came from over five leagues away to take part, and the penitential aspect was emphasised by the bare feet and indeed, in some cases, the complete nakedness, of the participants. According to the chronicler, similar processions took place in the dioceses of Chartres and Rouen, as well as in other parts of France.[62] The French peasantry had been able to bear the weight of monarchical and noble pretensions in the thirteenth century because the agrarian economy was expanding. Only a few peasants had benefited markedly from this, but the upper classes had come to expect a much more expensive way of life than their predecessors of the eleventh and twelfth centuries. They continued to expect this as the economy began to contract and the population began to fall during the fourteenth century.[63] There are signs of tension before 1320. In the spring of 1315 there was unrest in Sens against 'the many vexations and unjust extortions' which the people had suffered at the hands of the archbishop's curial officials. The people apparently elected their own king, pope and cardinals and administered the sacraments themselves or forced priests to act for them under threat of death. Here, there is a hint of the coalescence of economic and religious discontents, as was to happen on a larger scale with the Pastoureaux.[64] The year 1320 does not itself seem to have been one of serious shortage; grain prices had fallen back to their pre-1316 levels.[65] Perhaps, therefore, the appearance of the Pastoureaux, which undoubtedly had a genuine crusade element irrespective of general social conditions, acted as a catalyst for economic discontents which had been present for a number of years.

The brunt of peasant violence fell upon the Jews, for they were the only non-Christians within reach of the Pastoureaux and they could be blamed for the economic hardships which the lower classes had recently been suffering. Again, exploitive leadership bears a heavy share of the responsibility. Expelled in July 1306 for ever, the Jews had been allowed to return to France in July 1315 by Louis X, because, according to the royal ordinance, among other reasons, of the 'common clamour of the people'. The charter granted to the Jews allowed their return for twelve years and, significantly, outstanding debts were to be collected, of which the Jews would receive one-third and the crown two-thirds.[66] This

[62] *Cont. Nangis*, i. 422.

[63] For a discussion of the issues involved see R. H. Hilton, 'Y-eût-il une crise générale de la féodalité?' in *Annales E.-s.-c.*, vi (1951), 23–30. The *Chronique Parisienne*, 28, is one of many accounts which described shortages during this time. In 1317 the price of wheat in Paris was so astronomical that '*le menu peuple* were badly burdened and oppressed'.

[64] *Cont. Nangis*, 1. 419–20.

[65] See H. S. Lucas, 'The great European famine of 1315, 1316 and 1317' in *Speculum*, v (1930), 376, who describes the crisis at its most intense in the winter of 1315–16, but shows prices returning to normal by the summer of 1318.

[66] *Ordonnances des roys de France de la troisième race*, ed. E. de Laurière, Paris 1723, i. 595–7. See R. Chazan, *Medieval Jewry in Northern France. A Political and Social History*, Baltimore and London 1973, chaps v and vi.

obviously gave the crown a vested interest in the rigorous investigation of those debts among people who, following the expulsion of 1306, must have believed that they would never be called upon to repay, for one reason why the Jews were allowed to return in 1315 was the hope that they would provide the crown officials with information on debts still outstanding. With the likely accumulation of further debts during the miserable years between 1315 and 1317, the Jewish 'usurer', as he was seen, was an almost certain target during any social disturbances.

By this time, indeed, it seems likely that a large proportion of debts to the Jews were small-scale. Limited confirmation of this general statement can be found in R. W. Emery's valuable study of the Jews in Perpignan based upon notarial registers between 1261 and 1287. The Jews in Perpignan were almost completely dependent upon money-lending for their economic support, and a large part of this business was in small-scale loans to the lower classes. Despite the fact that the notarial records do not record very small loans nor do they deal with pawnbroking, since there was no need for a written record when the creditor held the security himself, Emery found that the inhabitants of villages in the region of Perpignan accounted for 65 per cent of all loans and 43 per cent of all money involved in them. Villagers also received 74 per cent of all recorded loans of 20s. or less and only 20 per cent of loans over 500s. Townsmen made up the bulk of the rest of the total, with 30 per cent of all loans and 41 per cent of the money loaned, although their median figure was higher than that of the villagers, at 75s. as opposed to 60s. Perpignan was to some extent a special case in Languedoc, since as an expanding town it seems to have attracted Jews with money-lending interests, for returns on money lent were higher than in a town with a stagnant economy, and therefore the proportion of the Jews dependent upon money-lending as opposed to other occupations was higher in Perpignan than in, for example, Narbonne, an older established centre. Nevertheless, even with this proviso, the figures do suggest that in a time of economic distress and religious excitement such Jews would be obvious victims of an enraged populace; in the circumstances of a riot the key figure is the number of debtors, not the total amount that they owed. The argument is strengthened by the fact that the trends shown by Emery's figures become stronger in the fourteenth century, for the registers show that debts to the feudal aristocracy and the clergy, already diminishing in the second half of the thirteenth century, are almost absent in the early fourteenth century, and that the Jews of Perpignan 'were moving towards exclusive pawnbroking'. By this time the upper classes generally had recourse to Christian creditors rather than to the Jews.[67] When the Jews

[67] See R. W. Emery, *The Jews of Perpignan in the Thirteenth Century*, New York 1959, esp. 40, 62, 98, 106–7, *et passim*. In a wider but less detailed survey, G. Nahon, 'Condition fiscale et économique des juifs', in *Cahiers de Fanjeaux*, xii (1977), 51–84, argues that the economic position of the Jews in Languedoc had suffered a crucial decline by the early fourteenth century and that this led directly to the expulsion of 1306. It seems unlikely, therefore,

returned in 1315, their opportunities of playing a major role in the economy must have largely disappeared, and it would be almost certain that these trends were reinforced.

Initially, the Jews who had returned in 1315 received royal protection, and indeed, in April 1317, Philip V issued a further charter which did not even adopt the pretence of 1315, when Louis X claimed that their presence was to be tolerated in order to convert them to the Catholic faith 'by conversation with Christians'. The clauses of the 1317 charter make quite overt the conditions which govern Jewish money-lending.[68] Royal officials were active in collecting debts; special commissions had been appointed by Louis X for this purpose.[69] Moreover, royal involvement added a cutting edge to collection, for bad debts which the Jews had been unable to regain were extorted by royal agents.[70] The fragility of royal protection, however, can be seen in the temporary success of a group of swindlers who, in 1319, travelled the country pretending that they had a commission from the king to ransom the Jews for cash payments.[71] Moreover, there are signs of complaint to the crown. On 29 March 1320, in response to a complaint from the consuls of Narbonne,[72] Philip V ordered the sénéchal of Carcassonne to cease all actions against the debtors of the Jews. Again hypocritical leadership contributed to the outburst of 1320.

This same leadership was rapidly inducing in France a morbid mental state which may have made its own contribution towards the inflaming of a superstitious peasantry. The monarchy and the upper nobility had given a lead by the attack on Enguerrand de Marigny, former chamberlain of Philip the Fair who, in 1315, under the cover of sorcery charges, became a sacrificial victim for the crown's financial policies.[73] The increasingly frequent use of sorcery charges as a cover for political and economic paralysis was merely an upper-class version of the mob attacks upon the Jews when the Holy Land became unattainable. Sorcery was the speciality

that the Jews who returned in 1315 would have been able to establish themselves as large-scale financiers; they must have relied on small loans and pawnbroking for a living. See also Hilton, 'Y-eût-t-il une crise?', on the position of peasantry in primitive agricultural societies, in particular their exploitation by usurers.

[68] *Ordonnances*, i. 646–7.

[69] For those of Languedoc, see G. Saige, *Les Juifs du Languedoc antérieurement au XIV siècle*, Paris 1881, *pièces justificatives*, no. LVII, pp. 330–1.

[70] See Emery, op. cit., 82–4, on the impact of the involvement of the Majorcan crown upon debtors of the Jews in Perpignan.

[71] Boutaric, *Actes*, no. 5713, p. 274.

[72] Saige, op. cit., no. LIX, pp. 333–4. The ability of the consuls to co-operate with Aymery de Cros, sénéchal of Carcassonne, against the Pastoureaux, may be related to this concession. Moreover, Narbonne was one of those towns whose economy was not sufficiently active to concentrate Jewish economic activity into money-lending.

[73] For his fall, see J. Favier, *Un Conseiller de Philippe le Bel: Enguerrand de Marigny*, Paris 1963, 191–220.

of Philip IV's sons, but Philip himself did more than any other Capetian to undermine the prevailing structure, especially by his attacks upon Boniface VIII and the Templars and by his oscillating monetary policies. Although the Pastoureaux disappeared as quickly as they had come, the extent to which the old stability had been shaken can be seen in the next year, when popular discontent once more broke loose, venting its fury not only upon the Jews, but also upon the many leper colonies spread across France in the early fourteenth century. This time the shock-wave was so great that, for a few months, it engulfed the monarchy and the nobility as well.

# VI

## THE TEMPLARS AND THE TURIN SHROUD

The disappearance of the relic known as the Turin Shroud between 1204, when the Latins plundered and seized Constantinople, and April, 1389, when it was put on display by Geoffroi de Charney, has been the subject of a recent investigation by Ian Wilson, the results of which were published in *The Turin Shroud* in 1978 (revised edition, 1979). If one grants that the cloth shown by the Charney family really was the same as today's "Turin Shroud," it still needs to be explained how the family came to possess it and to find reasons for the family's apparent reluctance to reveal the means by which it obtained that possession. If it is also conceded that both modern scientific evidence and historical research suggest that the Shroud is much older than the fourteenth century and thus undermine contemporary criticisms—especially those by Pierre d'Arcis, Bishop of Troyes—that the Shroud was a forgery, some other explanation needs to be sought for the behavior of the Charney family. In Chapters 19 and 20 of his book Mr. Wilson postulates that the relic had come into the possession of the Order of the Temple and thence, during or after the trial and suppression of the Order between 1307 and 1314, passed to the Charney family, possibly via Geoffroi de Charney, Preceptor of the Templars in Normandy, who was burned to death as a relapsed heretic in March, 1314. The Charney family was reticent about the Shroud's recent location, Mr. Wilson argues, both because it wanted "to suppress the family's association with a fallen order" and because the reigning Avignonese pope, Clement VII, to whom the Charney family was related by marriage, feared that if "French passions about the reputed innocence of the Templars" were stirred again, the pope's authority "would be worth nothing."[1]

Mr. Wilson supports his theory with four main hypotheses: (1) that the cloth was taken to the West after 1204 and then "went underground" in the possession of the Templars, who, as a wealthy, exclusive, and secretive

---

[1]Ian Wilson, *The Turin Shroud* (rev. ed.; Harmondsworth, 1979), p. 235.

order, were able to resist the temptation to exploit it for monetary gain;
(2) that it was not found during the Templars' trial because during "fierce
resistance" put up in the course of the arrests, it was secretly taken away,
and that its later possession by the Charney family was because of the connection with the Temple through the Preceptor of Normandy; (3) that
the idols in the form of heads which, in the trial, the Templars were accused of having adored at receptions and chapter-meetings were really the
Shroud and a number of copies of it and that this had become the center
of a secret Templar cult; and (4) that the Charney family was reluctant to
reveal its origins, despite contemporary accusations of fraud. This paper
aims to examine the validity of these hypotheses.

There is no evidence to support point one independently of points two
and three. Robert of Clari has a brief reference to the Shroud: "...there
was another of the churches which they called My Lady Saint Mary of
Blachernae, where was kept the *sydoine* in which Our Lord had been
wrapped, which stood up straight every Friday so that the features of Our
Lord could be plainly seen there. And no one, either Greek or French,
ever knew what became of the *sydoine* after the city was taken." Robert's
translator, E. H. McNeal, suggests that he confuses the *sudarium* (the
sweat cloth or napkin, the True Image of St. Veronica) with the *sindon*
(the Shroud), and that he has wrongly identified their location as the
church in the palace of Blachernae instead of the church of the Blessed
Virgin in the Great Palace. These mistakes suggest that Robert was writing from report rather than personal observation.[2] Robert, whether correct with the details of his identification or not, apparently had no idea
what happened to it after the sack. The major Latin sources do not mention the presence of the Templars at the siege; so if it did come into the
order's possession, it seems likely to have done so through a third party.[3]
Mr. Wilson does not suggest who this might have been, nor why no news
of this emerged at the time, for as he himself points out, relics stolen
from Constantinople were openly displayed once they had been brought
back to the West.[4]

The account of the Cistercian Gunther of Pairis provides an example of
contemporary attitudes. In 1207-1208 he described what he presented as

[2]Robert of Clari, *The Conquest of Constantinople*, tr. Edgar H. McNeal (New York,
1936), p. 112. Mr. Wilson believes that the cloth had been moved to Blachernae so that it
could serve as a rallying point for the Greeks under attack by the Crusaders (*op. cit.*, p. 192).
[3]Professional relic thieves appear throughout the Middle Ages. See Patrick J. Geary, *Furta
Sacra. Thefts of Relics in the Central Middle Ages* (Princeton, 1978), chap. 3.
[4]Wilson, *op. cit.*, p. 199.

VI

the triumphs of his abbot, Martin, in snatching relics during the sack of Constantinople. Although such an action did not pass without criticism in the West, Gunther justified the translation of the relics to Pairis as God's will, for impious Greeks were not fit to hold them.[5] Abbot Martin was no renegade clerk or unscrupulous adventurer. When he heard the Venetian plan for the crusade army to attack the Christian city of Zara on the Dalmatian coast in 1202, he was horrified, and unavailingly begged the papal legate who was with the army at Venice to release him from his crusade vow.[6] Yet he was proud of the relics which he had collected. The only evidence that the Templars, a respected and respectable order, contemporary criticisms notwithstanding, would have acted any differently had they obtained such relics, rests upon certain trial documents whose value in this context will be assessed below.

However, even if it is accepted that the Templars really did gain possession of the cloth, then the mystery of its concealment remains to be solved. It cannot be disputed that the Templars were often, although not invariably, secretive in their reception ceremonies and chapters.[7] There had been good reason for such secrecy in the Holy Land, for it made little sense to allow information to pass freely to the enemy, and it is likely that the practice was also adopted in the western preceptories in imitation, perhaps even as a preparation for recruits about to be transferred to Outremer. The Templars also held chapter-meetings at night and their accusers made much of this, for it was a popular cliché that heretics held orgies under the cover of darkness. Nevertheless, too much should not be made of alleged night assemblies, for it was, after all, common practice for monks to observe the canonical hours, which necessarily involved

[5]Gunther of Pairis, *Historia Captae a Latinis Constantinopoleos*, in Migne, *Patrologia Latina*, Vol. 212, col. 233–234. See Francis R. Swietek, "Gunther of Pairis and the *Historia Constantinopolitana*," *Speculum*, LIII (January, 1978), 49–79, who shows the weaknesses of the *Historia* as a source for the Fourth Crusade, but accepts that the work was written partly to authenticate the relics, pp. 62–63. He also presents some contemporary arguments for and against Martin's action, pp. 70–71.

[6]Gunther of Pairis, *op. cit.*, col. 232. See the comments of Donald Queller, *The Fourth Crusade. The Conquest of Constantinople, 1201–4* (Leicester, 1978), pp. 54–55, 78, 81. This is not, however, to argue that Martin's life was blameless, for he was later accused of some violations of Cistercian practices, see Swietek, *op. cit.*, p. 14.

[7]See, for example, the witness of Imbert Blanke, Templar Preceptor in the Auvergne, during the proceedings in England. He agreed that the Templars had, as he now saw it, foolishly kept secrecy, but denied that anything occurred that "the whole world could not see," David Wilkins, *Concilia Magnae Britanniae et Hiberniae*, Vol. II (London, 1737), p. 338.

some worship in the chapels during the hours of darkness. Moreover, it does not follow that the Templars were secretive in all their activities or that they would neglect opportunities for raising money for the cause of the Holy Land. Papal privileges granted them extensive rights for such purposes. The bull *Milites Templi* of January, 1144, which was confirmed many times afterwards, refers to "the brothers of the Temple, who have been appointed for the purpose of receiving a contribution." So important was this function that when such brothers came to a city, castle, or village, even an interdict could be lifted once a year "for the honor of the Temple and reverence of their knighthood" and the divine offices celebrated.[8]

Just as they were for Abbot Martin, relics would be both objects of pride and power and a means of attracting devotion and thereby gifts to the order. The Christians in the Holy Land, including the Templars, followed the True Cross into battle with great devotion;[9] for an order of Christian warrior monks to conceal an equally powerful relic such as the Shroud suggests behavior which, at the very least, can be described as inconsistent. An interesting illustration of the importance of relics in Templar possession does not, however, support this charge. This is a passage in the deposition of Antonio Sicci di Vercelli, an Italian notary who had worked for the order for forty years, and who, in March, 1311, appeared before the papal commission inquiring into the guilt of the order. Inquisitorial investigations have to be judged in the light of accusations that were made and pressures employed to produce confessions, but it does not follow that observations about everyday life need be rejected. Antonio Sicci described the role of relics as follows:

> I saw many times a certain cross, which at first sight seemed to be of no monetary value, and was said to be from the tub or trough in which Christ bathed, which the said brothers kept in their treasury; and several times I saw that, when excessive heat or drought occurred, the people of Acre asked the brothers of the Temple that that cross should be carried in a procession of the clergy of Acre. Also I saw that whenever the patriarch of Jerusalem walked in processions of this kind with one of the knights of the order, the Templar carried the said cross with fitting devotion. When these processions were carried out in this way, by the co-operation of divine clemency, water came from the sky and moistened the land and tempered the heat of the air. Item, I saw

[8]Marquis d'Albon (ed.), *Cartulaire Général de l'Ordre du Temple, 1119?-1150* (Paris, 1913), *Bullaire*, no. VIII, p. 381.

[9]See Jonathan Riley-Smith, "Peace Never Established: The Case of the Kingdom of Jerusalem," *Transactions of the Royal Historical Society*, 28 (1978), 89–93.

many sick persons, both men and women, carried and brought to the church
of the house of the Temple at Acre, vexed by a malign spirit. When at length
this cross was brought before them, chaplains and clergy having given assent
on oath, they replied in the vernacular as well as in Latin, saying to some of
the chaplains and clergy sometimes: "How can you, who are such a son,
speak?" and sometimes: "You have committed such crimes and sins," and
seeing the cross by them, they shouted: "Lo the cross, lo the cross, we must
not stay here any longer, but must go away." And thus the malign spirit
spoke in them, so that at length these sick persons, lying as if completely
dead, were afflicted by foaming mouths and freed from the malign spirits.[10]

A relic powerful enough to bring rain during a drought and drive out evil
spirits from the sick was assuredly powerful enough to attract offerings
from a grateful populace. The activities described by Antonio Sicci were
normal procedure for the period; there needs to be positive proof as to
why the Templars should have acted abnormally in the case of the
Shroud.

The second point is based upon an inference drawn from a mistake and
backed by an assumption. Most of the Templars were caught by surprise
by the arrests, which occurred in the early hours of the morning of October 13, 1307. About two dozen escaped.[11] Mr. Wilson agrees that the arrests were a surprise, but nevertheless postulates Templar resistance so
that the Shroud could be smuggled away. However, contemporary French
chroniclers fail to mention any resistance. For Jean de Saint-Victor it was
"an extraordinary event, unheard of since ancient times," when all the
Templars throughout France were unexpectedly (ex improviso) captured
on the same day. Bernard Gui calls it "an astonishing thing" and says that
they were captured "very unexpectedly" (inopinate sane). Amalric Auger
describes how the royal officials, having opened their sealed orders, armed
themselves, and by night arrested all the Templars whom they could find,
at which "the whole world was astonished."[12] Moreover, although during

---

[10]Jules Michelet (ed.), Le Procès des Templiers, 1 ("Collection de documents inédits sur
l'histoire de France" [Paris, 1841]), pp. 646–647. Occasionally in this deposition the witness
seems to be referring to a house at Ancona, but the context suggests that this is a mistake by
the notary for Acre.
   [11]For a discussion of this issue see Malcolm Barber, The Trial of the Templars (Cambridge, 1978), pp. 46–47.
   [12]Chronique Latine de Guillaume de Nangis de 1113 à 1300 avec les Continuations de
cette chronique de 1300 à 1368, I, ed. Hercule Géraud (Société de l'Histoire de France
[Paris, 1843]), p. 360; Jean de Saint-Victor, in Etienne Baluze, Vitae Paparum Avenionensium, ed. Guillaume Mollat, I, p. 8; Bernard Gui, Flores Chronicorum, in Baluze, I, p. 63;
Amalric Auger, in Baluze, I, p. 95.

the trial several Templars referred to deaths and injuries caused by torture, they said nothing of any losses sustained actually during the arrests.[13] In fact the trial depositions and the inventories of Templar property suggest that many Templars were not in any physical condition to offer "fierce resistance," nor were they heavily armed.[14]

If, however, it is accepted that the Templars were keeping the Shroud itself at the Paris Temple, then a case for defense can be made, for the building was a fortress, strong enough to keep out the mob in 1306 when Parisians rioted against the king who was hiding there.[15] There is, nevertheless, no evidence for resistance here either. Jacques de Molay, the Grand Master, appears to have felt himself reasonably secure from arbitrary arrest, for he had persuaded the pope to begin an inquiry into allegations circulating about the order, which it was hoped would satisfy the king.[16] On the day before the arrests, October 12, Molay had been one of the pallbearers at a royal funeral, that of Catherine, wife of the king's brother.[17] At this distance of time it is easy to underestimate the enormity of the step which the king took in instituting the arrests. Before the event it would have taken considerable evidence to convince contemporaries that the king was prepared to go that far, especially with an unfinished papal inquiry in existence. If the Templars had held the Shroud and its copies, it seems most unlikely that they would have had time to smuggle it away at the moment of the arrests, while if they had foreknowledge of the impending action it seems strange that they took no other precau-

[13]See, for instance, the statements of Ponsard de Gizy and Jacques de Soci. Ponsard said that thirty-six brothers died through the effects of jail and torture in Paris, while many others died elsewhere, *Procès*, I, p. 36. Jacques said that twenty-five brothers had died on account of torture and suffering, *ibid.*, I, p. 69. However, neither of them refers to resistance and bloodshed at the time of the arrests, nor do the many other Templars who claimed that they had been tortured after the arrests.

[14]For the age-structure of the Templars in France in 1307 and the nature of their preceptories, see Barber, *op. cit.*, pp. 53–54. See also Léopold Delisle, *Etudes sur la condition de la classe agricole et l'état de l'agriculture en Normandie au moyen-âge* (Paris, 1903), pp. 721–728, who gives five examples of inventories taken on Templar estates in Normandy. These were predominantly "granges" which the Templars farmed to produce livestock, grain, and fruit, and not military establishments.

[15]Jacques Hillairet, *Evocation du Vieux Paris*, 1: *Moyen Age et Renaissance* (Paris, 1951), pp. 295–298, describes the Temple as a fortified enclosure, within which was a large keep, fifteen meters square. The Paris Temple was not quite so close to the Louvre as Mr. Wilson assumes, p. 212. For its location to the north of Philip II's walls, see the map in Hercule Géraud, *Paris sous Philippe-le-Bel* ("Collection de documents inédits" [Paris, 1837]).

[16]Baluze, *op. cit.*, III, ed. Mollat (Paris, 1921), p. 60.

[17]*Cont. Nangis*, I, p. 360.

tions. The only action taken was the flight of a few individual Templars who may have been warned by friends among local royal officials or actually escaped at the moment of the arrest owing to local incompetence. In contrast, the Templars in Aragon, who did have advance warning, since they had seen what had happened in France, fortified castles, changed goods into gold which could be more easily concealed and, it was suspected, chartered a ship in which to make their escape.[18]

It is, of course, possible that the Shroud was not kept at the Paris Temple or indeed even in France, for if it was so important to the Templars that they had kept it secret for perhaps a century and had used it as the center of their own secret cult, it would surely have been preserved at the order's headquarters, where such a powerful relic would have been most efficacious in the war against Islam. These headquarters were in Cyprus and had not been transferred to France as Mr. Wilson assumes,[19] for Molay, who had worked hard to revive enthusiasm for the crusade after the loss of Acre in 1291, had only come to France at the request of Clement V on a short-term mission to discuss crusading projects.[20] It seems improbable that he would have brought the Shroud with him. This would certainly explain its absence from the inventories of Templar goods, but would hardly support the thesis that the Shroud was transferred to the Charney family or indeed Mr. Wilson's argument that various Templars had seen the Shroud during chapters held in Paris.[21]

This leads to Mr. Wilson's assumption that Geoffroi de Charney, Preceptor of the Templars in Normandy, belonged to the same family as Geoffroi de Charney of Lirey, killed at the battle of Poitiers in 1356, and father of the Geoffroi de Charney who exhibited the Shroud in 1389.[22]

---

[18]Heinrich Finke, *Papsttum und Untergang des Templerordens*, II (Münster, 1907), pp. 52–53, 54–55, 60–63, 121–122.

[19]Wilson, *op. cit.*, p. 212. Among the Templars arrested in Cyprus on the pope's orders were the marshal, the preceptor, the turcopolier, the draper, and the treasurer. See Clement V's account of a letter received from Amalric, lord of Tyre, the governor of Cyprus, August 20, 1308, Baluze, *op. cit.*, III, p. 85.

[20]Clement, V, *Regestum Clementis Papae V...cura et studio Monachorum Ordinis S. Benedicti*, year I (Rome, 1885), no. 1033, cols. 190–191, for the request to the Grand Master of the Hospital, which must have been similar to that received by Molay, although the latter is not extant. For Molay's efforts on behalf of the crusade after 1291, see Barber, "James of Molay, the Last Grand Master of the Order of the Temple," *Studia Monastica*, 14 (1972), 94–96, 98–100.

[21]Wilson, *loc. cit.*

[22]Mr. Wilson believes that the Shroud had already been exhibited by Jeanne de Vergy, Geoffroi de Charney's widow, in c. 1357 (p. 226). This is possible, but is not directly relevant to the argument in this paragraph.

According to Mr. Wilson no genealogical evidence has so far been found for this connection, and so his argument is based on the coincidence of name. Geographical links are equally inconclusive, for he suggests that the Preceptor of Normandy originated from Anjou, "a province just to the other side of Paris from Champagne" (where Lirey is to be found). This is really little different from saying that Somerset is just to the other side of London from Essex and is a fragile connection indeed for the transmission of a relic the location of which is totally unknown during this period.[23]

Points one and two, therefore, are speculative; for the historian it is point three which must provide the foundation for the other arguments, for it relates to existing historical documents. Between October, 1307, and August, 1308, the Templars were charged with various heretical and obscene practices, among which was the worship of an idol in the form of a head.[24] Mr. Wilson is not inclined to believe most of the accusations, but does, however, accept the validity of the charge that the Templars worshiped a magic head in nighttime activities of a secret cult.[25] This cult he finds contained in the articles of accusation (August 12, 1308), and he groups together those which are relevant so that its elements can be discerned: that they venerated the idols in the form of heads as their God and Savior, that they said that the head could save them, that it had given the order its riches, that it made the trees flower and the land fruitful, and that they encircled or touched the idol with cords which they wore around themselves.[26] According to Mr. Wilson, "viewing of the

[23]Ibid., p. 216; Procès, II, pp. 295–296. According to his deposition, the Templar Geoffroi de Charney was received into the order "apud Stampas," which probably means Etampes (Seine-et-Oise, Ar. Rambouillet). This is nearer to Lirey (south of Troyes) than the province of Anjou and perhaps makes a family connection a little more likely. This is the identification given in Orbis Latinus, ed. Graesse, although there is also an Etampes-sur-Marne, near Château-Thierry (Aisne).

[24]Georges Lizerand (ed. and tr.), Le Dossier de l'Affaire des Templiers (Paris, 1923), pp. 16–24; Procès, I, pp. 89–96.

[25]Wilson, op. cit., pp. 211, 202. He believes that St. Bernard, who drew up the Rule of the Templars and sent them encouragement in the form of the tract "In Praise of the New Knighthood," unwittingly laid the basis for this cult in that he "may have intended the Templars as an elite, privileged to enjoy a fleeting foretaste of the 'newness of life' upon earth," p. 210. However, he must first prove that a later cult existed at all before St. Bernard's Rule becomes of any relevance and for this he is forced to use unreliable trial depositions.

[26]Ibid., pp. 201–202; Procès, I, p. 92, articles 46–61.

head was the privilege of only a special inner circle."[27] He believes that the "head" was none other than the Shroud, displayed in the "disembodied" form favored by the Byzantines, together with a number of special copies.

Mr. Wilson uses five depositions from the trial to illustrate the existence of a head: those of Rainier de Larchant, a serving brother from the diocese of Sens; Jean Taylafer de Gêne, a serving brother from the diocese of Langres; Raoul de Gizy, a serving brother who was preceptor of the houses of Lagny-le-Sec and Sommereux; Etienne de Troyes, a serving brother from the diocese of Meaux; and Robert of Oteringham, a Franciscan. In addition he quotes article 3 from the eleven articles of accusation against the Templars given in *Les Grandes Chroniques de France*, a vernacular narrative emanating from the Abbey of St. Denis. "Clues" to the identity of the head as the "divine likeness" are (1) that it was regarded as having "fertility properties," for articles 56 and 57 of the accusations of August 12, 1308, charge that they worshiped an idol which they said could make the trees flower and the land germinate, which Mr. Wilson associates with the portrayal of the Templars as guardians of the grail in Wolfram von Eschenbach's *Parzival*; (2) that "some accounts" speak of it being displayed just after the Feast of SS. Peter and Paul (June 29) which Mr. Wilson believes is significant because the next medieval feast was that "dedicated to the Holy Face, celebrated just two days later on 1 July"; and (3) that a remark attributed by Mr. Wilson to Deodatus, Abbot of Lagny, one of the papal inquisitors in the trial in England, should be noted, which was that Templar priests had nothing to do but repeat the psalm "God be merciful to us" (Psalm 67) at the end of a chapter-meeting, for it contains the line "and cause his face to shine upon us," which "is highly suggestive of the object of Templar adoration."[28] He backs this with evidence drawn from a painting in a Templar preceptory at Templecombe in Somerset and with an "idol" supposedly found by the Mameluk Sultan Baibars in the tower of the Temple at Jerusalem in 1277.

The four Templars whose depositions are quoted were not of the

---

[27]This idea derives from an allegation in Philip IV's order for the arrest of the Templars (September 14, 1307) that the Templars wore cords around their waists which had touched or encircled "an idol which is in the form of a man with a large beard" and that they kiss and adore this head in their provincial chapters, "but this not all the brothers know, except for the Grand Master and the older members," Lizerand, *op. cit.*, p. 28. However, accusations which derive from this document cannot be accepted as evidence for the activities of the Templars without convincing, independent corroboration.

[28]Wilson, *op. cit.*, pp. 205–206.

knightly class, nor were they among the leaders of the order. Only Raoul de Gizy held a post of any importance, for he was preceptor of two houses and had acted as a royal tax-collector. Etienne de Troyes claimed that he was no longer even a Templar; his deposition suggests that he was an apostate who appears to have harbored a grudge against Hugues de Pairaud, the Visitor and effective commander in the West. These seem inappropriate witnesses to use as evidence for the existence of a head which could only be viewed by a special inner circle. If these men had seen it or even knew of it, then the knowledge must have been widespread in the order, and it is therefore inconceivable that security could have been maintained throughout the whole order for more than a century, threats or no threats.

The circumstances in which the depositions were made do not encourage any greater confidence in their validity. Rainier de Larchant was only the second Templar to appear before the inquisitor, Guillaume de Paris, in the hearings which followed the arrests. The first had been a priest, Jean de Folliaco, who appeared on October 19. Folliaco seems to have been selected as the first witness because Philip the Fair's advisers had reason to believe that he would make an incriminating statement, for he claimed that he had previously tried to leave the order because it was "not pleasing to him" and that he had already spoken to the curia of the *prévôt* of Paris and to the Bishop of Paris before the arrests. It was imperative for Philip the Fair to obtain rapid confessions if the arrests were to be justified; he could not have intended to take any risks with the early witnesses. They must have been chosen because they could be relied upon to confess the order's guilt, either because of a grudge or because of bribes or intimidation. The position of Rainier de Larchant in the hearings of October/November, 1307, therefore, puts him in the same suspect category. His later conduct during the trial certainly suggests that he was susceptible to pressure, for although he joined the defenders of the order at the height of Templar resistance in February and March, 1310, he rapidly retreated from this position following the burning of a number of Templars from the province of Sens as relapsed heretics on May 12.[29] Raoul de Gizy was not even prepared to join the defenders, but made a series of confessions between November 9, 1307, and January 11, 1311, when he anxiously stated that he in no way wished to retract his previous confession made before the bishop of Paris.[30] Raoul de Gizy made very full confes-

[29]*Procès*, II, pp. 278–279; I, pp. 78, 115, 283.
[30]*Ibid.*, II, p. 364; I, pp. 36, 82, 394–402.

VI

sions, clinging to the hope that he might ingratiate himself with his accusers. Etienne de Troyes is a similar case to Jean de Folliaco. He claimed
that he had already confessed before the arrests to the king and his con-
fessor, and again to the bishops of Bayeux and Coutances.[31] Moreover,
together with Jean de Folliaco, he was among a group of seventy-two
Templars picked by Philip the Fair to appear before the pope during the
meeting between the pope and the king at Poitiers between May and July,
1308. The pope had suspended the hearings against the Templars earlier
in the year and the Poitiers meeting was the culmination of the pressure
being brought by the French crown for them to be reopened. The
seventy-two Templars were selected from the many hundreds in royal custody to appear between June 29 and July 2. These were the men whom
the king hoped would make the most sweeping confessions and thus provide Clement V with an ostensibly respectable reason for reopening the
proceedings. Jean Taylafer de Gêne appeared before the papal commission inquiring into the guilt of the order as a whole on April 14, 1310. He
can be placed within a group of Templars brought forward by the French
government, together with some hostile outside witnesses, with the intention of countering the effects of the Templar defense which was at its
height during April.[32]

   The fifth witness is Robert of Oteringham, a Franciscan, who claimed
to know something of the activities of the Templars in Yorkshire. His observations are of little relevance as proof of the existence of an idol or the
Shroud or its copy. He was simply one of sixty outside witnesses called
during the trial in England in an effort to offset the denials of guilt by the
Templars from the English preceptories. He had three main stories
against them. He had heard at Ribston a Templar chaplain loudly rebuke
some brothers saying, "The devil burn you," or similar words, and, hearing a tumult, he had seen, "as far as he could remember," a Templar fac-
ing west with his posterior turned toward the altar. Secondly, about twenty
years before at Wetherby he had heard that, one evening, a grand preceptor of the order intended to show to the brothers various relics which he
had brought from the East. The witness had later heard noise coming
from the chapel and, peering through the keyhole, had seen a great light
from a fire or candle. When, the next morning, he had asked a certain
brother whose feast they had been celebrating, the brother had turned
pale, "as if stupified" and, "fearing that he had seen something of their

[31]Finke, op. cit., II, p. 336.
[32]Procès, I, pp. 187–193.

acts," told him to be on his way and, "as you love me and your life," never to speak of it. Finally, the witness had seen, at Ribston again, a cross thrown upon the altar and he had told one of the brothers that it was improper that it should be lying in that way and should at least be stood up. The brother replied: "Put aside the cross and depart in peace."[33] Such tales are fairly typical of these outside witnesses, who had nothing of substance to contribute; it seems to stretch the evidence indeed to suggest that the second of these stories is evidence that the Templars were terrified that outsiders might discover that they possessed the Shroud.

The eleven articles reproduced in *Les Grandes Chroniques* are equally suspect, for the close association of St. Denis with the French kings suggests that their contents emanated from sources near to the French government and not from the members of the Temple. Material included in them should therefore be examined in the light of Capetian propaganda rather than viewed as a possible source for the Shroud.[34]

To sum up: all four Templar witnesses had, within the context of the trial, strong motivation to invent their stories, while the Franciscan does not actually mention an idol at all. The article extracted from *Les Grandes Chroniques* has no direct connection with the Templars. These documents make very insecure foundations upon which to base the existence of a mystery cult centered on the Shroud which had been kept secret for more than a century.

Evidence identifying the idol head with the Shroud is no more convincing. The accusation of belief in an idol which could make the trees flower and the land germinate comes from the articles drawn up against the order. The accusations against the Templars have strong links with past and contemporary beliefs about heretics which colored the outlook of the inquisitors. In this case, it is implied that the order had been tinged with Catharism, which postulated an evil creator responsible for all material things. For instance, the Franciscan, James Capelli, writing c. 1240, interpreted this Cathar belief to mean that "they believe the devil divided the elements and gave fertility to the earth so that it might bear fruit."[35] The

[33]Wilkins, *op. cit.*, II, p. 359.
[34]*Les Grandes Chroniques de France*, ed. Jules Viard (Société de l'histoire de France, Vol. 8 [Paris, 1934]), p. 274.
[35]James Capelli, *Summa contra haereticos*, in *Heresies of the High Middle Ages*, tr. Walter L. Wakefield and Austin P. Evans (New York and London, 1969), p. 305. This seems a more likely origin for this idea than Wolfram von Eschenbach's Templars guarding the Grail, which is unique to Wolfram.

VI

content of this accusation, therefore, perhaps tells the historian more about the inquisitorial mentality and Capetian propaganda than about the real practices of the Templars.

Little significance can be squeezed from the dating of the appearance of the head. Only three witnesses seem to be pointing to a date on or near the Feast of the Holy Face: Rainier de Larchant saw it at a chapter in Paris on the Tuesday after the Feast of the Apostles Peter and Paul; Etienne de Troyes saw it at the end of a three-day chapter in Paris which began on the Feast of Saints Peter and Paul; and Raoul de Gizy also saw it at Paris in the week after the Feast of the Apostles Peter and Paul. This may mean no more than that the Templars in France were accustomed to hold a major chapter-meeting at Paris in the middle of the year, and certainly cannot stand on its own as independent evidence of the existence of the Shroud among the Templars. Most witnesses are not so specific, although Guillaume de Giaco believed that it was between the Feast of Pentecost and the Nativity of John the Baptist (June 24) at Limassol, and four other Templars, who had seen a head at their receptions, gave particular dates for those receptions: the Feast of Circumcision (January 1),[36] the Feast of All Saints (November 1), on the Wednesday after Easter, and at Christmas. None of the other Templars who claimed to have seen the head identify any particular part of the year as the time when they saw it.

The remark that in Templar chapter-meetings the priest "stood like a beast, and intervened in nothing, except that he said the psalm 'God be merciful to us' at the end of the chapter" is not in fact by the Abbot of Lagny, but is taken from the deposition of a serving brother called Thomas de Thoroldeby during his confession on June 29, 1311.[37] He is claiming that in Templar chapters the master absolved them from "great sins" and therefore that the priest had no function to perform other than to close the chapter with the psalm. This is a reference to the charge that, in the order, laymen usurped the priestly function by granting absolution, an accusation which was particularly pressed in England because of the difficulties experienced by the inquisitors in gaining any more serious

[36]It is perhaps frivolous to draw attention to the connection of this date with heathen and idolatrous practices against which Christian writers often inveighed.

[37]Wilson, op. cit., p. 206. The deposition is in Wilkins, op. cit., II, p. 386. Mr. Wilson brings in H. C. Lea to support his hypothesis, claiming that Lea said that it was strange to find such a chant among men alleged to be idolaters. So it is, but it does not indicate that the object of their adoration was the Shroud either. Incidentally, the comment seems to have come from Charles G. Addison, The History of the Knights Templars (London, 1842), p. 265, and not Lea.

confessions. In this context it seems unlikely that the inclusion of Psalm 67 in chapters has any special significance which connects it with a Templar cult.

If as Mr. Wilson says, the majority of the charges were trumped up, why can the descriptions of idols or heads be accepted? Mr. Wilson would answer: there really was a Shroud in the possession of the Templars which would then distinguish their worship of a "head" from the other charges. But the evidence for this is based upon descriptions of idols by trial witnesses such as those above and upon the articles of accusation, so that the argument is circular.

It is necessary, therefore, to examine the descriptions of the Templar idols more closely. According to Mr. Wilson, "while there is a wide variation in the accounts of the 'head,' " the consistent picture is that it was "about the natural size of a man's head, with a fierce-looking face and beard."[38] It should be remembered too that the cult of the Shroud was supposed to be confined to an inner elite of the order. It must, however, be considered doubtful that the picture is consistent even in the descriptions selected by Mr. Wilson. Rainier de Larchant said that it was a head with a beard "which they adored, kissed, and called their savior." Raoul de Gizy was struck by its terrible appearance, in that it "seemed to him that it was the figure of a certain demon, called in French *un maufé*, and that whenever he saw it such a great fear overcame him that he could scarcely look at it except with the greatest fear and trembling." They adored it since they had taken an oath denying Jesus Christ. On another occasion he thought that he saw the head brought in in a bag, but could not recall if it was as large as that of a man's, made of metal or wood, or that of a dead man. Etienne de Troyes claimed that it was brought into chapter with great ceremony, preceded by two brothers and carried by a priest, who placed it upon the altar upon a silk tapestry. It was bearded and seemed to be of flesh, although from the nape of the neck to the shoulders it was encrusted with precious stones. He thought that it was the head of Hugues de Payns, the first grand master of the order. Jean Taylafer thought that it was an effigy of a human face, colored red, but he did not know in whose veneration it was made. In *Les Grandes Chroniques* the idol had the skin of an old man, embalmed and polished with paste (*de cole polie*), with a beard and hollowed eyes in which carbuncles

---

[38]Wilson, *op. cit.*, pp. 202–203. The reference for this quotation is from Jean Taylafer de Gêne, *Procès*, I, p. 190, but, although he says that it was about the size of a human head, he does not describe it as fierce-looking or bearded.

glowed "like the light of the sky." These descriptions do have some common features, but do not entirely accord. Where they are consistent they suggest not a piece of cloth with an effigy upon it, but a three-dimensional object shaped like an actual head.

Descriptions given by other Templars offer further variations. At the Parisian hearings of October and November, 1307, apart from the bearded version, it was referred to as "that head which they adored," as being made of wood, silver, and gold leaf with a beard or an imitation of a beard, as being painted on a beam, and as having four legs, two at the front and two at the back.[39] Hearings at Carcassonne in November, 1307, produced an "idol of brass in the shape of a man" dressed in what appeared to be a dalmatic, two figures called Bahomet, one of which was gilded and bearded, a black and white figure, and a wooden idol.[40] At Poitiers in June and July, 1308, it was "very foul and black, having the form of a human head," "a white head with a beard," and an idol with three faces,[41] while before the papal commission between November, 1309, and June, 1311, it was "a certain painted board hanging in the chapel" on which was "an image of a man," a head resembling a Templar with a cap and a long, grey beard, a copper object, and "a small picture of base gold or gold, which seemed to be a picture of a woman."[42] These descriptions suggest that some of the Templars, through fear or a desire to please questioners whom they believed wanted them to describe such a thing, supplied an imaginary head, some of them basing it upon various objects with which they were familiar such as reliquaries or panel paintings. Guillaume d'Arreblay, Preceptor of Soissy, who appeared before the papal commission on February 5, 1311, identified the silver-gilt head seen on the altar at chapter-meetings as one of the eleven thousand virgins of Cologne, and only changed his description to a two-faced, bearded countenance under pressure, even then admitting that it was shown to the people, along with other relics, on feast days;[43] Bartholomew Bochier, who testified on April 19, 1311, betrays his source when he actually describes the "idol" as being next to the reliquaries on the altar;[44] Pierre Maurin told the papal commission on May 19, 1311, that, while at

[39]Procès, II, pp. 290, 299, 300, 313, 315, 363, 364, 367.
[40]Finke, op. cit., II, pp. 322–324.
[41]Konrad Schottmüller, Der Untergang des Templer-Ordens, Vol. II (Berlin, 1887), pp. 28–29, 30, 50, 59, 68, 70.
[42]Procès, I, pp. 257, 597; II, 192–193, 203, 212, 240, 249.
[43]Ibid., I, p. 502.
[44]Ibid., II, pp. 192–193.

Château Pèlerin in Outremer, he had heard of a head kept in the treasury of the Temple, adding however that his informant, Brother Pierre de Vienne, had said that the head was either that of St. Peter or St. Blaise.[45]

Finally, if the four hearings surveyed are taken as a whole, it will be seen that twenty-eight different Templars claimed to have seen idols.[46] One, Hugues de Pairaud, was Visitor of the Templar houses in the West, second only to Molay, but none of the others can be seen as members of an inner circle. Three can be identified as knights and sixteen as serving brothers. While seven of these Templars were preceptors, one was a treasurer at Paris, and another an almoner of the king, such positions did not automatically mean high status, for such responsibilities often devolved upon serving brothers as well as upon knights. In nine cases the head was shown to recruits at their receptions. If the idol was indeed the Shroud or a copy of it, the Templars with knowledge of it or access to it seem an odd collection; they certainly do not suggest an exclusive, privileged elite.

Mr. Wilson brings forward two further pieces of evidence which could help to break the circular nature of his arguments. The first of these is that in 1951 a painting of a male bearded head was discovered in a building at Templecombe in Somerset, which he believes belonged to the Templars. He further believes that this was a copy of Christ's head as seen on the Shroud, a belief strengthened by the absence of the traditional halo. He expands the argument to suggest that copies were made of the original Shroud for use in Templar preceptories and that others existed which had not been recognized as such, there being four such copies in England, apart from Templecombe. The variations in the descriptions of the head could presumably be explained by this means, while the cords described in the articles of accusation as having encircled or touched the idols before being given to Templars to wear around themselves, could actually be a means of contact with the original.[47] This explanation, however, raises more questions than it answers and does not appear to be consistent with Mr. Wilson's argument that the cult was kept secret. How could this secrecy be maintained if copies had been made, even for places as peripheral to the mainstream of Templar affairs as Templecombe? Who made the copies? Does this imply a special cadre of Templar crafts-

---

[45]*Ibid.*, II, p. 240.

[46]This excludes the depositions of Antonio Sicci, Hugues de Faure, and Guillaume April, which refer to a popular myth about the destructive power of a magic head, which has no direct connection with Templar receptions or chapters.

[47]However, the accusation concerning the cords may be an attempt to associate the Templars with the Cathars or the Moslems or both; see Barber, *Trial*, p. 188.

men sworn to secrecy? Why were some copies in the form of a three-dimensional head, while others were painted, if so much care was taken to reproduce the original? Even if it is argued that the Templecombe head has similarities to the Shroud, which itself, Mr. Wilson claims, influenced the way that Christ was portrayed in Byzantium and the medieval West,[48] does this say anything more than that the Templecombe artist had also seen the traditional medieval representations of Christ? Indeed, unless it can be shown that the Templar idol was the Shroud, there is no reason to assume that the painting was intended to represent Christ in the first place. It was, after all, not unknown for medieval artists to copy portrayals of Christ both in appearance and pose, while representing other figures, such as saints. In the case of saints they simply omitted the cross within the halo.

The second prop to the argument which is independent of the trial evidence is the discovery by Baibars of an "idol" in the former "castle" of the Templars at Jerusalem in 1277. For Mr. Wilson this too could have been a copy of the Mandylion.[49] This seems to be a mistake, for the reference given indicates that the Sultan found the object at the castle of Safed in 1267.[50] Even so, the castle at Safed had belonged to the Templars and it might, therefore, be possible that the object concerned was of Templar origin. It is, however, difficult to take the argument much farther, for in Islamic terms almost any implement of Christian worship might be considered as an idol by adherents of a faith that forbids representational art of any kind.[51]

The fourth and last point concerning the reticence of the Charney family about the origins of the Shroud is based on speculation. There is no definite evidence to link the Geoffroi de Charney who was killed at Poitiers in 1356 with his namesake who was burnt as a relapsed heretic in 1314. But even if some connection were found it cannot be used as proof that Geoffroi was "a man struggling to regain some lost family honor"[52]

[48]Wilson, op. cit., p. 208.

[49]Ibid., pp. 207, 362, n.21.

[50]Reinhold Röhricht, "Etudes sur les derniers temps du Royaume de Jérusalem. Les Combats du Sultan Baibars contre les Chrétiens en Syrie (1261–1277)," Archives de l'Orient latin, Vol. II (Paris, 1884), pp. 388–389. See Charles F. Defrémery, Mémoires d'Histoire Orientale, seconde partie (Paris, 1862), pp. 363–364, where a French translation of the relevant passage from Noweiri is given.

[51]See, for instance, 'Imad ad-Din's description of those Christians trying to defend the True Cross at the battle of Hattin as idolaters, 'Imad ad-Din, in Francesco Gabrieli (ed. and tr.), Arab Historians of the Crusades, tr. E. J. Costello (London, 1969), p. 136.

[52]Wilson, op. cit., p. 216.

and, taking this one huge step further, that this lost family honor was none other than kinship with a condemned leader of the dissolved order. The connection is in no way strengthened by Mr. Wilson's argument that the association of Geoffroi de Charney of Lirey with the foundation of the secular knighthood known as the Order of the Star, may have been "an attempt to revive the Templars under a different name." Mr. Wilson places Geoffroi among "the founder knights" of the order, which is credible, but this is not the same as identifying him as its co-founder with "his similarly religiously minded king, John the Good," as he does in the next sentence.[53] The history of the Order of the Star has been reviewed by Professor Renouard, in whose opinion such secular knighthoods were founded in reaction against the failures of the religious orders, rather than being connected to them.[54] In 1344, John the Good, at this time Duke of Normandy, and Eudes IV, Duke of Burgundy, put forward the idea of a communion or congregation of 200 knights under the patronage of the Virgin and St. George. This was confirmed by Pope Clement VI. Because of the French defeats during the 1340's, the plan was not implemented until 1351, by which time John had become king. Eudes of Burgundy had died the previous year. It was intended that the new order should consist of 500 knights, now with the patronage of the Virgin alone, since St. George had already been appropriated by Edward III's recently founded Order of the Garter. In fact the Order of the Star never reached anything like its planned recruitment, while the existing membership was virtually wiped out at Poitiers in 1356, a blow from which the order never recovered. It is difficult to see that the idea for this order came from Geoffroi de Charney or that it had any relationship to the Templars. Indeed, as a secular knighthood of the mid-fourteenth century it had much stronger roots in the Arthurian romances then fashionable than in the religious orders of the era of the Templars. Moreover, rivalry first with Edward III's Order of the Round Table and then with his successful Order of the Garter seems to have been a stronger impetus than nostalgic longing for a revived Temple. Clearly, the Order of the Star did have a devotional or religious character, for Clement VI seems to have welcomed it and encouraged the foundation of a collegiate church, served by canons and priests, as its centerpiece. Nevertheless, there were political and dynastic ends in mind too, particularly in the 1351 manifestation, for John II was attempting to group an elite knighthood around his person, both stress-

[53] *Ibid.*, pp. 222-223.
[54] On the reasons for the foundation of the Order of the Star, see Yves Renouard, "L'Ordre de la Jarretière et l'Ordre de l'Etoile," *Le Moyen Age*, LV (1949), 281-300.

ing his position as rightful king in the face of his competitors, especially Edward III, and creating a small and loyal army at the same time. The Order of the Star should be related to contemporary knightly values and political realities rather than connected with the defunct Templars.

Mr. Wilson's argument contains a further implication: that the fall of the Templars was still a live issue in the second half of the fourteenth century. But following the ravages of the Black Death and the French disasters of the Hundred Years' War, would the dissolution of an order, most of whose members were dead, still have been capable of raising passions? Papal interest in the matter seems to have petered out by the late 1320's, and it cannot be imagined that when the Shroud was exhibited in 1389 the Templars and their fate were a major consideration to the Avignonese pope, Clement VII. Mr. Wilson argues that Clement was a party to the true facts of the Shroud's origin, but did not wish to reveal his knowledge,[55] for if the issue of the Templars had been revived "the entire shaky foundations of the Avignon papacy" would be threatened.[56] This is a misunderstanding of the issues raised by the Schism. The scandal of the Schism endured because there was no easy solution, either politically or legally. The secular powers aligned themselves behind the two popes, thus consolidating the political divisions of western Christendom, while existing canon law hindered the application of conciliar ideas which were put forward during this period.[57] The position of Clement VII was not affected by the fact that an earlier Avignon pope had played a prominent part in the suppression of the Templars.[58]

However, even if it is accepted that the fate of the Templars retained a latent power to arouse deep passions as late as 1389, a number of unanswered questions remain. If the two Geoffroi de Charneys, father and son, really were related to the man who was burned in 1314, and the issue was still regarded as important in their time, then it would have been very difficult to suppress this association. Indeed, the fact of that association would have been generally known in the first place and, if it had mattered, would already have had some influence on the social standing of the Charney family. Perhaps, therefore, a better reason for hiding the origin and authenticity of the cloth was that the king of France might have claimed it for himself, arguing that the family had no legal or moral

---

[55]Wilson, op. cit., p. 231.

[56]Ibid., p. 235.

[57]See, for instance, the comments of Walter Ullmann, Origins of the Great Schism (London, 1967), especially Chapters I and X.

[58]Wilson, op. cit., p. 235.

right to it. Equally, the pope, who, Mr. Wilson argues, believed in its authenticity, might have claimed it, for the Templars had been an order directly responsible to the Holy See. If, on the other hand, the pope did not know of its connection with the Templars, then what was he told when he asked about its history and why was he supposedly convinced that it was genuine, especially in the face of the pertinent and cogent attacks of Pierre d'Arcis, the contemporary bishop of Troyes, who believed so strongly that it was a fraud?[59] Finally, how did those who apparently knew that the Templars had the Shroud in the thirteenth century keep silent, for this involved a large number of people, including those Templars who survived the trial, the later members of the Charney family, Pope Clement VII and his confidants, and any descendants or relatives that any of these might have told?

This paper is not concerned with the debate about the authenticity of the Shroud, but only with a link forged in the chain of its history by Mr. Wilson. This link seems brittle since ultimately it depends upon the depositions of the trial of the Templars which, while a fascinating historical source, need to be handled with considerable care if they are not to be misinterpreted. Without the idols described in the trial, the other pieces of evidence gathered by Mr. Wilson have no central core, but remain a series of fragments with no coherence of their own, leaving the episode of the missing years still to be satisfactorily explained.

[59]*Ibid.*, pp. 236–237.

# The world picture of Philip the Fair

*During the arrest and early months of the trial of the Templars in 1307 and 1308, a number of documents emanated from Philip IV's chancery which are not only valuable evidence of the regime's administrative concerns during the trial, but also, in the language used, convey a sense of contemporary concepts of the medieval world order as seen either by the king himself or by his chief advisers. Royal motivation for the arrests is still a matter of controversy, but it does not seem inconsistent to believe that Philip both sought the Templars' wealth to alleviate immediate financial problems and came to convince himself that the Templars had transgressed the laws upon which the whole ordering of society was based. It is upon this second aspect of Philip's mental outlook that this discussion concentrates. This paper aims to examine these concepts and to relate them to other contemporary polemical views on the trial.*

In Shakespeare's version of the reign of Richard II, the author puts a key speech in the mouth of the ageing duke of York. With the death of John of Gaunt the king can see no barrier to his seizure of the rights and revenues of John of Gaunt's heir, Hereford, who has already been banished abroad. But the duke of York tries to persuade Richard of the folly of this act, for its implications are much wider than the inexperienced and short-sighted king recognizes.

Take Hereford's rights away, and take from Time
His charters and his customary rights;
Let not to-morrow then ensue to-day;
Be not thyself. For how art thou a King
But by fair sequence and succession?
Now afore God, God forbid I say true,
If you do wrongfully seize Hereford's rights,
Call in the letters-patents that he hath
By his attorneys-general to sue
His livery, and deny his offered homage,
You pluck a thousand dangers on your head,
You lose a thousand well-disposed hearts,
And prick my tender patience to those thoughts
Which honour and allegiance cannot think.

In this speech, Shakespeare admirably sums up the situation of another medieval monarch, Philip IV of France, when faced with the problems with which the arrest and trial of the Templars was fraught. But whereas Shakespeare portrays Richard II as being too immature to grasp the implications of York's warning, there is no doubt that such an admonition was repeatedly drummed into every Capetian ruler from childhood onwards. It was for this reason that Philip IV, in his essentially arbitrary seizure of the lands and persons of the Templars in October 1307, took every care to present the action in the trappings of legality and to convey to the world that the alleged heresies and depravities of the Templars were blows intended to destroy the proper ordering of

Reprinted from the *Journal of Medieval History* 8 (1982) 13–27, with kind permission from Elsevier Science B.V., Amsterdam, The Netherlands.

society based on faith and reason. The following paper is intended to illustrate the world view of Philip IV and his advisers as reflected in seven important documents in the trial of the Templars.[1]

The relevant documents fall within the early phase of the trial, between the decision to arrest the Templars, which had been taken by 14 September 1307, and the meeting between Philip IV and Clement V at Poitiers between May and July 1308, which resulted in the re-opening of the trial after its suspension by the pope in February 1308. During this period, the king sought to convince both the pope and the wider world of the righteousness of his action in instigating, through the inquisitor, Guillaume de Paris, the Templars' trial. In this attempt, the king reveals in considerable detail his conception of his role and of the world in which he was called upon to play that role. The documents which will be used to illustrate these points are the order for the arrests (14 September 1307), the seven questions put to the Masters of Theology at the University of Paris (early 1308), a convocation of representatives of the towns to a meeting of the Estates at Tours (25 March 1308), and two speeches made by the royal minister, Guillaume de Plaisians, before the pope at Poitiers (29 May and 14 June 1308) (Lizerand 1964:16–24, 56–62, 102–6, 110–36). In addition, these will be set in the context of two contemporary tracts in which opposite points of view on royal rights over the case of the Templars are adopted: the *Tractatus de facto Templariorum* written by Augustinus Triumphus of Ancona (ed. Scholz 1903:508–16), and an anonymous *Supplication*, allegedly emanating from the French people and addressed to the king.[2]

The king saw, or claimed that he saw, in the crimes of which the Templars were accused, a dire threat to the fundamental unity of God's creation and, in his description of the character of this threat, he portrayed the nature of that creation. The cement of the structure was provided by the Catholic faith. This is expressed most clearly in the convocation of the Estates:

You know that it is the Catholic faith by which we remain that which we are in Christ; by which we live, by which in this way we, exiled and liable to death, are ennobled in the Lord Jesus Christ, in order that we may be with Christ the true sons of the living God, our eternal father, and also heirs to the Kingdom of Heaven. This most beautiful hope comforts us; this then is our whole substance. If someone therefore strives to break this chain, he tries to kill us Catholics; Christ is the way to us, the life and the truth. Who then can deny him, by whom and in whom we subsist, who is not acting to destroy us?

This chain linked the created world with God. In the first speech of Guillaume de Plaisians, he describes how Christ "rules all living [things] under the sun, even the angels and the good and evil spirits, even all the elements, and is commanded by no one". This parallels the frequent portrayal in Gothic sculpture of Christ as the creator through whom the thought of the Father was translated into the visible world order (Mâle 1972:29). In Plaisians' second speech, the iniquity of any threat to this 'chain of being' is forcefully emphasized: "who can deny or pervert the Catholic faith, who does not by this means touch all the life and all the substance of each of us?"

Within this created world there is a constitutive hierarchy, from human beings, blessed with the power of reason, down to the irrational beings which make up the lower links of the chain. This is stressed by the Masters of Theology in their reply to Philip's questions on 25 March 1308, in which they acknowledge that the king is "inflamed with zeal for the faith, [but is] nevertheless wishing indeed to defend the faith with the proper rule of reason" (Lizerand 1964:62). The elucidation of the faith by reason was, of course, a governing principle of the scholastic world and there is no doubt that the Masters were correct to perceive Philip's acceptance of this framework. In the refined scholasticism of the thirteenth century, this determined the presentation of the argument as well as the philosophy behind it. Plaisians' first oration is a clear demonstration of what Professor Panofsky has called *manifestatio* and which he has shown applied equally to High Gothic architecture in Capetian France (Panofsky 1957:27–60). In the speech, Plaisians adopts the scholastic scheme of division and subdivision, in his words, "to announce and elucidate the substance and form of the said victory" over the heresy of the Templars. The aim is the logical presentation of the argument within a homologous arrangement and so this victory is divided into stages: at the beginning it was horrible and terrible, for which four reasons are given, in its progress pleasing and marvellous, for which there are eight reasons, and at the end clear, well-known and undoubted, for which there are a further eight reasons. Finally, even without these preceding points, he contends that there are seven reasons which make the matter indisputable. The speech is the verbal and written equivalent of the High Gothic portal and reflects the belief in a logically ordered universe under God which characterized the period.

The heresy of the Templars is heinous because, according to the order for the arrests, "it is a thing almost inhuman, indeed set apart from all humanity". It shatters the gift of reason granted to the highest of God's corporeal creatures.

Indeed, the spirit of reason, having been stretched beyond the limits of nature, suffers and, in suffering, is disturbed by that which, having forgotten its origins, not knowing its own condition, ignorant of its worth, squandering itself and given to reprobate feeling, has not understood why it has been held in honour.

The Templars have deliberately upset the symmetry of the Gothic world order. Because they have abandoned the struggle to achieve humanity's created potential, they have shown their scorn for rationality and, worse than this, have acted in a way which even beings lower in the chain of creation, and not blessed with reason, would have refused. The Templars had contravened 'natural law' by breaking laws which made it possible for man to live in a mature way, that is in an orderly community. John of Salisbury expressed this concept in the *Policraticus*: "they [that is, the different occupations of the commonwealth] should not transgress the limits of the law, and should in all things observe constant reference to the public utility". (Dickinson 1963:bk.6, c.20). In the emotive language of the order for the arrests the action of the Templars is:

to be compared with foolish beasts, indeed transcending the stupidity of the beasts themselves by its stupendous bestiality, it exposes itself to all those kinds of evil that abhor and flee the sensibility of the irrational beasts themselves. It has forsaken God its maker, it has retreated from God its saviour, it has forgotten God its creator, it has made an offering to demons and not to God, . . .

Thus, the indecent kissing of which the Templars were accused is described in the order for the arrests as "in shame of human dignity" and in the convocation for the Estates as "in contempt of God's creation". For the same reason their alleged sodomy is stigmatized in the convocation for the Estates as "against nature, that which brute animals refuse", which merits just punishment, as it says in the order for the arrests, "on account of which the wrath of God falls upon the sons of infidelity".[3] The lower orders of creation demonstrate to erring man the virtues which he should maintain, but the Templars have ignored this lesson.

Proof of the evil of their actions is found in the fact that the Templars held chapters at night. In Plaisians' first speech, this is held to be one of the reasons why they are suspect, for it is "the custom of heretics, and [he] who acts evilly hates the light". This was not only intended to feed suspicions that heretics conducted secret and obscene rites under the cover of darkness, but also to convey a basic religious and philosophical tenet of the period: that God is Light and it is from God that each order of the created universe receives light, which in turn is reflected back to the Creator. This concept of the role of light in the universe was an integral part of the Gothic world (Panofsky 1946:18–24, 46–8); those who shunned it, shunned the faith which bound Christians together. Gothic architecture and sculpture is the three-dimensional expression of the ideas put forward in the trial documents, demonstrating in stone the orderliness upon which thirteenth-century men believed their world to be founded. Crimes like those of the Templars undermined the architecture of the universe, and therefore attacked God, the supreme architect, who, as was shown in Genesis, had given form to the earth and created the heavens, the earth, the sun, the

moon and the elements. Through light he gave beauty to this creation.

The acts of the Templars in disrupting the universal order must, therefore, demand vengeance since, in the words of the order for the arrests, "not only by their acts and detestable works, but also by unlooked-for words, they defile the land with their filth, remove the benefits of the dew and infect the purity of the air, and spread confusion in our faith". As such they are "enemies of God, faith and nature, and the opponents of human society". Indeed, according to Plaisians in his first speech: "On account of the inhumanity of the crimes, . . . divine and human nature were overturned". In the convocation of the Estates, the same theme recurs: "Heaven and earth are moved by the arrogance of such great wickedness and the elements are disturbed". Reaction is, therefore, inevitable: "Against a pestilence so evil [everything] ought to rise up, laws and arms, beasts and all four elements". John of Salisbury again provides a convenient reference point (Dickinson 1963: bk. 6, c.25):

an injury to the head, . . . is brought home to all the members, and that a wound unjustly inflicted on any member tends to the injury of the head. Furthermore whatsoever is attempted foully and with malice against the head, or corporate community of members, is a crime of the greatest gravity and nearest to sacrilege; for as the latter is an attempt against God, so the former is an attack upon the prince, who is admitted to be as it were the likeness of deity upon earth.

The phrases used in Philip the Fair's documents were not mere rhetoric therefore, for medieval men inherited from the ancient world a conception of the ordering of the universe which the crimes alleged against the Templars clearly violated. In the Platonic view, a Supreme Being who was perfection completed that perfection by its production of other beings, so that every conceivable being was realized. In the Neo-Platonic interpretation, these beings formed a hierarchy of unbroken links down to the very least of creation. According to Macrobius in the fifth century (Stahl 1952: 145):

... Mind emanates from the Supreme God and Soul from Mind, and Mind, indeed, forms and suffuses all below with life, and since this is the one splendour lighting up everything and visible in all, like a countenance reflected in many mirrors arranged in a row, and since all follow in continuous succession, degenerating step by step in their downward course, the close observer will find that from the Supreme God even to the bottommost dregs of the universe there is one tie, binding at every link and never broken.

While the conception of the fecundity of God was Platonic, it was Aristotle who provided a graded scale rising from plants eventually to man, with each level containing both the elements of those that were below it as well as a distinctive element of its own. Man was distinguished by his faculty of reason (Lovejoy 1942:35–97). The Templars were accused of crimes which forsook the gift of reason and, therefore, they can be seen as having abandoned their proper place in the universal order. *Inhumanitas* therefore involved actions contrary to the nature of man and his position in the divine ordering and could not be more serious, for the Templars had ignored God's scheme of the universe and thus denied the perfection of his creation.

In his depiction of creation in terms of what later came to be described as 'the chain of being' (Tillyard 1943:37–102), the king's perspective was one that was common to both the ecclesiastical and secular powers of the medieval world. However, the respec-

tive rights of the powers within this world were the subject of much greater doubt, and these rights form a second major theme of the trial documents of this period. Throughout most of the thirteenth century, despite challenge, the papal-hierocratic view of society as unified under papal headship but containing within it a duality of powers spiritual and temporal, maintained itself as the predominant vision of how Christendom was constructed. But, towards the end of the century, in particular in response to the reappearance of Aristotelian political ideas in the west, there emerged proponents of an idea of Christendom as a body which slowly divided itself and reproduced as many smaller bodies, the form of which could no longer be determined by immutable moral laws since these smaller bodies were themselves regarded as natural formations. Emergent lay power of the late thirteenth century was, therefore, able to draw upon supporting theories more in keeping with what had become the actual distribution of power than with the ideas of papal supremacy. This does not mean, of course, that Aristotelian ideas at once shattered the papal-hierocratic view of society in which each had a functional role; Aristotelian ideas are very appropriately described by M. Wilks as "seeping" into the political thought of the period and as having a "corrosive" effect upon the traditional Christian concept of society as a single universal political entity (1964:87, 431). In the trial documents, this "corrosion" can be clearly seen, yet at the same time new ideas are brought forward within the old framework of the organic society, for, as Professor Leff has pointed out, all the writers who followed Aristotle "in accepting society as natural to man" were not necessarily of the same school (Leff 1967:66). The value of Aristotelian ideas to the French monarchy perhaps lies in their confirmation of the view which already existed in the twelfth and thirteenth centuries, that the state was a natural organism and that kingship approved by God, as the sacrosanct nature of the office showed, was positively meritorious (Post 1964:498–561). Nevertheless, the very existence of the debate suggests that in neither theoretical nor practical terms was the papal view completely overthrown, and indeed, the king's need to force the pope to take action on the issue of the Templars was itself an acceptance of papal competence in this field.

The traditional view of the competence of secular and ecclesiastical powers within their own fields can be seen in Question 1 to the Masters of Theology. The function of the Church is to preach the faith and instruct the people, and if doubt arises about the faith or a heresy then "the recognition and decision appertains to the Church". If someone acts contrary to the faith, then the Church should proceed "towards the spiritual end of penitence and reconciliation". Relapsed and contumacious persons however the Church hands over to the secular arm. "It may not judge or condemn them temporally", says Philip. "About this however no one doubts." This view was quite acceptable within the papal-hierocratic structure of society. The same attitude is expressed in both of Plaisians' speeches. In the first, the king is described as coming to Poitiers with his Estates

not intending to assume the part of accuser, denunciator, instructor or promoter in the form of a trial against them, but as zealots of the Catholic faith, defenders of the Church, the wall of Jerusalem, and

the purgers of heretical depravity, to announce and elucidate to you [that is, the pope] the substance and form of the said victory.

The second speech repeats that the king comes "not as accuser, denunciator or special mover, but as minister of God, fighter for the Catholic faith, zealot of the divine law, for the purpose of defending the Church, according to the traditions of the holy fathers . . .".

The speeches emphasize the existence of the community of the faithful of which the pope is the head. In the first speech, the king comes to Poitiers to show the victory

to you most holy father, who is the universal bishop of the city [namely Rome] and the world, spiritual vicar on earth of the most high bishop Jesus Christ, and to your brothers, who are the columns of the holy Church of God, and through you and through them to all Christians.

This, too, shows adherence to the hierocratic view, although Plaisians is careful to balance it with the phrase "my lord king of France, temporal vicar of the said Jesus Christ in his kingdom . . .". Plaisians goes on to say that the Order of the Temple had been exposed and that nothing else remains to be done except for "its expulsion by you, pious father". The pope can do this without difficulty because in this he is "loosed from all restraints", which implies, although does not say so explicitly, that papal plenitude of power, upon which the thirteenth-century popes had increasingly depended, could overcome any legal obstacles to expulsion. Equally, the second speech is full of conventional images of the house of God and of the one body of the faithful, which are consistent with the traditional medieval world order: the pope is "father of the family of the house of God", a house into which the Devil has furtively entered and committed robbery, a house built upon the stones of the faithful and founded upon the cornerstone of Christ. This symbolism of the building is rooted in traditional, biblical images (Frankl 1960:211–12). Similarly, in the comparison with the body, Christ is the head of the body of the faithful in which the right hand is the ecclesiastical power, the left hand is temporal justice, and the feet are the people. In essence, this is little different from the organic view of society delineated most strikingly by John of Salisbury and, in a less detailed fashion, in a letter, written in the 1120s, aimed at stiffening Templar morale in the face of doubts among the early members about God's approval of their profession, which compared the interdependence of the various elements within society with the functioning of the body. "If all the members of the body performed only one function, the body itself could not entirely subsist." They should beware of the wiles of the Devil which were aimed at creating discontent with one's functional role and thus ultimately at destroying Christian society (Leclercq 1957:81–91).[4] At the end of the speech, Plaisians changes the image from robbery to fire, the fire which has gained strength in proportion to the time which it had lain hidden without being extinguished, and finally he combines the two, claiming that if the pope does not act, "the walls of neighbours will be broken down, the houses burned. . .".

Nevertheless, within this conventional structure the possibility that temporal authority within the state might be able to act independently against heretics such as the Templars is canvassed. After covering the common ground concerning the role of the Church, the first question to the Masters

of Theology continues by asking what happens when "the secular prince or people exercising jurisdiction hear the name of God blasphemed and the Catholic faith being blown away by heretics or schismatics or other infidels". Should the king exercise his powers of justice against heretics if the matter is public, or institute an enquiry if the matter is not public knowledge? Is the intervention of a secular prince restricted in any way if by his action the generation of a scandal can be prevented? Question 2 concentrates upon the specific issue of the Templars: should the king eradicate this obvious disease "in consequence of his office"? Here, the king is referring to his obligation to uphold the law as enshrined in his coronation oath, yet if the crimes were true then, in the words of Plaisians' first speech, "divine and human nature were overturned". The king's office necessarily involved the protection of divine and human law; indeed, it was upon this that the stability of his own position rested. The Templars were, therefore, attacking the legal structure which protected all the subjective rights that go to make up the objective rule of law (Kern 1939:163). Even so, the king again showed himself reluctant to make a clean break with past convention, for he suggests that perhaps he could act against the Templars because they might be seen "as a college of knights and not principally of clerks". This last idea was not at all acceptable to the Masters as they made clear in their reply, so Plaisians' second and more menacing speech picks up the theme of independent action again, irrespective of such distinctions. "By very many it has been suggested to him [that is the king] that he may extirpate the perfidy of the Templars on his own authority", but the king is "a respectful son" and, therefore, has requested certain remedies in the affair from the pope. One important source of such suggestions was an anonymous *Supplication* supposedly from "the people of France", which argued that the case fell within the scope of royal jurisdiction, although, as will be seen, even here the authority of the Church over 'true' heresy is still accepted and the argument is couched in biblical rather than Aristotelian terms.

The presentation of the case for the exercise of independent secular power in the affair of the Templars is, therefore, heavily qualified; nevertheless, the documents do suggest a view of sovereignty that is rooted in the natural formation of the state in which all are participants. Thus, in the first question to the Masters of Theology, the alternative of either "the secular prince" or "the people exercising jurisdiction" is suggested. More forcefully, the king demands the attendance of the towns at the Estates by insisting that in this "holy work we wish you to be participants, you who are participants and most faithful zealots of the Christian faith". Once again, however, the idea emerges most strikingly from the Plaisians' speeches. In the first speech, the king has come to Poitiers "full and whole, that is with all his members, prelates, chapters and the clergy and the Church, barons and knights, communities and faithful of the people of the kingdom", a statement in which the clergy appear simply as one element in the Christian community of the kingdom for which, as will be seen, Philip IV regarded himself as having overall care. It is the presence of the various parts of the community which makes the king "full and whole". This interdependent community re-

appears in the second speech (1 Cor. 12:26):

for we are one body in Christ, we are members who suffer the one for the other 'for how can one of the members of the body suffer if the others do not suffer', as the Apostle appropriately told us elsewhere.

In these statements, the king's ideas encompass more than merely the conventional image of the body of Christ, of the faithful under the pope, for the second speech develops the theme in a significant way which demonstrates again how the new ideas were 'seeping' into contemporary consciousness. Here, not only is the existence of the community of the state asserted, but it is given powers of action. If the spiritual and secular arms are deficient, should not the people act against heresy, since all their souls are threatened, asks Plaisians. "For what is committed against God, brings injury to all, as it is written." This contrasts with the essentially acquiescent role of the parts of the communal body envisaged by John of Salisbury. More than this, as John of Paris argued in his *Tractatus de potestate regia et papali*, a pope who was an incorrigible criminal who refused to heed warning could be forced to resign by a secular ruler acting with the people, although equally the pope could take similar action against a secular ruler which would lead the people to depose him.[5] "You give to another your glory in the service of God, which to you was shameful", says Plaisians to Clement V in the second speech. This is backed later in the speech by historical analogy and by quotation from Revelation: "the Lord said, "I wish that you were warm or cold; but since you are neither warm nor cold but tepid, I began to vomit you from my mouth". Here, Plaisians again returns to conventional biblical illustration to aid his arguments. Finally, the participatory theme provides the climax of the speech, but it owes more to feudal ideas of consent than Aristotelian theory. Here, Plaisians, consciously making a parallel with the familiar tag, drawn from Roman and canon law and frequently applied to consultative assemblies in the middle ages, *quod omnes tangit, ab omnibus approbetur* (Marongiu 1968:33–7), declared that "all whom the affair touches, all are called to the defence of the faith" (*quos omnes tangit negocium, omnes ad fidei deffensionem vocantur*). The use of *tangere* or *contingere* was a notable feature of convocations to assemblies involving business of a difficult or arduous nature in both France and England in the thirteenth century, and was applied quite flexibly in senses that were not necessarily consistent with Roman usage (Post 1964: 163–228). Here Plaisians exploits this flexibility to apply his own version of the tag to an affair of "heretical depravity", portrayed as a threat to the body politic.

The striking feature of the justificatory discourses contained in the royal documents is the variety of allusion which is encompassed: Aristotelian ideas on the formation of the state mingle with a concept of constitutive unity reminiscent of St Bernard, with conventional recourse to biblical authority, and with Roman, ecclesiastical and feudal jargon used for consultative institutions.

This same ambiguity can be seen in the king's justification of the role of monarchy and its duties in protecting subjects from the dire results of heretical depravity. For writers like John of Paris, the formulation of the idea of the state naturally assumed some form of government. For him, as Aquinas before him, monarchy seemed the best form for achieving the harmony and

peace which was the goal of the social organisation of the state (Leclercq 1942: 177). Philip IV leaves little doubt concerning his agreement with this, but once again the traditional and the new intermingle in the ideas expressed in the trial documents. No king who could boast ten ancestors in the direct male line would overlook the value of tradition in strengthening his position. In the convocation to the Estates he stresses that:

Our predecessors were always concerned to drive out heresies and other errors from the Church of God, and especially from the kingdom of France, before other princes of their time, defending the most precious stone of the Catholic faith, as an incomparable treasure from robbers and brigands.

In this he is "giving heed to the rock from which we are cut, inheriting the characteristics of our predecessors. . .". This is emphasized in rhetorical and dramatic fashion by Plaisians in the opening words of the first speech: *Christus vincit, Christus regnat, Christus imperat!*, imagery which had been used by the Carolingians, deriving it from both Roman and biblical sources (Wallace-Hadrill 1975:181–9), and, more recently, as a formula employed by Louis IX on his coinage (Kantorowicz 1958:4). It can, therefore, be seen as a conscious attempt to link Philip IV not only with his prestigious grandfather, but also with the imperial greatness of the preceding Carolingian dynasty.

Professor Strayer has traced these careful attempts by the later Capetians to create a cult of French kings: the acceptance of the kings as sacred rulers, their anointing by a special oil brought from heaven, the miraculous curing of scrofula, their leadership of the crusade in Christendom (1971:300–14).

VII

Indeed, it could be justly claimed that Philip's three immediate predecessors had died on or returning from a crusade of some kind, and that his five immediate predecessors had all been on crusade. The Masters of Theology, despite their fundamental disagreement with the king over jurisdictional rights in heresy cases, nevertheless show their awareness of this tradition in designating him "the principal fighter and defender" of the faith (Lizerand 1964:68).[6] Plaisians did not fail to emphasize this; in the first speech the king is "so great and so Catholic a prince, minister of Christ in this affair" and in the second speech "the most Catholic king". This king rules over the kingdom of France, described in the first speech as "chosen and blessed by the Lord before the other kingdoms of the world".

The importance of the king's role is shown by the responsibilities which it carries, as in the order for the arrests:

we, who are established upon the watch-tower of regal eminence for the defence of the liberty of the faith of the Church, and strive before all the desires of our mind for the augmentation of the Catholic faith.

The origins of this were deep-rooted. The German coronation-order of the tenth century required the archbishop to question the prince, "Wilt thou uphold the holy faith transmitted to thee by Catholic men, and follow after righteous works?", and the prince to answer, "I will" (Kern 1939:76). Plaisians follows this up logically in his first speech when he presents the king as having no alternative but to act against the Templars because he is held to do this "most importantly because he swore (an oath) in his coronation", and, in his second speech, by saying that the king comes to Poitiers "for

the purpose of defending the Church, according to the traditions of the holy fathers, by which he is held to render account to God". In the Capetian coronation-order of the thirteenth century, after the king swore to observe "the laws of the bishops and the churches", he promised to act in accordance with an injunction of the Lateran Council "concerning the extirpation of heretics from his kingdom".[7] Interestingly, Plaisians' implication that, in certain circumstances this might force the king to act against heresy, is included in the same sentence, already described above, as the disclaimer that the king had come as accuser or promoter in the case. The king cannot, in fact, effectively defend the Church when heresy is rampant, yet the pope is reluctant to act in such an obvious matter as the Templar depravity. The logical conclusion is that the king cannot fulfil his coronation oath and his duty as "minister of Christ", unless he controls the Roman Church, or at least takes jurisdiction over heresy. Philip's organic community is not, therefore, the whole of Christendom, but rather the regnum of France, presided over by the Capetians, the most Christian kings.

This step is, however, implied rather than fulfilled for, as has been seen, the king expended huge effort coercing Clement into reopening the trial of the Templars on papal authority. Even if this was only a sham, it seems that Philip still felt that it was a necessary sham, that he needed to relate his legal standing to the traditional order, despite the fact that he was prepared to use arguments deriving from the newer political ideas of his time as elements in the coercion. In short, the tension in the relationship between secular and ecclesiastical power, which had

22

been evident since the Gregorian era, was still present, for the power of the papacy had not yet been broken, although the balance of the argument had now begun to swing inexorably in favour of the secular monarch, whose view of the world began to change appropriately.

For a number of substantial reasons, therefore, the king was reluctant unequivocally to override the papacy's well-established jurisdiction over heretics, but outside the immediate area of debate between Philip IV and Clement V the battle-lines can be seen to be much more sharply drawn, thus providing a backcloth for Philip's world view. Plaisians' reference to those who had suggested that the king could eliminate heretics on his own authority seems particularly to relate to an anonymous tract, which must have been in circulation before the meeting at Poitiers, in which "the people of the kingdom of France" address a *Supplication* to their king. This has been ascribed to the Norman lawyer, Pierre Dubois (Lizerand 1964:97 n.1), but even if Dubois was the author, a connection with royal sources should not be discounted, since he may have been employed to put into circulation views which the king considered too extreme to be overtly connected with his government. The content of this document seems to suggest that it was produced in response to the arguments in the pro-papal tract by the theologian Augustinus Triumphus, *Tractatus de facto Templariorum.*

Augustinus first sets out the arguments which had been adduced in support of the view that, without any request from the Church, secular princes could judge heretics, make enquiry concerning heresy, and condemn for the crime of heresy those convicted

by their judgement. He draws his examples from the Old Testament. In Exodus 22 it is written that evil-doers shall not be suffered to live, meaning idolators and those who "sin against nature". Since it is also written that brother killed brother and neighbour killed neighbour for the sin of idolatry, therefore "it is even more strongly permitted to kings and princes". Equally, in Deuteronomy 7, the people of Israel are called upon to overturn the altars of the heretics, "since you are the holy people of God"; therefore, kings and princes are even more bound to act on this. The same applies to the burning of the bodies of heretics already dead, for in 4 Kings 23, King Josiah did precisely this, having had the bones of the heretics brought down from their burial place in the mountains. At the same time he broke their statues and ornaments. Asa, king of Judah, in 3 Kings 15, "purged all the filth of idols which his fathers had made" and burned them. Indeed, each king and prince is held to 'purify' his kingdom in this way, as a religious duty. Moreover, an offence committed against God is greater than one committed against one's neighbour, but kings and princes can punish the latter on their own judgement. It therefore follows that "they can much more strongly punish an offence which man commits against God".

In Augustinus' view, however, there was a fundamental objection to these arguments, which was that kings and princes cannot punish on their own judgement those who were not of their jurisdiction, except after they had been relinquished to them by the Church. But heretics did not fall within their jurisdiction for in Corinthians 12(11) it is written that there shall be heresies within the

Church, and it is for the Church to judge them, having taken into account all the circumstances. Augustinus, therefore, intended to show that neither the Templars, "who were persons immediately subject to the Church", nor any other heretics, could be captured and judged by any secular authority without the request of the Church. To this end he set out "to prove the truth" by authorities taken from both the Old and New Testaments and by reasons.

From the Old Testament he takes the cases which are considered to show the right of kings to act independently in heresy cases, and tries to show that these authorities do not justify such a use. In Exodus 32, Moses ordered the killing of the sons of Israel who had worshipped the golden calf, in his capacity as high priest, and it followed that no secular prince could condemn anyone for heresy without the precept of the pope. Equally, the injunction in Exodus 22 that evil-doers should not be suffered to live was "at the precept and mandate of Moses". The destruction of the idols of the heretics in Deuteronomy 7 was at the command of Moses, while the burning of the bodies of the heretics by Josiah was on the authority of the Lord, "whose place on earth the high pontiff bears". Finally, he seeks to prove that even a just war cannot be fought without permission of the Lord, as is shown in 2 Kings 5 by David, in consulting the Lord before doing battle with the Philistines. If a just war was not licit without ecclesiastical permission, then how much more true was this in relation to jurisdiction over heretics.

However, even if it was to be granted that these authorities conceded the king's jurisdiction over heretics, they could not be con-sidered as definitive, since they were judicial precepts concerned with specific matters in the past, which could be overruled by new law made since then. Such law is contained in the New Testament, or at least in the Book of Canticles which is concerned with Christ and his Church, and "thus the testimonies taken from it can appertain to the New Testament". The authority of the Church in heresy cases is specifically stated in the second Canticle where Christ invites the Church to capture heretics, saying, "seize for yourselves the little foxes who destroyed the vines, for your vineyard is flowering". The role of the pastors of the Church is, therefore, not only to set a good example and to preach, but also to correct those who err, which means capturing "the little foxes", that is heretics and schismatics. It was Paul the Apostle who, after the first and second corrections, finally ordered the heretic to be shunned, in a letter to Titus, which was done on the authority of the Church since Titus was a bishop. In the same way, in Corinthians 5, Paul ordered, on his authority, the enemies of Christ "to be surrendered to Satan". A major reason why secular princes should not be allowed to judge heretics is that they might proceed 'incautiously' in such a judgement, and eradicate the wheat with the tares, a mistake which the Lord warned against in Matthew 13. Finally, authority over heretics was conceded by the Lord to the Apostles, "whose persons the prelates of the Church represent", as is shown in Mark, where the Lord tells the Apostles to go into the world and preach the gospel, baptizing those who believe and condemning those who will not.

Augustinus lastly sets out to support his case by reasons, of which he has four. Firstly, no one is allowed to interfere with matters the Church reserves for itself, and heresy is such a case. Secondly, the secular prince is to be compared to the Church as is the body to the spirit, and "everything spiritual has direct power over that of the body". Since heresy is opposed to the faith, it is a spiritual matter and reserved to the Church. The only way that a secular prince can act in this is as the instrument of the Church. Thirdly, it follows that the Church has to decide who is the proper authority over heresy, as no-one can consider the faith without the mandate of the Church. Finally, it is licit for secular rulers to capture heretics only when they are not able to consult the Church quickly and conveniently, while at the same time seeing manifest danger to their kingdom, but then only with the purpose of restoring them to the power of the Church. In the case of the Templars, Augustinus makes comparison with the doctor, cited in the second Metaphysics, who first gave medical aid to a sick person and then looked at a book to see if he had done well. However, afterwards, when he returned, the sick person was dead. He does not seek to excuse the Templars, "since if the things which are imputed to them are true, the Church ought truly to extirpate and condemn that order as an iniquitous sect", but he simply wants to stress that it is not licit for a secular prince to intervene in matters of heresy without "the mandate and request of the Church".

Augustinus' arguments represent the traditionally held view of jurisdiction over heresy, a view which the Masters of Theology had confirmed in their reply to the king's questions on this issue on 25 March 1308 (Lizerand 1964:64). It would, therefore, take some ingenuity to counter them. The

*Supplication* of the people of France attempted to do precisely this, but with limited success. Among other reasons, the difficulty of establishing this case within the context of the mores of the period must have been a powerful disincentive to Philip to allow Plaisians to make claims too extravagant at Poitiers. The author of the *Supplication* begins by trying to make a distinction between heresies which differed from the Catholic faith "only in one or several articles", rather like the Greeks, and cases like the Templars. In the former case, the laws clearly oppose the king's intention, but he does not concede that the Templars are in the same category, arguing that they ought not to be called heretics, "but on the contrary [ought] to be placed entirely beyond the power of the Church".

Once again he turned to the episode of Moses and the golden calf to illustrate the action which should be taken. Moses had ordered that neighbour should kill neighbour, causing the deaths of 22,000 people because of the apostasy. Significantly, he had not consulted Aaron, his brother, even though he was God's high priest. It seemed, therefore, that there was no barrier to the king in such a case; indeed, the author went further, even claiming that "the most Christian prince" could proceed against the entire clergy if they were sustaining error. Do not the Apostles and the canons of the holy fathers shout out that the Templars' crime demands the same punishment, he asks rhetorically. Does not "ease of pardon give back an incentive for transgressing?" It might be said that Moses was himself a priest when he ordered the killing – and indeed this is what Augustinus Triumphus argued – "for it is written 'Moses and Aaron

in their priesthood'". But this is only acceptable in the sense that Moses was a legislator
and the giving of law is regarded as a sacred
act. In no other way could he be seen as a
priest; indeed, if he had been he could
neither have had a high priest above him,
nor could he have ordered the killing of so
many people. The Lord had prevented
David from building a Temple to him for
this reason. In short, Moses was not a priest,
yet had been able to act against the crimes of
idolatry and apostasy without clerical permission. One should not, therefore, believe
"those perverting the Scriptures" – a remark
presumably directed at Augustinus Triumphus – and justice should not be delayed
because of them.

There is here no attempt to justify the
king's action in terms of his priestly qualities,
for considerable pains are taken to show that
Moses was not a priest, nor to argue that the
king had general jurisdiction over heresy,
nor even to pick up John of Paris' argument
that there was nothing to show that Christ
had commissioned the Apostles to exercise
jurisdiction (Leclercq 1942:197). Instead,
the author concentrates upon the specific
case of the Templars, for which he is forced
to invent a special category which places
their crimes beyond the pale of all Christian
society. It is clear which party felt itself to
be the more innovatory and, consequently,
in the medieval context, on the weaker
ground. The tract, which was not overtly
connected with the government, was useful
propaganda for the king, but he had no
intention of committing himself directly and
without reservation to such a view.

The polemics of the Templars' trial
demonstrate in microcosm the fundamental
problems faced by the secular powers of the

early fourteenth century in their struggle to
perceive the proper order of the world
around them. Despite his greatly increased
practical power compared with that of his
predecessors, Philip IV did not succeed in
convincing the world that he had a right to
ignore traditional and established procedures or to defy conventional power relationships. A central reason for this failure lay
in the nature of the royal power itself; the
king had too great a stake in the established
order to attack it with the conviction needed
to overthrow it.

## Notes

1 I am particularly grateful to Miss Patricia
McNulty for her comments on this paper.
2 Lizerand 1964:96–100. It has been argued that
Pierre Dubois was the author of the *Supplication*, but
the case is not entirely convincing (Wailly 1855: 491–
2).
3 The influence of Justinian's *Novellae* is evident
here, for Philip's lawyers are using phrases similar to
those in *Nov.* 77 and 141 (ed. Schoell 1928:382, 704). I
am grateful to Professor James Brundage of the University of Wisconsin-Milwaukee for drawing my attention to this point.
4 There are some doubts concerning the authorship, which may be attributable to Hugh of St Victor
or perhaps to Hugh of Payens, the first Grand Master
of the Order.
5 Ed. Leclercq 1942:214. See also the *Remonstrance
du peuple de France* (Lizerand 1964:84–94), a vernacular
tract circulated a little earlier in 1308 than the *Supplication*, in which papal corruption is attacked in such a
way as to suggest Clement's moral weakness and
administrative incompetence.
6 This was the tradition of Charlemagne. See a
letter of Charlemagne to Pope Leo III in 796 (Wallach
1959:18–19).
7 Schreuer 1911:176. The Fourth Lateran Council,
to which this refers, assumed that a secular power
would act at the behest of the Church (canon 3), but
it did not make provision for the dilemma in which
Philip claimed to find himself.

## Literature

Dickinson, J. (tr.) 1963. John of Salisbury, The states-man's book of John of Salisbury. Being the fourth, fifth and sixth books and selections from the seventh and eighth books, of the Policraticus. New York.

Frankl, P. 1960. The Gothic. Literary sources and interpretations during eight centuries. Princeton, N.J.

Kantorowicz, E. H. 1958. Laudes regiae: a study in liturgical acclamations and medieval ruler worship. Berkeley, California.

Kern, F. 1939. Kingship and law in the middle ages. Translated by S. B. Chrimes. Oxford.

Leclercq, J. 1942. Jean de Paris, Tractatus de potestate regia et papali. In: Jean de Paris et l'ecclésiologie du XIIIe siècle. Paris.

Leclercq, J. (ed.) 1957. Un document sur les débuts des Templiers. Revue d'histoire ecclésiastique 52: 81–91.

Leff, G. 1967. The apostolic ideal in later medieval ecclesiology. Journal of theological studies 18:58–82.

Lizerand, G. (ed.) 1964. Le dossier de l'affaire des Templiers. Paris.

Lovejoy, A. O. 1942. The great chain of being. A study of the history of an idea. Cambridge, Mass.

Mâle, E. 1972. The Gothic image. Religious art in France of the thirteenth century. Translated by D. Nussey. London.

Marongiu, A. 1968. Medieval parliaments. Translated by S. J. Woolf. London.

Panofsky, E. (tr.) 1946. Abbot Suger on the abbey church of St. Denis and its art treasures. Princeton, N.J.

Panofsky, E. 1957. Gothic architecture and scholasticism. New York.

Post, G. 1964. Studies in medieval legal thought, public law and the state, 1100–1322. Princeton, N.J.

Schoell, R. (ed.) 1928. Iustiniani Novellae Corpus iuris civilis, 3. Berlin.

Scholz, R. (ed.) 1903. Augustinus Triumphus of Ancona, Tractatus de facto Templariorum. Die Publizistik zur Zeit Philipps des Schönen und Bonifaz' VIII. Stuttgart.

Schreuer, H. 1911. Die rechtlichen Grundedanken der französischen Königskronung. Weimar.

Stahl, W. H. (tr.) 1952. Macrobius, Commentary on the dream of Scipio. New York.

Strayer, J. R. 1971. France: the holy land, the chosen people and the most Christian king. In: Medieval statecraft and the perspectives of history. Essays by Joseph R. Strayer, Edited by J. F. Benton and T. H. Bisson: 300–14. Princeton, N.J.

Tillyard, E. M. W. 1943. The Elizabethan world picture. London.

Wailly, N. de. 1855. Mémoire sur un opuscule anonyme intitulé Summaria brevis et compendiosa doctrina felicis expeditionis et abbreviationis guerrarum ac litium regni Francorum. Mémoires de l'Académie des Inscriptions et Belles-lettres, 18.

Wallace-Hadrill, J. M. 1975. The Via regia of the Carolingian age. In: Early medieval history: 181–200. Oxford.

Wallach, L. 1959. Alcuin and Charlemagne: studies in Carolingian history and literature. New York.

Wilks, M. 1964. The problem of sovereignty in the later middle ages. Cambridge.

# THE SOCIAL CONTEXT OF THE TEMPLARS

REPLYING, on 13 January 1308, to letters of Philip IV of France describing the arrest of the Templars, Albert of Habsburg, King of the Germans, after expressing the customary sadness at the turn of events and extolling his own role as the leading prince in defence of the faith, remarked that 'although a crime of such evil infamy ought to be reprehensible and damnable in all persons, nevertheless it is known to be more reprehensible among the religious, who ought by the splendour of their life to be mirror for others and an example'.[1] Throughout the 193 years of its history the Order had indeed been in a position where it was 'a mirror for others and an example', a position which made it a particularly sensitive indicator and, in its turn, promoter, of social change.[2] This paper is an attempt to trace this interrelationship.

The Romanesque world of the late eleventh and early twelfth centuries portrayed the virtues and the vices locked in a struggle for possession of men's souls, with the vices striving to overcome the virtues either in battle or by temptation. After a fierce struggle the two most prevalent vices of mankind, Luxuria and Avaritia, are overcome, and Sapientia is enthroned above a world of peace and concord, which is the end to which temporal concerns must be directed.[3] This world—the world in which the crusades were born—was one in which these conflicts were continuous, both on the metaphysical plane and in the literal sense, challenging in particular the first generation of settlers in the crusader states after 1099 with a directness not met elsewhere in Christendom. The two knights who, in 1119, founded what was to become the Order of the Temple, Hugues de Payns and Godefroi de S. Omer, manifested a direct response to this challenge when, according to William of Tyre, they vowed before the Patriarch of Jerusalem to follow quasi-monastic

---

[1] *Litterae ad regem Franciae de causa Templariorum*, ed. J. Schwalm, *Monumenta Germaniae Historica, Constitutiones*, IV (Hanover, 1906), no. 229, 196.

[2] See how M. Bloch, *Feudal Society*, trans. L.A. Manyon (1962), 320, uses the different editions of the Rule to encapsulate changes in noble class-consciousness between c. 1130 and c. 1250.

[3] See A. Katzenellenbogen, *Allegories of the Virtues and Vices in Medieval Art* (New York, 1964), 1-3.

lives of poverty, chastity, and obedience, a dedication seen as a preliminary to a self-imposed charitable task, that of protecting the pilgrims who came regularly from the west to visit the Holy Places. Here the abstract and the literal merge. Life was a pilgrimage in which faith and hope were means by which charity—that is true love of God—could be achieved and the future existence be assured, while at the same time the crusading movement had itself arisen directly from actual pilgrimages made to the Holy Places. Charity is the goal of the pilgrimage and these first Templars set out to protect those seeking this goal.[4]

Their dedication was the product of an impulse which had overtaken many others of their generation. Fired by the enthusiasm for cleansing the Church and Christian society which the papal reformers of the eleventh century had set in train, by the spread of the peace movements in feudal society, and by the success of the First Crusade, many men, either in groups or individually, had undertaken to lead purer lives, sometimes with a specific charitable task in mind, sometimes simply in an attempt to escape the material accretions and corruptions of life on earth. From these sources had emerged durable orders, like the Carthusians and the Cistercians, but at the same time too there had been many more obscure and short-lived ventures, as well as agitation through popular heresy, which derived from the same sources. The first Templars were typical of their generation; pious laymen seeking an outlet for their religious impulses. However, the nature of their action was directly inspired by one particular aspect of the reformist impetus of the eleventh century, that of the idea of the *miles Christi*, an idea which, as Professor Duby has shown, was forged particularly to canalise the warlike impulses of a noble class no longer subject to any effective royal or judicial restraint.[5] The peace and truce of God movements and their more positive partner, the crusade, were the practical expressions of this idea. They aimed firstly, to reduce the damage and suffering caused by the noble class within Christian society, and secondly, to employ this bellicosity against the infidel, and indeed against papal enemies in general. This reflects acceptance of the simple fact that the noble instinct for warfare could not be abolished; indeed, the point has been made that the very emergence of the word *miles* as a description used by all members of this class in France shows that its self-image was indissolubly bound to military

[4] See also J. Riley-Smith, 'Crusading as an Act of Love', *History*, lxv (1980), 177-92.

[5] G. Duby, *The Three Orders. Feudal Society Imagined*, trans. A. Goldhammer (Chicago, 1980), 152-66. See also C. Morris, '*Equestris Ordo:* Chivalry as a Vocation in the Twelfth Century', *Studies in Church History*, ed. D. Baker, 15 (1978), 87-96.

VIII

activity.⁶ It is significant that this too was the appellation of the Templars in their Latin Rule which is headed *Incipit prologus Regule pauperum commilitorum Christi Templique Salomonici* and goes on to appeal in clause two 'o Christi miles'.⁷

The development of the concept of the *miles Christi* was accompanied by strenuous attempts to find a justificatory ideology for Christian warfare and thus overcome the moral dilemmas inherent in the idea. The work of theologians and later, canonists, in developing this ideology, has been very ably analysed by Professor Frederick Russell, who shows that, basing themselves on Augustine, they argued that war was necessary as a remedy for sin, for the just warrior had a duty to prevent evil-doers from inflicting harm upon society. Put in terms of the allegories of the virtues and vices, it meant that the world of peace and concord presided over by Sapientia would only be achieved when the perpetrators of vice had been overcome. It was of central importance, however, that the motives of the warrior were unimpeachable and that he acted only upon the command of legitimate authority, which, by the era of Gregory VII, was coming to be seen to reside in the papacy.⁸ Dr Ian Robinson has shown how Gregory VII put theory into practice by using military force to support the proprietary rights of the papacy, thus converting the early medieval idea of the 'soldier of Christ' as a monastic figure waging war against the devil by prayer and the mass, into a soldier who fought in the literal sense with material weapons.⁹

That these ideas had become part of the intellectual accoutrement of the educated cleric associated with the crusade in the early twelfth century can be shown by two quotations (from several which could have been chosen) from Fulcher of Chartres, chaplain to Baldwin, the first king of Jerusalem. Baldwin's army, travelling from Edessa to claim the kingship in 1100, was held up by Moslems defending a pass just to the north of Beirut. After several times being near defeat the Christians eventually fought their way through, a victory which, in Fulcher's view, was evidently a miracle of God.

Truly for us, and with us, and in us was fulfilled what He said through the prophet to the Israelites, 'If you shall have obeyed my laws I shall enrich you with this gift, that five of you shall succeed against one hundred of the enemy, and one hundred of

⁶ G. Duby, 'Lineage, nobility and knighthood', *The Chivalrous Society*, trans. C. Postan (1977), 80.
⁷ *La Règle du Temple*, ed. H. de Curzon (Société de l'histoire de France) (Paris, 1886), 11-12.
⁸ F.H. Russell, *The Just War in the Middle Ages* (Cambridge, 1975), chap. 1.
⁹ I.S. Robinson, 'Gregory VII and the Soldiers of Christ', *History*, lviii (1973), 169-92.

30

you against ten thousand' (Levit. 26:8). And because we endured much suffering day and night in His service, and trusted no one else, He wondrously broke the pride of enemy. And because we served the Lord with devout hearts in tribulation He hath regard for our humility.

The following year, in September, King Baldwin harangued his troops before a battle with the Egyptians near Ramla. Fulcher puts the following words in his mouth:

"Come then, soldiers of Christ, be of good cheer and fear nothing! Conduct yourselves manfully and you shall be mighty in battle. Fight, I beseech you, for the salvation of your souls; exalt everywhere the name of Christ whom these degenerate ones always vigorously revile and reproach, believing in neither his Nativity nor Resurrection. If you be slain here, you will surely be among the blessed. Already the gate of the Kingdom of Heaven is open to you. If you survive as victors you will shine in glory among all Christians".

He then adds, almost bathetically bringing the whole speech down to the level of the mundane, ' "If, however, you wish to flee remember that France is indeed a long distance away" '.[10] Purity of motive in pursuit of the just destruction of the opponents of the true faith in obedience to the law is the way to win God's approval for the militant Christian. Christian humility drove out pagan pride.

The Templar Rule expresses with precision this concept of the *miles Christi*. The Prologue begins: 'Our sermon is especially directed to all who scorn to follow their own will and who desire to fight in high and true purity of soul for the king, in that they might choose to assume and fulfil the noble armour of obedience, fulfilling and preserving (it) with the most eager care.' The special nature of their calling is emphasised by a contrast with those who do not fight with the security of this purity of motive. 'Therefore we exhort you who until now were a secular knighthood, in which Christ was not the cause, but esteemed by human favour alone, to hurry to be involved in perpetuity in the company of those whom God has chosen from the mass of perdition and arranges for the defence of the holy church of God in spontaneous piety.' In clause two the Rule might almost be invoking the peace movements of the eleventh century: 'For the order of knighthood already flowers again and revives in itself, which lacking in zeal for justice, sought not to defend the poor and the

[10] Fulcher of Chartres, *A History of the Expedition to Jerusalem, 1095-1127*, trans. F.R. Ryan, ed. H.S. Fink (Knoxville, 1970), 141, 157-8. Latin text in *Recueil des Historiens des Croisades, Historiens Occidentaux*, III, lib. II, cap. iii. 376; cap. xi. 392.

churches, which was its (function), but to thieve, despoil, kill.' The sense that membership confers an exclusive status in the eyes of God is heightened by clause nine in which the Templars are enjoined to hear matins and the whole of the divine service, leaving them in a proper spiritual condition for the holy war: '... since, despising the light of the present life, being contemptuous of the torment which is of your bodies, you have promised in perpetuity to hold cheap worldly matters for the love of God: restored by the divine flesh, and consecrated, enlightened and confirmed in the Lord's precepts, after the consummation of the divine mystery no one should be afraid to fight, but prepared for the crown.' The symbolism of the granting of the white habit only to professed knights of the Order gave visual confirmation of this internal state. Clause fifty-seven provides an appropriate summary: 'Divine providence, as we believe, has undertaken through you the beginning of this new type of order in the holy places, that you might mix knighthood with religion and thus religion should proceed armed through knighthood (and) should strike the enemy without sin.' So closely does this reflect contemporary preoccupations that it appears that there were, even at this early date, inferior imitators 'in parts beyond the mountains' which the Rule calls 'certain pseudo-brothers'.[11]

The emergence of this Order should therefore be seen as an important expression of the ideology of knighthood which the Church had been vigorously promoting since the era of Leo IX. Even so, the infant did not grow to maturity unaided, for the premises upon which the Order was based needed justification. The Rule itself describes the Temple as 'a new type of order', while a letter of encouragement and comfort apparently intended for some of the original members and therefore probably dating from the late 1120s is testimony of both Templar doubts and contemporary criticism.[12] This letter is important in that its very existence warns against accepting too readily a thesis of inevitable Templar success, while, nevertheless its actual contents reinforce the links between the appearance of such an order and contemporary clerical and knightly values. The letter falls back on a functional scheme, various versions of which had become familiar during the eleventh century.[13] It reminds the Templars of the continuing battle for their souls in

[11] *Règle*, paras. 1, 2, 9(1), 17(20), 57(51), 68(21).
[12] J. Leclercq, 'Un document sur les débuts des Templiers', *Revue d'histoire ecclésiastique*, lii (1957), 81-91. Leclercq argues that this letter was written by Hugues de Payns, but some doubts remain. See C. Sclafert, 'Lettre inédite de Hugues de Saint-Victor aux Chevaliers du Temple', *Revue d'ascétique et de mystique*, xxxiv (1958), 279, and M. Bulst-Thiele, *Sacrae Domus Militiae Templi Hierosolymitani Magistri* (Göttingen, 1974), 23, n. 13.
[13] See G. Duby, *Three Orders, passim*.

32

which the devil seeks to entrap them by diverting them from God's purpose, but his cunning should be resisted. 'Do not deceive yourselves: each receives recompense in accordance with his work. The roofs of the houses receive the rain and the hail and the winds, but if there were no roofs, how could the ceilings be adorned?' Their profession was an honourable one. 'We say this for this reason brothers, because we have heard that certain of you have been troubled by some persons of little wisdom, as if your profession, by which you have dedicated your life to carry arms for the defence of Christians against the enemies of the faith and of peace, as if, I say, that profession were either illicit or pernicious, that is either a sin or an impediment to a great conception.' Once more the Christian ideology of the just war is thrust forward: '... and since he (the devil) labours to corrupt the end of causes through intention, he suggests hatred and fury when you kill, he suggests greed when you pick up the spoils; you repel on all sides this snare because, in killing you do not hate unfairly and in despoiling you do not covert unjustly. Thus I now say: "You do not hate unfairly", because you do not hate the man but the iniquity. Thus I say: "You do not covert unjustly", because you take that which, for their sins, is justly taken and, seeing your work, is justly owed.' If the devil cannot succeed by corrupting the intention, he pretends that the role should be abandoned in order to seek a higher goal. Once again this is a fallacy, for God judges not upon externals, but upon inward disposition. Nevertheless, they should not be deceived by the more subtle temptation of the devil which is to argue that the external cares with which the Templars are often involved are an unnecessary diversion from a desirable life of contemplation. It is not for mere men to make such arbitrary decisions: 'He is the Lord and we are His servants; and, in His great house, He has put each in His place, having the law that whoever was the most humble in the duty of service should be the highest in the recompense of the retribution.' The Templars are to fulfil their duty even if no temporal recognition is to be gained. 'For I judge that there is no man of wisdom among you who does not know that all virtue is the more secure when it is the more hidden.' The theme throughout therefore is in keeping with the contemporary preoccupation with the importance of what the letter calls 'inward disposition' or motive.[14]

This letter was however essentially private in nature; the really public justification of the concept which the Templars represented is to be found in St Bernard's tract *Liber ad milites Templi de laude novae militiae* which, produced in the early 1130s, was a response to

[14] See C. Morris, *The Discovery of the Individual, 1050–1200* (London, 1972), esp. 73-5.

Hugues de Payns' appeal to write 'a sermon of exhortation for you
and your fellow knights.'[15] This is of central importance to the subject because it sets down in much greater depth and with much
greater eloquence the contemporary ideals of knighthood which had
been formulated through the peace movements and the crusades
and with which the development of the Order of the Temple is so
closely interconnected. His theme is that of the double conflict which
so thoroughly permeated the mentality of this world, a conflict
against both flesh and blood and against evil spirits. The Templars
are 'a new species of knighthood' which is better than both those
who fight the enemy solely through bodily strength—'this indeed I
do not judge amazing, nor do I think it rare'—and those who wage
the war against vices or demons which, although praiseworthy, is
not to be marvelled at, 'since the whole world is seen to be filled
with monks'. But the new knights need fear neither demon nor man
since they cannot lose, for death makes them happy martyrs and
survival gives them glorious victory. The crusaders' self-image almost exactly as portrayed by Fulcher of Chartres in 1100 is here
incorporated in a permanent institution. Bernard then, just as in the
Rule, contrasts the Templars with the secular knights who do not
fight for Christ's cause. If they kill the enemy their own soul dies, or
if they are killed themselves then both body and soul die. 'O safe
life when the conscience is pure! ... If the cause of the fighting be
good, the end of the fighting cannot be evil, just as the end cannot
be judged good, when the cause is not good and the right intention
does not precede (it).' If the motive is wrong, so that in battle the
knight is dominated by anger or pride, then whether he lives or dies
he is a 'homicide'. Here again is the crusader ethic as understood by
Fulcher of Chartres. For Fulcher, the wearing of crosses was 'the
outward sign in order that they might obtain the inner reality. It is
evident indeed that because a good intention brings about the ac-
complishment of a good work, a good work brings about the salvation of the soul.'[16]

Equally, the inner motives of secular knights who do not fight for
the Lord can be discerned from their outward appearance: silk cloths
over the horses, painted lances, shields and saddles, reins and spurs
ornamented with gold and silver gems. 'Are these the insignia of

[15] Bernard of Clairvaux, *Liber ad Milites Templi de Laude Novae Militiae*, S. Bernardi
*Opera*, III, ed. J. Leclercq (Rome, 1963), 213.
[16] Fulcher of Chartres, 68. Latin text, lib. I, cap. iv, p. 325. See Leclercq, 'Saint
Bernard's Attitude toward War', *Studies in Medieval Cistercian History*, ii, 1976 (*Cistercian
Studies Series:* 24), 24-5, who stresses that ultimately St Bernard was interested in
these 'higher realities', in that death gained in this fashion enables the soldier-monk
to achieve 'an encounter with God'. Thus the last two-thirds of *De Laude* is devoted
to 'the mysteries to which the Holy Places bear witness'.

34

knighthood or are they the ornaments of women?' Bernard demands. They pile their hair high 'in the feminine manner'—in the catalogue of vices and virtues, this is the high coiffure of pride[17]—they entangle their steps with long flowing robes and they bury delicate and soft hands in full and flowing sleeves. Doubtless this is, as Dom Jean Leclercq has said, an exaggerated satire and, indeed, this whole passage has a rhetorical structure which suggests that a love of word play and the balanced sentence were only slightly subordinate to Bernard's desire to convey his message.[18] Nevertheless, the basic argument is firm: evil causes bring evil results and, in Bernard's view, the secular knights exhibit the three worst of such vices, 'the irrational movement of anger, or appetite for vainglory, or cupidity for some kind of earthly possessions'.

Christ's soldiers do not run these dangers for they are the ministers of God, engaging not in homicide but in malicide, the killing of evil-doers. Of course it would not be necessary for such killing if the pagans did not harass and oppress the faithful, but since they do, 'it is better that they be killed, than certainly the rod of the sinners be left upon the fate of the just, in case by chance the just extend their hands to iniquity'. This was calculated to overcome the moral dilemma which faced the Christian who used violence. 'If it is completely forbidden to the Christian to strike with the sword, why therefore did the herald of the Saviour say that they should be content with the wages of soldiers, and rather altogether forbid them the military occupation?'[19] The idea, central to Urban II's speech at Clermont,[20] is repeated here, which is that the just war against the infidel is essentially of a defensive nature, to repel wrongs done to the Christians and the Holy Places. The true Christian knight, encapsulated in the Templar, fights for this reason only.

In order to show 'how the knighthood of God and that of the secular world mutually differ', Bernard then sets out to describe 'the customs and life of the knighthood of Christ'. It is a disciplined order in which individual wills are subordinate to the common good, for, quoting Luke, chapter 7, 'it is the sin of witchcraft to rebel and it is like the evil of idolatry to refuse to obey', a quotation which seems to reflect a growing sense of the need for Christian unity in the face of increased threats to the faith, internal as well as external. The acceptance of the virtue of mutual help is a microcosm of the

[17] E. Mâle, *Religious Art in France, XIII century: a study in medieval iconography and its sources of inspiration*, trans. D. Nussey (1913), 100.

[18] *De Laude*, 216. See esp. *militia* and *malitia*, *occisor* and *occisus*, *pudendo* and *impudenti*, *militaria* and *muliebra*, and *occidere* and *occumbere*, among others.

[19] F. Russell, *Just War*, 58, 61, on Gratian's reiteration of this.

[20] D. C. Munro 'The Speech of Urban II at Clermont', *American Historical Review*, xi (1906), 231-42.

ideal Christian society. Within the Temple therefore, Bernard claims, no account of personal status is taken, for, true to the spirit of the Benedictine Rule, it is the best not the most noble who count for the most. Here Bernard incorporates the apostolic ideal which characterised the thinking of the early Cistercians.[21] Not surprisingly, such a society is not interested in the frivolities of games and hunting nor in the vanities of personal appearance. The Templars are unkempt, dusty, their faces blackened by dirt and sunburn, almost like the hermits of the early Christian centuries. The ascetic, anti-materialist drive which fired the Cistercians, is similarly the goal of the warrior monks, so that Bernard sees in them elements of both the reformed monasticism of the early twelfth century and the equally reconstituted knighthood of the same era. 'They are seen (to be) both more gentle than lambs, and more ferocious than lions, that I almost doubt what I should prefer them to be called, namely monks or knights, unless I should call them in fact most suitably by both (names), in whom neither is known to be lacking, neither the gentleness of the monk nor the strength of the knight.'

These knights are the occupants of Solomon's Temple and their use of the building compares favourably with that of his time. 'Indeed, all the magnificence of that was contained in corruptible gold and silver, in dressed stone and in the variety of woods', but now it was entirely in 'the religious piety and most orderly conduct of the inhabitants'. God 'delights not in polished marble but in ornate morals, and loves pure minds over golden walls'. Their function is to drive out from Jerusalem those who would threaten the faith, a function Bernard compares, significantly for this period, with the chasing of the money-changers from the Temple by Christ. The language is that of disgust with material things, for Christ judged it unworthy that the house of prayer should be 'infested (*incestari*) by markets of this kind';[22] therefore, how much more intolerable was it for the Holy Places to be 'polluted' (*pollui*) by the infidel, which followed 'a filthy and tyrannical madness' (*spurca et tyrannica rabie*). This is the imagery of corruption and decay in which the transitory nature of material things and the disease-ridden body of infidelity are associated in a powerful rejection of the two great preoccupations of twelfth-century moralists, faced, on the one hand, by the quickening economic tempo and, on the other, by the spread of what many saw as the cancer of heretical unbelief and pagan uncleanliness.[23] Moreover, by employing the imagery associated with

[21] C. Morris, 'Equestris Ordo', 94–5.
[22] See the examples cited by L.K. Little, *Religious Poverty and the Profit Economy in Medieval Europe* (1978), 34.
[23] Compare C. Davies, 'Sexual Taboos and Social Boundaries', *American Journal of Sociology*, lxxxvii (1982), 1032–63.

36

the Cleansing of the Temple Bernard reinforces the role of the Order as a vehicle for reformist impulses, for the Gregorians had laid particular stress on this event as a representation of the Church Militant using force against its enemies as a means of purifying the Church.[24]

One further benefit had been gained from the formation of the Templars, for the Order could provide the means of salvation for those who, in secular life, were sinners, 'evil and impious men, ravishers and sacrilegious men, murderers, perjurers, and adulterers', so that a double benefit is achieved in that Jerusalem received its 'most-faithful defenders', while the oppressed society of the west lost its 'most cruel devastators'. This again quite overtly made the Templars the centrepiece of the general crusade ethic. One of the best-known passages from Fulcher of Chartres' version of Urban II's speech has the pope demand, ' "Let those who are accustomed wantonly to wage private war against the faithful march against the infidel. ... Let those who have long been robbers now be soldiers of Christ. ... Let those who have been exhausting themselves to the detriment of body and soul now labour for a double glory." '.[25] All are drawn by the excitement of Jerusalem. Bernard says: 'The islands hear, and people from afar take notice, and they surge from East and West, like a glorious flowing river ...' Here is the theology which was made manifest in the great contemporary sculpture on the tympanum in the narthex at Vézelay showing the Ascension and the Mission of the Apostles, where peoples of all kinds, lining the lintel and crowding the archivolt, come from afar.[26] The tympanum shows how the world had been conquered for the Christian faith by the Apostles, but at the same time it acted as a reminder to contemporary Christians of the need to take up the task once again, to continue with the renewed mission of the crusades, because since the time of the Apostles the rise of Islam had undone much of the work. In the words of *De Laude*, God had suffered Jerusalem to be attacked from the beginning, so that it might be the occasion for the bravery of strong men and thus their means of salvation. In this context the Templars are seen as the vehicle for channelling some of the most powerful social forces of the age, indeed, as essential instruments of the Divine plan for Mankind.

The Temple was particularly suited to this role because, like the other new monastic orders of the first half of the twelfth century, it was essentially an adult order, whose members had experience, often wide experience, of life outside the monastery. Dom Jean Leclercq,

[24] R.H. Rough, *The Reformist Illuminations in the Gospels of Matilda, Countess of Tuscany* (The Hague, 1973), esp. chap. 5.

[25] Fulcher of Chartres, 66-7. Latin text, lib. I, cap. iii. 324.

[26] A. Katzenellenbogen, 'The Central Tympanum at Vézelay: Its Encyclopedic Meaning and its Relation to the First Crusade', *Art Bulletin*, xxvi (1944), 141-51.

examining this characteristic in relation to the Cistercians, makes comparison with the established black monk Benedictine houses, many of whose members had been oblates and known no other life. Leclercq points out that the psychological difference is profound, for the new orders tailored their appeal and their literature to the experiences of the sinners in outside life whom they hoped to attract and reform.[27] Such orders therefore demonstrate a two-way process in which seculars are influenced by the monastic environment, but equally, when recruited, these seculars bring their outside experience to bear within the monastery. In the case of the Templars, then, the virtues of the Templar knight represent the Church's ideal of knightly behaviour in the twelfth century.

This was soon reflected in contemporary world pictures of society as a whole, as can be seen from examples taken from the works of two of the most famous intellectuals of the mid-twelfth century, Otto of Freising and John of Salisbury. Otto, in the *Two Cities*, writing between 1143 and 1147, when describing the mood of the early twelfth century, says that 'some, for Christ's sake, despising their own interests and considering that it was not for naught that they were wearing the girdle of knighthood, set out for Jerusalem and there, undertaking a new kind of warfare, so conducted themselves against the enemies of the Cross of Christ that, continually bearing about in their bodies the death of the Cross, they appeared by their life and conversation to be not soldiers but monks'.[28] The extract from John of Salisbury is from his *Policraticus*, completed in 1159. In his picture of the truly organic society he is talking of the proper function of knighthood and the bearing of arms.

For wherein do they partake of the character of the true knight, who, although they may have been called, yet do not obey the law according to their oath, but deem the glory of their military service to consist in bringing contempt upon the priesthood, in cheapening the authority of the Church, in so extending the kingdom of man as to narrow the empire of Christ, and in proclaiming their own praises and flattering and extolling themselves with false commendations, thus imitating the braggart soldier to the amusement of all who hear them? Their valour shines forth chiefly in stabbing with swords or tongues the clergy and the unarmed. But what is the office of the duly ordained knighthood? To defend the Church, to assail infidelity, to venerate the priesthood, to protect

---

[27] J. Leclercq, *Monks and Love in Twelfth-Century France* (Oxford, 1979), chap. 2.
[28] Otto, bishop of Freising, *The Two Cities. A Chronicle of Universal History to the Year 1146 A.D.*, trans. C. C. Mierow (New York, 1966), 414–15. Latin text, *Ottonis episcopi Frisingensis Chronicon*, ed. R. Wilmans, *Mon. Germ. Hist., Script.*, xx (Hanover, 1868), 252–3.

38

the poor from injuries, to pacify the province, to pour out their blood for their brothers (as the formula of the oath instructs them), and, if need be, to lay down their lives.[29]

These then were the standards to which the whole knightly class should adhere, not simply the Templars or even the knights on the special mission of the crusade. A short comparison can serve to illustrate this. Professor Southern has suggested that, in some circles, the ceremonies of knighthood acquired a religious connotation between the late 1120s and the late 1150s,[30] a development which cannot be unconnected with the publicity surrounding the recognition of the Temple. When a Templar entered the Order, part of the Latin formula was laid out in the following way, 'and in order that this petition of my profession be firmly held, I surrender this pledged obedience in the presence of my brothers in perpetuity, and I place my hand under the altar, which is consecrated in honour of the Omnipotent God and Blessed Mary and all the saints'.[31] John of Salisbury's description of 'the solemn custom' which had appeared when a man was girt with the belt of knighthood should be read in this light. The man 'goes solemnly to the church, and placing his sword on the altar like a sacrificial offering, and making as it were a public profession, he dedicates himself to the service of the altar and vows to God the never-failing obedience of his sword, that is to say, of the performance of the duties of his office'.[32]

The role of the Templars as a channel for transmitting the Church's ideology to lay aristocratic society is especially important in view of the fact that, when John of Salisbury wrote, the clergy had already been promoting various versons of the ethical code for knighthood for over a century, yet secular literature in the form of the *chansons de geste* of which the aristocracy were reputedly so fond, had been slow to take up these themes.[33] There was a need for the

[29] *The Statesman's Book of John Salisbury*, trans. J. Dickinson (New York, 1963), 199. Latin text, *Ioannis Saresberiensis Episcopi Carnotensis Policratici*, ed. C.C. Webb, introd. P. McNulty (New York, 1979), II. 22-3.
[30] R.W. Southern, *The Making of the Middle Ages* (1953), 112-13.
[31] *Règle*, 167.
[32] John of Salisbury, 203-4. Latin text, II. 25. This was not exclusive to Latin texts. Religious ceremonial associated with dubbing can be seen in vernacular literature during the later decades of the twelfth century, although it is not an invariable component. For example, *Girart de Vienne par Bertrand de Bar-sur-Aube*, ed. W. van Emden (*Société des Anciens Textes Français*) (Paris, 1977), ll. 41-3, 2912, for the religious element, but l. 2359 for a battlefield dubbing in which it is absent. The text strongly reflects baronial interests. Professor van Emden dates it 1180 3.
[33] See J. Flori, 'La notion de Chevalerie dans les Chansons de Geste du XIIᵉ siècle. Etude historique de vocabulaire', *Le Moyen Age*, lxxxi (1975), 211-44. 407-45. The pattern of the geographical spread of these ideas tends to confirm the thesis that the Military Orders were important in this process. The adoption of this essentially French knightly code in Brabant, Lotharingia and Germany seems to follow the

Church to maintain its vigorous propagation of the message, for, despite the First Crusade, acceptance of its ideas among seculars was often partial and transitory. The *chansons* frequently portray a brutal and callous world of noble superiority in which other classses are not acknowledged to have any role or significance and in which the ideals expressed are only those affecting the relations between the nobles themselves or the nobles and the king, and are not concerned with noble conduct towards the rest of society.[34] It is precisely this attitude, to which the *jongleurs* pandered, that the Church sought to combat and against which the Templars were such a useful instrument.

The Templars therefore offered an institutional means of imposing moral restraint on the knightly class as well as providing that class with a suitable way of expressing contrition for actions taken which were contrary to Christian ethics. This greater systematisation of the ethical ideas seen in a more disjointed form in the peace of God movements and in the chronicles of the First Crusade is in turn in keeping with the nature of the intellectual frameworks being created in the twelfth century. *De Laude*, however, for all its potent and evocative language and persuasive power does represent only an image; it was not the substance of the Order. This substance was rooted in contemporary economic realities. Such realities, as Professor Duby has shown, can both influence and be influenced by, the image.[35] Evidence of the bridge between these two closely related but not quite matching worlds is to be found in the Templar charters and wills which, through the frequent statements of motive when making a donation or joining the Order, show how the donor was influenced by the image so that he or she saw the Order as an efficacious means of conveying them to paradise, while, at the same time, providing the Order with the solid economic foundation which turned it into a massive international corporation. 'No member of the faithful ought to doubt', wrote the anonymous author of the letter of support for the Templars, 'that whoever places himself among those who serve Christ in any community, sharing in the work, will unequivocally share the recompense which they will receive.'[36]

---

establishment of the Templars and the Hospitallers in these regions during the last quarter of the twelfth century, see G. Duby, 'Une enquête à poursuivre: la noblesse dans la France médiévale', *Revue historique*, ccxxvi (1961), 13.

[34] P. Noble, 'Attitudes to Social Class as revealed by some of the older Chansons de Geste', *Romania*, xciv (1973), 359–85. I have greatly benefited from discussions with Dr Noble about the ideas displayed in vernacular French literature of the twelfth century. The views expressed in the paper are, however, entirely my responsibility.

[35] G. Duby, *Chivalrous Society*, vii.

[36] J. Leclercq, 'Un document', 89.

40

Elbert, bishop of Châlons, in an early grant of 1132, makes the case. 'The knights of the Temple of the holy city of Jerusalem, having professed a knighthood of the most high and pacific king, furnish so great a relief and so much safety to the needy, pilgrims, poor and all wishing to go to the Sepulchre of the Lord, (which) we do not believe to be unrecognised by the charity of the faithful.'[37] Many of the faithful did indeed believe that association with piety of this kind would bring spiritual recompense. Three examples drawn from a single year, 1134, underline the point. Gerallus, knowing himself near death in May, 1134, prefaced his will with a simple statement of faith: 'Since the Lord and our Saviour through his mercy descended from the heavenly heights, in order that he might redeem us from the bonds of the devil. Because I, Gerallus, lie in my sickness of body and I fear the penalties of Hell and I desire to arrive cleansed to the joys of Paradise, I make my will ...' He then made a series of grants to religious orders, including the Hospital, but at the head of the list—'in the first place' as he says—as well as the largest single grant of 40 *miguera* of barley, he left his body to the Templars at their house of Gardeny in Aragon.[38] Two other circumstances particularly drew men to contemplate their mortality: the imminence of battle and departure on a long and hazardous pilgrimage. Only a few months after Gerallus realised that his natural span was at an end, a Spanish knight called Lop Kaixal gave, as he put it, his body and soul to the Templars, and his manor, his horse and weapons at his death, for he was about to take part in battle with the Moslems. 'This done and said Lop Kaixal died in that battle of Fraga (17 July) by the hand of the Saracens, enemies of God, and that horse and arms remained in their hands.'[39] In August of that year, farther to the north at Douzens, east of Carcassonne, in the region of the Aude, Guillaume Pierre was about to set out for Jerusalem. Among his preparations he 'put aside to the Omnipotent God and to the brothers of the knighthood of the Temple, for the remission of my sins and the safety of my soul and those of my father and mother, some of my allod, ... if I remain in Jerusalem at my death or in any other manner'.[40] Thierry, Count of Flanders, and his wife, Sibylla, with the benefit of a staff of learned clerks in their household, were able to say explicitly what is implicit in these charters. In a grant sometime between 1134 and 1147 they conceded in perpetuity various reliefs and lands to the

---

[37] Marquis D'Albon, *Cartulaire générale de l'Ordre du Temple, 1119?-1150* (Paris, 1913), no. XLVI, p. 35.
[38] Ibid., no. LXXXII, p. 63.
[39] Ibid., no. LXXXIV, p. 64.
[40] Ibid., no. LXXXV, pp. 64-5.

Templars, 'giving heed through religious persons that it is written: "If what is given to God, so by subtle consideration it is thought, is not a gift but a loan, since by fruitful multiplication, it will revert to the giver".'[41]

Indeed, the interrelationship with lay society was, from the Order's earliest days, facilitated by arrangements of considerable flexibility which enabled knights to share in the benefits of association with the Temple. Membership would be for a set term and need not involve the renunciation of secular relationships. The Latin Rule gives an official place in the Templar scheme to *milites ad terminum* and *fratres coniugati*.[42] Elisabeth Magnou has studied these arrangements in detail in the charters of certain perceptories in Douzens, Albi and the Rouergue,[43] but the idea of service for a limited term was not confined to these regions. The universality of the arrangement can perhaps best be demonstrated by a casual reference in a popular French tale of the first half of the thirteenth century called *The Count of Ponthieu's Daughter*, where it is evident that the author expected his audience to be fully conversant with the idea of lay knights in associate membership with the Temple. The count, haunted by guilt at the way he had treated his daughter—for reasons of great interest to students of traditional masculine morality but which are not directly relevant here, he had enclosed her in a barrel and thrown the barrel in the Mediterranean—decides to go on pilgrimage to Jerusalem. He and his companions

made their pilgrimage with great devotion, visiting every place where they learned that God was to be served. And when the count had done that much he felt that he would like to do still more, and offered his services and those of his companions to the Knights Templar for a twelvemonth. When the year was up he felt a wish to see his land and his friends once more, so he sent orders to Acre for a ship to be made ready and, bidding farewell to the Holy Land, journeyed to Acre and there embarked.[44]

This rather primitive vernacular folktale—described by its translator as 'a sort of fairy tale in a naturalistic setting'—is far removed from

---

[41] Ibid., no. XCVIII, p. 72.

[42] *Règle*, paras. 9, 69. See also E. Lourie, 'The confraternity of Belchite, the Ribāt, and the Temple', *Viator*, xiii (1982), 159-76, who argues that the concept of temporary membership may have been adapted from the Islamic ribat. She suggests that the most probable date for the inclusion of these regulations is 1130.

[43] E. Magnou, 'Oblature, classe chevaleresque et servage dans les maison méridionales du Temple au XII^me siècle', *Annales du Midi*, lxxiii (1961), 377-97.

[44] *The Count of Ponthieu's Daughter*, in *Aucassin and Nicolette and other tales*, trans. P. Matarasso (Harmondsworth, 1971), 121-2. Text in *La Fille du comte de Ponthieu. Nouvelle du XIII^e siècle*, ed. C. Brunel (*Les Classiques Français du Moyen Age*) (Paris, 1926), 22.

42

*De Laude*, yet the idea of the Temple as instrument of repentance for the noble class is evident in both.

The evidence which has been considered suggests strongly that, as would be expected, the primary appeal of the Templars was to the knightly class and to the ethic around which this class had been coalescing. Nevertheless, Templar social interconnections encompassed more than this. Women and children were not allowed to join the Order, but they could be embraced within the *familia* of each house. Over the years Templar houses extended and consolidated their position within local society so that they became an integral part of the scene. Thus, for example, in 1133, a woman called Laureta made a grant to the house at Douzens, with the same motives and presumably the same hopes as the men who had associated themselves with the Temple, 'fearing a day in the future, namely the Day of Judgement, when there will be my Redeemer sitting on His seat of majesty and repaying each as he will have brought forth, for the redemption of my soul as well as those of my parents, so that, by the compassion of the Redeemer, we can avoid the punishments of Hell'.[45] A more complicated arrangement was made by a woman called Odelina who had offered to the Templars of Provins her son, Renald, with all her property, including that which Renald would inherit on his mother's death. In 1241, Renald, described as 'healthy and sound and sane in the head, arriving at the years of adulthood (*ad annos puberes perventus*) and free from the tutelage of his parents', renewed this agreement and confirmed his wish to assume the habit of the Temple.[46]

The *familia* achieved an even broader base by establishing links of dependence of varying degrees.[47] Most commonly, local persons sought security in their old age by granting their property to the Order in return for sustenance. These could be men or women, but the possession of sufficient property for such an arrangement to have a long-term attraction for the Templars suggests relatively high social status. An example drawn from Barcelona, 1136, is fairly typical. 'I, Sancia, who was the daughter of Raymond Miron of Palaccio, now deceased, long and strongly desired to give and offer to the holy knighthood of Jerusalem of the Temple of Solomon, all my hereditary lands and rights which happen to appertain to me by right of my father and mother ...' The lands are then described and the charter continues: 'For the knights will give to me, while I

[45] D'Albon, no. LXII, p. 45.
[46] V. Carrière, *Histoire et Cartulaire des Templiers de Provins* (Paris, 1919), no. XII, pp. 49-50. Magnou, p. 390, shows cases of children who actually entered the Order while under-age, but this practice seems to have been confined to the remoter preceptories.
[47] For an anaiagous case, see G. Duby, 'The Manor and the Peasant Economy. The Southern Alps in 1338', *The Chivalrous Society*, 214-15.

live, victuals and clothing for the donation, in accordance with what is necessary for me ...'[48] Lower down the social scale, those who had nothing except their own bodies might, as Elisabeth Magnou has shown, voluntarily enter servitude to the Temple in return for security,[49] while beneath even this level the Order gained a host of serfs, dependent craftsmen and artisans who came as part and parcel of the grants made by their owners.[50]

These charters show the donors to have been persuaded by the Templar image, an image which, in the twelfth century at least, helped to shape contemporary attitudes. However, the gifts could not conceivably be allowed simply to accumulate and lie idle, for they were made in a world of vibrant economic activity from which one could only secede by the adoption of forms of poverty so absolute as at once to excite the suspicion of authority. Indeed, the function of the Templars demanded the provision of a financial and economic system which could equip and maintain fighting men in the field for whatever periods were necessary. This had always been—and continues to be—a very costly business. It has been shown that a minimum of 150 hectares of good land was needed to support a knight on his own domains; for the Templars there must be added the overheads arising from the costs of transport, buildings and the state of readiness required in Outremer.[51] Thus, just as the ideology of the Templars drew donations which provided an economic base, so the realities of the economy and the demands of society came to affect the image, a situation which was similarly faced by contemporary Cistercians and later by the Franciscans. This in itself did not ruin the Templars, any more than it did the Cistercians or the Franciscans, but it did attract criticism which, after 1291, had an identifiable focus in the crusading failures with which the Templars had been associated.[52] It was a situation which could be exploited by Philip IV's advisers. Guillaume de Plaisians told the pope in

[48] D'Albon, no. CXXVII, 88.
[49] E. Magnou, 390-5.
[50] See, for example, Carrière, pp. lxxv-lxxvii, no. LXIV, pp. 90-1.
[51] See the summary of research in G. Fourquin, *Lordship and Feudalism in the Middle Ages* (1976), 84-7, and the specific case in Provence analysed by G. Duby, *Chivalrous Society*, 186-215. See A.J. Forey, 'The Military Orders in the Crusading Proposals of the Late-Thirteenth and Early-Fourteenth Centuries', *Traditio*, xxxvi (1980), 325-33, for a review of contemporary opinions about the Templars' use of their properties.
[52] See A.J. Forey, 317-45. Moreover, it does seem that the Cistercians, for instance, showed greater self-awareness than the Templars, as a comparison between Stephen Lexington's criticisms of his Order in the 1230s and 40s and Jacques de Molay's *mémoire* on proposals for a union of the Military Orders in 1306-7 shows. For Lexington, see L.J. Lekai, *The Cistercians. Ideals and Reality* (Kent State University, 1977), 80, and for Molay, see *Le Dossier de l'Affaire des Templiers*, ed. and trans. G. Lizerand (Paris, 1964), 1-14.

VIII

44

1308: 'We are able to know them by their fruits, because by their defection the Holy Land is said to have been lost and they are said often to have made secret agreements with the sultan, nor did they offer hospitality, nor alms, nor other works of charity in their houses: their whole aim was in acquisition and litigation and contention and in this way they promised to act, legally or illegally...'[53]

The cartulary of the Templar houses at Provins, both established by the 1190s, provides material from which an illuminating case history can be constructed. It is a world of hard bargaining and heavy pressures, of monetary calculation and territorial acquisition, a world which seems to bear only a tenuous relation to that of St Bernard's knights purifying the Temple, a task which, it will be remembered, the saint judged to constitute a higher calling even than Christ's expulsion of the money-changers. Yet it does link with the image for, until c. 1225, donations were plentiful and the two houses prospered. After this date however, the flow of gifts faltered and this was perhaps not unconnected with the fact that, by the 1240s, it was distinctly uncomfortable to be a neighbour of these Templars. In June, 1240, Etienne de Rouilly leased a vineyard from the Templars at an annual rent of 100 *sous provins*, to be paid from the fruits of that vineyard, which were not to be gathered without the Templars' knowledge. If the value of the harvest was insufficient to cover the rent, then Etienne could be expelled from his own property 'by lay hand', at the wish of the Templars, until he made good the debt. If he in any other way transgressed the agreement, then at the petition of the Templars, 'on each Sunday and feast-day, candles being lit, bells ringing, in whatever place he makes residence, we (i.e. the local ecclesiastical authorities) should excommunicate and cause him to be excommunicated until he will have made full satisfaction.... And it is to be believed on the word of the brothers alone concerning the want of rent and damages and expenses without the onus of any other proof'.[54] About eighteen months later, Gilbert, described as 'a man of the Hospitallers', leased from the Templars a certain house called 'la Tuilerie' with its associated buildings for the purpose of making embossed tiles. The lease was to run for eleven years at six *livres provins* annual rent. Gilbert was held to maintain the works 'in the good state and even better than he found it' and he was obliged to provide the Templars with as many tiles as they needed at a set price of 14 *sous provins* per

[53] *Le Dossier*, 122. Nevertheless, it should be stressed that, while many of the proposals described by Dr Forey show discontent with the activities and condition of the Military Orders, the favourite solution—that of some type of merger—hardly suggests that a belief in the 'heretical depravity' of the Templars was widespread before 1307, since this would only have served to spread the 'disease' still further.

[54] Carrière, no. XXX, pp. 63-4.

VIII

thousand. Moreover, since he was unable to provide sufficient pledges, he was constrained to invest in the works to the value of 30 *livres provins* from his moveable goods, so that should Gilbert defect, the Templars 'are able to seize the said moveables, without (re-course) to lay justice or without any contradiction from Gilbert' until satisfaction was made. Finally, 'if it should happen, God forbid! that the house and building should be burnt by fire, Gilbert is not held to repair it, but nevertheless he is held to render the sum of money to the brothers, as is written, on each year.'[55]

The Templars of Provins were therefore prepared to bring the full weight of lay and ecclesiastical power to prevent any default in contracts which were essentially no risk ventures for the Order in the first place. Moreover, from these two contracts alone they were assured of a supply of both the vintage and of tiles for which they did not work. Yet these same Templars, so vigorous in the protection of their own rights, could be careless of the rights of others. The Templars possessed certain mills on the Seine at Varennes, which must have been lucrative. However, they were not content with these, for they fished in the sluices and cuts of the mills, they used a boat to collect their catch, they took earth and turf from the surrounding area to build up their causeways and barrages and to make new ditches, and they built a house on this land to accom-modate the brothers and their *familia* associated with the mills. All these actions are known because they were seen by the local land-owner, Droco, lord of Trainel, as infringements of his jurisdiction, yet 'at length, moved by the advice of good men', in 1248, he had to concede all these alleged transgressions, saving only that a servant of the Templars who steered the boat should swear to him once a year that 'he should not use the boat other than in the affairs of the brothers'.[56]

These documents emphasise what Professor L.K. Little sees as one of the central moral dilemmas of the era, that of applying Christian concepts which insisted that extensive contact with money and com-merce was defiling, to a period when economic change drew the successful landowner into just such a commercial ambience.[57] In many ways the gifts described in this paper—such as that of Thierry of Flanders—display some of the literal elements which characterised

---

[55] Ibid., no. XVI, pp. 53-5.
[56] Ibid., no. CXLII, pp. 146-8.
[57] Little, chap. 2. Professor Little's distinctions between a gift and a profit economy and between the characteristics of the early and high middle ages seem to me over-simplified; nevertheless, it does seem likely that the application of pious gifts to pro-fitable purposes was, in the twelfth and thirteenth centuries, both a greater tempta-tion to the recipients and a greater provocation to potential critics than had pre-viously been the case.

46

early medieval social and religious attitudes, and which in the more economically advanced regions of Western Christendom, were being superseded by a more sophisticated outlook in which credit and risk capital played a major part.[58] In these changing circumstances the Templars benefitted from this literal-mindedness, yet increasingly displayed the attitudes associated with the developing economy. The Templars of Provins were doubtless not unique among contemporary landlords, but the original social context of the Order made it more likely that a different scale of values would be applied. When the Templars became great landlords and international bankers where were St Bernard's unkempt enthusiasts who cared nothing for the vanities of this world but strove only for holy martyrdom? The very ambiguity of their position—were they monks or knights?— which St Bernard had seen as a source of strength, was to become a point of weakness when Philip IV, seeking to pluck them from ecclesiastical jurisdiction, demanded of the Parisian masters of theology whether they were 'more a college of knights and not principally of clerks'.[59] The Templars had been established as a living ideal of Christian chivalry, whose standards had been set with great vividness by Bernard of Clairvaux. The Order's material success stemmed from this, for it received donations and recruits on a large scale, as well as a number of exclusive privileges from the papacy. But ultimately the Templars were no more likely to be able to maintain such a religious ideal than the secular knighthood actually intended to ride out and search for dragons. This is not to say that the ideal was unconnected with reality, only that ideology and substance could not be exactly matched, nor could they be expected to be. While most secular knights did not or could not adhere to the codes of conduct to which they professed allegiance, society nevertheless expected those who symbolised those codes to maintain standards. The empathy between the Templars and the interests of lay aristocratic society which can be seen in the twelfth century had its dangers, for when it began to be believed that the Templars fell short of the ideal, the reaction could be as hostile as the initial reception had been enthusiastic.

[58] See the discussion of M.B. Becker, *Medieval Italy. Constraints and Creativity* (Bloomington, 1981), chap. 1.
[59] *Le Dossier*, 58.

# IX

## THE CRUSADE OF THE SHEPHERDS IN 1251

"Eminent and discerning men and prelates of profound mind," asserted the St. Albans' chronicler Matthew Paris, "said that since the time of Mahommed, there had never crept into the church of Christ so dreadful a plague."[1] "Consider, therefore, from these matters which have been narrated," warned the Dominican Thomas of Cantimpré, "how many people, Antichrist, when he comes, will gather to himself, from among the Christian population."[2] "It was said of them," wrote a correspondent of the Franciscan Adam Marsh, "that they intended that firstly they should extirpate the clergy from the earth, secondly that they should wipe out the monks, [and] afterwards that they should attack the knights and nobles, so that the land being thus desolate of all defense, it would easily lie open to the errors and incursions of the pagans. Which seemed near to the truth; especially since a certain multitude of unknown knights, who were dressed in white, began to appear in German regions."[3] This is a selection of just three opinions among the apocalyptic, moralizing or simply denigratory views which can be found among chroniclers who were contemporaries of the rising in France in the spring and summer of 1251 known as the Crusade of the Shepherds or Pastoureaux. Reference is made to this movement in at least thirty-four chronicles, annals and letters of the thirteenth century,[4] as well as the register of Odo Rigaud, Archbishop of Rouen, which range encompasses writers from France, the Low Countries, England, Germany and Italy. Nor were the events quickly forgotten. Bernard Gui, Inquisitor in the Toulousain, writing sometime between 1305 and 1328, recalled the disruption caused by "certain vagabond tricksters" in 1251, the Swabian chronicler, John of Winterthur, a Franciscan, compiling material for sermons in the mid-fourteenth century, thought the events significant enough to copy up a paragraph about them, while Froissart makes allusion to such movements when he alleges that many of the English peasants in the revolt of 1381 had no more idea what to do than follow each other about like beasts, just like the Pastoureaux of former times.[5]

What happened which so shocked and impressed these writers? It is, of course, only possible to piece together the events from these same sources, and thus perhaps the historian is trapped by narratives in which the authors free their imaginations to dwell upon their worst social fantasies and then, having thoroughly frightened themselves, give vent to deep lamentations and portentous warnings. Moreover, the chroniclers are all clerical and they naturally stress the anticlerical aspects of the movement. These are very real problems, but they need not be as serious as they seem, for whether or not the threat was real there clearly was a widespread disturbance and, equally evidently, at least one estate of the established order felt itself threatened to a degree well beyond the ordinary. This was much more than a local conflict between village peasants and their lord; indeed, some modern historians are prepared to invest it with as deep a significance as clerical contemporaries, although their language is that of social change and not of religious feeling. Professor Hilton, for instance,

sees it as "an episode which seems to bridge the movements of pure
enthusiasm for the freeing of Jerusalem with those to come, which aimed
to free the unfree and the poor."[6]

The geographical spread certainly carried it beyond the merely
parochial. At various stages of the movement, bodies of both its
victims and its participants ended up in the Seine, the Loire and the
Garonne. Richer of Senones gives Lotharingia, Burgundy and Francia;[7]
many chroniclers simply say that it affected all of France. It began in
the Low Countries and northwestern France, in Flanders, Picardy, Brabant
and Hainault,[8] regions which for more than 150 years had been
susceptible to calls from religious enthusiasts. This fact did not pass
unnoticed by contemporaries, for the author of the Chroniques de Saint-
Denis describes their leader or "master" as leaving Outremer for France
and alleges that when he arrived "he thought where and in what part he
could achieve his end; thus he went right into Picardy. . . ."[9]

This leader is called variously Master Jacob, the "Master of
Hungary," and, less often, Roger, which probably refers to two different
persons, for several leaders appeared in the course of the crusade, and
Roger is described as a shepherd, whereas Jacob seems to have had
intellectual pretensions.[10] Jacob was undoubtedly the central figure.
According to Matthew Paris' informant he was Hungarian by birth and
about 60 years old. He knew French, German and Latin.[11] Some authors
said that he was an apostate from the Cistercian Order. He began
preaching at or soon after Easter which, in 1251, fell on 16 April,
claiming "that he had received an order of such a kind from the Blessed
Mary, mother of God, namely that he should assemble the shepherds of the
sheep and other animals, through whom, in their humility and simplicity,
Heaven, as he said, had granted that the Holy Land, with all the slaves,
would be acquired from the power of the infidel. . . ."[12] He and others
had seen, in the words of Guillaume de Nangis, "a vision of angels and
[said] that the Blessed Virgin Mary had appeared, and had ordered that
they take up crosses."[13] The resulting army should then set out to aid
the king of France in Outremer where he had sailed after the military
disasters and imprisonment of his Egyptian campaign in 1249-1250. The
Master of Hungary claimed that he actually had a written command
(cartulam et mandatum) from the Virgin Mary authorising him to act, a
document which he kept clasped in his hand.[14]

This preaching quickly caught the imagination of the shepherds and
the herdsmen, most of whom were young, for the chroniclers say that they
left without asking their parents,[15] and consequently, as Hilton points
out, were among the most mobile of the medieval rural population.[16] The
author of the Chroniques de Saint-Denis says that, by this means, within
eight days, there had gathered a crowd of more than 30,000 which began
to move through the fields and towns, attracting more supporters along
the way, until they reached their first major city, that of Amiens.
"The inhabitants of the town gave them wine and meat and everything that
they asked for; for they were so infatuated [enfantosmé] that they
believed that there could be no more saintly people. Thus they asked
who was their leader and they showed them. And he came before them with
a great beard, also as if he were a man of penitence; and he had a pale

and thin face. When they saw him with such a countenance, they prayed
that he lead their host and [do] with their goods what he wished. Some
knelt before him, as if he were a saint, and gave him whatever he wished
to demand." "There were many," says Matthew Paris, "who showed them
favour as well as aid, saying that frequently the Lord chose the weak of
the world in order that they might confound the strong, nor was it in
the strength of one's legs that it was pleasing to the Almighty. . . ."
Bearing banners of the lamb and the cross, "the lamb being a sign of
humility and innocence, the standard with the cross a sign of
victory,"[17] and of the Virgin Mary as she was supposed to have appeared
in the vision,[18] they moved towards Paris in force sufficient to draw
forth the usual breathless estimates of medieval chroniclers, who claim
60 or even 100,000.[19] Apart from their standards--which numbered as
many as 500 according to Matthew Paris--they were armed with swords,
axes and knives. They were equally well-received in Paris, in
particular being favored by Blanche, the Queen-Regent, who "commanded
that no one should be so bold as to contradict them in anything; for she
believed, as others believed, that they were good people of Our Lord,"
says the Saint-Denis chronicler. The Master of Hungary was honored by a[20]
personal audience with the queen who made him great gifts. Primat
thought that "she hoped that they would bring some aid to King Louis,
her son, who still remained in Outremer."

About this time a new dimension was added to the crusade, that of
violent anticlericalism. The Chroniques de Saint-Denis describes how
their leader "invested himself as a bishop in the Church of Saint-
Eustace in Paris, and placed a mitre on his head like a bishop, and did
himself great honour and service. The other shepherds went all over
Paris and killed all the clergy that they could find. . . ." They would
have attacked the university masters and students on the left bank, who
held clerical status, had not the Petit-Pont been closed against them.
Adam Marsh's Parisian correspondent also detected a change of emphasis,
writing that their leader "seeing himself surrounded by so great a
crowd, with the support of the people, was not able to continue anymore
with the original purpose, [but] on the contrary began to attack the
ecclesiastical dignity, execrating the sacraments, preaching, giving the
cross, sprinkling water in a new manner, indeed slaughtering
ecclesiastics. Then on their arrival in Paris, together with their
forerunners and followers, so great a commotion of the people was made
against the clergy that in a few days many clerics were killed, some
being thrown into the river, but more were wounded. . . ."

Although Adam Marsh's correspondent ˙implied that attacks on the
clergy had begun before the Pastoureaux had reached Paris, the apparent
approval of the queen tends to support the sequence of events described
by the Saint-Denis chronicle. It has recently been argued by Professor
Jordan that the major acts of violence against the clergy occurred after
the interview with Blanche, a view supported by his belief that, after
leaving Paris, there was more than one band of Pastoureaux for, whereas
the Master of Hungary led one party south to Orléans, others either on
their way to join him or splitting away from him westwards, disrupted
the Pentecostal synod being held at Rouen by the Archbishop, Odo
Rigaud.[21] The Chroniques de Saint-Denis gives some limited confirmation

of this, stating that their leader considered their numbers too great for any one town and that they should divide into three groups. A cryptic entry in Odo Rigaud's register for 11-12 June says that the synod was held in the archbishop's own hall "on account of the multitude of shepherds and the commotion of the people."[22] That this means the Pastoureaux is suggested by the fact that two local chroniclers report that the shepherds forced Odo out of the church at Rouen, together with members of the synod.[23]

The real action was taking place at Orléans. "On St. Barnabas's Day [11 June]," says Matthew Paris, "arriving with great pomp and strength at Orléans, against the will of the clergy, but favourably accepted by the citizens, they entered the city. And when their leader, by means of the town herald, just like a miracle-working prophet, declared that he intended to preach . . . the people came to him in an infinite multitude." The bishop forbade any clerks to go to listen to him, an order which most of the clergy wisely obeyed, barring and bolting their doors. However, some scholars of the university, largely out of curiosity according to Matthew Paris, did venture out to listen to him. Indeed, Matthew marvels that, in a city with such a flourishing intellectual community, the master could command such a following. But opposition was dangerous for the leader's power was at its height. When one of the scholars attempted to contradict his preaching, "one of their vagabonds rushed at him, lifted a certain pointed axe [and] split his head apart. . . ." This was the signal for a general riot which led to a battle with the students and resulted in a number of deaths.[24] Matthew continues: "With the pretence of closed eyes by the people of the city and more truly by their consent, from which they deserve to be called dogs, they butchered many and submerged many others in the Loire; however they wounded others and some they robbed. When those who had hidden shut up in their homes saw this they left secretly in droves by night. Therefore the whole community was disturbed, and it emerged that about twenty-five clerics had been wretchedly killed, without [counting] those wounded and injured in various ways." The bishop, who had kept in hiding, emerged to lay the city under interdict for the help the inhabitants had given the Pastoureaux, while the shepherds themselves moved on, frightened lest the citizens should turn on them following the uproar.

It appears that by this time if not before, Queen Blanche had lost faith in them and ordered that they be excommunicated and that force be used against them.[25] It was, however, of little immediate value in stopping the movement for, says Primat, "when they entered Berry they divided themselves here and there throughout the region," although some of their leaders were captured and hung at this time. Tours and Bourges were the most important towns that they reached. The letter to Adam Marsh says that they attacked the Dominican school-house at Tours, wounding some of the friars and capturing others, "but what is horrible to hear and relate, but more horrendous to see, when they entered a church where that undefiled and most holy sacrament of the body of Christ was venerably lying on the altar, they threw [it] contemptuously, and cut off the nose of the image of the glorious Virgin and gouged out the eyes and, with evil hands, took away whatever they pleased." The

4

<u>Chronica Universalis Mettensis</u> sees their anger as particularly aimed at the Dominicans, against whom they preached, wounding four of them, breaking the seats in the choir of their church, and "beating to death eleven brothers in the middle of the town in the presence of all."[26] They broke into the small Franciscan house in the city also, injuring the friars, but, laments Adam Marsh's correspondent, "there was no concern for all these things among the French."

The reporting of their time at Bourges is more widespread, probably because it was either in Bourges or shortly after leaving the city that the Master of Hungary was killed and the movement began to break up. The clergy were amply forewarned here and, when the Pastoureaux appeared, were not to be found. However, despite letters from the archbishop prohibiting their entry, the citizens opened the gates. So great were the numbers, says Matthew Paris, that some had to remain in the vineyards outside, for "the city could not conveniently receive them." The disappearance of their erstwhile victims, the clergy, seems to have brought out the latent anti-Semitism present in most movements of this kind in the Middle Ages. They entered Jewish synagogues, destroyed their books,[27] and seized their goods, "without just cause," says Guillaume de Nangis.

It is not easy to piece together the exact sequence of events from this point. Matthew Paris, who does not mention the attacks on the Jews, says that the Master of Hungary, having gathered together a huge multitude on the promise that he would work miracles, was revealed as an imposter and that, as a result, he was struck on the head by a butcher with an axe which "sent him brainless to Hell." His body was thrown on a crossroads and left to rot. Adam Marsh's correspondent sees this incident as the result of provocation by the Master who struck down with his sword a holy man who had dared to contradict him, at which the citizens of Bourges cut the Master to pieces. The canon Baldwin of Nivone also places the leader's destruction in Bourges saying that a certain citizen detected his iniquity and "with others of his group, placed in chains and condemned by the archbishop of the town, he perished by hanging."[28] The <u>Chroniques de Saint-Denis</u> agree with Primat that they divided forces after they had left Paris, one part going to Bourges, another to Marseilles, where they should await the Master's arrival. Those who went to Bourges could not find the clergy but instead began to plunder the city and to rape young women and girls. No reference is made to attacks on the Jews. The disorders persuaded the <u>bailli</u> to act against them and the leaders were captured and hung. "The children returned all abashed, each to his <u>pays</u>." Meanwhile, the <u>bailli</u> sent messages at high speed to the <u>viguier</u> at Marseilles warning him of what was to come. Indeed, a later chronicler, the Flemish monk John of Ypres, writing in the mid-fourteenth century, believed that some had reached Aigues-Mortes and Beaucaire.[29] "Thus," says the St. Denis chronicler, "many were taken and hung on high branches; and the shepherds who followed him [the Master of Hungary] returned poor and begging. . . ." Other chroniclers, however, describe how the Master and his followers had actually left Bourges before the reckoning, but were overtaken and killed by bourgeois from the town to the south-west between Villeneuve-sur-Cher and Morthomiers.[30] Primat relates this to

the attacks on the Jews: "And then when the commonalty of the town saw
. . . they were destroying the Jews in this manner, who were in the
guard of the king, they closed the gates of the city in order to avenge
the injury to the king made to the Jews. . . ." But the Pastoureaux
broke out into the fields, pursued by members of the bourgeois on
horseback. When they caught up with the Master one of them "pierced his
entrails with a blow from a point of a lance," and then the others set
upon him and "tore him limb from limb."

For most of the chroniclers the crusade ended here. All of them
emphasize its collapse. Guillaume de Nangis is typical: ". . . after
which event the others dispersed to various places, [and] on account of
their evil they were killed or hung; others disappeared like smoke."
However, Matthew Paris, having an informant with English connections,
tells how one group converged upon Bordeaux, probably passing through
Limoges en route.[31] At Bordeaux, when challenged by Simon de Montfort,
Earl of Leicester, Henry III's lieutenant in Gascony, as to whose
authority they acted upon, replied, "We do not extend the authority of
pope or bishop, but of Omnipotent God and the Blessed Mary, his mother,
which is greater." Simon de Montfort, "justly considering such things
to be frivolous," threatened to decapitate them if they did not disperse
and, says Matthew Paris, they scattered in all directions, becoming, in
one of his favorite phrases "like sand without lime." Meanwhile, their
leader secretly took ship, "but the sailors discovering him to be the
traitor and companion of the above-mentioned Hungarian whom the
inhabitants of Bourges had killed, having bound him hand and foot, threw
the wretched vagrant into the Garonne. And thus escaping from Scylla,
he fell into Charybdis." A third leader managed to land at Shoreham
where he gathered a following of about five hundred, apparently largely
composed of herdsmen much as had been the case in France. But it was
discovered that he was associated with the Master of Hungary and his
listeners rose up against him. Says Matthew Paris with apparent relish,
"he, fleeing into a certain wood, was quickly captured and not only
dismembered but cut into tiny pieces, his cadaver being left exposed as
food for the ravens."[32] This probably took place in early July for, on
the 8th, Henry III ordered B. de Crioll, Warden of the Cinque Ports, to
expel any of the Pastoureaux who tried to land or to seize any who were
already present, thus preventing them congregating. He could, if
necessary, call on the help of the Sheriff of Kent, who had been sent a
similar order.[33] Not all the would-be crusaders were killed or
dispersed however. Some did accept penance and receive the cross, "from
the hands of good men," says Matthew Paris. They set out for the Holy
Land where they entered the service of Louis IX.

Contemporary and later medieval writers are unanimous in seeing this
movement as a crusade, the prime aim of whose participants was to bring
aid to Louis IX in the Holy Land. The Franciscan Salimbene de Adam:
"They said that they wished to cross to kill the Saracens and avenge the
king of France." He continues, "For their leader said to them that it
was revealed by God that the sea would open up, and he ought to lead
that multitude to avenge the king of France. And I say, when I hear
such things: 'Woe to the shepherds who leave their flock! Where the
king of France is not sufficient, can these be?'"[34] This, however,

according to some chroniclers, was precisely the point.   The anonymous
Chronica Universalis Mettensis says that "a great multitude of shepherds
assembled expectantly, that the Holy Land which could not  be  recovered
by so many French knights, would be returned by the shepherds." Matthew
Paris puts it more forcefully; their leader told  them  that  they  were
specially  chosen, "for the pride of the French knights was not pleasing
to God." Indeed, the chroniclers thought that Master  Jacob gained  such
a  large  following by stressing the positive virtues of the humble who,
because of their lowly status, gained God's approval and therefore  his
invincible  help.  The St. Denis chronicler has the Master of Hungary
going to "the shepherds and the children who guarded  the  animals,  and
[he] said to them that he was a man of God:  'By you, my sweet children,
the land of Outremer will be delivered from the enemies of the Christian
faith.'"  The  Norman  chronicler  of  St.  Laud  has  him telling "the
shepherds and simple  persons"  that  they  were  chosen by God.   The
Chronique  Anonyme  des  Rois  de  France  says that the shepherd leader
called Roger "gave the cross to all who wished to take it,  as  much  to
women  and children as to men," while Bernard Gui calls it "a crusade of
shepherds and many  boys  and  girls."   Indeed,  the  annalist  of  St.
Benignus  at  Dijon  makes  explicit  the  obvious connection with the
Nativity story:  the shepherds wished to cross to Outremer "saying  that
the  Lord  in  his  nativity wished to manifest himself to the shepherds
through an angel, and for that reason they wished to  go  to  the  place
where  he  was born and to conquer his enemies."[35]  Reinforcement of the
message was achieved therefore by claiming renewed  contact  with  God's
agents,  either  the  Virgin  Mary  herself  or unspecified angels.  The
leaders, asserts Primat, "said that  they  had  taken  the  office  of
preacher  of  the  cross  on  the  command of the Lord; and some of them
affirmed that they had been admonished by the Blessed Virgin Mary  in  a
vision,  and  in  order  to  do this they carried ensigns and banners in
front of them like the princes of  the  host."   One  version  gave  the
revelation  astrological  origin;   the  Flores Temporum Imperatores says
that Jacob pretended that a star told him that  the  king  ought  to  be
liberated by the Pastoureaux.

However,  none of the chroniclers was prepared to accept the aims of
the leaders of the Pastoureaux at  their  face value.  Adam  Marsh's
correspondent  is one among several who see the leader acting "under the
pretext of the cross and the appearance of piety."  Matthew  Paris  say
bluntly that the Master was lying when he asserted that he had a message
from the Virgin Mary  and  calls  him  "an  imposter."   The  St.  Laud
chronicler thought that they only "pretended that they had seen a vision
of angels." The more charitable of the chroniclers believed  that  the
rank-and-file  had  been misled; in the words of the Chronica Universalis
Mettensis, "a multitude of evil men associated with them made a  mockery
of  their  simplicity."  Matthew  Paris  compared the deception to the
Children's Crusade of 1212:  "Indeed,  in  generating  that  evil  he
employed the means which he had formerly used in France, once again with
shepherds and adolescents when,  about  forty  years  before,  he  had
infatuated  all  the  people of France, assembling an infinite number of
boys who followed him on foot singing. . . ."  Guillaume  de  Nangis
believed  that  "the  shepherds  and  simple  persons, although not in
accordance with wisdom, did this with  good  intention,"  but  had  been

victims of "deceiving exhortations." Bernard Gui calls the leaders "pestiferous inventors of fraud,"[36] and Primat, describing the collapse of the movement, ends by saying that "those who had put hope in them were defrauded in their hope." As these quotations show, the leaders, especially the Master of Hungary, were consistently blamed. Matthew Paris apparently believed that he had made a career of it since his youth in 1212. Adam Marsh's correspondent describes him as "this damned man" and "this son of perdition," the chronicler of St. Martin of Tours as "a certain excommunicate," John Taxster, a monk at Bury St. Edmunds, as "a certain seducer," and a Senonais chronicler, the Benedictine Geoffroy de Courlon, accuses him of "saying that he was [acting] on behalf of God; but leading a most shameful life, he was censured by the wise and honoured by the stupid."[37] Jacob was not alone in his evil-doing, for the St. Laud chronicler castigates all the leaders as "these princes of thieves," a view which reflects the general opinion of the chroniclers that even if many of the simple were deceived, there were many others who used the circumstances as a cover for their wickedness. The Chronica Universalis Mettensis describes them as "a multitude of evil men. . . . namely thieves, outlaws, apostates, pagans, heretics and prostitutes." Guillaume de Nangis claims that there were "among them many thieves and murderers with knowledge of secret crime, by whose advice the host of the masters was ruled."

The reason for such harsh judgments of course lies in what these writers see as the anticlerical nature of the movement, if not from the outset, at least in its course. Adam Marsh's correspondent had conceded that perhaps the movement had been diverted from its original aim, but this is no more than a prelude to his denunciation of it as being led by hypocrites and supported by the demented. "It is not sufficient to narrate the blasphemies of the evil-doers and the contempt of the people for the divine word of God, the injuries brought to monks and clerics," he says, but also to describe "the madness of the common people" whom he apparently sees as gullibly falling for the line of "such men as murderers, assassins and thieves, offering to cure the sick and when they were not cured [and] did not become better, preaching the virtues of wretched persons." Matthew Paris had been told the content of "these blasphemies." "And when their chief leader preached, attended on all sides by armed men, he condemned as reprehensible all orders except their own conventicles; especially however the Preachers and Minors, calling them vagrants and hypocrites; asserting that the monks of the Cistercian Order were the most avaricious lovers of flocks and lands; that the Black Monks were gluttonous and proud; that the canons were half-secular and devourers of flesh; that the bishops and their officials were only hunters of money and wallowing in all kinds of pleasures. Moreover, concerning the Roman Court, he preached unmentionable shameful things, so that they were clearly seen to be heretics and schismatics."[38]

The chroniclers were particularly vehement because this anticlericalism generated wide popular support. The people, says Matthew Paris, listened favorably to "these ravings . . . in hatred and contempt of the clergy." One writer comes close to seeing this as an expected consequence; the Pastoureaux "despising the clergy and thus

[ideo] very mucn received by the laity,"[39] and Bernard Gui, while accepting that many favored the attacks on the clergy "because they hoped that this would turn out to a good end," nevertheless thought that most of the support came "since they enjoyed [gaudebant] the persecution of the clergy." Salimbene connects these feelings with the crusading fervor of the movement, in that the clergy was being held responsible for the disasters of Louis' expedition, although the forms which this took seem to have involved a certain loss of consistency. "The French masses . . . surged up terribly against the regulars, especially the Dominicans and Franciscans, because they had preached the crusade and men had taken the cross to make the passage with the king, who was defeated by the Saracens. Therefore, the French who had remained in France were angry then at that time against Christ, to the extent that they presumed to blaspheme the blessed name of Christ above all names. For they hissed through their teeth at those Dominicans and Franciscans at that time collecting alms in the name of Christ, and in their sight calling to another poor person, they gave denarii to him and said: 'Take [these] in the name of Mahomet, who is more powerful than Christ.' Whence it was implanted in them what was fulfilled in the Lord, Luke 8: At the time believe, and in the time of temptation retreat [from belief]." Several chroniclers record that the attacks were at least partially provoked because of opposition voiced by the clergy to Master Jacob's preaching. "The people would not suffer these reprimands," says Primat. The masters commanded the shepherds "to kill all the priests and the clergy that they could find" because they had contradicted him, says the St. Denis chronicler. For Guillaume de Nangis, clerics killed in this way were "martyrs as we believe." The depth of anticlerical feeling exhibited is perhaps demonstrated by the comparatively few references made to anti-Semitism which, in movements of this kind, both before and after the 1251 crusade, was a marked feature. This time it seems to have been a poor alternative to attacks on the clergy and arose only when the clerics of Bourges prudently went into hiding on the arrival of the Pastoureaux.[40]

In many of these writers the accusation of anticlericalism shades into one of heresy. Adam Marsh's correspondent describes the leader as "a certain heretic or pagan" who "came with extraordinary customs and doctrine and huge lies, in hypocrisy just like a wolf not entering into the fold by the gate, nevertheless dressed in sheep's clothing. . . ." The annalist of the house of Austin canons at Osney (Oxfordshire), commented that "there erupted in France certain heretics who were called pastores" and Thomas Wykes, a later chronicler of the same house, claimed that it was "ascertained by the confession of their master and others of their company that they were heretics."[41] To the extent that a consistent picture emerges of the nature of the heresy it appears in the form of a usurpation of clerical function, a lack of respect for and a twisting of the sacraments, and immoral and blasphemous behavior. Matthew Paris' account keeps returning to these themes: ". . . they caused illicit marriages to be contracted. And in their preaching their leaders and masters who, although laymen, presumed to preach, deviated enormously from the articles and manifest rules of truth of the Christian faith." He reports a scholar at Orléans, who was struck down for his audacity, as interrupting the preaching of Master Jacob with the cry, "O most iniquitous heretic and enemy of the truth, you lie on your own head, deceiving innocent people with your false and fallacious preaching." Primat says that "they began little by little to go into a new heresy and to envelop the people in a very serious error; that they espoused eleven men to one woman as if by an alliance of marriage," adding, a little unnecessarily after the enormity of this accusation, that "it is certain that marriage ought not to be made except by the hand of the priest, and three banns should be solemnly published in church, as is the custom." "These people," he says, "believed in the vanity of this false religion." Absolution was allegedly freely given. The Chronica Universalis Mettenis: ". . . at Tours they preached publicly that the sacraments of the church were nothing, and he who killed a clerk or a priest was absolved by the drinking of good wine." Primat ascribed their growing confidence in their views to the lack of opposition, especially in Paris, the city where it would be most expected, a place where "there was the fountain of the seven liberal arts, and a great abundance of wise men of the Faculty of Theology."

Anticlericalism and heresy were apparently accompanied by the claim to work miracles. Primat again: "And they vaunted themselves that they could make the blind see, and cure the lame and impotent, and return to health those tormented by all maladies." The chronicler of St. Martin of Tours however had a very cynical view as to how these "cures" were achieved: Jacob "restored the lame to health violently in this way: he grasped the sick by the shins and limbs and pressed them so strongly, that on account of the sadness which they had they said that they were healthy, so that they could escape from his hands." Several chroniclers report a claim that the leaders could cause food and drink and other necessities to increase and not diminish by consumption, while the Dominican John of Columna says that "on behalf of false miracles, they opened churches, [and] rang bells, saying that they saw angelic visions and delighted in assemblies of angels." No credence was placed in any of these claims by the chroniclers, who condemn them as pretence and mendacity, accusations proved at Bourges, according to Matthew Paris, when the Master attracted huge crowds "in order to hear things previously unheard of and to see things which they had not seen before. And when the traitor made certain deranged assertions, and the miracles he promised were found to be fraudulent," he was struck down by a member of the crowd.

By these condemnations the chroniclers intended to show that the "crusade" had soon undergone a radical change of objective from the original intention of aiding the king. However, not content with this, some writers asserted that the movement was the very opposite of what it ostensibly claimed to be, a kind of reverse-image of the crusade, in that it was in reality a Moslem plot to conquer France. Adam Marsh's correspondent says that the leader died "invoking Mahomet." It had been intended that the elimination of the established authorities through the attacks of the Pastoureaux would have left France defenseless in the face of Moslem attack. According to the Tewskesbury annalist, Mahommed was "his [i.e., the leader's] God."[42] Others fill in more detail. Baldwin of Nivone: "A certain apostate and evil man who, renouncing the Christian faith, and crossing over to paganism, promised to the king of the Saracens an infinite multitude of Christian people to be led to him under this agreement, that for each Christian he would receive five besants. . . ." Richer of Senones compares this to the sale of the children to Saracen slave-traders in 1212, an event which he had already described earlier in his work. The St. Denis chronicler claimed to know that the agreement was made before the attack on Egypt in 1249, while the king was still at his base in Cyprus, for so great was the sultan's fear of Louis' attack "he prayed him [the Master of Hungary] to put into action that which he had promised, and he gave gold and silver in great quantity, and kissed him on the mouth as a sign of great love." According to this account the master promised not only a large number of Christian youths at four besants a head, but also the delivery of the king into Saracen hands. The most comprehensive description of the plot however derives from Matthew Paris who says that the Master had been an apostate from Christianity from his early years and that he "had most fully drawn out from the sulphurous pit of Toledo the fallacious subtleties of magic." The situation was ripe for the intervention of the Devil, "the enemy of the human race, having faith that the Jordan would flow into his mouth, since he had already drunk from it through the Sultan of Babylon, and when he saw that the Christian faith was tottering and falling even in the regions of sweet France, he strove to incite a new type of fallacy. . . ."[43] In these circumstances therefore it was not surprising that the Master, who was "a slave and disciple of Mahomet, had certainly promised to the Sultan of Babylon, whose slave he was, that he would present to him as captives an infinite number of Christians, so that France being empty and its king absent, entrance into the lands of the Christians would be more easily attainable for the Saracens." Nor was Master Jacob the only conspirator, for after his death, the unnamed leader who went to Bordeaux "strove in haste to travel to the lands of the pagans from which he had come," but he was captured and drowned in the Garonne. "However, there was found in his packs, with not a little money, many charters inscribed with letters in Arabic and Chaldean with strange characters and poisonous powders for making many types of potions. The tenor of some of these letters, as was afterwards discovered [was] that the Sultan exhorted him most carefully to devote himself to gaining captives under hope of great reward; indeed, the purport of some letters was that innumerable people would be presented by him to the Sultan. And thus the two magi perished ensnared in the toils of Satan."[44]

The reference to the leaders as magi is not an isolated one. Magic was linked in the popular mind with the Moslems and four other writers apart from Matthew Paris thought that they detected the employment of magic arts. Geoffrey de Courlon calls the master "a certain necromancer," Richer describes the leaders collectively as "certain magicians," who "wished to delude by their art these shepherds since they were believed to be rather simple," while the Waverley annalist says that the shepherds were "seduced by the magic art."[45] The idea is most strongly implanted in the mind of the St. Denis chronicler however, who, wishing to reinforce his allegation of a Moslem plot, claimed that the Master knew magic and that he would bring the French youth to the Sultan "by the force of his art." His means of achieving this were to go to Picardy, where he "took a powder that he carried and threw it all about in the air among the fields in the name of the sacrifice which he made to the Devil."

The historian seeking a balanced picture of the movement is therefore faced with a barrage of hostile reporting in which few concessions are made to the participants. The most that these clerical writers are prepared to admit is that the shepherds had been deceived and that therefore more blame fell on the shoulders of the leaders than on their followers. Yet there are indications that at the time that the movement began contemporaries did view it as an expression of genuine crusading piety and did not make the distinctions that, with the advantage of hindsight, later appeared to them so obvious. The Waverley annalist, anxious to show that magic had been used, nevertheless prefaces his allegation with the comment "not having been inspired by Heaven as was first thought." More telling is the initial faith in the movement apparently shown by Blanche of Castile, a faith which has puzzled historians,[46] for none would dispute that she was a shrewd and experienced politician who had weathered many storms, especially during her son's minority. Matthew Paris says that Blanche gave her support "hoping they would gain possession of the Holy Land and avenge her sons," a sentiment expressed in similar fashion by Primat and Guillaume de Nangis. It was for these reasons, says the St. Laud chronicler, that she allowed them to cross Paris without opposition. The St. Denis chronicler is equally revealing. No one was to oppose them, said the queen, "for she believed, as others believed, that these were good people of our Lord." Finally, Matthew Paris records that even after the disasters which the movement brought upon the clergy, the Jews and its own participants, there were still those among them with a genuine desire to travel to Outremer who "putting aside the crosses which they had received from the hands of the traitors, [and] reassuming them from the hands of good men, made the pilgrimage in the proper manner [rite]."

The queen's interest cannot be dismissed as a form of desperate love for her son which, in the evening of her life, warped her judgment, for there is little other evidence that in her last years her powers were failing. Professor Lerner argues that Blanche's actions were the result of "her embittered state of mind,"[47] a condition engendered by Pope Innocent IV's apparently greater interest in his war against the Hohenstaufen, for[48] which he offered full crusade indulgences, than in helping Louis IX, but, while this may have contributed to her attitude, it is still a judgment which implicitly accepts the chroniclers' final view of the danger of the movement. However, Blanche's support can be seen in more positive light for, as the quotations in the previous paragraph suggest, distinctions between noble and military expeditions to Outremer and the mass pilgrimage of an armed populace may not always have been so obvious to contemporaries as they sometimes appear to modern historians.

In this context Joinville's description of his departure for the king's expedition in 1248 suggests that society's concept of the crusader was not necessarily very different from that of the Pastoureaux movement in its early stages. The shepherds' feelings lacked organizational form, but tapped the same reserves of medieval piety which was the crusade's ultimate source.[49] Joinville's account is as follows: "This abbot of Cheminon gave me my wallet and pilgrim's staff: and then I departed from Joinville without entering my château until my return, on foot, without breeches and in my shirt; and dressed thus I went to Blécourt and Saint-Urbain, and to other places where relics were kept."[50] Here Joinville draws on a strand reaching back to the First Crusade. Two examples will suffice. The author of the Gesta Francorum, describing the defeat of an Egyptian army in August, 1099, has a Moslem emir say, "Sad and miserable man that I am! . . . I have been beaten by a force of beggars, unarmed and poverty-stricken, who have nothing but a bag and a scrip."[51] Louis VII's preparations for the Second Crusade in 1147, as described by Odo of Deuil, convey the same self-image. "Upon setting out he did a praiseworthy thing, which few, perhaps no one of his lofty rank, could imitate; for, first having visited some monks in Paris, he went outside the gates to the leper colony. There I myself saw him enter, with only two companions, and shut out the rest of his great retinue for a long time. Meanwhile his mother and his wife and countless others went ahead to St. Denis. When the king arrived there presently, he found the pope and the abbot and the monks of the church gathered together. Then he prostrated himself most humbly on the ground; he venerated his patron saint. Indeed the pope and the abbot opened the small golden door and drew out the silver reliquary a little way so that the king might be rendered the more eager for his task by seeing and kissing the relic of him whom his soul venerated. Then, when the banner had been taken from above the altar, after he had received the pilgrim's wallet and a blessing from the pope, he withdrew from the crowd to the monks' dormitory."[52] Many crusaders therefore maintained the idea of themselves as poor pilgrims who would gain the Holy Land by their devotion, without which the elaborate organization and the sophisticated system of spiritual and temporal privileges were of no value.

The differences between the poor and humble of 1251 and the highly organized royal and noble expeditions of the time were therefore more superficial to the medieval mind than perhaps it appears to a modern reader more attuned to practical problems than appreciative of the power of religious fervor.[53] The Pastoureaux were roused because their leaders convinced them that they could maintain the proper purity of motive which should have been common to all crusaders, but which, it was alleged, had been forsaken by those who had accompanied Louis IX. Here again the roots were deep. An instance can be taken from the description of Raymond of Aguilers of the vision of St. Andrew as it appeared to Peter Bartholomew, the Provençal pilgrim who, in 1098, claimed to have been told where the Holy Lance was hidden. St. Andrew tells Peter: "Do you know God's reason in leading you here, the greatness of his love for you, and his especial care in the choice of you? He ordered you here to vindicate the scorn of Him as well as His chosen ones. His love for you is so great that the saints now resting in peace, aware of the favor of divine will, desired to return in the flesh and fight by your side. God has selected you from all mankind as grains of wheat are gathered from oats, because you stand out above all who have come before or shall come after you in merit and grace as the price of gold exceeds that of silver."[54] The Master of Hungary drew on

13

this same sense of the poor as chosen in the face of the abandonment of crusading ideals by the high-born as Raymond of Aguilers seeks to demonstrate here. Their banner with the Lamb Triumphant symbolized their belief in ultimate victory and, as Professor Jordan suggests, is perhaps the reason for their enduring image as a movement of shepherds.

It is clear too that the would-be crusaders of 1251 were not completely toothless, for the arms that they carried further blur the dividing line between organized military strength and popular enthusiasm. The chronicler of St. Laud is typical in showing that they did in fact carry more than a bag and a scrip, for "they brandished swords and axes and other tools," and, according to Richer of Senones, they expected ships to be waiting for them at the ports. Even if their arms seem more agricultural than military the numbers involved were great enough and their equipment sufficiently fiercesome to frighten or overcome or convince the authorities, for as Guillaume de Nangis says, "there was scarcely anyone of judicial power who did not dread to contradict them in anything."[55] As for the shepherds themselves there was no reason why they should not view themselves as perfectly legitimate crusaders. Had they not taken the cross at the hands of the Master of Hungary and his lieutenants? Were they not to receive indulgences for this act, just as members of the king's army had done? All this had, after all, taken place in a world in which fraudulent sellers of indulgences were not unusual and in which even official preachers raised money by granting the cross and then commuting it for cash to a whole range of persons, suitable or not.[56] The self-appointed crusade leaders were only extending actions which were already commonplace. It is conceivable therefore that the explanation for Blanche of Castile's initial favor is that she--and other contemporaries--had a broader concept of a crusader than that encompassed by the image of the fully equipped knight replete with his official privileges and obligations. Clerical writers such as Adam Marsh, who describes the movement as "unbridled madness,"[57] did so with knowledge of the ultimate direction and fate of the Pastoureaux.

While the movement can therefore be placed within the crusade and pilgrimage tradition it nevertheless clearly did not in practice provide Louis IX with any aid, but instead provoked widespread social disorder within France itself. Even allowing for the bias of the chroniclers, it does reveal popular anticlericalism as being strong, indeed violent, within society; it is apparently assumed by clerical writers as a fact of life which from time to time went beyond its usual day-to-day manifestations. This perhaps emphasizes a basic difference between Francia and Languedoc in the twelfth and thirteenth centuries in that northern demonstrations of anticlerical feeling tend to appear in uncoordinated outbursts like that of 1251, whereas until the conquest and resettlement of Languedoc was assured, in the south heresy was embedded in society and acted as a regular vehicle for anticlerical feeling. The Cathars, in particular, had enjoyed widespread support in town and country and much of their preaching had been aimed at the wickedness of the Catholic Church which they frequently denounced, calling the clergy liars, condemning the Franciscans and Dominicans as false prophets and dismissing images of the saints as being of no value.

Crusade of the Shepherds in 1251

Until the advent of the Inquisition lack of coordinated repression meant that in Languedoc anticlerical feeling found a ready means of expression through the Cathar Church which, incidentally, did not demand tithes or expect landed endowments from its followers. This regional difference helps to explain the geographical origins of the movement and the nature of its development.

Not surprisingly therefore the northern chroniclers quickly detected heresy in the 1251 movement and, equally predictably, their descriptions betray a certain stereotyping common to twelfth and thirteenth-century popular movements.[58] Matthew Paris uses the appellation pestis, a contemporary cliché when describing heresy, while the charismatic leader whose demeanor and appearance is that of the penitent, the heavenly letter, the unlicensed public preaching, especially of an antisacramental nature, the unruly following, and the immoral sexual behavior, in particular the blasphemous "marriage" of numbers of men to a female supposedly representing the Virgin Mary in a parody of devotion to her, are all elements which could be constructed, for instance, from a conflation of descriptions of the preaching of Peter the Hermit in 1095 and the disturbances inspired by Tanchelm of Utrecht between 1110 and 1115.[59] The same tendencies are evident in the idea of the Moslem plot. Anti-Moslem propaganda associated with the crusades was the result of the same mental processes; once a link with the Moslems was imagined, then it was not difficult to believe that the leaders were necromancers or magicians,[60] while papal propaganda against Frederick II had already implanted the idea that false Christians might make secret alliances with the Moslems.[61]

That the chroniclers possessed a set of inherited preconceptions as to the nature and behavior of popular anticlerical disturbances does not however disguise the fact that, although the cruder elements of typecasting need not be given much credibility, the 1251 movement does display some of the characteristics of past heresy, most obviously that of the Waldensians, who attacked clerical luxury and hypocrisy, were anti-sacramental, and denied the efficacy of clerical intercession. Adam Marsh's correspondent says that at Bourges the Master preached that people should not believe what they were told by clerks "since their doctrine was not in keeping with their way of life." It is perhaps no coincidence that the friars, supposedly the orthodox guardians of the concept of apostolic poverty, seem to have suffered more than most of the clergy,[62] since for the popular preacher they could provide the most conspicuous examples of clerical hypocrisy. Indeed, in another context, Matthew Paris himself indulged his own prejudicies against the friars, launching a blistering attack on what he considered to be the abuses of the Dominicans and Franciscans, bestowing the cross one day and redeeming it for money from the same people the next. Simple people, he said, found this "unbefitting and senseless."[63]

In fact, it is clear that the guardians of the established order were not themselves devoid of responsibility for what happened. Matthew Paris compared the leaders of the Pastoureaux to the heresy-hunter Robert le Bourge who, initially with papal and secular approval, raged against alleged heretics in northern France between 1232 and ca. 1244.[64]

15

"By the same deceit, Robert, called Bugre, a false brother of the Order of Preachers, was said to have infatuated an infinite number of persons and to have surrendered innocents thus infatuated to the fire and with [the help of] the secular power of the king of France, whom he inclined to this, to have caused enormous ruin." Similarly, the anti-Semitic aspects of the movement can also be linked to governmental activities, for book-burning was a notable feature of Louis IX's policies towards the Jews, as in 1242 when he decided that all talmudic writings should be destroyed.[65]

All contemporaries therefore see the movement in religious terms; none offers a direct economic or social explanation. Only in the sense that Matthew Paris reports on the categories of clerical greed and Adam Marsh's correspondent alleges a plot to eliminate the clerical and noble ruling classes might such motives be inferred, but neither writer gives these views such a gloss. The Low Countries and northwest France were however characterised by rapid urban growth and the consequent need for rural communities to make adjustments to meet an ever-changing situation.[66] Matthew Paris describes how the Pastoureaux left without asking their lords or parents, an action fundamentally disruptive of the basic ties of seigneurie and kin, but more likely to occur in these regions which, because of economic change, must have contained a high proportion of the _pueri_ or _pastores_, whom Professor Duby sees as the new poor of the thirteenth century, a rural proletariat with no prospect of an inherited and stable position within the local hierarchy.[67]

It is equally difficult to extract any signs of a coherent social program from the sources. As Hilton points out, Adam Marsh's letter is hardly adequate evidence for a movement of social radicalism; in no way can the shepherds of 1251 be placed in the category of those late medieval movements "whose declared aims were often explicitly social and political."[68] It was, however, a phenomenon of wide geographical significance, united, it seems, not only in resentment of the clergy, but in the more positive affirmation of support for the king. But, as the opening quotations show, the former aspect was more striking to contemporaries than the latter, and it was therefore a matter of alarm. Perhaps "social radicalism" can be interpreted in a way too modern to be appropriate; thirteenth-century peasants were not social theorists. It is rather than the chroniclers betray signs of the social fear which Duby associates with "a crisis of feudalism" in the thirteenth century.[69] The clerics were, after all, proponents of social ideologies which, by means of various versions of trifunctional schemes, justified the seigneurial exploitation of the peasantry; indeed, by the thirteenth century the most vigorous proponents of these ideologies were to be found in the scholastic centers of northern France. The hierarchial society, ordained by God, was overturned when rustics dispensed with the intercession of the clergy and took up arms in a grotesque imitation of society's true defenders, the knights. Self-appointed "crusade leaders" who usurped and even parodied clerical functions and claimed miraculous powers had no right to the role of intermediaries between the heavenly and the earthly kingdoms, a role which was variously claimed for the monks, the secular clergy or the king. What had not been clear at the outset of the crusade hardened into certainty when the events were being described in retrospect. Shepherds should not leave their flocks; if the king and the knights were insufficient to achieve crusading success then God did not will it. He could not possibly be calling on the peasantry to rectify the defeats. The only other explanation was that anti-Christian forces--either heretics or Moslems or even Antichrist-- were trying to take advantage of the absence of the true defenders of France, the king and the knights. In its outcome the movement of 1251 is a demonstration of what Duby calls "the stark reality that society was divided into two antagonistic classes."[70]

The evidence available for the study of the "Shepherds' Crusade" of 1251 is almost exclusively that of chronicles and annals, the authors of which were all clerical. They were deeply imbued with the bookish culture of their age and were as likely to describe a phenomenon such as this in terms of past literary stereotypes as they were to report contemporary observations. Moreover, they judged this movement by its ultimate outcome and here the violence against the clergy, together with the admonitory course which so many of the chroniclers set themselves, inevitably led them to condemn it, whatever the initial aims, and despite the fact that there are distinct signs that it was not at first seen in an unfavorable light. Both Richer and Salimbene draw on the same Biblical reference in a way which underlines the point. Here is Richer's version: "And thus as St. Gamaliel, teacher of St. Paul the Apostle, attested concerning the apostles when they were held in Jerusalem by the Jews: if the apostles were from the Lord it would remain their kingdom, if otherwise it would be dissolved: thus concerning these shepherds, since their action was not of God, as we have said above, it was at once dissolved." At the same time they wrote in a world which, during the twelfth century, the schoolmen had struggled to classify within a universal order; outbreaks of undisciplined enthusiasm were not likely to be received kindly by proponents of such schema. Finally, their writing is more likely to reflect their own preoccupations than those of the movement being described: the inability to achieve a successful crusade, clerical corruption, and deepseated fears of internal and external threats in the form of popular sedition, of heresy and of Islam. Ultimately the chroniclers' evidence is as important for what it reveals about these writers' own mental horizons as it is as a source of facts about the movement of the shepherds in 1251.

NOTES

1. Matthew Paris, Chronica Majora, ed. H. R. Luard (Rolls Series), vol. 5, A.D. 1248-1259, R.S. 57 (London, 1880), p. 254. Matthew says that he gained his information from Thomas of Sherborne, a Norman monk, who had been captured by them while on royal business in France. Thomas had been held for several days and then escaped to England, where he met the king at Winchester, at which Matthew was present. This is therefore a contemporary account probably written at the time in rough draft, see R. Vaughan, Matthew Paris (Cambridge, 1958), p. 9.

IX

2. Thomas of Cantimpré, Bonum Universale de Apibus (Douai, 1627), book 2, chap. 3, paragraph 15, pp. 140-41. A treatise on virtues and vices, which explains the tone adopted here, written ca. 1258.

3. Annales Monastici, vol. 1, Annales de Burton, ed. H. R. Luard, R.S. 36 (London, 1864), pp. 292-93. The letter is dated Paris, 1251, and is from the warden of the Franciscan house in Paris. Adam Marsh passed on letters on the subject to Robert Grosseteste, Bishop of Lincoln, Monumenta Franciscana, vol. 1, Epistolae, Chronicles and Memorials of Great Britain and Ireland during the Middle Ages (London, 1858), no. 24, p. 109. This letter was probably among them.

4. In addition to those cited elsewhere in the notes brief references in the thirteenth century in Extraits de la Chronique attribuée à Baudoin d'Avesnes, in R.H.G., 21:169; E Chronico Girardi ab Avernia, canonici claromontensis, et anonyma ejusdem chronici continuatione, in R.H.G., 21:215; and W. Wattenbach, ed., Chronicon Rythmicum Austriacum, in M.G.H. SS., 25:361. For the early fourteenth century, Chronique rimée dite de Saint-Magloire, in R.H.G., 22:83; and Guillaume Guiart, La Branche des Royaus Lingnages, in R.H.G., 22:191-92.

5. Bernard Gui, E Floribus Chronicorum, seu Catalogo Romanorum Pontificum, in R.H.G., 21:697; F. Baethgen, ed., Die Chronik Johanns von Winterthur, in M.G.H.SS., 3:18; and G. Raynaud, ed., Chroniques de J. Froissart, Société de l'Histoire de France, vol. 10 (Paris, 1897), p. 98.

6. R. Hilton, Bond Men Made Free. Medieval Peasant Movements and the English Rising of 1381 (London, 1973), pp. 99-100. Other useful accounts are R. Röhricht, "Die Pastorellen (1251)," Zeitschrift für Kirchengeschichte 6 (1884): 290-96; E. Berger, Histoire de Blanche de Castille, Reine de France (Paris, 1895), pp. 393-401; W. L. Kerov, "The Uprising of the Pastoureaux in Southern Netherlands and France in 1251," Questions of History 6 (1956): 115-23 (in Russian); N. Cohn, The Pursuit of the Millenium (rev. ed., London, 1970), pp. 94-98; and W. C. Jordan, Louis IX and the Challenge of the Crusade (Princeton, 1979), pp. 113-16.

7. G. Waitz, ed., Richeri Gesta Senonensis Ecclesiae, in M.G.H. SS., 25:310. Richer was a Benedictine monk at the abbey of Senones in the Vosges. He is not noted for his factual accuracy, but his local knowledge makes this information more credible, as does the fact that he was a contemporary (d.c. 1267).

8. Chronique de Primat traduite par Jean de Vignay, in R.H.G., 23:8. The chronicle was originally in Latin, but the surviving part is known through this translation, beginning in 1250. Primat was a monk at St. Denis who had previously been married, but little else is known about him. His chronicle is an important source for the Pastoureaux. On him, see G. Spiegel, The Chronicle Tradition of St. Denis: A Survey (Brookline, Mass. and Leyden, 1978), pp. 89-92. H. Géraud, ed., Chronique Latine de Guillaume de Nangis de 1113 à 1300 avec les Continuations de cette chronique de 1300 à 1368, Société de l'Histoire de France, vol. 1 (Paris, 1843), p. 435. The author was also a monk at

18

St. Denis, c. 1289-99. There are two descriptions of the event in this chronicle, of which this is the second and more detailed. The editor believes the first and briefer account to be the original reading. It is likely that he expanded his original account through the use of Primat. Chronique Anonyme des Rois de France, in R.H.G., 21:83, which was probably written before 1297.

9. Extraits des Chroniques de Saint-Denis, in R.H.G., 21:115. See Röhricht, "Die Pastorellen (1251)," p. 293.

10. O. Holder-Egger, ed., Chronica Minor Auctore Minorita Erphordiensi, in M.G.H.SS., 24:200; O. Holder-Egger, ed., Flores Temporum Imperatores, in M.G.H.SS., 24:241; and Ex Continuatione Chronici S. Martini Abbreviati, in M.G.H. SS., 26:476, call him Jacob. Guillaume de Nangis, Vita Sancti Ludovici Regis Franciae, in R.H.G., 20:382, says "a master whom they called the master of Hungary." Chronique Anonyme des Rois de France, says their leader was a shepherd called Roger. Most of the chroniclers, while not naming the leader, designate him "master," although some appear sceptical as to his right to such a title.

11. O. Holder-Egger, ed., Chronica Minor; and O. Holder-Egger, ed., Flores Temporum Imperatores.

12. Matthew Paris, Chronica Majora, pp. 247-48; and Annales de Burton, p. 290.

13. Chronique Latine de Nangis, p. 435.

14. Matthew Paris, Chronica Majora, p. 247.

15. Ibid; and Chronique de Primat.

16. Hilton, Bond Men Made Free, p. 101.

17. Matthew Paris, Chronica Majora, p. 248. On the significance of the symbol of the lamb, see W. C. Jordan, "The Lamb Triumphant and the Municipal Seals of Western Languedoc in the early thirteenth century," Revue belge de Numismatique 123 (1977): 218.

18. Chronique de Primat; and Chronique Latine de Nangis.

19. Chronique de Saint-Denis, and Annales Monastici, vol. 2, Annales Monasterii de Waverleia, ed. H. R. Luard, R.S. 36 (London, 1865), p. 344, giving 60,000. The latter were the annals of the Cistercian house near Farnham, Surrey. During this period they were written contemporaneously with events. Matthew Paris, Chronica Majora.

20. Chronique de Saint-Denis.

21. Jordan, Louis IX.

22. T. Bonnin, ed., Registrum Visitationum Archiepiscopi Rothomagensis (Rouen, 1852), p. 112.

23. E Chronico Sancti Laudi Rotomagensis, in R.H.G., 23:396; and E Chronico Sanctae Catharinae de Monte Rotomagi, in R.H.G., 23:401-2.

24. Chronique de Primat, p. 9; and Annales de Burton, p. 291.

25. Matthew Paris, Chronica Majora, p. 251.

26. G. Waitz, ed., Chronica Universalis Mettensis, in M.G.H.SS., 24:522. The local chronicle of St. Martin of Tours stresses the particular damage caused in the city, E Continuatione Chronici S. Martini Abbreviati.

27. Chronique Latine de Nangis, p. 208 (first version) and p. 436, who thinks that the attacks started between Orléans and Bourges. Chronique de Primat, pp. 9-10, says that they began at Bourges, as does the St. Laud chronicle, p. 396.

28. O. Holder-Egger, ed., Balduini Nivonensis Chronicon, in M.G.H. SS., 25:544. Nivone was a Premonstratensian house on the borders of Flanders and Brabant, and the author was probably a Fleming.

29. O. Holder-Egger, ed., Chronica Monasterii Sancti Bertini Auctore Johanne Longo de Ipra, in M.G.H.SS., 25:846.

30. Nangis, Vita S. Ludovici, p. 382; E Mari Historiarum Auctore Johanne de Columna, Ordinis Praedicatorum, in R.H.G., 23:124. John was a Dominican from a noble Roman family, closely connected with the papacy and the cardinals' college. His value as a source is somewhat reduced by the fact that his chief experience of affairs was in Tuscany and Sicily, but he had spent about a decade studying in the Parisian schools. He died ca. 1285.

31. H. Duplès-Agier, ed., Brevissimum Chronicon 1251-1299, in Chroniques de Saint-Martial de Limoges, Société de l'Histoire de France (Paris, 1874), p. 184. An anonymous monk of St. Martial recorded their presence in Limoges in a cryptic one-liner.

32. The text says that this took place at "Monstreolum," which could be Minster in Thanet, although this seems a long way from Shoreham.

33. Close Rolls of the Reign of Henry III, A.D. 1247-1251 (London, 1922), p. 549.

34. Salimbene de Adam, Chronica, ed. G. Scalia; vol. 2 (Bari, 1966), p. 645. Salimbene died in 1288.

35. G. Waitz, ed., Annales S. Benigni Divionensis, in M.G.H. SS., 5:50.

36. These views were shared by an anonymous French chronicler who called the leader "a cheat" (un trompeur), who only seemed to be a "homme de bien et bon predomme," Extraits d'une chronique anonyme finissant M.CCC.L.XXX, in R.H.G., 21:141 and by an anonymous Rouen observer who calls those involved "quidam ribaldi," E Chronico

Crusade of the Shepherds in 1251

Rotomagense, in R.H.G., 23:339. There is also a paragraph in a similar vein by Marino Sanudo, the Venetian Senator, writing in 1321, but it seems simply to be a condensed version of Bernard Gui's description. Marinus Sanutus, Liber Secretorum Fidelium Crucis (Gesta Dei per Francos, vol. 2) (Hannover, 1611), p. 219.

37.   Ex Iohannis de Tayster Annalibus, in M.G.H.SS., 28:589. He was received as a monk in 1244 and his history extends to 1265. He probably used Matthew Paris. M. G. Julliot, ed., Chronique de l'Abbaye de Saint-Pierre-Le-Vif de Sens redigée vers la fin du XIIIe siècle par Geoffroy de Courlon (Sens, 1876), p. 524. The work itself is largely a compilation and not an original account. The chief interest lies in the opinion expressed. The author died ca. 1295.

38.   See R. E. Lerner, The Heresy of the Free Spirit in the Later Middle Ages (London, 1972), p. 42, who shows that clerical writers were particularly severe on what they regarded as hypocrisy which they connected with Antichrist, whose sway would be achieved by deceit.

39.   E Chronico Normanniae, in R.H.G., 23:214.

40.   Only four writers (Primat, Nangis, the St. Laud Chronicler and John of Columna) mention attacks on the Jews and none give many details.

41.   Annales Monastici, vol. 4, Annales Monasterii de Osneneia (A.D. 1016-1347) et Chronicon vulgo dictum Chronicon Thome Wykes (A.D. 1066-1289), ed. H. R. Luard, R.S. 36 (London, 1869), pp. 100-1. These annals are similar for this period, since they both knew Matthew Paris. Wykes, who entered Osney in 1282, was probably the author of the second one. This seems to have been a general idea among the annalists of English monastic houses, e.g. the Winchester annalist says that they preached "against the faith in an heretical manner," again probably following Matthew Paris, Annales Monastici, vol. 2, Annales Monasterii de Wintonia, 519-1277, ed. H.R. Luard, R.S. 36 (London, 1865), p. 92.

42.   Annales Monastici, vol. 1, Annales de Theokesberia, ed. H. R. Luard, R.S. 36 (London, 1864), p. 145. A chronicle concerned not only with local monastic affairs, but also with contemporary events in the wider world.

43.   The Biblical quotation from Job 40, 18, was a favorite of Matthew Paris, since he had employed it before, under the year 1236, when describing the reasons for the success of Islam, 3:356. The Pastoureaux "plot" fitted into his conception of the Moslems as prepared to seize any opportunity to spread their beliefs.

44.   The idea that Moslems were necromancers was also already firmly fixed in Matthew's mind. See under the year 1240, 4:62-63.

45.   Ann. Monast. de Waverleia, p. 344.

46.   E.g., Berger, Blanche de Castille, p. 401.

47. Lerner, "The Uses of Heterodoxy: The French Monarchy and Unbelief in the Thirteenth Century," French Historical Studies 4 (1965): 199-202.

48. See Röhricht, "Die Pastorellen (1251)," p. 293, and P. A. Throop, Criticism of the Crusade (Amsterdam, 1940), pp. 56-59.

49. See M. Purcell, Papal Crusading Policy 1244-1291 (Leiden, 1975), p. 78, who accepts that the movement represented a genuine expression of religious feeling channelled into a desire to rescue the king.

50. Jean de Joinville, Histoire de Saint Louis, ed. N. de Wailly (Paris, 1874), chap. 27, p. 68.

51. Gesta Francorum, ed. and trans. R. Hill (London, 1962), p. 96.

52. Odo of Deuil, De Profectione Ludovici VII in Orientem, ed. and trans. V. G. Berry (New York, 1948), pp. 17-19.

53. See G. Duby, The Three Orders. Feudal Society Imagined, trans. A. Goldhammer (Chicago and London, 1980), pp. 327-36, on the movement of the White Capes in 1182-1183, which began as a peace movement with clerical support, but ended, in the view of contemporary commentators, as an attack upon the proper social order. There are several interesting parallels between the reactions to the movements of 1182 and 1251.

54. Raymundi de Aguilers Historia Francorum, in R.H. Cr. Occid., vol. 3, chap. 10, p. 254. Translation from Raymond of Aguilers, The History of the Frankish Conquerors of Jerusalem, trans. J. and L. L. Hill (Philadelphia, 1968), p. 53.

55. Chronique Latine de Nangis, p. 435.

56. See, for instance, Throop, pp. 82-100, who shows the connection between anticlericalism and clerical abuses of crusade indulgences. See also Matthew Paris, Chronica Majora, 3:374, who, although he can hardly be seen as an unbiased source, seems unlikely to have been expressing a unique opinion.

57. Epistolae, no. 286, p. 121.

58. On the general methodological problems, see Lerner, Free Spirit, pp. 1-34.

59. For Peter, Guibert of Nogent, Gesta Dei per Francos, in R.H. Cr., Occid., vol. 4, chap. 8, pp. 142-43 and Albert of Aix, Historia Hierosolymitana, in R.H.Cr., Occid., vol. 4, chaps. 2-5, pp. 272-73; for Tanchelm, see R. I. Moore, The Birth of Popular Heresy (London, 1975), pp. 28-32.

60. See the analysis of the thought processes which led Christians to represent Islam in this way in N. Daniel, Islam and the West. The Making of an Image (Edinburgh, 1960), esp. pp. 244-49.

61. Matthew Paris, Chronica Majora, 3:520-21. Indeed, the idea of a plot against Christendom was often in Matthew's mind, for he even claimed that the Jews had conspired with the Mongols, believing them to be a branch of their race, 4:131-33.

62. On the general context of this, see L. K. Little, "St. Louis' Involvement with the Friars," Church History 33 (1964): 125-48.

63. Matthew Paris, Historia Anglorum, ed. F. Madden, vol. 3 (1246-1253), R.S. 44 (London, 1869), pp. 51-52. He apparently had second thoughts about this and later pasted a favorable interpretation of the same passage over the top, see Vaughan, Matthew Paris, p. 122.

64. See C. H. Haskins, "Robert le Bougre and the Beginnings of the Inquisition in Northern France," in Studies in Medieval Culture (New York, 1929), pp. 193-244.

65. See M. Riquet, "Saint Louis Roi de France et les Juifs," Septième Centenaire de la mort de Saint Louis: actes des Colloques de Royaumont et de Paris (21-27 Mai) (Paris, 1976), pp. 345-50.

66. See B. Lyon, "Encore le problème de la Chronologie des Corvées," Le Moyen Age 69 (1963): 615-30, for a discussion of the impact of economic growth upon the traditional economic and social structures of the Low Countries.

67. Duby, "Les Pauvres des Campagnes dans l'Occident médiéval jusqu'au XIII$^e$ siècle," Revue d'Histoire de l'Eglise de France 52 (1966):30. These were probably similar to participants in the "Children's Crusade," see P. Raedts, "The Children's Crusade of 1212," The Journal of Medieval History 3 (1977): esp. 298-300. For an analysis of the connections between religious upheaval and social and economic change, see J. L. Nelson, "Society, Theodicy and the Origins of Heresy: Towards a Reassessment of the Medieval Evidence," Studies in Church History 9 (1972): 65-77.

68. Hilton, Bond Men Made Free, p. 109.

69. Duby, The Three Orders, pp. 326-36.

70. Ibid., p. 328.

# X

# Western Attitudes to Frankish Greece in the Thirteenth Century

Then indeed you might have seen that the Queen of Cities was a vast field of desolation, full of rubbish and heaps of stones: some buildings were destroyed and little remained of others gutted by the great fire. For the violence of the flames had often consumed its beauty and its most potent decoration since the time that it had first been menaced with the slavery of the Latins. They had taken so little care in imposing that subjugation that they destroyed it in every way, day and night. For it was as if the Latins despaired of the possibility that they could keep possession of it forever; God, I believe, in secret words told them what the future would be. ... The first and special occupation of the emperor was therefore that he should at once cleanse it and restore order to the confusion that had prevailed by propping up the churches which had not completely collapsed and filling the empty houses with inhabitants.[1]

This extract from the fourteenth-century Greek historian Nicephorus Gregoras, describes how Michael Palaeologus was supposed to have found Constantinople when he entered it in July 1261, after its fifty-seven years of Latin occupation. It provides a striking contrast to two letters written by Innocent III in May 1205, a year after the Fourth Crusade, for to read these is to be left with the impression that, even after such a short time, the Latins in Romania and Greece were close to the culmination of a great triumph in Byzantium. It needed only the help of those Westerners appropriately qualified for the task to be complete. Writing to the prelates of France, Innocent exulted that 'a great part of the eastern Church, namely almost all of Greece' had been brought to the proper obedience of its mother, the Roman Church. The emperor Baldwin was now labouring to ensure 'that the edifice, already largely built, should not fall down' and, to this end, requested that the pope send 'religious and prudent men from the orders of the Cistercians, Cluniacs, canons regular, and other religious' to the region of Constantinople. He asked too that 'missals, breviaries and other books in which is contained the ecclesiastical office in accordance with that instituted by the Holy Roman Church ... should be sent to these parts.'[2] In a second letter to the masters and scholars of the University of Paris the pope spoke alluringly of 'a land crammed with silver and gold and gems, founded upon grain, wine, and oil, and overflowing with supplies of all good things.' Moreover, if they settled in these lands they would receive 'apart from temporal riches and honours, the rewards of eternal glory'. The emperor Baldwin, he said, had humbly asked us 'that we might think fit to induce and admonish you through apostolic letters to go to Greece, where you might strive to reform the study of letters in the place where it is known to have had its beginning.'[3]

This apparent reference to Athens, which had been captured by Boniface of Montferrat in 1204, became explicit in 1209. By this time Innocent's vision had become even more grandiose, for he placed the Latin conquest within the Christian scheme for the destiny of mankind, claiming that the Athens of the antique world was simply a fore-shadowing of this new and glorious epoch. In a privilege placing the church of Athens under the protection of St Peter, Innocent declared that the three pagan divinities of Athens were 'like a figure of modern religion' in a city which now worshipped the three persons of the Trinity. Having changed 'from the study of profane science to the desire for divine wisdom', this city of 'famous name and perfect beauty' now gave its trust to 'the most glorious mother of the true God', rather than to the most famous Pallas. Previously learned in the philosophical art, it was now instructed in the apostolic faith.[4] In the papal rhetoric of the years immediately following 1204, the capture of Constantinople and the creation of the Latin empire of Constantinople, together with the consequent establishment of the Latin states in Thessalonica, Negroponte, and the Morea, constituted a triumph comparable to the capture of Jerusalem in 1099. William of Tyre, while profoundly pessimistic about the future of the crusader states in his own time, nevertheless offered the following retrospective on the arrival of the 'pilgrims' of the First Crusade before Jerusalem: 'There seemed to be fulfilled the prophetic word of the Lord delivered in sacred history, which had been sent through the prophet: Lift up your eyes, Jerusalem, and see the power of the Lord: Behold, your Saviour comes to release you from your chains ...'[5]

But just as the fervour which made the First Crusade the most fully-chronicled event in the Christian world since the fourth century gave way to a growing realization of the practical difficulties, so too did Innocent III's glowing images of Constantinople and Athens begin to fade as western Christians became aware that another new burden had been added to those already carried in provisioning and defending the crusader states. Indeed, as early as 1211, Innocent was writing to the emperor Henry, despite his military prowess, complaining that 'since you and other crusaders have striven to capture and keep the empire of Romania principally in order that by this means you may bring help more easily to the Holy Land, you have not only failed to provide any assistance for this, but have also brought trouble and damage to the brothers of the Temple, who are labouring with all their strength for the defence of this land ...' Threats that assistance would cease unless Henry mended his ways reinforced papal indignation.[6]

The fact was that, throughout the thirteenth century, the parties of western Christendom chiefly interested in these lands were those who sought the extension of their own religious, economic or political power: the papacy, actuated by its desire to dominate the Greek Church and to protect communications with Syria; the Venetians, whose wealth had been founded upon their entrenchment within the eastern empire; the Angevin kings of Sicily, heirs to the Norman lust for Byzantine possessions. For most other western Christians attitudes were far more likely to be shaped by the sight of the pathetic and incompetent emperor Baldwin II trundling the begging bowl around the courts of Europe than by papal dreams of prophecies fulfilled. There was, in fact, some limited monastic settlement in Romania and Latin Greece – Cistercian houses, for instance, eventually reached 12 in number, while the Franciscans took the conquest sufficiently seriously to act both as papal envoys to the Greeks and to advise the emperors John and Baldwin II.[7] However, it is clear that the academics of Paris did not see much prospect of furthering their careers in such places, nor do they seem to have been at all convinced that it was Athens and not Paris which, in Innocent's words, was 'the mother of the arts and the city of letters'.[8]

Innocent III's successors, however, were in no position to adopt the detached attitude of the Parisian masters. After the emperor Henry died in 1216, the papacy found itself in constant need of men and money to activate new crusades, for neither Constantinople nor Athens provided an emotional focus comparable to Jerusalem. The size of the problem can be seen by the labour put in by Honorius III between 1217 and 1225 to organize the crusade to Thessalonica under William IV of Montferrat, and to provide support for the Latin emperor Robert of Courtenay who ascended the throne of Constantinople in 1219. Different emphases were placed on the appeals made. Three letters sent in 1224, for instance, illustrate this approach. Honorius told the prelates of northern and central Italy to exhort their subjects to cross over to help William in the kingdom of Thessalonica because by this means there would be great profit to both 'the emperor of Constantinople and the affair of the Holy Land'. This appeal had

X

echoes of the regular papal claim, increasingly less credible, that help for Latin Greece was a preliminary stage in the crusade to the Holy Land, and may perhaps be seen as an attempt to generate enthusiasm among groups with no vested interest in Latin Greece as such. To Geoffrey I of Villehardouin, Prince of Achaea, Honorius wrote that he hoped that, when the marquis arrived, the conjunction of their two strong forces would 'with divine help, abase the schismatics of Romania to such an extent that, in the future, they would not presume to erect a barrier against the Roman Church and the Latins', concentrating here on the prospect of direct military help rather than on any vague benefits to the Holy Land. Finally, he asked Blanche of Castile that she persuade Louis VIII to bring aid to Robert of Courtenay, both as a relative of the French royal house and because, unless help was brought quickly, he feared irreparable damage would be done to the empire which, in the time of his father, had been acquired by the great valour of the Frankish people. In this case he played on Capetian pride in their role as the most Christian kings ruling over a chosen race.[9] In fact, only the rulers of the principality of Achaea managed to maintain any coherent military activity. Thessalonica was lost to Theodore of Epirus in 1224, and by 1228 all the principal proponents of these plans – Pope Honorius III, William of Montferrat, and Robert of Courtenay – had died, having achieved nothing.[10]

Pope Gregory IX, however, had no alternative but to follow his predecessors in publicizing the importance of the Latin empire. When, in 1234, an attempt to reach a negotiated settlement over church union with the Greeks under John Vatatzes, the ruler of Nicaea, broke down,[11] he too turned to Crusader rhetoric, reinforcing his appeals for men by offers of indulgences and by heavy imposts on the Latin hierarchy in Greece. He seems, too, to have tried to add an extra dimension to the appeal by accusing the Greeks not only of being schismatics, but also of infecting the land with heresy, an accusation which accords with this pope's general policy of severity towards what he regarded as deviations from the faith and which provided added justification for the use of force.[12]

Several potential crusader leaders did emerge, but none made much real progress. Gregory IX nevertheless adopted an aggressive stance. In 1237 he wrote to warn John Vatatzes, now the most dangerous enemy of the Latins, not to impede the Latin emperor John of Brienne. He should take especial care, it was implied, because 'by the inspiration of divine grace, so many *nobiles* and *potentes* and so many vigorous *bellatores* have taken the sign of the cross, that the number of them is almost uncountable.'[13] Indeed, the anonymous author of the *Annals of Erfurt* thought that he could count them, claiming that 2,000 French crusaders had had their vow to travel to the Holy Land commuted, so they could aid the Latin empire instead.[14] One such French crusader was Peter of Dreux who, according to the pope, was intending to furnish 2,000 *milites* and 10,000 foot-soldiers in aid of the Latin empire. However, by January 1238 Gregory was urging him to lead a majority of these, amounting to 1,500 *milites* and 6,000 foot-soldiers, to Constantinople as soon as possible, apparently fearing that the intended date of departure, the Feast of St John the Baptist, would be too late.[15]

A letter to the upper clergy of the Morea, written a week after the appeal to Peter of Dreux, shows why the pope was so concerned. 'We have heard sad reports concerning the city of Constantinople, from which, having suffered not a little grief, we have rushed to apply an opportune remedy for these reported dangers'. Apart from the many problems for the city created by Vatatzes, 'enemy of God and the Church', it was oppressed by such a lack of food that, making a comparison with the situation of the Israelites in Judges, chapter 7, the pope said that 'it mourned and grieved to pass over to the enemy'. The sting was that the pope wanted to levy a tax of a third on clerical moveable goods. To those who brought help to the city he conceded a pardon of their sins equivalent to that 'which was conceded in the general council to those aiding the Holy Land'.[16] Within a year he was asking for another third on account of 'the wretched necessity and state of the empire of Romania'.[17] But the cause seemed to absorb resources like a sponge. By 1241 he was levying a tithe on the clergy, Latin and Greek, of the Morea, Negroponte and the other islands subject to the patriarchate of Constantinople, for the city was now on the brink of destitution, 'neither did anyone wish nor was able to stretch forth his hand to it with subsidies'.[18] It is not altogether surprising to find that John Vatatzes, in replying to the pope's letter of 1237, had purported to believe that it could not have come from the pope but from 'a man suffering from extreme madness'.[19]

Gregory IX's efforts illustrate problems common to all the thirteenth-century pontificates. Nevertheless, after his death in 1241, some of the urgency seems to have disappeared from papal directives because once more the seductive prospect of Church union was being canvassed, especially by the rulers of Nicaea who had most to gain by undermining papal loyalty to Latin Constantinople.[20] This policy was to be used to considerable effect by Michael Palaeologus after 1261, but for a brief period after the loss of the city papal indignation overrode any such prospects. Urban IV became pope just over a month after the fall of Constantinople and at once began a vigorous campaign to rouse the West, in particular pinning his hopes on the French monarchy by appealing to those Frankish sensibilities which the popes of the twelfth and thirteenth centuries cultivated with such success. If France, 'which is the mirror and examplar of all the Christian kingdoms', was to take the lead, then, argued Urban, others would be inspired to undertake the work as well.[21]

In his letter ordering the provincial ministers of the Franciscans in France to organize the preaching of a crusade, probably in 1262, Urban compared the impact of the news from Romania upon him to that of spears piercing 'the innermost parts of our heart', and followed this up with a lament which would not have been out of place on the lips of late eleventh-century preachers calling upon the faithful to recover Jerusalem from the Muslims:

> In that region the sword of the schismatics has arisen against the population of the faithful; on all sides the storm of persecution breaks out to overturn the position of the Catholics of Greece, as a result of which the devotees of the Orthodox faith there are suffering the insults of enemies and the Christian religion is being attacked by various and diverse adversaries. ...

The Church had shed bitter tears when news had come of the loss of Constantinople, but there was a further danger that Michael Palaeologus, 'who calls himself emperor of the Greeks', was aiming to seize the Frankish lands in Achaea as well. The Franciscan preachers were therefore to tell their audiences that the doge of Venice would provide all Crusaders with a naval passage 'without fare', a material concession which the pope matched with an indulgence equivalent to that granted to those going to the Holy Land. The preachers themselves were given discretion as to how to gather crowds to hear this message, and were permitted to offer an indulgence of between 40 and 100 days 'to all those, being truly penitent and having made confession, who come to assemblies and preaching of this kind'.[22] There is a note of desperation here. The offer of a free passage and the grant of indulgences simply to gather a crowd make an interesting comparison with the conditions before the Fourth Crusade, when the Venetians insisted upon the commercial price for their services and Fulk of Neuilly was able to gather large numbers of people in quite spontaneous demonstrations of enthusiasm.

Although there are isolated signs of support for the papal call – the poet Rutebeuf, for instance, repeated the pope's words almost exactly when he warned that Achaea and Morea would be next[23] – the fall of Constantinople of 1261 was not the battle of Hattin. The following entries in the register of Eudes Rigaud, archbishop of Rouen, under the

X

year 1262, may serve to put in context the words of a pope afflicted to the very depths of his being:

30 August. This is the Wednesday on the morrow of [the Feast] of the decapitation of John the Baptist, at Paris, and we celebrated a mass of the Holy Spirit in our chapel. Afterwards we went to the Holy Council of the venerable father, the bishop of Agen, legate of the lord pope. This same father firstly expounded a sermon in which he laid out the need which the Roman Church had for a subvention, both to remedy the dangers which already threatened it, namely to recover the land of Constantinople which had already been lost, and to avoid dangers it feared would happen, namely to preserve the land of Achaea, which was in danger of being lost, and if it happened that it was lost, Christians would not have any means of going to the Holy Land, so the same father said. When these things had been proposed and explained, the said father concluded that on account of this he was deputed by the Holy See in order that, having assembled in one place all the prelates of the kingdom of France, he should ask from them an appropriate subvention to remedy or avoid the dangers mentioned above. Also he showed apostolic letters, through which he said that he had the power to do and ask such things; but with the consent of the legate, the reply of the prelates was put off until the next day.

The next day, namely 31 August, at Paris, we assembled with the other bishops in the episcopal *aula*, in order to give a response to the legate, where, having deliberated among ourselves and with the procurators of the chapters, we made our reply through the reverend Father G., archbishop of Tours. He, however, showing the heavy burdens which for a long time had oppressed the Gallican Church because of the subventions which it had granted at other times at the request of the lord pope for the relief of the Holy Land, namely the tenths and the twelfths which it had granted for a long period, and on account of other special subventions which at other times the pope had made, and also others for the land of Constantinople, with the general assent of all, replied that at the present time we could not help that land.[24]

Two years later the pope was still trying to persuade the faithful by telling the world that the schismatic Greeks, inflated with pride because of their capture of Constantinople, were reaching into Achaea, which was being denuded of its faithful population as a result, a population in which 'scarcely any security or hope was present, as it was without help from others of Christ's faithful'.[25] In fact, the only real participant was William II of Achaea, recently released from prison by Michael Palaeologus. By 1266 he had gravitated towards Charles of Anjou, whom he saw as the one power likely to intervene effectively. From this time on there was an underlying tension between a papacy increasingly inclined to listen to Byzantine overtures on union, especially after the lukewarm response to the events of 1261, culminating in the agreement at Lyons in 1274, and Charles of Anjou, more and more consumed with a desire to conquer the eastern empire. Not until the accession of the pro-Angevin Martin IV in 1281 did Charles have a real opportunity to put his plans into action, only for the whole venture to be indefinitely postponed by the Sicilian Vespers of Easter 1282. Thereafter, both popes and Angevins were largely occupied with the seemingly endless campaigns and tortuous diplomacy which, it seemed to them, the recovery of Sicily merited.[26] By the mid-1280s even the papacy had abandoned the Latins of Greece. In the light of Innocent III's initiative of 1205, it is perhaps symptomatic that by 1276 only three of the Cistercian houses established still remained, and only one of these – at Daphne – was on the mainland.[27]

While the attitudes of the papacy had some claim to represent the higher aspirations of Christian society as a whole, there was no such dimension to the Venetian view. The capture of Constantinople in 1204 had re-established Venetian commercial dominance and had given her shipping direct access to the Black Sea. Despite papal opposition the Venetians had forced their candidate into the patriarchate. During the next three years these successes were consolidated by the acquisition of vital intermediate ports and islands, including Modon and Coron in the Morea, Crete, and Naxos, together with the overlordship of Cephalonia in the west and Negroponte in the east. It may, however, be true to say, as Thiriet has suggested, that the Latin conquest was not as obviously beneficial to Venice as has often been thought, for the new lands brought heavy administrative and defensive responsibilities, while the subject populations did not always prove amenable to Venetian government, where inexperience in dealing with rural societies, especially in Crete, led to instability. Although Venice had established itself quite firmly by *circa* 1220, these circumstances seem nevertheless to have led to a 'romaniot' policy by the doges, especially from the time of Giacomo Tiepolo, doge from 1224, a policy which meant naval help for the Latin states and enthusiasm, real or feigned, for the papacy's crusading plans.[28]

Matters came to a head after the victory of Michael Palaeologus at Pelagonia in 1259, a victory which made the Venetians sufficiently uneasy to try and organize a common defence policy with the Latin barons of the Morea, Negroponte, and the islands. The idea, which apparently appealed to no-one else since it was never implemented, was that 'a thousand men should be placed in Constantinople and retained there continuously', paid for communally.[29] Indeed, the contemporary author of the chronicle of the Marches of Treviso and Lombardy, probably from Verona, alleged that, after the imprisonment of William II of Villehardouin, 'only the Catholic people of the Venetians with infinite expenses and dangers and with the very greatest labour were defending [Constantinople]'.[30]

The Venetians were particularly concerned about the consolidation of the links between Michael Palaeologus and the Genoese, especially as demonstrated by the Treaty of Nymphaeum of March 1261. According to the Venetian chronicler Martino da Canal, the Genoese were motivated entirely by their rivalry with Venice:

> ... the Genoese held a council, and in the council decided that in no way, neither by promise of peace nor by an agreed pact, would they forbear from revenging themselves on the Venetians ... They sent messengers into Romania to a clever man, called Michael Palaeologus, who had not long ago had the lordship of Anatolia. That man was an enemy of the Venetians, and the Genoese promised to furnish galleys and men against the Venetians; and messer Palaeologo promised to give them all payment; and just as was promised on both sides so it was done.[31]

Venetian fears were realized when Michael Palaeologus recovered the city in July 1261, even though this was achieved without Genoese help. Not surprisingly, Venice became particularly enthusiastic about the crusading cause from this time on. By 1264 the doge Ranieri Zeno seems actually to have been promoting the crusade to the pope, declaring 'how great, how honourable and how excellent the Empire of Romania was and is to the strength of the Christian faith, and with what great labour and cost, and loss of people, it was acquired in favour of the Roman Church, and afterwards defended. ...' Although at this time of tribulation Venice, 'almost alone, as is recognized, remains for its maintenance and defence', the doge had heard that the Holy See had offered a full indulgence to those who would set out in its defence. A key element in that defence, he alleged, was the island of Crete which is 'the power and strength of that part of the empire at present possessed by the Latins, concerning which, if, God forbid, anything adverse should happen, there would be no hope for the remainder. ...' Help in the form of men and money must be sent at once, since, without it, the faithful who live on the island have said very forcefully that they have no hope of recovery in the face of the growing strength of Michael Palaeologus.[32] Crete was indeed important to crusaders taking the sea route to the Holy Land, and in that sense the doge's letter was calculated to appeal to a papacy which had always argued that Latin Greece was vital to the crusading effort, but in practice the Venetian attitude was determined largely by self-interest, for the island was even more vital to the Republic.[33] Indeed, the Republic's envoys were negotiating with the Byzantines even as the letter to Urban IV was being dispatched, a policy which eventually led to a ten-year truce with Andronicus II, Michael Palaeologus's successor, in 1285.[34]

However, before this apparent acceptance that western Christians could not or would not help Frankish Greece, Venice had investigated the possible value of an alliance with Charles of Anjou, the one ruler who seemed to be both serious and effective in his determination to drive out the Byzantines. With the defeat and death of Manfred in 1266, Charles had been able to secure his hold on the kingdom of Sicily. To the beleaguered William of Achaea and the dispossessed emperor Baldwin, Charles offered the best prospect of salvation and, in May 1267, at Viterbo, they both signed treaties with him which, in the extent of the rights conceded, illustrate their lack of viable alternatives. The essence of the terms was contained in the marriages arranged between the children of William and Charles on the one hand and those of Baldwin and Charles on the other. By these means both the Morea and the empire would ultimately devolve upon either Charles or his heirs. In the preamble to the first treaty William II explained that, threatened with grave danger by the schismatic Michael Palaeologus, he had tried unsuccessfully to find a remedy 'by various ways and means, and we also asked among the princes and magnates of the world, at length having recourse to you, most serene prince, lord Charles ... both on account of the prerogative of strength conceded to you by God and on account of the power and position of your kingdom, not only to help us and our land, but to attain the recovery and defence of the orthodox faith and the Holy Land ...' Charles, for his part, borrowing the papal imagery of the unified body of Christendom, committed himself to the re-creation of the Latin empire. According to the second Viterbo treaty, made with Baldwin II, 'We, therefore, considering that the aforesaid empire, which is a noble member of the holy Roman Church, has been separated from its body by schismatics, and wishing that this member might be restored to its body through our office, taking on a labour both pious and useful, promise to recover the empire. ...'[35]

From this point, Charles set about preparations for the reconquest with a commitment shown by no other western ruler, either before or after. The oppressive fiscality of his government in the kingdom of Sicily, and his policy of raising loans from Florentine bankers in return for allowing them access to the valuable raw materials of Apulia and the island of Sicily, owe much to the cost of these invasion plans.[36] The Angevin registers, despite the fact that we have only a fraction of the total numbers of documents produced, still provide ample evidence of the export of food, horses, arms, precious metals, and cash, as well as payments for mercenaries and the dispatch of specialist personnel like doctors and engineers. Under license, others, like Hugh of Brienne, were allowed to export needed materials to the Morea through these ports.[37]

Nevertheless, even for a man of Charles's energy and resources the obstacles were formidable. Acts of God like the destruction of his fleet in a storm off Trapani in November 1270, were compounded by the efforts of God's representative on earth, Gregory X, to secure the union of the Churches at Lyons in 1274, the success of which blocked any overt attack upon Constantinople. Moreover, when William II died in 1278, the Morea came directly under Charles's rule, but his absentee administration was not a success, and it has been argued that this persuaded him to think in terms of a land attack via Albania, Epirus, and Thessalonica, rather than a naval expedition.[38] Marino Sanudo writes that King Charles, 'intending to acquire the empire of Romania, sent messer Rosso de Solino (Hugh of Sully) ... with more than 2,000 men-at-arms and about 6,000 foot-soldiers, among whom were many Saracens, and caused them to go Avlona and Durazzo'.[39] However, the defeat and capture of Sully at Berat in 1281 effectively undermined this strategy and probably encouraged Charles's alliance with the Venetians shortly after.

In retrospect it can be seen that any realistic chance that the Angevins would be the saviours of the Latin empire ended with the Vespers in 1282. Inevitably, the focus of Charles II's attention was the recovery of Sicily and, in practice, the Morea was restored to the Villehardouin line through the person of William II's daughter Isabelle. Charles II, nevertheless, seems to have been ready to grant licenses to others to export via the Adriatic ports, especially Brindisi and Otranto, to both the Morea and the Holy Land. The scale of these exports can be quite surprising. There was, for instance, a very brisk trade in horses and pack-animals. To take three examples from the mid-1290s: in 1293 and 1295 Hugh of Brienne was allowed to send 82 and 160 animals respectively, while in the intervening year, Florent of Hainault, Isabelle's husband, was given permission to export 200 animals. These included the whole range of beasts from war-horses to mules.[40]

The papacy, the Venetians, and the Angevins all had specific reasons for their policies towards Frankish Greece, but it is clear that for western Christendom as a whole their fate failed to fire the popular imagination. As early as 1212 the Emperor Henry, having defeated Theodore Lascaris – the ruler of Nicaea – the previous year, wrote that 'nothing is lacking for the achievement of complete victory and for the possession of the empire, except an abundance of Latins ... since, as you know, there is little use in acquiring [land], unless there are those who can conserve it'.[41] Henry's problem was not dissimilar to that described by Fulcher of Chartres in the kingdom of Jerusalem over a century earlier. Following the crusade of 1101, he wrote that 'then some remained in the Holy Land, others however returned to their own countries. As a result, the land of Jerusalem remained empty of people, nor was there anyone who could defend it from the Saracens if only they dared to attack us'.[42] However, except for the dire emergency caused by the events of 1261, even the popes saw help to the Latins in Greece as essentially less important than recovering the Holy Land and, increasingly, than their problems within Italy itself. Most often they presented this conquest of a large part of the lands of fellow Christians as a means of giving greater help to the Holy Land. Only William II of Villehardouin, in his enthusiastic participation in Louis IX's crusade to Egypt in 1249–50, ever came near to justifying this pious hope.

Henry, at least, presented the image of a vigorous and clear-sighted ruler, but his successors as emperors did little to enhance a failing cause by their personal demeanour and character. His immediate successor, Peter of Courtenay, never reached Constantinople, dying in the prison of Theodore of Epirus, but his son, Robert did receive the crown in 1221. Alberic of Trois Fontaines dismissed him as the emperor 'in whose time many of the acquisitions of the Latins in Greece were lost, since that man was ignorant and almost simple'.[43] John of Brienne, ejected from the regency of Jerusalem by Frederick II, became co-emperor with Baldwin II in 1229, although he did not arrive in Constantinople until 1231. He was, despite his age, recognized as a more formidable figure, both by the western chroniclers and by John Vatatzes. The Franciscan, Salimbene, picking up the propaganda in favour of the empire put out by Pope Gregory IX, described him as follows:

> No one dared to face this King John when he entered the fray and was roused to battle, but avoided him, seeing that he was a valiant and strong fighter. It is appropriate to quote about him what was written about Judas Maccabeus: *He was like a lion in his works, and as the young of the lion roaring in the chase.*[44]

Nevertheless, whatever some may have thought of John's personal qualities, an account of the state of the empire given by a group of Franciscans in 1233–34 shows why Michael Palaeologus found Constantinople in such a sorry state in 1261:

> The land of Constantinople was almost entirely destitute of all protection: the lord Emperor John was a pauper. All the mercenary soldiers had left. The ships of the Venetians, Pisans, Anconitans, and other nations were preparing to leave and some had already done so. Considering therefore the desolation of the land, we feared danger since the land is situated in the midst of its enemies.[45]

Not surprisingly, when war with Vatatzes recommenced the following year, in the words of Martino da Canal it was

> ... hard and bitter. And messer Vatatzes, the lord of the Greeks, who was always thinking as to how he could have possession of Constantinople, put together a great army, both by sea and land, and directed it with all his arms towards Constantinople. And to tell the truth messer Baldwin, the noble emperor, was then so lacking in knights that he did not dare confront messer Vatatzes in the field. ...[46]

Baldwin II had married John's daughter and became sole emperor on John's death in 1237. Heavily in debt and desperate for manpower, he came to France between 1236 and 1239 and again from 1244 to 1248. In 1245 he appeared at the courts of Louis IX and Henry III and at the Council of Lyons. Contemporary observers were not impressed. The anonymous writer known as the Minstrel of Reims, whose work can be dated to *circa* 1260, has justly been described as a writer of historical romance, but the very fact that he was aiming at a popular audience suggests that he knew something of that audience's susceptibilities. Moreover, his wilder stories date from the twelfth century and not from his own time. Here is the relevant passage:

> And the emperor Baldwin was young and childish; he spent liberally, and did not keep a watch on his affairs; he was poor and in debt, and was not able to give anything to his knights and sergeants. As a result, the majority of them left him and returned to their own *pays*. And when the emperor realized what a state he was in, he decided that he would come to France, to the pope who was at Lyons, and to the queen [Blanche], who was his wife's aunt, and ask help from them. And he took ship as soon as he could, for Vatatzes was making war on him, and was pressing him closely; and he desired to conquer Constantinople and the empire. And Baldwin came to Marseilles, and went down to La Roche, and came as quickly as he could to Lyons, where he found the pope; and he demonstrated to him his need. And the pope was very moved and gave him the clerical tithe for three years. And he went

to the queen who saw him very readily; and he told her his problems. And the queen said that she would gladly give it some thought; and kept him with her for a long time, and she found that he spoke in a childish fashion; and he displeased her greatly, for to retain an empire requires a man who is wise and vigorous.[47]

Both his visits to England were recorded by Matthew Paris, who used them as a vehicle to express his anti-papal and anti-French prejudices. According to Matthew, in 1238, when he first came to England he was not well-received, for the king recalled how many benefits and honours had been bestowed on King John when he had visited, only for him to return to France and plot against the kingdom. However, when Baldwin recognized that this had happened, Henry III relented and the emperor was honourably received. He left 'enriched with many and precious gifts, reported to be worth 700 marks'. Under the year 1247 Matthew included a letter from the clergy and people of Canterbury to the cardinals, complaining about papal taxation, and claiming that the province could not afford to pay. Part of this money 'is for the use of the French, who persecute us and our people, for the conquest of the empire of the Greeks', a sour aside which belies Urban IV's claim that France was the exemplar for all the Christian kingdoms, and suggests that the association of the Latin empire with Frenchmen and Italians did its cause no good in England. In such an atmosphere it is not altogether surprising to find the following mordant comment on Baldwin himself when he arrived the following year:

> Also there came into England at this time certain foreign magnates, worthless and hungry, gaping with open mouths for the king's treasure, namely Baldwin, emperor of Constantinople, with certain of his accomplices, who had been violently ejected from the territories of the Greeks. This man, having, a few years before, sold all the sacred relics he could find and raised loans from wherever he could, had fled from there most ignominiously, a pauper, an exile, and despoiled of all his goods, although the lord pope had begun to favour him and had helped as far as possible, promoting most effectively wars against Vatatzes, the son-in-law of Frederick. Certainly, he began to be in need, and to ask for monetary aid from the lord king, whose munificence he had enjoyed before; and in order to obtain greater favour he asserted that he was his relative.[48]

Again, Matthew Paris is a prejudiced observer, but his view does perhaps reflect attitudes in a way that differs from a court chronicler. In 1261 Baldwin was forced to flee again, but this time his departure was final. He spent the next six years looking for a sponsor, which he finally found in the person of Charles of Anjou. The following passage from Marino Sanudo, although not entirely accurate, conveys a strong sense of his wanderings:

> The emperor, going from there [Negroponte], went to Apulia and found there King Manfred, who, with his barons, received him with great honour and gave him great presents. From there the emperor left and went to France, to his own country, which was in Hainault, where he was with the King of France and the other princes and barons of that kingdom, and finally he was given for a wife the daughter of Charles I, King of Jerusalem and Sicily, and to his son Philip was given as wife Charles's daughter.[49]

Martino da Canal describes a similar perambulation, although he adds the additional detail that Baldwin sent a letter to the doge of Venice, 'imploring him to send messengers to the pope and to the king of France and to the other kings of the West'.[50] The contact with Manfred was a mistake, serving only to irritate Urban IV as heir to the papacy's long antipathy towards the Hohenstaufen, but he did manage to extract money from other courts, not mentioned by Sanudo, when he made agreements with Theobald of Champagne in 1269 and with Ferrante Sancho, a son of James of Aragon, in 1270.[51]

The only real interest incited in the West beyond those directly involved in the politics of Romania and Greece seems to have been in the Villehardouin court in the Morea, for the Villehardouin princes were quite evidently the most competent Latin leaders. David Jacoby has shown that the French chivalric values displayed in the Morea served as an attraction to French knights, encouraging them at least to visit, if not to settle in, Latin Greece. Honorius III's optimistic description of the empire of Romania as a place where 'almost a new Francia had been created'[52] might more appropriately have been applied here, where a much stronger sense of affinity with a mother country shows through.[53] The Greek version of the *Chronicle of Morea*, although produced in the second half of the fourteenth century, derived ultimately from an earlier original in French, and provides some justification for what might at first sight be taken as Matthew Paris's xenophobia. Prince William, having heard of the victory of Charles of Anjou at Benevento in 1266 and the death of Manfred, is presented as approving of it highly, 'because the Frankish race, to which he, too, belonged, had come closer to Morea, his own land'.[54]

The history of western attitudes towards the Frankish settlements in Romania and Greece needs to be placed within the wider context of thirteenth-century crusader history. The relative indifference or even

X

126

hostility of westerners to the appeals for men and money for Latin Greece suggests that this region had a low priority in the minds of most western Christians. The pattern of response is much more like the rather specific crusades of the fourteenth century, where the parties involved had close connections with the region concerned, rather than the more universalist appeal of the twelfth century. It shows too that thirteenth-century Latins did have in their own minds a hierarchy of crusading priorities, which meant that they by no means viewed every 'expedition of the cross' in the same light. From almost the beginning of the Latin empire the popes found it difficult to promote Constantinople; their frequent linking of aid to Romania and Greece with the ultimate goal of the Holy Land was a tacit recognition of which held the greater attraction.

NOTES

1. Nicephorus Gregoras, *Byzantina historia*, Vol. 1, ed. L. Schopen, Corpus Scriptorum Historiae Byzantinae, Vol. 4 (Bonn, 1829), pp.87–8.
2. *Patrologia Latina cursus completus ...*, ed. J.-P. Migne, 221 vols. (Paris, 1844–) (hereafter *PL*), 215, cols. 636–7.
3. *Chartularium universitatis parisiensis*, Vol. 1, ed. H. Denifle and E. Chatelain (Paris, 1889), pp.62–3.
4. *PL*, 215, cols. 1559–60: to the Archbishop of Athens and chapter.
5. Guillaume de Tyr, *Chronique*, ed. R.B.C. Huygens, Corpus Christianorum, Continuatio mediaevalis, Vol. 63A (Turnhout, 1986), p.378.
6. *PL*, 216, col. 470.
7. E.A.R. Brown, 'The Cistercians in the Latin Empire of Constantinople and Greece, 1204–1276', *Traditio*, 14 (1958), 78; R.L. Wolff, 'The Latin Empire of Constantinople and the Franciscans', *Traditio*, 2 (1944), 213–37.
8. *PL*, 215, col. 1560.
9. *Regesta Honorii Papae III*, Vol. 2, ed. P. Pressutti (Rome, 1895), Nos. 4753, 4758, 5006; *Recueil des historiens des Gaules et de la France* (hereafter *RHG*), Vol. 19 (Paris, 1879), pp.754–5.
10. See D. Nicol, *The Despotate of Epirus* (Oxford, 1957), pp.60–64, for this crusade, and K.M. Setton, *The Papacy and the Levant (1204–1571)*, Vol. 1 (Philadelphia, 1976), Chs. 1–8, for papal policy towards the Latins in Greece in the thirteenth century.
11. See Wolff, 'Latin Empire', 224–7.
12. See R. Spence, 'Gregory IX's Attempted Expeditions to the Latin Empire of Constantinople: The Crusade for the Union of the Latin and Greek Churches', *Journal of Medieval History*, 5 (1979), 163–76.
13. *Les Registres de Grégoire IX*, Vol. 2, ed. L. Auvray, Bibliothèque des Ecoles Françaises d'Athènes et de Rome, 2nd. ser., Vol. 9 (Paris, 1907), No. 3693.
14. *Annales Erphordenses*, ed. G.H. Pertz, Monumenta Germaniae Historica, Scriptores (hereafter *MGH SS*), Vol. 16 (Hanover, 1859), p.33.
15. *Les Registres de Grégoire IX*, No. 4027.
16. Ibid., No. 4035.
17. Ibid., No. 4711.
18. Ibid., No. 6035.
19. On this letter, see V. Grumel, 'L'authenticité de la lettre de Jean Vatatzès, empereur de Nicée, au Pape Grégoire IX', *Echos d'Orient* 29 (1930), 452–6, and F.

Dölger, *Regesten der Kaiserurkunden des oströmischen Reiches* (Munich, 1925), Pt. 3, p.16, No. 1757.

20. See M. Angold, *A Byzantine Government in Exile: Government and Society under the Laskarids of Nicaea (1204–1261)* (Oxford, 1975), pp.14–16.
21. O. Raynaldus, *Annales Ecclesiastici*, Vol. 14 (Cologne, 1694), ann. 1262, pp.79–80.
22. *Les Registres d'Urbain IV (1261–64)*, Vol. 2, ed. J. Guiraud, Bibliothèque des Ecoles Françaises d'Athènes et de Rome, 2nd ser., Vol. 13 (Paris, 1901), No. 131.
23. 'La complainte de Constantinople', in J. Bastin and E. Faral (eds.), *Onze poèmes de Rutebeuf concernant la croisade*, Documents relatifs à l'histoire des croisades, Vol. 1 (Paris, 1946), v.13–20, p.36.
24. *Registrum visitationum archiepiscopi rothomagensis*, ed. T. Bonnin (Rouen, 1852), p.440.
25. *Les Registres d'Urbain IV*, No. 577.
26. See N. Housley, *The Italian Crusades* (Oxford, 1982), pp.75–97, for the various attempts to force the papacy to focus on the problems of the Holy Land and Latin Greece rather than on Italian affairs.
27. Brown, 'The Cistercians in the Latin Empire', 116–17.
28. See F. Thiriet, *La Romanie vénitienne au Moyen Age* (Paris, 1959), pp.64, 96, 122–39.
29. W. Norden, *Das Papsttum und Byzanz* (Berlin, 1903), App. No. 13, pp.759–60.
30. *Chronicon Marchiae Tarvisinae et Lombardiae*, ed. L.A. Botteghi, in Rerum Italicarum Scriptores, new edn. (hereafter RIS), Vol. 8 (Città di Castello, 1916), p.47.
31. Martin da Canal, *Les Estoires de Venise, Cronica veneziana in lingua francese della origini al 1275*, ed. A. Limentani, Civiltà Veneziana, Fonti e Testi, Vol. 3 (Florence, 1972), pp.180–81.
32. Andrea Dandolo, *Chronica Brevis*, ed. E. Pastorello, in RIS, 12/1 (Bologna, 1938), App. I, p.392.
33. On the importance of Crete, see L.B. Robbert, 'Venice and the Crusades', in K.M. Setton (ed.), *A History of the Crusades*, Vol. 5, *The Impact of the Crusades on the Near East*, ed. N.P. Zacour and H.W. Hazard (Madison, WI, 1985), pp.422–4.
34. See Thiriet, *Romanie vénitienne*, p.148.
35. *Actes relatifs à la Principauté de Morée 1289–1300*, ed. C. Perrat and J. Longnon, Collection de documents inédits sur l'histoire de France, Vol. 6 (Paris, 1967), App., pp.207–11; *I Registri della Cancellaria Angioina*, Vol. 1, ed. R. Filangieri (Naples, 1950), pp.94–6, No.3.
36. See D.H.S. Abulafia, 'Southern Italy and the Florentine Economy, 1265–1370', *Economic History Review*, 2nd ser., 33 (1981), 377–88.
37. For examples, among others, see *I Registri*, 3, p.182; 10, p.240; 12, p.515; 15, p.81; 20, pp.199–200; 21, p.314; 24, p.79.
38. See D.J. Geanakoplos, *Emperor Michael Palaeologus and the West, 1258–1282* (Hamden, CT, 1973), pp.325–6.
39. Marino Sanudo Torsello, *Istoria del Regno di Romania*, Chroniques greco-romanes, ed. C. Hopf (Paris, 1873), p.129.
40. *Actes relatifs à la Principauté de Morée*, Nos. 58, 114, 132.
41. *RHG*, Vol. 18 (Paris, 1879), p.533.
42. Fulcher of Chartres, *Historia Hierosolymitani*, Recueil des Historiens des Croisades, Historiens occidentaux, Vol. 3 (Paris, 1866), Bk. 2.6, p.383.
43. *Chronica Albrici Monachi Trium Fontium*, ed. P. Scheffer-Boichorst, MGH SS, 23 (Leipzig, 1925), p.910.
44. Salimbene de Adam, *Chronica*, Vol. 1, ed. G. Scalia, Scrittori d'Italia, Vol. 232 (Bari, 1966), p.60.
45. H. Golubovich, 'Disputatio Latinorum et Graecorum', *Archivum Franciscanum Historicum*, 12 (1919), 446.
46. Martin da Canal, *Les Estoires de Venise*, pp.84–5.
47. *Récits d'un ménestrel de Reims au treizième siècle*, ed. N. de Wailly (Paris, 1876), pp.224–5.

128

48. Matthew Paris, *Chronica Majora*, Vol. 4, ed. H.R. Luard, Rolls series, Rerum britannicarum medii aevi scriptores..., 244 vols. (London, 1858–96), Vol. 57 (1877), pp.480–81, 597, 625–6.
49. Sanudo, *Istoria*, p.115.
50. Martin da Canal, *Les Estoires de Venise*, pp.196–7.
51. See Geanakoplos, *Michael Palaeologus*, pp.219–20.
52. *RHG*, Vol. 19, 754; *Regesta Honorii Papae III*, No. 5006.
53. See D. Jacoby, 'Knightly Values and Class Consciousness in the Crusader States of the Eastern Mediterranean', *Mediterranean Historical Review*, 1 (1986), 158–86.
54. *Crusaders as Conquerors: The Chronicle of the Morea*, trans. H.E. Lurier (London, 1964), pp.250–52.

# Catharism and the Occitan Nobility:
## The Lordships of Cabaret, Minerve and Termes *

'Now matrimony is the legitimate union of man and woman who seek an inseparable community of life under faith and worship of one God. Against this the ferocious rabies of the heretics foams out false phrases full of idle superstition. They babble that no one can ever be saved in matrimony. Indeed, these most stupid of people, seeking the purity of virginity and chastity, say that all carnal coition is shameful, base and odious, and thus damnable.'[1] Thus wrote James Capelli, Franciscan lector at Milan, in c.1240. His view is based on the idea that the Cathars regarded each new birth as yet another triumph for the lord of material creation, another soul trapped in the prison of the body; marriage simply institutionalised this gross form of productivity. The famous historian of the Inquisition, H. C. Lea, seems to have found this aspect of Catharism the most shocking of all, believing that, had the Cathar view prevailed, it would have led either to the extinction of the race or, more likely, given human nature, to 'lawless concubinage and the destruction of the family'.[2]

It might indeed be felt that within their own society, the Cathars managed to achieve their own self-destruction. The last known Cathar *bonhomme* was executed in 1321 and thereafter there is little sign of dualist belief in the West, apart from some fitful and dubious examples in Thuringia in the sixteenth

* I am grateful to the Wolfson Foundation for a grant which enabled me both to study the Doat collection at the *Bibliothèque Nationale* and to visit the sites of the castles possessed by these families in the south of France.

[1] This translation by W. L. Wakefield and A. P. Evans, *Heresies of the High Middle Ages*, 1969, 305, from the manuscript in the *Biblioteca Malatestiana* at Cesena.
[2] H. C. Lea, *A History of the Inquisition in the Middle Ages*, i, Philadelphia 1887, 106.

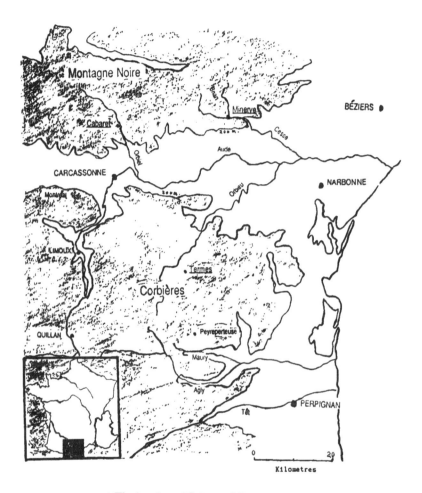

1 The location of Cabaret, Minerve and Termes.

century.[3] On the face of it this might be regarded as a kind of success; in fact, quite the opposite is the case. The Cathars thrived when their organisation was underpinned by the powerful network of interlinked family structures of the Occitan nobility. They declined when those structures were broken up, so that the old rural nobility was replaced by new colonials from the north or, like Olivier de Termes, adapted themselves to the new régime. Cathar leaders were then driven into exile or forced to exist on the run, no longer welcome at the noble courts of the Toulousain, Carcassès or Narbonnais, and in constant fear of betrayal to the Inquisition. The aim of this paper is to examine this network in the first half of the thirteenth century through the examples of three prominent lordships – those of Cabaret, Termes and Minerve (see fig. 1) – and by this means to try to show the relationship between social structure and heresy in the region.

In late August 1209, Simon de Montfort was chosen as leader of the Albigensian Crusade. It was an honour more apparent than real, for during the following months the great army which had assaulted Béziers and had massacred its inhabitants and which had forced the submission of Carcassonne, melted away. Crusades were essentially temporary phenomena, and once the spiritual benefits had been gained and some trophies seized, home exercised a very strong pull on the wanderer. However, in the autumn of 1209, this attraction was, for many, greatly reinforced by the prospect of future dangers for those who stayed. According to Guillaume de Tudela, a local cleric who was the author of the first part of the *Chanson de la Croisade Albigeoise*, Montfort was in a very difficult position. 'For few of his friends agreed to stay with him; most wished to return to the region of Paris: the mountains were savage and the gorges terrifying; they had no wish to be killed in this *pays*.'[4] The Cistercian chronicler, Pierre des Vaux-de-Cernay, is more specific. After his election, Montfort and the Abbot of Cîteaux tried to persuade the two leading crusaders, the Duke of Burgundy and the Count of Nevers, to prolong their stay, 'for there were still very many strong castles of the heretics to be conquered. There were, among others, three very strongly fortified places around Carcassonne, in which lived the chief enemies of our faith at that time: these were, on one side, Minerve, on another, the castle of Termes, and on another, Cabaret'.

Pierre, like Geoffroi de Villehardouin at Venice in 1202, believed that if only the entire army could have been assembled, all would have been well. 'The army of the crusaders which was at the siege of Carcassonne was so large and strong that, if they had wished to go on and together pursue the enemies of the orthodox faith, they would not have found anybody to resist them and

---

[3] See C. P. Clasen, 'Medieval Heresies of the Reformation', *Church History* xxxii, 1963, 392-414.
[4] *La Chanson de la Croisade Albigeoise*, ed. and trans. E. Martin-Chabot, i, *La Chanson de Guillaume de Tudèle*, Paris 1931 (henceforth *Chanson*), 36. 89.

2 Termes: views from the castle: (i) looking east; (ii) looking north-east.

XI

would have acquired the whole land in a short time.' The devil, however, had prevented this by sowing dissent between the Duke of Burgundy and the Count of Nevers.[5]

But Béziers and Carcassonne, although large and defended by formidable walls, were both set in relatively accessible country, in which a large army could hope to operate with some success. The task which faced Simon de Montfort was quite different, as Pierre himself realised when he first saw Termes in August 1210 (see pl. 2). 'The castle of Termes is in the territory of Narbonne, about five leagues from Carcassonne. It was of such astonishing and unbelievable strength that to human eyes it seemed almost impregnable. Indeed, it was sited on the summit of a high mountain upon a great and natural rock and completely surrounded by the most deep and inaccessible ravines, in which flowed the water which surrounded the castle. The rocks surrounding these valleys were so great and, as I have already said, unclimbable, that, if anyone wished to go up to the castle, it would be necessary for him to precipitate himself into the abyss and then, as I have said, to crawl towards the sky. Moreover, near the castle, a stone's throw away, situated on the summit of a rock, was a fortified tower, small but very strong, which is commonly called Termenet. The castle of Termes, thus sited, could only be approached from one side, since from that side the rocks were smaller and more accessible.'[6] According to Guillaume de Tudela, its defenders were entirely confident: 'Raymond, the lord of Termes, did not think them (the crusaders) worth a button; for he did not believe that one could ever see a castle as strong as this . . . If the Lord God had not sent illness to them, as he did in giving them dysentery, they would never have been taken.'[7] Montfort brought a large and impressive army to the siege, but as the weeks passed with little effect upon the defenders, morale sank and some contingents began to leave. Pierre des Vaux-de-Cernay reflects a deepening gloom at the prospect of a winter siege: 'Moreover, winter was imminent, which in those parts was usually very severe. Indeed, in the mountains in which Termes was situated, as we have already said, the deluges of rain, the whirling of the winds, the abundance of snow, made this a place cold beyond measure and almost uninhabitable.'[8]

Cabaret, set above the valley of the Orbiel in the Black Mountains to the north of Carcassonne, occupied a similarly dramatic site (see pl. 3). 'Even if all the men in the world assembled to besiege it,' said Guillaume de Tudela, 'the people of the castle would have given them less concern than a peeled apple.' It only submitted, he says, because of God's will, against which no city

[5] Pierre des Vaux-de-Cernay, *Hystoria Albigensis*, ed. P. Guébin and E. Lyon, 3 vols., Paris 1926-39 (henceforth *VC*), i, 108-9. 112-14.
[6] *VC*, 171. 173-4.
[7] *Chanson*, 56. 133-7.
[8] *VC*, 187-8. 190.

5

3 Lastours, looking north. Cabaret is at the north end of the ridge.

**4** Minerve: (i) gorge of the River Brian, looking north; (ii) gorge of the River Cesse, looking north-east.

or castle could hold out.[9] Indeed, the countryside around Cabaret was so difficult that even men from neighbouring lordships could get lost. Pierre des Vaux-de-Cernay describes how the Count of Toulouse sent men from Castelnaudary to regain Cabaret from the crusaders to whom its lord, Pierre-Roger, had submitted in April 1211. The distance was only five leagues, yet 'by the disposition of divine clemency, they lost the way which led to Cabaret and, straying for a long time into impassable country, were unable to find the castle of Cabaret, and therefore after prolonged wandering they returned to the castles from which they had come'.[10]

As for the castle of Minerve (see pl. 4), according to Guillaume de Tudela, it 'does not sit on the plain, but (that Faith may assist me!) on a high mountain: there is not as far as the Spanish mountains, a stronger castle, except those of Cabaret and Termes . . . Guillaume de Minerve (its lord) took his repose and had an agreeable time there, (and) was enclosed there with all his company'.[11] Pierre des Vaux-de-Cernay describes how it was 'surrounded by very deep and natural valleys'. These ravines, created by the Rivers Cesse and Brian, were of such a kind, says Pierre, that one body of besiegers was unable to bring help to another without exposing itself to very great dangers.[12] Again Guillaume de Tudela could see only the hand of God in its fall. 'If it had been the King of Morocco with his Saracens making the siege, by Saint Catherine, he would not have done damage worth more than an *angevine*; but against the army of Christ, the sovereign judge of the human race, there are no rocks, however high or steep, nor castle perched on a mountain which can protect (themselves).'[13]

The political, social and religious characteristics of this region owe much to this spectacular topography. In the early thirteenth century the lordships of Cabaret, Minerve and Termes were typical: relatively independent of higher overlordship, strongly linked together by intermarriage, governed by apparently antiquated inheritance systems which often determined that patrimonies should be shared by co-heirs rather than descending in a single line, and markedly anti-Catholic and pro-Cathar in their religious sympathies.

During the twelfth century the most important territorial rulers, the counts of Toulouse and their rivals, the Trencavel family, *vicomtes* of Béziers, north of the Pyrenees, and the kings of Aragon to the south, had been unable to impose their overlordship upon the castellans of the Black Mountains and the Pyrenean foothills to a degree at all comparable with their counterparts in the gentler countryside of the north. Here, among others, by the late twelfth

[9] *Chanson*, 65-6. 158-63.
[10] *VC*, 260. 259.
[11] *Chanson*, 49. 116-19.
[12] *VC*, 152. 156.
[13] *Chanson*, 48. 115-16.

century, the counts of Anjou, the dukes of Normandy and, above all, the Capetian kings, had succeeded in curbing the independence of their lesser vassals. In one sense, therefore, Montfort's problems were not dissimilar to those of the Capetians, Philip I and Louis VI, a century earlier in the Ile-de-France, but with the added difficulty that the castellans whom he had to overcome had entrenched themselves in castles which improved upon some of the most formidable natural defences in Europe. Raymond de Termes, for instance, according to Pierre des Vaux-de-Cernay, 'placed such confidence in the fortifications of his castle that he used to fight sometimes with the king of Aragon, sometimes with the count of Toulouse, and sometimes with his own lord, namely the *vicomte* of Béziers'.[14] This confidence made the lords of Termes equally determined to protect their economic position from encroachments by their overlords. In the late twelfth century claims to half the products of the mines of Polairac by the *vicomte* of Béziers had resulted in conflict with Raymond de Termes, even though theoretically these products appertained to the suzerain of the lands in which they were found. In 1191 the Trencavel lords had to settle for a quarter.[15]

The *vicomtes* had similar problems with the lords of Cabaret. Although they clearly accepted the Trencavels as their overlords and indeed Pierre-Roger and his brother Jourdain are listed among the principal vassals of Roger II, *vicomte* of Béziers, in 1191 and 1194, past history suggests that this involved little real diminution of power. Some time before 1153, for instance, the lords of Cabaret had added a third castle – that of Surdespine – to the two that they already possessed along their rocky ridge above the River Orbiel at Lastours. Raymond Trencavel had little alternative but to accept this, even though it evidently strengthened an already powerful position. 'He gave them license to build and have a castle in *castlar de Surdaspina*, as the lord Roger formerly gave this castle to them, and if by chance they will have erected a fortification in this *castlar*, saving the fidelity and jurisdiction of Raymond Trencavel and his descendants they should make and hold it there, and putting aside all opportunities for harm, they should swear faithfully to him and his posterity for it.'[16] The site had been fortified as early as the sixth century;[17] there was little chance of undermining this position in the twelfth century, even when its lords built adulterine castles.

These castellans were reluctant to give up this independence to anybody, even under the considerable military pressure exerted by Simon de Montfort. According to Pierre des Vaux-de-Cernay, Pierre-Roger de Cabaret, Raymond de Termes and Aimery de Montréal approached Peter II of Aragon, with the

[14] *VC*, 172. 174.
[15] C. Devic and J. Vaissete, *Histoire générale de Languedoc*, ed. A. Molinier *et al.* (henceforth *HGL*), vii (i), Toulouse 1879, 184.
[16] *HGL*, viii, col. 411; vi, 155; v, col. 1139.
[17] *Gregorii Episcopi Turonensis Historia Francorum*, ed. W. Arndt, in *MGH, Scriptorum Rerum Merovingicarum* i, Hanover 1884, 8. 30, 345.

intention of offering him homage, probably in May and June 1210. The reason was, says Pierre, 'so that by this means they could expel the count of Montfort from that land'. But the price demanded was apparently too high and the negotiations failed, emphasising the nature of the position enjoyed by such lords. 'The king, however, as soon as they came to him, wanted them to surrender the castle of Cabaret to him; moreover, he said that he would receive them as his men on the condition that they would render to him all their fortified places, as many times as he wished. When they had taken counsel among themselves the knights again asked the king to enter Montréal and (said) that they would render to him what they had promised. But the king in no way wished to enter except (on condition that) they should first do what he wished. Since they were unwilling to do it, each of them left the place of the conference in confusion.'[18] It is noticeable that when these lords were eventually forced out of their strongholds by the crusaders and apparently reconciled to orthodoxy, they were resettled in country much more amenable to control from above, such as the territories around Béziers.[19]

The political and economic independence of these nobles was emphasised when needed, by considerable military force, as the crusaders found to their cost. Pierre-Roger, lord of Cabaret, was particularly powerful. In November 1209 soldiers from Cabaret defeated some fifty men led by Bouchard de Marly, a close associate of Simon de Montfort, killing many of them and capturing Bouchard himself, so that he spent the next sixteen months in prison in the castle of Cabaret. Guillaume de Tudela estimated the defenders of Cabaret who had defeated them as numbering at least ninety, both horse and foot, as well as about forty archers.[20] The following summer Pierre-Roger, with the aid of his own vassals, such as Guillaume Cat and Raimond Mir and their relations, put together a force of over 300. At the end of July, 1210, Montfort had assembled siege machines and other equipment outside the walls of Carcassonne, preparatory to the planned attack on Termes. Pierre-Roger and his men twice attempted to destroy them during night raids, although they were eventually beaten off.[21] The failure of this attack did not deter them from further forays. When Montfort's army set itself to besiege Termes, it was harassed day and night, says Pierre, by the defenders of Cabaret, 'the

[18] *VC*, 148-9. 152-3. Peter II here seems to be trying to apply the principle of rendability in which the lord could take over a castle whenever and for as long as it suited him, but without diminishing his vassal's rights to it. This policy was being used with some success by Philip II in the north, but it was unacceptable to the lord of Cabaret, a point which underlines the independence of these mountain lords. See C. Coulson, 'Fortress policy in Capetian Tradition and Angevin Practice: aspects of the conquest of Normandy by Philip II', in *Anglo-Norman Studies VI, Proceedings of the Battle Conference 1983*, ed. R. A. Brown, Woodbridge 1984, 13-38. My thanks to Richard Eales for drawing my attention to this point.
[19] *VC*, 157. 161.
[20] *Chanson*, 41. 102-5; *VC*, 123. 127.
[21] *Chanson*, 54-5. 126-31; *VC*, 169. 172.

principal and most cruel enemies of the Christian religion at that time'.[22] The ironic epitaph on Simon de Montfort, so strikingly expressed by the anonymous author of the second part of the *Chanson* is often quoted and makes dramatic reading,[23] but it should not be overlooked that his opponents were equally ruthless. There seems no reason to doubt Pierre des Vaux-de-Cernay's description of atrocities inflicted on prisoners by Pierre-Roger's troops: 'by night and day they went round the public roads and, whichever of our men they were able to find, either condemned them to a most foul death or, in contempt of the Lord and us, sent them back to the army with their eyes, noses and other members most cruelly mutilated'.[24] Bouchard de Marly, captured in the skirmish already mentioned, was not held in comfortable captivity, but imprisoned in irons for sixteen months, irons which had to be struck off by a blacksmith.[25] The elaborate courtesies supposedly surrounding his release, preliminary to Pierre-Roger's submission to Montfort in April 1211, seem superficial and contrived in this context.

Not surprisingly, since it lacked strong overall authority, this was often an unstable and lawless society. The chronicler Guillaume de Puylaurens, chaplain to Raymond VII of Toulouse, although not pro-Cathar, was brought up in the Toulousain and knew well the mode of life of the region. He characterised it as a land of 'brigands, *routiers*, robbers, homicides, adulterers and manifest usurers'.[26] A comparison with the Normandy of Duke Robert as seen by Orderic Vitalis a century before is revealing. 'The whole province was in disorder; troops of bandits were at large in the villages and all over the countryside, and robber bands pillaged the weak mercilessly. Duke Robert made no attempt to bring the malefactors to justice, and for eight years under the weak duke scoundrels were free to treat the innocent with the utmost hostility . . . Crimes of arson, rapine, and murder were committed daily, and the wretched populace bewailed its unspeakable misfortunes.'[27] Any suzerain wishing to impose his control over the southern mountain lands therefore needed not only a long purse to sustain the large forces and the extensive equipment needed for sieges, but also a strong nerve to operate in country in which ambushes and guerilla warfare were second nature to its inhabitants. The slowness of the progress made by the suzerains of the south during the twelfth century in comparison with their northern counterparts is surely more related to the nature of the terrain which made men like Pierre-Roger so difficult to subordinate, rather than to the idea that the south was insufficiently 'feudalised'. As Elizabeth Brown has pointed out, all rulers wanted to

---

[22] *VC*, 173. 175-6.
[23] *Chanson* iii, 208. 228-9.
[24] *VC*, 173. 176.
[25] *Chanson*, 63. 156-9.
[26] *Chronica magistri Guillelmi de Podio Laurentii*,ed. and trans. J. Duvernoy, Paris 1976, 24-5.
[27] *OV* iv, 147.

establish their control as effectively as they could and, to this end they utilised whatever means were available to them.[28] While the vertical links were relatively weak, horizontal ties were far stronger for, naturally, these families intermarried. Witness-lists to charters and records of homages in the twelfth century, together with inquisitorial depositions in the thirteenth century, reveal a network of formidable complexity.[29] The genealogies of the three families in question underline this point, for they show that the more northerly lordships of Cabaret and Minerve were strongly bound up with the important families of the Corbières in the Pyrenean foothills, in that the lords of Cabaret had married into the families of Niort and Peyrepertuse, while sometime before 1191, Guillaume de Minerve had married Rixovende de Termes, sister of Raymond de Termes.[30] The lordships themselves were sometimes held by co-seigneurs. At Cabaret, Pierre-Roger shared with Jourdain de Cabaret, who was probably his younger brother. Jourdain himself had, among other possessions, a *castrum* at Sallèles in the Orbiel Valley.[31] Termes, while apparently unified at the time of the crusade, had been divided in the past. An arbitration of 1163, for instance, by *vicomte* Raymond Trencavel, had apportioned two-thirds to Raymond de Termes, and a third to his brother Guillaume. Rixovende, their sister, was to share Raymond's part.[32]

This was the society which the pope and, in his train, the crusaders, believed had become thoroughly infected by heresy. Pierre des Vaux-de-Cernay provides striking pen portraits of the lords of Cabaret, Minerve and Termes and their vassals from the point of view of an outsider committed to the cause of the crusade. Cabaret was 'a fountain of heresy' and its lord, Pierre-Roger, 'a veteran of evil days' who was 'a heretic and manifest enemy of the Church'. Guillaume de Minerve, despite his capitulation and the grant of a new lordship near Béziers, 'not long after, breaking the fidelity he had promised to God and the count, . . . joined up with the enemies of the faith'. Raymond de Termes was 'an old man twisted in reprobate feeling and a manifest heretic'. Citing Luke 18.4, he concluded, 'if we can sum up his malice, he neither feared God nor respected man'.[33]

These descriptions of specific individuals fit into a context of what orthodox ecclesiastics saw as a total lack of respect for the Church and its institutions. According to Guillaume de Puylaurens, 'if the clergy went out in public, they hid their timid tonsures by bringing over their hair from the back of the head,

[28] See E. A. R. Brown, 'The Tyranny of a Construct: Feudalism and Historians of Medieval Europe', *American Historical Review* lxxix, 1974, 1063-88.
[29] See M. C. Barber, 'Women and Catharism', *Reading Medieval Studies* iii, 1977, 45-62, and A. Termens, 'Généalogie de la Maison de Termes', *Cahiers d'Études Cathares* xxxviii, 1987, 38-57.
[30] *HGL* viii, cols. 412-14.
[31] *HGL* vii (ii), cols. 222, 329.
[32] *HGL* v, col. 1277.
[33] *VC*, 123. 127; 157. 161; 172. 174.

and the nobles rarely offered their children to the clergy. But they presented the sons of their dependents to the churches in which they perceived there were tithes, and the bishops made clerks such as they were able according to circumstances'.[34] Orderic Vitalis's view of Norman anarchy under Duke Robert is not very different. 'They sorely abused Holy Church, seizing by violence or devastating the properties which their worthy ancestors had freely given. The ruined monasteries lamented; monks and nuns suffered great privation. As these outrages spread like the plague no honour or reverence was shown to consecrated persons or things.'[35] In the south however, according to Guillaume de Puylaurens, the situation had passed beyond anti-clericalism and noble greed into one of active support for heresy. 'The same nobles, in abusive contempt of their lordship, at their wish and without opposition from anyone, adhered to one or other of the heretics. The heretics were held in such respect that they had cemeteries in which they publicly buried those whom they had hereticated, from whom they received complete beds and clothes. More was left to them than to the people of the Church; they went neither to ecclesiastical offices nor provided *tailles*.'[36] According to Raymond V, count of Toulouse, it was a pattern already well-established forty years before the coming of the crusaders. In 1177 he wrote: 'This putrid disease of heresy has indeed prevailed to such an extent . . . that it has divided wife from husband, son from father, daughter-in-law from father-in-law . . .'. He lamented that '. . . against an evil so great and of such a kind I know my strength to be deficient'.[37]

In the first place, therefore, the structure of the Church in these regions was weak, for it had no strong secular authority upon which it could rely as an ally, leaving it open to the more predatory local nobles. Such nobles were not peculiar to the south; it was simply that a social and political structure had persisted which placed no effective restraints upon them. Georges Duby has shown that such circumstances were fairly general in eleventh-century France[38], but for the reasons already suggested, this situation continued in the south into the late twelfth century, leaving a vacuum which from the 1170s at least, came to be filled by heretical preachers, welcomed by some for their conviction and sincerity, and by others because they made few material demands upon seculars. It seems that Catharism was coming to replace the Catholic Church as a framework for social control in a society that, in many other ways, was deficient in this respect. Guillaume de Puylaurens claimed

[34] Puylaurens, 24-5.
[35] *OV* iv, 147.
[36] Puylaurens, 24-7.
[37] Gervase of Canterbury, *Chronica*, ed. W. Stubbs, in *The Historical Works of Gervase of Canterbury*, i, RS 73, 1879, 270 (letter to the General Chapter of the Cistercians).
[38] See G. Duby, *The Three Orders. Feudal Society Imagined*, trans. C. Postan, 1980, part 3.

that 'if any man of war going along a road with them (*i.e.* heretics) was found by his enemies, he was protected (*tutus*)'.[39]

This seems to have operated not only in the nobles' relations with each other, but also as an aid to their own local domination. Raymond V wrote in 1177 that 'the nobles of my lands, already having caught the infection of infidelity, have succumbed, and with them a very great multitude of men have been corrupted in the faith, so that I do not have the strength to overcome it'.[40] Looked at in this way, Catharism was an élitist heresy imposed from above by a local nobility as an aid to its continued social pre-eminence. For various reasons this nobility found the Catholic Church of the late twelfth century inadequate for this purpose, yet, partly because of their own religious needs and partly because of self-interest, could not have conceived of a secular society in which religious functions and services were not provided. Not surprisingly the Cathar ministry recruited heavily from these families, just as the Catholic hierarchy did elsewhere. Catharism could have taken root in the north if eleventh-century circumstances had continued to prevail, but the powerful alliance between the ecclesiastical and the secular, of which the identification of the Capetian kings with Saint Denis is the archetype, ensured that no such development could take place. Indeed, it has, on the contrary, recently been argued that in the north-west persecution of heretics was one weapon used by the new administrative régimes to consolidate their power.[41]

Depositions taken before the inquisitors at Toulouse in 1243 and 1244 show in detail how a castle like Cabaret functioned as a centre for Catharism. Two witnesses who deposed within a few days of each other towards the end of 1243 (on 14 November and 7 December respectively) are particularly interesting. The first, a knight called Raymond Aiffre, retained detailed recollections of the 1220s during the period before the Treaty of Paris of 1229 placed Cabaret in the hands of royal agents. Raymond Aiffre came from the lordship of Laure in the Minervois, itself a dependency of Cabaret. He had been present at Cabaret in 1223 when Pierre Isarn, Cathar bishop of Carcassonne, and his companion, had preached there, and had been among those who 'adored' them, which in effect meant an exchange of blessings and a kiss of peace. Among others present on this occasion were the lords of the castle, Pierre de Laure and Pierre-Roger de Cabaret, as well as Raymond de Cabaret, who was probably another brother. Raymond Aiffre had also seen heretics preach there on other occasions and had indeed been present when, in 1227, the perfect Guiraud Abith had administered the *consolamentum* to a dying knight, Frédol de Miraval, in a house within the castle. Frédol was his own nephew and there were several other members of the family present at the bedside.

---

[39] Puylaurens, 26-7.
[40] Gervase of Canterbury, 270-1.
[41] See R. I. Moore, *The Formation of a Persecuting Society. Power and Deviance in Western Europe 950-1250*, Oxford 1987, 134, 152-3.

Raymond Aiffre was a Cathar believer, while his wife, Bernarda, received the *consolamentum* at the castle of Roquefort shortly before her death.[42] The second witness was Gaucelin de Miraval of Puylaurens, who gave an account of this world a generation earlier, for he himself had received the *consolamentum* in 1199, a decade before the beginning of the crusade. It had been administered at Cabaret by Pons Bernard, a *bonhomme* who lived in a house within the castle. He had, according to his own witness, taken this step, 'led by fear because he had killed a certain man'. When Gaucelin had confirmed that he wished 'to return to God and the Gospel', he promised henceforth not to eat meat, eggs, cheese or any oil, except for olive oil and fish, and that 'he would not swear nor lie nor engage in sexual intercourse, nor desert the sect for fear of fire, or water, or any other type of death'. The heretics then placed their hands and a book on the witness's head and made several genuflections and prayed, while Gaucelin himself said the Lord's Prayer in accordance with their rite. Several male and female heretics were present at his *consolamentum*, which was followed by the 'adoration' and a meal at which the bread and drink were blessed. Both his mother and his wife had been *perfectae*, although he himself had remained a Cathar for only two years, one of which he spent at Cabaret. During that time the Cathar deacon, Arnaud Hot, was a frequent visitor to the castle where he preached sermons to audiences which included Pierre-Roger, lord of the castle, and his son, Pierre de Laure, as well as other named lords and knights from the region.[43]

Other witnesses testify to the continuity of Cathar influence at Cabaret, broken only during the Montfort presence between 1211 and 1223. Isarn de Hautpoul had been at Cabaret 'at the time of the war', apparently meaning c.1227. Many *faidit* knights, including Raymond de Cabaret, and male and female heretics here been there and they had listened to a sermon by Guiraud Abith, Cathar bishop of Carcassonne.[44] The presence of Guiraud Abith at this time was confirmed by another witness, Raymond de Miraval of Hautpoul, who said that Guiraud and other heretics 'openly kept their houses and preached frequently both in the streets and in the houses'. The lords of Miraval had been closely associated with the heretics, giving them food and shelter, while Raymond's father had been hereticated on his death-bed. At the time that the castle of Cabaret was to be handed over to the king and the Church, that is with the signing of the Treaty of Paris, he and his brother Bernard, together with Vasco de Laure and Vasco's squire, took two female heretics called Marcellina and Raymonde away from the castle and found them a hiding place in the village of La Tourette.[45] As this incident shows, Cabaret could no longer function as a haven after 1229 and by the 1230s those

[42] Bibliothèque Nationale, *Collection Doat* 23, fo. 80v-85.
[43] *Ibid.*, 23, fos. 106v-108v.
[44] *Ibid.*, 23, fos. 226-227v.
[45] *Ibid.*, 23, fos. 230v-235v.

who had lived and preached there were on the run. Jean Blanch d'Hautpoul, for instance, described how, in 1235, he had received three female heretics into his house and kept them there for four months before they had been moved on. These were Beatrice, sister of Roger de Cabaret, and her companions, Arsende and Raymonde, the last of whom was probably the same woman who had escaped from Cabaret before the hand-over to royal officials. Among those who came to visit the women were Roger's wife, Astruga, and the elderly Brunissende, wife of Pierre-Roger II, lord of Cabaret before and during the crusade.[46]

Witness to the presence of heretics at Minerve comes from Pierre des Vaux-de-Cernay rather than from depositions. When Guillaume de Minerve capitulated to Simon de Montfort on 22 July 1210, after a seven-week siege, Pierre describes how the count 'coming to the house where the heretics were congregated together, being a Catholic man and wishing all to be saved and to come to the acceptance of the truth, began to exhort them to convert to the Catholic faith. But when he had achieved almost nothing, he made them come out of the castle. There were 140 or more *perfecti*. A large fire was therefore prepared and all were thrown on to it; indeed, it was not necessary for our men to throw them since, being obstinate in their evil, all threw themselves on voluntarily . . .'. Only three women saved themselves, although the other inhabitants of the town were reconciled to the Church.[47] Guillaume de Tudela too describes how the many stubborn and foolish heretics there were recalcitrant and were burnt to death; 'not a brave chestnut was left'.[48]

At Termes Pierre des Vaux-de-Cernay discerned the mysterious hand of God in a series of events which led, in his view, to the just punishment of its lord, Raymond. Termes had proved extremely difficult to take, despite some successes against the settlements and fortifications outside its walls. However, in mid-October 1210, having run short of water, Raymond indicated that he was prepared to hand over the castle for the winter, only to renege on his promise the next day after an overnight downpour. Here is Pierre's interpretation: 'However, divine justice wished and provided for that delay in their surrender, as the outcome of the matter most manifestly proved. For God, the most just judge, did not wish that man who had brought so many and such great evils to His Holy Church (and would continue to do so still, if he could) to escape immune and unpunished after so great an exercise of cruelty: for, setting aside his other evils, for thirty years or more, as we have heard from persons dignified in the faith, divine sacraments were not celebrated in the church of the castle of Termes . . .'. Understandably, the defenders saw the downpour in a different light, as a sign of divine aid in their time of need, an idea that Pierre indignantly calls 'fatuous and wicked

---

[46] *Ibid.*, 23, fos. 239v-241.
[47] *VC*, 156. 160-1.
[48] *Chanson*, 49. 116-19.

presumption'. An attempt was made to reopen negotiations in which Bernard-Raymond de Roquefort, bishop of Carcassonne was prominent, since he came from the region and, indeed, his mother and brother, both heretics, were at that time inside the castle. The eventual abandonment of the castle on 22 November following an attack of dysentery, however, provided Pierre with the means of showing the subtle working of the hand of God.[49] Although lacking the detail available for Cabaret, inquisitorial depositions also indicate the presence of heretics at Termes, most notably Benoît de Termes, who may have been a brother of Raymond. Benoît eventually died in c.1241 after having received the *consolamentum* as long ago as 1207 and, during the 1220s, rising to become Cathar bishop of the Razès.[50]

These depositions and chronicles underline a fundamental point. The milieu of Catharism in the south was the *familia* in the broad sense which includes relatives, friends and other dependents, covering a wide social range. Not all members of the family were equally committed as the depositions concerning Cabaret show, but they were brought up in an environment in which Catharism was tolerated and accepted and probably did not trouble to pursue the logical implications of absolute dualism in the way which Catholic theologians had been trained to do.[51] Until these groupings were broken up, it was difficult to stamp out heresy, not only because some of its adherents were so totally committed that they were prepared to die for their beliefs, but also because it was an integral part of the social and institutional structure of the region.

Despite the successes of Montfort's forces in the three lordships under consideration it took time to smash this infrastructure. At Cabaret the Cathars were driven out by the submission of 1211, but they returned very quickly after 1223, for the lords of Cabaret still held lands and *castra*, and the clan still existed. Even though the old lord, Pierre-Roger II, died sometime after the loss of his castle in 1211, his two sons, Pierre de Laure and Pierre-Roger III, and his brother, Jourdain, one of the co-seigneurs of the castle, were still active, resurfacing in 1224 in support of the Trencavels. Pierre de Laure agreed to joint lordship of Cabaret with his uncle, Jourdain, at this time. However, Jourdain took seriously an attempt to come to an agreement with royal agents in 1226 and thereafter was regarded as a traitor to the cause. Pierre de Laure and Pierre-Roger nevertheless fared no better, for they lost all their lands after the treaty of 1229, living as *faidit* lords during the 1230s before joining the hapless Trencavel revolt of 1240.[52] The royal inquiry of 1259-62

[49] *VC*, 182-3. 185-7.
[50] *Doat*, 23, fo. 270v; 24, fo. 100v. See A. Termens, 'L'évêque cathare du Razès: Benoît de Termes', *Cahiers d'Études Cathares* xxxviii, 1987, 44-59. Termens finds no proof of relationship to the lords of Termes, 44-5.
[51] See M. Roquebert, 'Le catharisme comme tradition dans la "familia" languedocienne', *Cahiers de Fanjeaux* xx, 1985, 221-41.
[52] See E. Griffe, *Le Languedoc Cathare au temps de la Croisade (1209-1229)*, Paris 1973, 208-9.

shows that Jourdain's son, also called Jourdain, eventually accepted possessions at Villarzel-Cabardès and Villarlong, although he never regained the bulk of his father's possessions in the Cabardès.[53]

After the horror of the mass burnings of the *perfecti* outside his castle, Guillaume de Minerve was, along with his followers, apparently reconciled to the Church and, although deprived of his castle and fiefs, compensated by lands near Béziers. He joined the Hospitallers in 1215, entering their house at Campagnolles, but it was a short-lived conversion.[54] By the summer of 1216, perhaps inspired by the increased level of resistance to Montfort, he was back in the fray, fighting the crusaders near Beaucaire. Three years later he was present at the siege of Marmande opposing the forces of Prince Louis.[55] These activities bear witness to the extent of his resistance, but he never regained his fief in the Corbières, and therefore had no chance of recreating the structure that had sustained heresy. Raymond de Termes had even less opportunity. His failure to keep his word to Simon de Montfort led to harsh retaliation. Pierre des Vaux-de-Cernay says that he was captured during the flight of 22 November 1211 and brought before Montfort. 'The count, receiving (him) like a splendid gift, did not in fact kill him, but caused him to be thrust into a dungeon in the tower of Carcassonne, where for many years he sustained the punishment and miseries which he deserved.'[56] No more is heard of him and he presumably died in prison.

After the treaty of 1229 these three lordships were entrusted to royal castellans. However, under Louis IX's policy of pacification and reconciliation, two of the three families gained partial restitutions. Guillaume de Minerve's son, also called Guillaume, and Olivier de Termes, Raymond's son, eventually accepted royal control and took part in Louis's crusade to Egypt and Palestine between 1248 and 1254, although both Olivier and his brother Bernard had played a prominent role in southern resistance movements in the 1230s and early 1240s.[57] In 1254 Guillaume de Minerve received 50 *livres* of *rente* in fief, assigned on lands confiscated from his father's lordship. He had continued the family connection with Termes, having married Blanche, sister of Olivier and Bernard, and in 1253 she too received 60 *livres* of *rente*, in her case assigned on her brother's confiscated property. However, this marriage only produced daughters and the family had died out in the direct male line by 1266.[58] Olivier de Termes received some of the family lands back while still on crusade in 1250, including the castle of Aguilar

[53] *HGL* vii (ii), cols. 221-2, 324-30.
[54] *HGL* viii, cols. 663-5.
[55] *Chanson*, ii, *Le Poème de l'Auteur Anonyme*, Paris 1957, 167. 176-7; 169. 190-1; iii, Paris 1961, 214. 304-5.
[56] *VC*, 189. 192.
[57] See A. Peal, 'Olivier de Termes and the Occitan Nobility in the Thirteenth Century', *Reading Medieval Studies* xii, 1986, 109-30.
[58] *HGL* vi, 840.

and revenues to the value of 250 *l.t.*, in recognition of the fact that he had now become a devoted and loyal servant of the king.[59]

Until the last quarter of the thirteenth century, the northern lords and royal castellans who replaced the long-standing families of these lands sought actively to suppress heresy and the remaining Cathar ministers were deprived of the opportunity for public preaching and continuous residence that had been offered them in the past. However, it is worth concluding with one ironic footnote. Friedlander's researches have found that from *c.*1275 Cathar *bonhommes*, in the persons of the perfects Guillaume Pagès and Bernard Coste, were once more seen at Cabaret, now protected by royal castellans resentful of the activities of the Inquisition.[60] It was too late to promote an effective Cathar revival, but it is testimony to the importance of this type of socio-political unit in the maintenance of heresy.

The role of these families in the protection and promotion of Catharism shows that there is no single social model which can explain the spread of heresy. It is clear though that heresy was not exclusively an urban phenomenon, accessible as the towns were to outside influence through the links created by the trade routes, but that it could also be sustained by the quite different environment of the rural mountain *castra*. This suggests that dualist belief had a latent existence in most medieval minds but that the key element is that in areas in which both the secular and ecclesiastical authorities perceived it to be a threat and therefore worked together to suppress it, it would make little headway. However, in the fractured society of the south no such common perception existed; it was only when the secular lords who tolerated the Cathars were either removed and replaced or coerced into acceptance of orthodoxy that dualism was overcome.

---

[59] *HGL* viii, cols. 1276-7.
[60] See A. Friedlander, 'Les agents du roi face aux crises de l'hérésie en Languedoc vers 1250-vers 1350', *Cahiers de Fanjeaux* xx, 1985, 199-220.

# XII

# Supplying the Crusader States: The Role of the Templars

The Military Orders, Richard of Mepham, dean of Lincoln, told Pope Gregory X in 1274, have the most abundant possessions everywhere throughout the world. If all these or even the greater part of them were properly directed, then they would be sufficient for the aid of the Holy Land towards which everybody labors so solicitously. "Many kings and princes," he added confidently, "publicly attest to this."[1] He was neither the first nor the last to criticize the use which the Military Orders made of their resources. Over forty years before, another armchair critic, the monk Matthew Paris, writing from the safety of St. Albans, had complained that the Military Orders ingested so much revenue from Christendom that it was "as if they plunged it into the abyss of the Lower World."[2]

Such criticisms became commonplace in the second half of the thirteenth century, but in fact it seems unlikely that many of these writers had any real idea what the sustenance of the crusader lands actually entailed.[3] To read, for instance, the Norman lawyer Pierre Dubois, writing in about 1306, is to be left with the impression that he thought trade and shipping between the West and the Levant to have been of negligible importance in the twelfth and thirteenth centuries.[4] In fact, the Military Orders bore huge financial burdens, for, among many other tasks, they were required to maintain and garrison castles; ship supplies of foodstuffs, clothing, armaments and horses; provide recruits to replace losses in battle and from old age; defend, transport, finance and ransom pilgrims and crusaders; and hire mercenaries. These duties had become

1  Maurice Powicke and Christopher Cheney, eds., *Councils and Synods with other documents relating to the English Church* 2, *AD 1205-1313* (Oxford, 1964), p. 815. Richard of Mepham, of course, had a case to make, for the kernel of his presentation was that the English clergy and people were over-taxed, an allegation which brought him papal censure and suspension from office.
2  Matthew Paris, *Chronica Majora*, ed. Henry R. Luard, RS 57 (London, 1872-83), 3:178.
3  See Alan J. Forey, "The Military Orders in the Crusading Proposals of the Late-Thirteenth and Early-Fourteenth Centuries," *Traditio* 36 (1980), esp. 324-329.
4  Pierre Dubois, *De recuperatione Terre Sancte*, ed. Charles V. Langlois, Collection de textes pour servir à l'étude et à l'enseignement de l'histoire (Paris, 1891), pp. 14-15.

XII

particularly heavy in the mid- and late-thirteenth century, for the diminished area of crusader territory, together with the losses incurred as some of the trade routes were diverted northwards, eroded income and supplies. A stream of letters from Outremer testify to the increasing depth of the crisis, and it has been shown that only the Military Orders could hope to sustain the Latins as, one after another, the secular lordships of the east faced financial ruin.[5] It is no coincidence that there are signs of increased pressure being applied by the administrators of Templar lands in the West from the 1220s and 1230s, pressure which did nothing to improve the Order's image.[6] However, this was only the culmination of a long process, for crusading had been ruinously expensive from the very beginning.[7] Small wonder that it seemed to Matthew Paris that money was disappearing into a bottomless pit.

The extent of the burden carried by the Templars can be demonstrated by looking at two of the more obvious needs: manpower and horses. After the battle of Ḥaṭṭīn, Terricus, grand commander and acting master, described how scarcely any brethren had escaped, for 230 had been beheaded and another 60 had already been killed at the Springs of Cresson on 1 May.[8] Others must have been killed at Ḥaṭṭīn itself, while still further losses must have been sustained defending castles like Safed, which held out for nearly a year after Ḥaṭṭīn. Indeed, at one time or another during the twelfth and thirteenth centuries the Templars garrisoned at least fifty-three castles or fortified places in the crusader states ranging from massive edifices like 'Athlit to small watchtowers in which pilgrims could take refuge. They had charge of castles as early as c. 1137 in the Amanus and from 1149 in Palestine.[9] They came to hold a substantial number of buildings in all the major cities, including Jerusalem, Caesarea, Acre, Tyre, Gibelet (Jubail), Tripoli, Tortosa, Jabala, and Antioch. They were particularly prominent in the north, for they dominated the region around Tortosa, where they were established by 1152, while north of Antioch they held an area of quasi-autonomy, from Port Bonel and La Roche de Roissel on the coast, inland to Baghras, Darbsak and La Roche Guillaume.[10]

5  Jonathan Riley-Smith, *The Feudal Nobility and the Latin Kingdom of Jerusalem, 1174-1277* (London, 1973), pp. 28-32.
6  See, for instance, the activities of the Templar administrators of the two houses at Provins: Victor Carrière, *Histoire et cartulaire des Templiers de Provins* (Paris, 1919), Nos. 16, 30, pp. 53-54, 63-64.
7  See Jonathan Riley-Smith, *The First Crusade and the Idea of Crusading* (London, 1986), pp. 130-134.
8  "Benedict of Peterborough," *Gesta Henrici II et Ricardi I*, ed. William Stubbs, RS 49 (London, 1867), 2:13-14. RRH No. 660.
9  See Jonathan Riley-Smith, "The Templars and the Teutonic Knights in Cilician Armenia," in *The Cilician Kingdom of Armenia*, ed. T.S.R. Boase (Edinburgh and London, 1978), pp. 92-97. WT 17.12, p. 776.
10  See Claude Cahen, *La Syrie du Nord à l'époque des croisades* (Paris, 1940), pp. 582-621, and Riley-Smith, "Templars and Teutonic Knights," pp. 92-93. It is more accurate to describe the Military Orders as possessing a series of buildings in the ports of Outremer rather than as holding distinct and exclusive quarters, as has sometimes been said, for in Acre "enclaves étrangères" penetrated what were once thought to be compact quarters.

Manpower, however, was of limited value without a constant supply of horses. The Military Orders were particularly vulnerable to losses because of their exposed position at the front and rear of the crusader columns. During Richard I's march from Acre in September 1191, the army was continually assailed; 3 September was especially gruelling. "The Templars," says the author of the *Itinerarium,* "on this day lost so many horses as a consequence of the attacks of the Turks at the rear, that they almost gave up hope."[11] The increasing adoption of long mailed coats for horses from the late twelfth century must have reduced such losses, but this in turn needs to be balanced against the cost, especially as it appears that most metal goods had to be imported into the Latin East.[12] Philip of Novara still thought that the sight of a German knight with a horse accoutred in this way sufficiently unusual for comment in 1232.[13] The Templars therefore made the provision of horses their especial concern, a fact noted by visitors to the East. In the early 1160s John of Würzburg observed that the Order in Jerusalem had space for 2,000 horses or 1,500 camels, while ten years later the German pilgrim, Theoderich, claimed that the stables in the Temple of Solomon could take 10,000 horses.[14]

Theoderich was perhaps trying too hard to amaze his readers, but it seems likely that John of Würzburg's figure represents a minimum, for the Templar Rule is full of references to horses, colts, pack animals, and camels, and it contains clauses on the number allowed to each official, their pasturage, fodder and upkeep, purchase and sale. All knights were allowed three horses, and squires and serjeants one each, although in the French versions of the Rule, produced when the Order had become richer, knights could, at the discretion of the Master, have an additional horse and squire. High officials had four horses each, while the five serjeants who held key posts in Jerusalem had two. Secular knights serving *ad terminum* were to be supplied with a horse (for which they paid), to be replaced by the Order if it was lost in service. The importance of these animals is underlined by the regulation that both at compline and at matins each brother was required to go and check his horses and rectify any problems which may have arisen. Mules too were needed in quantity, for during the twelfth and thirteenth centuries there was a great increase in their use as pack

The Military Orders had less impact on Acre than the Italian maritime cities. See David Jacoby, "Les communes italiennes et les ordres militaires à Acre: aspects juridiques, territoriaux et militaires (1104-1187, 1191-1291)," in *Etat et colonisation au Moyen Age et à la Renaissance,* ed. Michel Balard (Lyon, 1989), pp. 193-214.

11  *Itinerarium peregrinorum et gesta regis Ricardi,* ed. William Stubbs, RS 38 (London, 1864), 1:257.

12  See John H. Pryor, *"In subsidium Terrae Sanctae:* Exports of Foodstuffs and War Materials from the Kingdom of Sicily to the Kingdom of Jerusalem, 1265-1284," *Asian and African Studies* 22 (1988), 127-146.

13  Philippe de Novare, *Mémoires, 1218-1243,* ed. Charles Kohler, Les Classiques Français du Moyen Age (Paris, 1913), p. 77.

14  *Johannis Wirzburgensis descriptio Terrae Sanctae,* in *Descriptiones Terrae Sanctae ex saec. VIII. IX. XII. et XV.,* ed. Titus Tobler (Leipzig, 1874), pp. 129-130. Theodericus, ed. Bulst, pp. 26-27.

XII

animals. According to the Rule, for instance, the commander of the city of Jerusalem was "obliged to have ten knights at his command to conduct and guard the pilgrims who go to the River Jordan... and to lead pack animals and to carry victuals and to bring back the pilgrims on the pack animals if need be." As the Rule makes clear, it was certainly possible to purchase horses and mules in the East,[15] but it is no more likely that local markets could produce sufficient numbers than that the Latin settlers could provide the Templars with an adequate supply of new recruits.

It was then imperative that the Order should create a network of support which would provide the backing to make this role viable and, from the Council of Troyes in 1129 onwards, vigorous efforts were made to recruit men and to establish commanderies in the West. The earliest leaders, Hugues de Payns and Geoffroi de Saint-Omer, together with some of their companions, embarked on a series of journeys in the West with these ends in mind. Between 1128 and 1130 Hugues alone traveled through Champagne, Anjou, Normandy, England and Scotland, and then back to Flanders, probably returning east via the Rhône Valley and Marseille. According to the entry in the Anglo-Saxon Chronicle, he collected more men than at any time since the First Crusade. Arnold of Torroja, the ninth Grand Master (1181-84), must have had similar aims in mind when, together with prominent crusade leaders, he set out on an embassy to the West in 1184. The intention was to alert Christian rulers and their people to the increasing threat presented by Saladin. The plan was to visit Italy, Germany, France, and England, but Arnold, already elderly, died at Verona in September 1184. In the last decade of the thirteenth century the Templars were still maintaining this policy. During 1294-95 Jacques de Molay, the last Grand Master, was in Italy, France, and England, visiting Boniface VIII in Rome and Philip IV in Paris. In 1306-07, at the request of Pope Clement V, he undertook a second visit, this time fatally for himself and his Order.[16]

By Molay's time the Grand Master was presiding over at least 970 houses, including commanderies and castles in both east and west, serviced by a membership which is unlikely to have been less than 7,000, excluding employees and dependants, who must have been seven or eight times that number.[17]

15  Henri de Curzon, ed., *La Règle du Temple*, Société de l'Histoire de France (Paris, 1886; repr. Geneva, 1977), clauses 51, 66, 77, 114, 121, 143, 283, 305.

16  On Hugues de Payns, see Malcolm Barber, "The Origins of the Order of the Temple," *Studia Monastica* 12 (1970), 234-236. On Arnold de Torroja, Radulf de Diceto, *Ymagines Historiarum*, ed. William Stubbs, RS 68 (London, 1876), 2:32, and Edouard de Barthélemy, ed., *Obituaire de la Commanderie du Temple de Reims*, in *Mélanges historiques. Choix de documents* 4, Collection de documents inédits sur l'histoire de France (Paris, 1882), p. 328. On Jacques de Molay, see Malcolm Barber, "James of Molay, The Last Grand Master of the Temple," *Studia Monastica* 14 (1972), 95-97, 108-109.

17  This figure is compiled from references to Templar houses and castles in a wide variety of sources. Major reference works for this include the maps and list in the *Grosser historischer Weltatlas*, 2: *Mittelalter* (Munich, 1970), maps 31a and b, p. 82 and R2-4; Emile Léonard, *Introduction au cartulaire manuscrit du Temple (1150-1317)* (Paris, 1930); Alan J. Forey, *The Templars in the Corona de Aragón* (London, 1973), p. 89; and David

318

Crusader sources suggest that, before Ḥaṭṭīn, the Templars had 600 or more knights in the East, in which case a figure of 2,000 serjeants, with perhaps 50 priests or chaplains, is not unreasonable.[18] A throwaway remark reportedly made by Clement V in February 1308 suggests that he thought that there were about 2,000 Templars in France at this time,[19] but as will be seen this figure is about 50% too low, for it seems unlikely that the Order could have functioned without much larger numbers of support personnel than frontline soldiers.

One possible way of estimating numbers might be to adopt the laborious method of counting heads, but not all the commanderies have left sufficient material to make this possible, nor does the existing evidence permit a figure to be produced for a distinct point in time. It is therefore necessary to find a figure which can be used as a basis for multiplication, but the problem is to find a "typical" house. Inventories of Templar property taken in 1307 show that many commanderies were simply small rural communities, run by perhaps two or three Templars, with a larger non-Templar staff.[20] Such houses must have formed the great majority in countries like France, the British Isles, and Italy, but interspersed with these were much larger houses like the great treasuries and administrative centers at Paris and London, while the fortified commanderies and castles of Aragon and Portugal would similarly have been much more heavily staffed.

More than one multiple is therefore necessary and this can be obtained by following the grouping of houses adopted by the Templars themselves. In some regions smaller houses seem to have been linked to a larger commanderie. Richerenches in the Vaucluse region of Provence seems to have been a house of the latter kind. It has a published cartulary which shows it to have been established as early as 1136.[21] The cartulary contains 262 documents, covering the period down to 1214, 249 of which refer by name to Templars present in the

Knowles and Richard Hadcock, *Medieval Religious Houses. England and Wales* (London, 1953), pp. 235-239. I am very grateful to Clive Porro for information on Portuguese houses. This map is intended to give a broad idea of the distribution of houses, but it represents only the present state of research and is not meant to be definitive.

18   WT 12.7, p. 554, giving 300 knights and presumably referring to the Kingdom of Jerusalem only. He says that the number of brothers other than knights was "almost infinite." Jean de Joinville, *Histoire de Saint-Louis,* ed. Natalis de Wailly (Paris, 1874), pp. 118-121, who claims that 280 Templars were killed in a single incident, that is the attack on Manṣūrah in February 1250. *The Itinerary of Benjamin of Tudela,* ed. and trans. Marcus Adler (London, 1907), p. 22, says that there were 300 knights quartered at the Temple of Solomon, c. 1169-71. On the proportion of knights to serjeants see the discussion in Raymond C. Smail, *Crusading Warfare 1097-1193* (Cambridge, 1956), pp. 89-91.

19   Heinrich Finke, *Papsttum und Untergang des Templerordens,* 2 (Münster, 1907), Nos. 74, 114.

20   For example, Léopold Delisle, *Etudes sur la condition de la classe agricole et l'état de agriculture en Normandie au moyen âge* (Paris, 1903), pp. 721-728, and Forey, *Aragón* (note 17 above), pp. 276-279.

21   Le Mis de Ripert-Monclar, ed., *Cartulaire de la Commanderie de Richerenches de l'Ordre du Temple (1136-1214)* (Paris-Avignon, 1907) [hereafter quoted *Cart. Rich.*], No. 128, pp. 121-122.

XII

house at that time. The numbers fluctuate in an arbitrary manner since in some transactions the presence of the preceptor and/or the "claviger" or treasurer is thought to be sufficient, whereas in others a much longer list of Templars is appended. As early as 1138 one document shows ten Templars at Richerenches; by 1163 there were as many as twenty brothers present. By c. 1180 it seems unlikely that the house had fewer than eighteen Templars in residence, a conservative figure based on an analysis of the names of the Templars mentioned and repeated in 1179 and 1180.[22]

According to Durbec, Richerenches had eight dependent houses,[23] perhaps similar to many of those shown in the trial inventories, with about three Templars in each. This little cluster of nine houses might then have contained about 42 Templars (i.e., 18 + 24). If such a calculation is applied to France as a whole on the basis that it had 660 houses,[24] divided into 73 main centers similar to Richerenches, with 587 dependencies, then a figure of 3,075 Templars is produced. It seems unlikely to have been lower than this, for Richerenches is exceptional in Provence in having as many as eight dependent houses.[25] The French houses, of course, are the majority, making up two-thirds of the total. Even so, if the overall figure of about 7,000 is accepted, this still leaves only about 1,300 Templars for houses in lands other than Outremer and France, regions which included some 250 houses. The Templar structure therefore seems to have provided slightly more than three support personnel to two frontline soldiers in the East, although since the number of non-Templar employees is very much greater, this may have been enough. It should be noted that this calculation assumes that Templars in Spain were all part of this support structure when of course some of them were evidently combatants as well.

To some extent these houses were scattered at random because of the arbitary nature of donations, but given these constraints the Templar command does seem to have tried to impose a rational pattern. According to the Rule there were ten provinces: Jerusalem, Tripoli, and Antioch in the East, France, England, Poitou, Aragon, Portugal, Apulia, and Hungary in the West. It is, however, evident that the pattern and emphasis were adapted over time in ways not recorded in the Rule, presumably in accordance with perceived needs.[26] Over

---

22  *Cart. Rich.*, Nos. 2, 189, pp. 4-5, 168-169. In 1179 and 1180, 23 Templars are mentioned as being present more than once, although in all reference is made to 47 different Templars during this period. The apparently arbitary choice of 18 was made because this was the largest single figure in the documents covering these two years, No. 242, p. 215.

23  J.-A. Durbec, "Les Templiers en Provence, Formation des commanderies at répartition géographique de leurs biens," *Provence historique* 9 (1959), 14.

24  Léonard, *Introduction* (note 17 above), pp. 13-173.

25  In fact, some of the dependencies quickly developed the scope of their operations, so that it is probable that an estimate of only three Templars per house is too low: Durbec, "Templiers en Provence," p. 16.

26  *Règle* (note 15 above), clause 87. However, at the trial, for instance, Geoffroi de Charney, preceptor of Normandy, was evidently regarded as one of the more important leaders, despite the omission of Normandy from this list, while at various times during the twelfth century "the master of Provence and Spain" appears at, among other places, Richerenches, a division which does not accord with any of these provinces.

and above the provincial preceptors there was "a master on this side of the sea" (deça mer), who appears to have had general command in the West, although this office was transmuted into that of Visitor in c. 1250. Dr. Forey has shown, however, that this was not a simple change of title, for it coincided with a grouping of the provinces into those of France, England, and Germany on the one hand, and the Iberian lands on the other, with two separate hierarchies.[27]

By means of this network the Templars supplied the crusader states with men, money, horses, and goods. Manpower came through local houses which acted both as centers for recruitment and as departure points for secular crusaders. If the age-pattern shown on the graph (fig. 1), which is based upon the depositions of 115 Templars at Paris in 1307, is in any way typical, it suggests that Templars of military age were being sent to the East, while the Western commanderies were being manned by a high proportion of the middle-aged and the elderly.[28] An analysis of the 76 depositions made by the Templars interrogated in Cyprus in 1310 shows that only five had entered the Order in the Crusader States, four in Cyprus and one in Cilicia. As might be expected, most, that is 40 of them, joined in France, but the others were drawn from all over Latin Christendom, including Aragon, Castile, Portugal, England, Germany, Italy, Dalmatia, and the Morea.[29] Once in the East release from the obligation to serve there was not easily granted. Clause 93 of the Rule lays down the procedures to be followed if a Templar is to return to the West. Only illness or "the needs of the house" justified this, and even then a written case had to be made out by a species of sub-committee, which included the marshal, the draper, the commander at Acre, and three or four experienced members of the Order.[30]

Perhaps just as important was that Templar houses provided facilities which eased the logistical problems of crusading and in this way contributed further to the supply of men to Outremer. The Richerenches cartulary provides the example of one Pons Lautier from Colonzelle who, in June 1160, was about to set out for the Holy Land. He left his lands in pledge to the Templars for fifteen years after which, if he died or did not return from Jerusalem, the Order would acquire proprietary rights. His expedition to Jerusalem, he says, was "a journey which the above-mentioned brothers have prepared for me."[31] The supply of men was probably an irregular affair, much affected by the vicissitudes of recruitment and the state of affairs in Outremer, but responsions, payments in both money and goods, were more regularized, for the Western houses were obliged to send the equivalent of a third of their revenues to the East, although

27 Forey, Aragón, pp. 328-329.
28 Jules Michelet, Le Procès des Templiers, 2, Collection de documents inédits sur l'histoire de France (Paris, 1851), pp. 277-418. This might, of course, indicate falling recruitment, but there is little to suggest this in the years of service given, which range from less than one month to 45 years. Despite the age structure shown in Figure 1, 35 of the 133 who give their length of service had been in the Order for 5 years or less. The average is 14.6 years.
29 Konrad Schottmüller, Der Untergang des Templer-Ordens, 2 (Berlin, 1887), pp. 166-218.
30 Règle, clause 93.
31 Cart. Rich., No. 163, pp. 145-146.

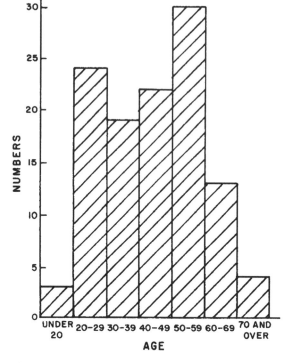

Fig. 1. Age distribution of Templars, derived from 115 depositions taken at Paris, October and November, 1307

the Iberian lands were an exception, since there was evidently a front line here too, and therefore the proportion was nearer a tenth.[32]

The Order had from an early date acquired juridical immunities from the papacy which greatly facilitated these policies. The bull *Omne Datum Optimum* of 1139 was the most sweeping of its privileges, but *Milites Templi* (1144) and *Milicia Dei* (1145) were especially important for the development of Templar functions in that they made it easier for the Order both to attract benefactors and to accumulate resources which could be used for the crusade. Take these two key clauses from *Milites Templi:*

32  See Forey, *Aragón,* pp. 322-324. Ironically, in view of contemporary criticism that the Templars were not doing enough for the Holy Land, the Order under Molay was pushed to even greater efforts, for additional sums and supplies were extracted over and above the usual responsions. See, on the other hand, the interesting discussion by David M. Metcalf, "The Templars as Bankers and Monetary Transfers between West and East in the Twelfth Century," in *Coinage in the Latin East. The Fourth Oxford Symposium on Coinage and Monetary History,* ed. Peter W. Edbury and David M. Metcalf, BAR International Series 77 (Oxford, 1980), pp. 1-13, who argues that the Order financed its Eastern responsibilities by means of shrewd management of its estates in Outremer, rather than through its links with the West.

XII

(i) "Whoever ... assists them and establishes a community for so holy a brotherhood and cedes to them benefits (*beneficia*) annually, we grant an indulgence of the seventh part of the penance enjoined on him";
(ii) "When, however, the brothers of the Temple, who are engaged in making a collection, shall arrive in a city, castle or village, if by chance the place should be under interdict, for the honor of the Temple and reverence to their knighthood, once a year churches shall be opened and, excommunicates having been excluded, divine offices can be celebrated."

*Milicia Dei* further strengthened the Order's independence by allowing Templars to build their own chapels and to bury their dead in the adjoining consecrated ground.[33] This in turn meant that commanderies could build up strong links with the local community, links which are very evident from an examination of their cartularies. The Richerenches cartulary, for instance, contains many grants from men who wanted to end their lives in the Order and to be buried in Templar cemeteries and who, for this privilege, made grants to the house. It was particularly common at Richerenches for men to promise their horse and arms when they died or the monetary equivalent if these were not available.[34]

The system had, of course, to provide the means to link up the constituent parts. The map shows particular concentrations in the rich lands of the Paris Basin and Champagne, and houses distributed along the major trade and pilgrimage routes, especially to Spain, southern France, and Italy. Provence seems to have been a key area. The Order had houses all along the Rhône-Saône corridor, including Richerenches, and at or near embarkation points for the East, including Arles, Saint-Gilles, Biot, Nice, and Toulon (fig. 2). Marseille was, however, the most important departure point in the region. In 1216 the consuls granted both the Temple and the Hospital the right to keep ships in the port which could be used for voyages to and from Outremer, Spain, or other regions "and to collect or receive in these ships or vessels pilgrims and merchants and their money, when they wished, with or without fares, in accordance with their judgment and wish." This sweeping privilege soon created tensions. By 1233 the Orders were complaining that these concessions were being disregarded, causing them great damage, and were claiming 2,000 marks of silver in compensation. Under the arbitration of Eudes de Montbéliard, constable of Jerusalem, and Jean d'Ibelin, Lord of Beirut, at Acre, a compromise was reached which was much more restrictive of the Orders' activities. From this time the Temple and the Hospital were each allowed two ships per year, one in the March or Easter passage, the other in August, "into which they could freely and without restriction load and unload their own goods and personnel, and receive in each ship up to 1,500 pilgrims and whatever

33 Marquis d'Albon, ed., *Cartulaire général de l'Ordre du Temple, 1119?-1150* (Paris, 1913), Bullaire, Nos. 5, 8, 10, pp. 375-379, 381, 382.
34 An index of the frequency of such arrangements can be seen by the fact that Innocent III became seriously disquieted, alleging in 1213 that some of these practices were equivalent to simony. See Joseph H. Lynch, *Simoniacal Entry into Religious Life from 1000 to 1260* (Columbus, Ohio, 1976), pp. 190-192.

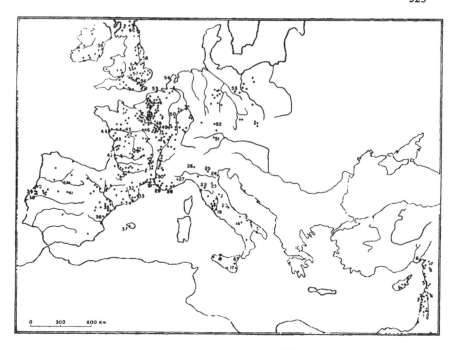

Fig. 2. Preliminary survey of Templar houses, circa 1300

1. Jerusalem; 2. 'Athlit; 3. Acre; 4. Safed; 5. Tortosa and Ruad; 6. Antioch; 7. Baghras (Gaston); 8. Ayas; 9. Limassol; 10. Lamia; 11. Andravida; 12. Barletta; 13. Bari; 14. Troia; 15. Taranto; 16. Messina; 17. Syracuse; 18. Palermo; 19. Rome; 20. Chieti; 21. Perugia; 22. Lucca; 23. Bologna; 24. Venice; 25. Verona; 26. Milan; 27. Asti; 28. Hyères; 29. Marseille; 30. Avignon; 31. Saint-Gilles; 32. Mas Deu; 33. Ampurias; 34. Barcelona; 35. Tortosa; 36. Valencia; 37. Mallorca; 38. Pombal; 39. Tomar; 40. Soure; 41. Segovia; 42. Bordeaux; 43. La Rochelle; 44. Nantes; 45. Angers; 46. Orléans; 47. Paris; 48. Provins; 49. Troyes; 50. Metz; 51. Augsburg; 52 Bamberg; 53. Tempelhof; 54. Haarlem; 55. Ostend; 56. London; 57. Sandford; 58. Willoughton; 59. Clontarf; 60. Balantrodoch

number of merchants they wished." The Orders were allowed further ships for their own personnel and goods, but could not take any more pilgrims or merchants, a restriction which suggests that they had been undercutting local shipping operators. Indeed the Grand Masters of the two Orders were obliged to accept that, on a wide stretch of the Mediterranean coast, from Collioure to Monaco, which the consuls evidently regarded as the city's legitimate sphere of interest, they could not transport pilgrims or merchants in their ships.[35]

35 Eduard Winkelmann, *Acta Imperii inedita saeculi XIII et XIV*, 1 (Innsbruck, 1880), Nos. 139, 117. Delaville, *Cartulaire*, Nos. 1464, 2067, pp. 186-187, 462-464. RRH Nos. 889, 1046.

XII

By the thirteenth century the Temple possessed houses in the major ports at both ends of the Mediterranean and on the Channel and Atlantic coasts. Apart from Provence, they had houses at London and Dover, La Rochelle and Bordeaux, Tortosa and Valencia, and Venice, Barletta, Bari, Taranto, Palermo, Messina, and Syracuse, among others. In the East they were established in the important cities, while at Acre they kept their own fleet of sea-going vessels.[36] As the major trade routes began to switch to the north in the second half of the thirteenth century, they adapted to circumstances, for in the 1270s and 1280s they had their own wharf at Ayas in Cilicia.[37]

As the documents from Marseille and Acre show, the Order both possessed its own ships and the resources to charter others, although the evidence for this derives largely from the thirteenth century. The Templars certainly imported essential raw materials like iron during the twelfth century, but they seem to have used commercial operators like the Mairano brothers of Venice, with whom they signed a contract through an agent in 1162. By 1207, however, there is a reference to a Templar ship at Constantinople[38] and from that time there are fairly frequent, if uneven, references to Templar shipping and, indeed, named Templar ships, not only in the Mediterranean, but also in the Channel and the Bay of Biscay.[39] The two agreements with Marseille suggest that in the early thirteenth century the fleets of the Military Orders had not been very large, but that after 1216 a considerable expansion both in the numbers and in the size of individual ships had taken place.

These ships were used for both warfare and supply. During the Egyptian campaigns of the thirteenth century Templar galleys with cash and arms hove to off the coast, while in 1279 the Templars at Acre were able to dispatch thirteen galleys in their conflict with Bohemund of Tripoli.[40] The exploits of Roger de Flor, the orphaned son of a German falconer in Apulia, who rose to command a great vessel built for the Order by the Genoese called *The Falcon,* were simply a flamboyant example of these activities. At the age of eight Roger had been taken on a Templar ship which had put into Brindisi. In time he became a serjeant in the Order and by the age of twenty was in command of his own ship. According to Ramon Muntaner, who knew him well, he is said to have gained a great deal

*Règle,* clause 119.
37 Cornelio Desimoni, "Actes passés en 1271, 1274 et 1279 à l'Aïas (Petite Arménie) et à Beyrouth par devant des notaires génois," *AOL* 1 (1881), No. 4, p. 495.
38 Raimondo Morozzo della Rocca and Antonio Lombardo, *Documenti del commercio veneziano nei secoli XI-XIII,* 2 vols. (Turin, 1940), 1:No. 158, 155-156; 2:No. 487, pp. 27-28.
39 See Thomas W. Parker, *The Knights Templars in England* (Tucson, Arizona, 1963), pp. 56-57.
40 Oliver of Paderborn, *Historia Damiatina,* in *Die Schriften des Kölner Domscholasters, späteren Bischofs von Paderborn und Kardinalbischofs von S. Sabina Oliverus,* ed. O. Hoogeweg, Bibliothek des litterarischen Vereins in Stuttgart 202 (Tübingen, 1894), pp. 181, 194; Joinville (note 18 above), pp. 206-211; Gaston Raynaud, ed., *Gestes des Chiprois* (Geneva, 1887), p. 207.

for the Temple with this ship, a phrase which implies piracy as well as legitimate trade. He was present at the fall of Acre in 1291 and apparently saved many women and children, although it may have been at a price, since he was afterwards pursued by the Order, apparently to regain certain sums of money which he had kept.[41]

More mundane was the regular transportation of needed supplies, especially in the second half of the thirteenth century when the shrinking crusader lands lacked almost all the necessities. By this time the transportation of horses by sea was well developed, although at the moment the Templar part in this is relatively obscure. In his detailed studies of sea transport to the crusader states based on the Angevin registers, Professor Pryor found only one instance of the Templars themselves transporting horses—in 1277—although it is clear that they were involved in this operation as the registers show horses and mules from Spain destined for the Templars in the East passing through Messina.[42] The Templar Rule shows too that officials had wide powers to purchase beasts that were needed, either in Outremer or by importation from the West.[43] The Templars are referred to more frequently in the transport of wheat and vegetables (sometimes specifically mentioned as being produced on their own estates), barley for horses, arms, especially crossbows, and cloth. They made particular use of the ports of Bari, Brindisi, and Manfredonia, in the late 1260s and 1270s,[44] while under Jacques de Molay, Grand Master from 1293, King Charles II issued a whole series of export licenses for the Templars, especially between 1295 and 1299.[45] Among the cargoes in the opposite direction must have been Muslim slaves, for in 1274 there was a dispute over the provenance of two such men whom the Templars claimed had escaped from their house at Bari to which they had been brought from overseas.[46]

Angevin Sicily evidently became a vital center of supply for the East, especially with Charles of Anjou's purchase of a claim to the kingship of Jerusalem in 1277. The links with the Templars had already been cemented when

---

41  Lady Goodenough, trans., *The Chronicle of Muntaner* 2, Hakluyt Society (London, 1920), pp. 466-469.
42  John Pryor, "Transportation of horses by sea during the era of the Crusades: Eighth Century to 1285 AD," *Mariner's Mirror* 68 (1982), 110. and *"In subsidium Terrae Sanctae"* (note 12 above).
43  *Règle,* clauses 84, 103, 107, 115, 135.
44  Ricardo Filangieri, *I registri della cancelleria angioina* 2 (Naples, 1951), No. 473, p. 124; 3 (1951), No. 715, p. 239; 5 (1953), No. 99, p. 234; 6 (1954), Nos. 706, 1270, pp. 140, 238-239; 7 (1955), Nos. 43, 99, 198, pp. 17-18, 45, 199; 9 (1957), Nos. 98, 22, pp. 215, 293-294; 11 (1958), No. 145, p. 122. Supplies sent from the Angevin lands in southern Italy would usually be intended for the consumption of the Templars only (compare the restrictions placed on the Templars sailing from Marseille after 1233). Special permission was needed if the Order wished to resell, for example, 26 (1979), No. 735, p. 207. I am very grateful to Professor Pryor and Professor Jacoby for their valuable comments on this issue. I owe the last reference to Professor Pryor.
45  See Barber, "Molay" (note 16 above), p. 95.
46  Filangieri, *Registri* 11, No. 143, p. 55.

XII

326

Guillaume de Beaujeu, Charles's kinsman, became Grand Master in 1273.[47] However, since the bulk of the references derive from southern Italy, these documents perhaps give a rather unbalanced picture, for Marseille continued to be used, as a reference to the export of grain and other merchandise in 1270 indicates, while the notarial registers of the city show regular movement of Templar ships to and from the East between 1229 and 1290, where they are evidently part of the normal commercial system, since they are seen carrying merchants fulfilling commenda contracts for other parties.[48] Other rulers were also active. Two orders from Edward I of England, for instance, made at Berwick in 1296, show the king granting permission for the export of horses, worsted cloth, and cash for the Templars from Dover.[49] Such supplies were not sent only during the crisis years of the late thirteenth century. The Rule shows that the Templars in the East expected to receive such imports in the normal course of events. Clause 609 states that, "If the commander of the vault brings ships loaded with wheat and the brother in charge of the corn loft says it is moist, then it needs to be laid to dry."[50]

Some general conclusions can perhaps be drawn from the evidence. It has been argued by Professor Giles Constable, without exaggeration, that the need for goods, services, and manpower generated by the crusades was one of the most significant contributions to the break-up of the old social and economic order.[51] It began on an *ad hoc* basis, with individual monasteries providing credit for would-be crusaders, but it developed into an institutionalized structure with the Hospital and Temple at its center.

47  Filangieri, *Registri* 9 (1957), No. 288, pp. 264-265; *Gestes des Chiprois* (note 40 above), pp. 201-202; *Eracles*, p. 463. RRH No. 1387.
48  Filangieri, *Registri* 6 (1954), No. 147, p. 42; Louis Blanchard, *Documents inédits sur le commerce de Marseille au Moyen Age* (Marseille, 1884), 1:28-29, 73, 103, 134-135, 314-315; 2:272, 436, 446.
49  See Barber, "Molay," p. 96.
50  *Règle*, clause 609.
51  Giles Constable, "The Financing of the Crusades in the Twelfth Century," in *Outremer*, p. 88.

# XIII

## THE ORDER OF SAINT LAZARUS AND THE CRUSADES

There is a privilege in the cartulary of the Hospital, granted by
Innocent IV in October, 1248, to Ebrard, Bishop-elect of Constance,
in which the pope restrains certain religious orders from exercising
their rights to celebrate Mass and bury the dead in their own cemeteries while the diocese was under interdict. Such actions had in the
past, he said, been the occasion of much discord.[1] The orders concerned are four: the Hospitallers, the Templars, the Teutonic Knights,
and the Knights of Saint Lazarus. The exemptions and power of the
first three are well known, but here it can be seen that a much less
conspicuous order, the community of lepers known as the Order of
Saint Lazarus, was possessed of the same kind of privileges granted,
for example, to the Templars over a century before. Moreover, since
it is grouped with the three great military orders of the age, it was
presumably regarded by the pope as an order of the same kind as
these. Other references in the papal registers of the thirteenth century

---

[1]*Cartulaire général de l'Ordre des Hospitaliers de Saint-Jean de Jérusalem 1100–
1310*, Vol. 2, ed. Joseph Delaville Le Roulx (Paris, 1894; reprint Munich, 1980) (henceforth *Cart.*), no. 2487, p. 676. Cf. no. 2806, p. 812 (Alexander IV, March 1256).

confirm this: Innocent IV, Alexander IV, and Clement IV were particularly assiduous in their efforts to encourage contributions from the faithful, as well as making over certain categories of papal revenues for the order's support.[2] The popes were indeed correct to see the order in these terms for, although not endowed on the same scale as the other three orders, the brothers of Saint Lazarus held lands in most of the countries of western Christendom, ranging from England to Hungary.[3] In some areas they were particularly well established; in Normandy, for example, they administered eight houses.[4]

Although the order, therefore, was firmly established in the mid-thirteenth century, its origins are very obscure. The first clearly dated reference to it in the surviving fragment of its cartulary is in 1142 in the Kingdom of Jerusalem. In that year, King Fulk, with the approval of Queen Melisende and their son, Baldwin, conceded to "the church of Saint Lazarus and the convent of the sick who are called *miselli*, an estate which Baldwin of Caesarea gave them in alms, . . . which is between the Mount of Olives and the Red Cistern on the road which leads to the River Jordan." [5] One possible earlier reference is the grant of a cistern by an Armenian monk called Abraham, who had held it "for the use of the poor." This grant must fall within the patriarchate of William I of Jerusalem between 1130 and 1145. Here the concession is quite explicitly to "the house of the lepers of Saint Lazarus."[6] These documents suggest that a hospitaller order caring mainly or exclusively for lepers was establishing itself in the Kingdom of Jerusalem during the 1130's. The Armenian monk, Abraham, became a dependent, receiving victuals and clothing during his lifetime in exchange for the cistern. Perhaps he had become leprous and had found it difficult to remain within his own community. The confirmation of 1142 shows that they were situated on the pilgrim route between the Mount of

---

[2]See below, pp.
[3]See René Pétiet, *Contribution à l'histoire de l'Ordre de Saint-Lazare de Jérusalem en France* (Paris, 1914), and John Walker, *The Patronage of the Templars and the Order of St. Lazarus in England in the Twelfth and Thirteenth Centuries* (Ph.D. thesis, University of St. Andrews, 1990) For evidence of their establishment in Hungary, see *Cart.*, Vol. 2, no. 2135, p. 497.
[4]See André Mutuel, "Recherches sur l'ordre de Saint-Lazare de Jérusalem en Normandie," *Annales de Normandie*, 33 (1983), 121–142.
[5]"Fragment d'un Cartulaire de l'Ordre de Saint-Lazare, en Terre Sainte," ed. Arthur de Marsy, in *Archives de l'Orient latin*, Vol. 2 (Paris, 1884; reprint New York, 1978), no. II, pp. 123–124.
[6]*Ibid.*, no. I, p. 123.

Olives and the Jordan, where they would have been well placed to
gather alms and from which they might travel to bathe in the supposedly curative waters of the River Jordan.[7] Two years later the order
had built a house on the site and had begun the cultivation of vines.[8]
By 1150 the brothers were wealthy enough to purchase land elsewhere, giving 1,500 besants and a horse for thirteen carucates of land
on the Bethlehem Plain.[9] It seems likely too that by this time they
were established in the house mentioned by the Old French continuation of Ernoul-Bernard as existing in 1187, when Saladin conquered
the city. This house abutted the walls of Jerusalem, on the northwest
corner of the city. Here a postern seems to have led directly from the
city into their hospital.[10] The site seems to have been granted to them
by the Ibelins. In 1148 the family confirmed the order in possession
of ten carucates of land "beside (*secus*) the walls of Jerusalem."[11]

During the next forty years the order, although not mentioned in
the accounts of pilgrim visitors like John of Würzburg or Theoderich,

---

[7]James of Vitry, Bishop of Acre between 1216 and 1228, described how it was the
custom of pilgrims to bathe in the Jordan, sanctified by the baptism of Christ, an event
which had "bestowed regenerative power upon all its waters." The consonance was
evident. "As a type of the purification which was to come, Naaman the Syrian was
cleansed of the leprosy in these waters, and his flesh came again in the flesh of a little
child." [2 Kings 5], *History of Jerusalem*, tr. Aubrey Stewart, *Palestine Pilgrims' Text
Society*, Vol. 11 (London, 1896), pp. 130–131. The tradition was well established by
Vitry's time, since Gregory of Tours describes how, in the sixth century, lepers traveled
to the East in the hope of gaining a cure by bathing in the Jordan at the place of Christ's
baptism beyond Jericho. Indeed, he claimed to know of a leper from Gaul, called John,
who had been restored to health as a result. Gregory of Tours, *Liber in Gloria Martyrum*,
ed. Bruno Krusch, in *Monumenta Germaniae Historica, Scriptorum Rerum Merovingicarum*, Vol. 1 (Hanover, 1885), caps. 16–18, pp. 498–499.
[8]"Fragment," no. III, pp. 124–125.
[9]*Ibid.*, no. VII, p. 128.
[10]*Chronique d'Ernoul et de Bernard le Trésorier*, ed. Louis de Mas Latrie, *Société de
l'Histoire de France* (Paris, 1871), p. 200; *Continuation de Guillaume de Tyr de 1229
à 1261, dite du manuscrit de Rothelin*, in *Recueil des Historiens des Croisades, Occidentaux (RHCr)*, Vol. 2 (Paris, 1859), p. 500. A reference to "a dwelling for lepers,"
situated between the Tower of Tancred and the Gate of St. Stephen, seems to have
been included in the anonymous *Work on Geography*, which has been reconstructed
by John Wilkinson in a version which can be dated between 1128 and 1137. Although
this passage dates from sometime after 1157 it appears to have been derived from the
*Work on Geography*, thus suggesting that a leper house existed at this spot in the early
1130's, *Jerusalem Pilgrimage 1099–1185*, ed. John Wilkinson (Hakluyt Society, Vol.
167 [London, 1988]), p. 143 and pp. 12–15 for a discussion of the source. See also *The
Atlas of the Crusades*, ed. Jonathan Riley-Smith (London, 1991), pp. 44–45.
[11]"Fragment," no. V, pp. 125–127.

# XIII

THE ORDER OF SAINT LAZARUS AND THE CRUSADES

nevertheless became increasingly important to the resident families of the Kingdom of Jerusalem. Even from the small part of the order's cartulary which survives, the interest of the royal house and the great barons can be seen. Kings Fulk, Baldwin III, and Amalric all made donations, as did Queen Melisende.[12] A particularly interesting example is Amalric's grant of, among other donations, an annual rent of fifty besants specifically for the support of one leper, the money to be transferred to another when the original recipient died. This was in 1171 which must have been about the time that the king became aware of his own son's infirmity.[13]

The great barons of the twelfth century are also well represented, for the lords of Beirut, Caesarea, Toron, Galilee, Jaffa, and Nablus, as well as the Count of Tripoli, all had links with the order. In March, 1164, Walter II Brisebarre, lord of Beirut, gave the brothers half of the vintage from a vineyard cultivated by a certain Master Lambert, concluding the donation with the possibility that he might enter the order, "if, by chance, I should wish to renounce the secular life." Walter, in fact, died later that year, but some months later his wife, Maria, *domina* of Beirut, granted the order an annual rent of fifteen besants on the revenues of a *casal* called Musecaqui. Four years later Walter III gave a further forty besants to be taken annually on the revenues derived from his money-changing rights at Beirut.[14] Hugh, lord of Caesarea, had a similarly close connection, since a donation of 1160, refers to the fact that his brother, Eustace, was already a member of the order, although the document does not say explicitly that Eustace was a leper.[15] Between 1148 and 1183 the lords of Toron, Humphrey II and Humphrey IV, made grants from their various properties in Hebron, Toron, and Acre,[16] and in 1170 Walter, Prince of Galilee, and his family granted them a rent at Tiberias.[17] As has been seen, the Ibelins, too, were involved: between 1148 and 1169, Rainier of Ramla, Ermengarde, Viscountess of Tiberias, and Hugh of Ibelin contributed lands near Jerusalem, Tiberias, and Ramla to the growing

---

[12]*Ibid.*, no. II, pp. 123–124 (1142); no. III, pp. 124–125 (1144); no. VII, p. 128 (1150); no. VIII, pp. 128–129 (1150); no. X, pp. 130–131 (1151); no. XIV, pp. 133–134 (1155); no. XV, pp. 134–135 (1155); no. XVI, p. 135 (1159); no. XXII, p. 140 (1164); no. XXVII, pp. 144–145 (1171); no. XXVIII, pp. 145–146 (1174).

[13]*Ibid.*, no. XXVII, pp. 144–145.

[14]*Ibid.*, no. XXI, p. 139; no. XXIII, p. 141; no. XXIV, pp. 141–142.

[15]*Ibid.*, no. XVIII, pp. 136–137.

[16]*Ibid.*, no. VI, p. 127 (1148); no. IX, pp. 129–130 (1151); no. XXIX, pp. 146–147 (1183).

[17]*Ibid.*, no. XXVI, pp. 143–144.

XIII

443

estates of the order.[18] In 1153 Philip of Nablus, later Master of the Temple, together with his family, donated ten carucates of land and the *casal* of Zaythar.[19] In 1185 Raymond of Tripoli, in a donation of twenty besants to be taken on the *funda* of Tripoli, is described as a *confrater* of the order, suggesting that he had become a lay associate of some kind, similar to those linked to the Templars.[20]

Most of the donors give conventional reasons for their grants, which are largely for the souls of departed relatives, but the personal links suggested in the donations of Walter Brisebarre, Hugh of Caesarea, and Raymond of Tripoli open the possibility that the order acted as a respectable refuge for Latin settlers in the kingdom who had become afflicted by leprosy.[21] This seems all the more probable in the light of the fact that the names of two thirteenth-century masters of the order, Walter of Chastel Neuf and Rainaud of Fleury, both of whom were lepers, suggest close ties with the native Latin aristocracy. The histories of the lordships of Toron and Chastel Neuf are interlinked in a very complicated manner,[22] and it is surely no coincidence that Walter's appearance in the order's cartulary in 1228 is a request for the Emperor Frederick II to confirm the grant made by Humphrey IV of Toron to Saint Lazarus in 1183.[23] Rainaud of Fleury, who appears in two charters of 1234, probably succeeded Walter as master of Saint Lazarus; he seems to have been related to the family which held the office of *vicomte* in Acre.[24] This close-knit, sometimes xenophobic community favored Saint Lazarus because leprosy was endemic in the region and the Latins were therefore far more aware of their susceptibility to the

[18]*Ibid.*, no. V, pp. 125–127 (1148); no. XIII, pp. 132–133 (1154); no. XXV, pp. 142–143 (1169).

[19]*Ibid.*, no. XIV, pp. 133–134.

[20]*Ibid.*, no. XXX, pp. 147–148.

[21]On this see the fundamental article on the order by Shulamith Shahar, "Des lépreux pas comme les autres. L'Ordre de Saint-Lazare dans le royaume latin de Jérusalem," *Revue historique*, 267 (1982), 19–41.

[22]See Steven Tibble, *Monarchy and Lordships in the Latin Kingdom of Jerusalem 1099–1291* (Oxford, 1989), pp. 13–23.

[23]"Fragment," no. XXXIV, pp. 150–151; no. XXXV, pp. 152–153. This same lordship also produced two other leading members of the military orders in the thirteenth century, William, Grand Master of the Hospital (1242–1258), see Jonathan Riley-Smith, *The Knights of St. John in Jerusalem and Cyprus c. 1050–1310* (London, 1967), pp. 180, 186, and Arnald, Grand Preceptor of the Temple (1277), *Regesta Regni Hierosolymitani (RRH)*, Vol. 1, ed. Reinhold Röhricht (Innsbruck, 1893; reprint New York, 1960), no. 1413, p. 367.

[24]"Fragment," no. XXXVI, p. 153; no. XXXVII, p. 154. See, for example, Gilbert of Fleury, *vicomte* of Acre, c. 1179–c. 1186, *RRH*, no. 582, p. 155; no. 657, p. 175.

disease than their contemporaries in the West. In 1159 Queen Melisende granted the order a *gastina* called Betana specifically to sustain
an additional leper beyond the existing complement,[25] a donation
which suggests that the support of lepers in the kingdom was a growing
and visible problem. This idea is supported by the late twelfth-century
law code known as the *Livre au Roi*, which provided that a knight or
sergeant who became leprous should join the Order of Saint Lazarus,
"where it is established that people with such an illness should be."
His wife should enter a convent and their property should devolve
upon their heirs, or failing heirs, upon their lord.[26] For the Templars
there was an equally explicit provision: their Rule shows that leprous
brothers could transfer to Saint Lazarus, although they were not to be
compelled to do so.[27] It was a refuge for which both the families of
Outremer and the Templars were prepared to pay. Hugh of Caesarea
and his family, for instance, gave an orchard and two houses, one of
which was formerly owned by his brother who was now a member
of the order,[28] while the Templars continued to pay for the upkeep
of sick brothers sent to Saint Lazarus. It is reasonable to suppose that

[25]"Fragment," no. XVI, p. 135. The exact nature of the *gastina* is not clear, but it
was probably a piece of uncultivated land dependent upon the villages of Magna Mahumeria and Parva Mahumeria, just to the north of Jerusalem, which were settlements
colonized by the Franks. It seems that the order was expected to develop or redevelop
the land. On the ambiguity of the term, see Jonathan Riley-Smith, *The Feudal Nobility
and the Kingdom of Jerusalem, 1174–1277* (London, 1973), pp. 43–44.

[26]"Le Livre au Roi," in *RHCr., Lois*, Vol. 1 (Paris, 1841), pp. 636–637. A woman
whose husband had entered a monastery was expected to lead a chaste life thereafter,
usually in an appropriate religious house. However, since there was a prevalent belief
that women could transmit the disease through sexual intercourse, the provision that
she enter a convent may have had added importance for contemporaries in these cases.
In the twelfth century, leprosy in the Kingdom of Jerusalem seems to have been regarded
as a male disease, there being no known provision for leprous women. The difference
in the treatment of men and women is underlined by the case of the Burgundian knight
who, in c. 1130, entered the Temple after his wife had contracted leprosy, leaving her
and his daughters in the care of a local monastic house at Dijon, *Cartulaire général de
l'ordre de Temple 1119?–1150*, ed. Marquis d'Albon (Paris, 1913), no. XXVII, p. 19.
This charter says much about contemporary confusion regarding leprosy, since his
wife's ailment was no barrier to the knight's entry into the Temple.

[27]*La Règle du Temple*, ed. Henri de Curzon, *Société de l'Histoire de France* (Paris,
1886), pp. 239–240. Those leprous brothers who refused to transfer to Saint Lazarus
were required to live apart from the other Templars, although the order would continue
to maintain them.

[28]As the houses were adjacent and were to be held free of service while they were
actually occupied by the brothers, Denys Pringle suggests that the aim was to establish
a house of Saint Lazarus in Caesarea, *The Churches of the Crusader Kingdom of Jerusalem. A Corpus*, Vol. 1 (Cambridge, 1993), p. 180.

well-known cases of leprosy in the East, like those of Robert the Leper, lord of Zerdana, and King Baldwin IV, give only a glimpse of the extent of the problem, and that for the Latin population Saint Lazarus, therefore, offered at least a partial solution.[29]

Since the order seems to have performed such an important function in Outremer, it needs to be defined more closely. In 1234 a grant of Peter of Limoges, Archbishop of Caesarea, laid down the necessity of obedience to the archbishop and his successors in matters regarding the property concerned, "saving the rule of your house."[30] This appears to have been the adaptable Augustinian Rule, referred to in bulls of Innocent IV in 1247 and Alexander IV eight years later. Alexander IV's bull in fact confirmed this Rule, "which you [the brothers of Saint Lazarus] assert to have professed and followed up to this time."[31] At the head of the Order was a master, first referred to in 1153, where he is called simply Bartholomew.[32] Until 1253 the masters were themselves lepers, for at that time, at the request of the brothers, Innocent IV released them from the custom hitherto observed, which was to choose a master who was a *miles leprosus.* He was able to do this since the members were not exclusively lepers; the pope's concession gave them the right to elect as master "any healthy knight from among the brothers of the house."[33] Membership had probably been open to the healthy throughout the Order's existence, for Humphrey of Toron's grant of 1183 refers to "all serving God in this house, both sick and healthy," while in 1234 Archbishop Peter had made his donation to the lepers and "others serving God there." The existence of healthy brothers, vowed to charitable service, is similar to the organization of contemporary houses in the West, the striking difference being that, until 1253, the master was himself a leper. There may too have been a class of brother priests, for among the witnesses to a grant of 1148

[29]Further evidence of the needs of the leper community can be seen in the existence of houses at Bethlehem and Beirut, unconnected with the Order of Saint Lazarus. See the legacies to these two houses in the will of Odo, Count of Nevers, who died at Acre in August, 1266, Alphonse-Martial Chazaud, "Inventaire et comptes de la succession d'Eudes, comte de Nevers," *Mémoires de la Société Nationale des Antiquaires de France,* 32 (1871), 199.
[30]"Fragment," no. XXXVII, p. 154.
[31]*Les Registres d'Innocent IV,* Vol. 1, ed. Elie Berger ("Bibliothèque des Ecoles françaises d'Athènes et de Rome" [henceforth *BEFAR*], ser. 2 [Paris, 1884]), no. 3156, pp. 476–477; *Bullarium Diplomatum et Privilegiorum Sanctorum Romanorum Pontificum Taurinensis Editio,* vol. 3, ed. S. Franco, H. Fory, and H. Dalmazzo (Turin, 1857), no. X, p. 602.
[32]"Fragment," no. XI, p. 131.
[33]*Reg. Inn. IV,* Vol. 3, no. 6204, p. 153.

XIII

is one "Frederick, *capellanus* of the church of Saint Lazarus,"[34] but since this reference is both isolated and ambiguous it cannot be regarded as certain. Nevertheless, it remains likely, since in the thirteenth century they held a church of their own, that of Saint Lawrence in the village of Painperdu, north of Caesarea, granted to them by the archbishop in 1235.[35] The interest taken in the order by the families of the Kingdom of Jerusalem ensured that this structure rested upon a modest economic base during the twelfth century. By 1187 it had agricultural estates and vineyards, and incomes from tithes, rents, markets, ports, and coinage, in or near most of the important centers of the kingdom. In 1164 it was even granted a tithe of slaves captured by King Amalric on royal expeditions.[36] In addition, a confirmation of 1216 by Ramond-Roupen, Prince of Antioch, of a grant by his grandfather, Bohemond III, shows that the brothers were drawing revenues from Antioch from at least 1201, although there is no evidence that the order was itself established there.[37]

During the twelfth century the house of Saint Lazarus at Jerusalem, therefore, became a familiar sight, and indeed its occupants were sometimes the object of the devotions of pious men intent on performing penance through service to the lepers. Gerard of Nazareth, Bishop of Latakia between 1139 and 1161, described three such cases in the mid-twelfth century, two of whom, Ralph, a Frankish nobleman of some importance, and Bartholomew, who became a Templar, were originally pilgrims from the West. The most spectacular case of devotion to the lepers, however, was that of Alberic, who "ate those things which the lepers had left, kissed each one daily after Mass, washed and wiped their feet, made their beds, and carried the weak on top of his shoulders." After he had washed their feet, "the water mixed with the blood and discharge moved him to nausea, but he at once immersed his face and, horrible to say, took away not the least part."[38] It was probably devotion such as this which attracted the

[34]"Fragment," no. VI, p. 127.
[35]*Ibid.*, no. XXXVIII, pp. 154–155.
[36]*Ibid.*, no. XXII, p. 140.
[37]*Ibid.*, no. XXXII, pp. 149–150. Raymond-Roupen was the son of Princess Alice of Armenia, who was a niece of Humphrey IV of Toron. Alice successfully claimed lordship over Toron in 1229 and, in 1234, confirmed the donation of Humphrey II of 1151, "Fragment," no. XXXVI, p. 153, showing once more the links between this family and the lepers.
[38]Gerard of Nazareth, *De conversatione servorum Dei*, ed. Benjamin Z. Kedar, in "Gerard of Nazareth. A Neglected Twelfth-Century Writer in the Latin East," *Dumbarton*

attention of King Louis VII during the Second Crusade, for he had originally conceived his expedition in terms of a penitential pilgrimage. Back in France, in an act dated 1154, he recalled that he had granted the house ten *livres* of rent while he had been on crusade, which "at the request and prayer" of the brothers, he now exchanged for an estate on the royal demesne at Boigny, near Orléans.[39] This house became the center of the order's structure in France, which suggests a conscious plan to plant houses in the West, perhaps with the idea of creating a network of support for the eastern establishment.

However, the loss of the city of Jerusalem in 1187 confronted the order with the same problems as the other Latin institutions based there. Saladin probably gave them a year to organize their evacuation,[40] and ultimately the order re-established itself at Acre. Although there is no clear evidence of Saint Lazarus at Acre until 1240, when the boundaries of their property in the northern suburb of Montmusard were defined,[41] nevertheless, between 1226 and 1234 they received confirmations of the properties granted to them by Walter Brisebarre and Humphrey of Toron in the twelfth century, the last of which was made to Rainaud of Fleury, Master of Saint Lazarus, at Acre. Therefore, it seems certain that they had set up a house of some kind there well before 1240.[42] The existence of a Gate of Saint Lazarus in Montmusard, which is attested by "the Templar of Tyre," who knew the late thirteenth-century city well, and by early fourteenth-century maps,[43] reinforces the case for believing that the order established itself there quite soon after 1187. David Jacoby has shown that sometime between 1198 and 1212 the defenses of Acre had been greatly strengthened by the building of a new outer wall around the city's landward side.

---

*Oaks Papers*, 37 (1983), 72. The text is derived from fragments quoted by the Centuriators of Magdeburg in 1569.

[39]"Fragment," no. XII, p. 132. Louis had made a conspicuous visit to the leper colony at Paris before setting out on crusade, Odo of Deuil, *De Profectione Ludovici VII in Orientem*, ed. and tr. Virginia G. Berry (New York, 1948), pp. 16–17.

[40]Saladin allowed ten Hospitallers to stay for up to a year to tend the sick, *Cart.*, Vol. 1, no. 847, p. 527. It is likely that the same privilege was extended to the Order of Saint Lazarus.

[41]"Fragment," no. XXXIX, pp. 155–157.

[42]*Ibid.*, no. XXXIII, p. 150; no. XXXIV, pp. 150–151; no. XXXV, pp. 152–153; no. XXXVI, p. 153.

[43]*Gestes des Chiprois*, ed. Gaston Raynaud (Geneva, 1887), p. 245. See also the maps of Marino Sanudo (probably by Pietro Vesconte) and Paolino Veneto, Bernard Dichter, *The Maps of Acre, An Historical Geography* (Acre, 1973), pp. 17–18, 22–30.

This involved erecting a double line around the growing suburb of Montmusard, which had previously been too insignificant for such defenses.[44] The Gate of Saint Lazarus was the most northerly of the three gates in the Montmusard section, situated just in front of the area delineated by the donation of 1240. The last known gifts which the brothers received at Acre can be found in two wills: those of Saliba, a Syrian merchant from Acre and *confrater* of the Hospitallers, who, in 1264, left them six besants, and of Odo, Count of Nevers, who, in 1266, included them in a list of religious houses to which he had bequeathed various items of clothing.[45]

All the evidence discussed so far suggests a hospitaller order of a slightly unconventional kind, both in the early date of its specialization and in the choice of a master who was a leper. There is, however, nothing in the twelfth-century documents to suggest that it was in fact a military order as well, and in this sense markedly different from the many small establishments founded to shelter the sick and pilgrims in the twelfth-century Latin kingdom.[46] Templar documents, for example, show the order's fighting role from the outset, but in 1155 the brothers of Saint Lazarus are simply described as "serving God in a conventual manner," while an act of 1164 speaks only of their "cloister" contiguous with the walls of Jerusalem.[47] The compilers of the *Livre au Roi*, dated between 1198 and 1205, evidently believed that leprous entrants to the order were no longer able to fight, since they were required to provide substitutes for this purpose.[48] However, in 1234, Gregory IX made a general appeal for aid for the order to clear debts contracted in the "defense of the Holy Land,"[49] while in the 1240's and 1250's narrative sources show that the brothers made a series of spectacular—perhaps disastrous would be a better word— interventions in military affairs. Despite their lack of military success, in 1255 Pope Alexander IV still described them in what appears to have been their own terms as "a convent of nobles, of active (*stre-*

[44]David Jacoby, "Montmusard, Suburb of Crusader Acre: The First Stage of its Development," in *Outremer. Studies in the History of the Crusading Kingdom of Jerusalem presented to Joshua Prawer*, ed. Benjamin Z. Kedar, Hans E. Mayer, and Raymond C. Smail (Jerusalem, 1982), pp. 205–217.

[45]*Cart.*, Vol. 3, no. 3105, p. 91; Chazaud, *op. cit.*, p. 198.

[46]See Jean Richard, "Hospitals and Hospital Congregations in the Latin Kingdom during the First Period of the Frankish Conquest," in *Outremer*, pp. 89–100.

[47]"Fragment," no. XV, p. 134; no. XXII, p. 140.

[48]"Livre au Roi," p. 636.

[49]*Les Registres de Grégoire IX*, ed. Lucien Auvray, *BEFAR*, ser. 2, Vol. 1 (Paris, 1896), no. 1708, p. 942.

*nuorum*) knights and others both healthy and leprous, [existing] for the purpose of driving out the enemies of the Christian name."[50] The adoption of this role seems to have been a response to the deteriorating military situation in the East. Manpower had always been short, and the order contained the fit as well as the sick. Moreover, leprosy is a progressive disease which, in some cases, shows its full effects only after many years; indeed, if it is of the tuberculoid type, then it can remain quiescent or even improve.[51] In 1119 Robert of Zerdana was still leading his troops in battle despite the fact that he was well known to be a leper even by his Muslim opponents, while King Baldwin IV led the Frankish army on several occasions.[52] While these may have been exceptional individuals, men in the early stages of the disease would still have been capable of fighting, and indeed those from the knightly classes might still have desired the dignity and prestige which combat could bring.

A need for all available manpower arose in 1244, when, at La Forbie, the crusaders met the Egyptian forces in the greatest battle since Hattin. The crushing defeat sustained there devastated the fighting strength of the kingdom; according to a letter of Robert of Nantes, Patriarch of Jerusalem, "all the leper knights of the house of Saint Lazarus were killed."[53] Nevertheless, Matthew Paris claims that they took part in Louis IX's Egyptian campaign between 1248 and 1250 (a claim which seems to be confirmed by Louis IX's grant to them of a house in Damietta in 1249),[54] and, in a brief but graphic passage, Joinville describes how in 1252 the Master of Saint Lazarus and his men attempted a *chevauchée* near Ramla in the hope of collecting

[50]*Les Registres d'Alexandre IV*, ed. Charles Bourel, Joseph de Loye, Pierre de Cenival, and Auguste Coulon, *BEFAR*, ser. 2, Vol. 1, no. 404, p. 122.

[51]See *The New Encyclopaedia Britannica, Micropaedia*, 15th ed., Vol. 7 (1986), p. 287, where the two main types of leprosy are described.

[52]For Robert, see Usamah Ibn-Munqidh, *An Arab-Syrian Gentleman and Warrior in the Period of the Crusades*, tr. Philip K. Hitti (Princeton, 1929; reprint London, 1987), p. 149, and Kemal ed-Din, "Extraits de la Chronique d'Alep," in *RHCr. Or*, Vol. 3 (Paris, 1884), pp. 621–622. For Baldwin see, for example, the battle of Montgisard (1177), Guillaume de Tyr, *Chronique*, ed. Robert B. C. Huygens, *Corpus Christianorum, Continuatio Medievalis*, LXIIIA (Turnhout, 1986), 21.21–2 (22–3), pp. 990–992. See also Steven Runciman, *A History of the Crusades*, Vol. 2 (Cambridge, 1952), pp. 417, 419–420, 432, 441.

[53]Salimbene de Adam, *Chronica*, Vol. 1, ed. Giuseppe Scalia (Bari, 1966), p. 255.

[54]Matthew Paris, *Chronica Majora*, Vol. 5, ed. Henry R. Luard, *Rolls Series*, 57 (London, 1880), p. 196; for their house in Damietta, see Jean Richard, "La fondation d'une église latine en Orient par saint Louis: Damietta," *Bibliothèque de l'École des Chartes*, CXX (1962), 41, 53.

# XIII

booty, but were so strongly attacked by the Muslims that only four of them escaped. Joinville personally gathered a contingent of Hospitallers and Templars in order to gain revenge.[55] The fighting strength of the order had by this time been thoroughly undermined and, shortly after the Ramla incident, in 1253, Innocent IV issued the bull allowing a non-leper to become master, "since all the leper knights of the said house have been miserably killed by the enemies of the faith." Louis IX's compliance, in the same year, with the brothers' request to be allowed to send a vessel to Aigues-Mortes free of taxes and restrictions almost certainly arose from the same circumstances.[56]

It is probable that they had originally been encouraged to take on military functions by their close association with the Templars.[57] Templars are prominent in two of the few surviving twelfth-century charters: the confirmation of Barisan of Ibelin in 1148 of the donation made by Rainier of Ramla, his brother-in-law, was sealed by the Templars "through the hand of Peter, brother and chaplain of their knighthood," and witnessed by Andrew of Montbard, the seneschal, and five other Templars, while Humphrey of Toron's grant of 1151 has three Templar witnesses, one of whom is again Andrew of Montbard.[58] Moreover, Bartholomew, one of the three devotees of the lepers described by Gerard of Nazareth, was himself a Templar, who was apparently allowed to spend his time ministering to the lepers rather than fighting for the faith. "That man, imitating Alberic, was accustomed to bring water from the ponds with great labor to the lepers at Jerusalem, whom he maintained in all necessities as far as he could."[59] Although Gerard of Nazareth says that he eventually abandoned this life to become a monk on the Black Mountain at Antioch, it is possible that this is the same Bartholomew recorded as master of Saint Lazarus in 1153. On the other hand, connections with the Hospital are much less evident. Although Saint Lazarus may have taken in leprous Hospitallers, there is no explicit reference to this in the Hospitaller statutes. Presumably the Hospital could provide facilities lacking in the

[55]Jean de Joinville, *Histoire de Saint Louis*, ed. Natalis de Wailly, 2nd ed. (Paris, 1874), paras. 540–542, pp. 294–297.

[56]*Gallia Christiana*, Vol. 7, p. 1045.

[57]Both the Hospitallers and the Templars were accustomed to maintaining client crusading societies in the form of confraternities, largely composed of burgesses; so the evolution of Saint Lazarus would not have seemed all that unusual; see Riley-Smith, "A Note on Confraternities in the Latin Kingdom of Jerusalem," *Bulletin of the Institute of Historical Research*, 44 (1971), 301–308.

[58]"Fragment," no. V, pp. 125–127; no. IX, pp. 129–130.

[59]Gerard of Nazareth, p. 72.

Temple; thus leprous Hospitallers were fed and clothed by their Order, but kept separate from other brothers.[60] Moreover, it is noticeable that whereas several of the other smaller hospitaller foundations within the Kingdom of Jerusalem were eventually absorbed by the Hospitallers,[61] the Order of Saint Lazarus remained independent of them.

The Templar links are equally evident in the thirteenth century. In 1240 it was the Templars who helped them to establish themselves at Montmusard. Here, for an annual rent of fifteen besants they received an area bounded by the public road on the east, the sea on the west, the house of Saint Thomas Martyr on the north, and the lane which descended to the sea near the house of Nicholas the Englishman on the south. If in the future the brothers intended to sell any buildings, then the Templars would have first refusal. One concession included was that they should have free access to a Templar water cistern situated on the other side of the public road next to the Templars' house. For their part the Templars guaranteed to defend and maintain the site on behalf of the master and brothers of Saint Lazarus "against all persons of the world."[62] The early fourteenth-century maps show this area, together with the Gate of Saint Lazarus, situated immediately behind the section of the walls of Montmusard labeled *Custodia Templariorum* on the northwest corner.[63] It is not surprising, therefore, to find the Order of Saint Lazarus involved in the civil strife known as the War of Saint Sabas between 1256 and 1258; indeed, in 1258 during this conflict Thomas Bérard, Master of the Temple, was obliged to take shelter from the Pisan war engines in the house of Saint Lazarus.[64] By the late 1260's the ties had become so close that it had become obligatory for a leprous Templar to transfer to Saint Lazarus,[65] whereas in the twelfth century he had retained his right to refuse. This change might well reflect a perception that Saint Lazarus was an order similar in kind to the Templars by this time, which does not appear to have been true in the twelfth century. However, as in the past, the Templars still provided support for their former brother, for he went with all his clothes, a slave, a donkey, and fifty besants.

[60]*Cart.*, Vol. 3 (Paris, 1899), para. 17, no. 3396, p. 229 (statutes of Hugh Revel, 1270).
[61]Richard, "Hospitals," pp. 90–91, 98–99.
[62]"Fragment," no. XXXIX, pp. 155–157.
[63]Dichter, *loc. cit.*
[64]Matthew Paris, Vol. 5, pp. 745; *Gestes des Chiprois*, p. 153.
[65]Joseph Delaville Le Roulx, "Un nouveau manuscrit de la Règle du Temple," *Annuaire-Bulletin de la Société de l'Histoire de France*, 26 (ii) (1889), cl. XIV, pp. 197–198.

# XIII

The Saint Lazarus' contingent could not, of course, compare with the forces mustered by the three leading military orders for the defense of Acre; nevertheless, Innocent IV had regarded them as a group in 1248, and indeed, throughout the thirteenth century, the papacy paid particular attention to the needs of the brothers, a policy in keeping with the papal desire to mobilize resources for the crusade on the widest possible scale.[66] Gregory IX's appeal for aid for the order in 1234 included grants of a twenty-day indulgence to those who would give to the order or its collectors.[67] In 1247 Innocent IV gave the master the further privilege of absolving brothers who had incurred excommunication for violent acts, an interesting concession in view of the confusion exhibited by the Templar leaders during the trial over what, at that time, seems to have been defined as lay absolution. Apparently the Templars did not possess such a privilege.[68] Alexander IV was particularly assiduous in encouraging the faithful to see the order as a worthy object of their charity. One of his bulls, in March, 1255, made clear the reason for papal concern: following the reversals of war, the greater part of their possessions had fallen into the hands of the pagans or had been occupied by the enemies of the Church, forcing them into a state of extreme poverty. Consequently, it was quite impossible for the order to recover without the help of the Holy See.[69] Such help was readily forthcoming: a hundred-day indulgence to those who would contribute to the order (a fivefold increase on the 1234 offer), proceeds of confiscations from usurers in cases where the original owners could not be found, and income from redemption of crusade vows up to the value of 200 marks of silver.[70] Moreover, in 1262, Urban IV placed them under the sole jurisdiction of the patriarch of Jerusalem, a decree which removed them from diocesan supervision, in particular the bishop of Acre.[71]

---

[66]The key pontificate is that of Innocent III, particularly notable for the pope's efforts to lift canonical restrictions on crusading; see James Brundage, *Medieval Canon Law and the Crusader* (Madison, Wisconsin, 1969), pp. 114–115. The efforts of Innocent III and Honorius III to find new sources of income for the crusade are described by James Powell, *Anatomy of a Crusade, 1213–1221* (Philadelphia, 1986), pp. 89–106.

[67]*Reg. Grég. IX*, Vol. 1, no. 1708, p. 942.

[68]*Reg. Inn. IV*, Vol. 1, no. 3156, pp. 476 477. For the Templars, see Henry Charles Lea, "The Absolution Formula of the Templars," in *Minor Historical Writings and Other Essays by Henry Charles Lea*, ed. Arthur C. Howland (London, 1942), pp. 97–112.

[69]*Reg. Alex. IV*, Vol. 1, no. 404, p. 122. In this case papal help took the form of the grant of the right of advowson over the church of Galby in Lincolnshire.

[70]*Reg. Alex. IV*, Vol. 2, no. 2340, p. 722 (indulgence), no. 2341, pp. 722–723 (confiscations, redemptions).

[71]*Les Registres d'Urbain IV*, ed. Jean Guiraud, *BEFAR*, ser. 2, Vol. 2 (Paris, 1901), no. 157, p. 61.

XIII

However, in many ways the most interesting initiatives taken by the papacy were those of Clement IV during his short pontificate between 1265 and 1268. One of the reasons for papal intervention on the order's behalf at this time may have been the need to counter a growth in clerical and public hostility, itself possibly a side effect of increased western discontent with the effectiveness of the military orders in general.[72] Clement's bull of April 27, 1265, right at the beginning of his pontificate, seems to have been intended as a summary of the privileges which the Order of Saint Lazarus had received in the course of the thirteenth century, which the pope desired to see reconfirmed and reinforced. The bull was addressed to all clergy from the level of archpriest upwards, many of whom, if the pope's perception was correct, seem to have been less than assiduous in defending the order's rights. The brothers of Saint Lazarus had, Clement says, been granted the right to enter churches once a year to collect alms by Pope Innocent (it is not clear whether Innocent III or Innocent IV is meant), but "certain of you, inflamed with the heat of avarice," had chosen to favor their own communities on the appointed day, and the brothers had been left with little or nothing. The pope, therefore, demanded that the clergy "receive them kindly and treat them honorably," particularly as they (the clergy) had daily access to their communities, whereas the Saint Lazarus brothers were able to do this only once a year. Moreover, it seems too that the order's houses had been pillaged and that the brothers had been forced to have recourse to the papacy in an attempt to gain redress. Clement evidently did not consider that the order had received sufficient support in these circumstances, and the clergy were ordered to ensure that the brothers' rights were defended and maintained. The order had been oppressed in other ways too: potential recruits had been impeded from joining; the brothers had been charged for burials contrary to conciliar decrees; tithes had been demanded despite papal exemption on all crops and animals produced by the brothers or at their expense; clerics had refused to dedicate oratories of the order; and they had on the one hand made little effort to apprehend apostates from the order while at the same time impeding priests who wished to join for short-term service of one or two years. Perhaps most controversially the pope insisted upon the special rights of the brothers in areas under interdict, allowing them to bury their dead and to send in their collectors, on whose arrival the churches were to be opened once annually and the divine

[72]See Joshua Prawer, "Military Orders and Crusader Politics in the Second Half of the XIIIth century," in *Die geistlichen Ritterorden Europas*, ed. Josef Fleckenstein and Manfred Hellmann (Sigmaringen, 1980), pp. 217–229.

office celebrated, two privileges which had been a constant source of friction between the secular clergy and the Hospital and Temple since the mid-twelfth century.[73]

This striking reaffirmation of the order's rights was evidently designed as a preliminary to Clement's bull of the following August, by which he apparently intended that all the lepers of western Christendom should be gathered together under the protection and governance of the Order of Saint Lazarus. This was justified in that it accorded with God's command expressed in the law of Moses that "all lepers should be expelled beyond the walls" (*eiiciantur extra castra*). Surprising as this seems at first sight, it was in fact consistent with the contemporary trend of rationalizing piecemeal provision for the sick, so that individual houses were grouped under specialized hospitaller orders.[74] There is no evidence that either the papacy or the order was ever able to turn this decree into reality, both because of the extreme practical difficulties and because of the opposition which it must have provoked,[75] especially from the episcopacy to whom the guard and inspection of leper houses usually appertained, but it does suggest continuing papal support for crusading institutions during a period when the Mamluk advance looked increasingly ominous.

The papal bulls do, as well, raise one final consideration, that of the status of the order in Christian society as a whole. When looking at the donations of the Jerusalem nobility in the twelfth century, or the stream of papal privileges in the thirteenth, it is easy to forget that the order was in essence an association of lepers. They were, moreover, not simply the recipients of the charity of outsiders nor a means of salvation for the healthy brothers and sisters who might take care of them, as in the typical leper house in the West, but lepers who to a considerable degree ran their own affairs. Yet many texts could be cited to show that leprosy was regarded with horror and that the word itself was a means of opprobrium. Two such examples from the *Ecclesiastical History* of Orderic Vitalis illustrate this point. In one place, referring to the death of Pope Gregory VII in 1085, he describes how, "Lepers begged for the water in which his body had been washed,

[73]*Bullarium Diplomatum*, Vol. 3, no. IV, pp. 727–729.

[74]*Ibid.*, no. VII, pp. 742–743.

[75]An attempt by Charles of Anjou to enforce the decree in the Kingdom of Sicily between 1268 and 1272 met with determined opposition. See *I registri della cancelleria angioina*, Vol. 2, ed. Ricardo Filangieri (Naples, 1951), no. 234, pp. 65–66; vol. 7, no. 29, pp. 274–275; vol. 8, no. 105, p. 110.

and on obtaining it washed in it with faith, and by God's grace were instantly cleansed." In another, he quotes from a sermon by Fulchred, a monk of the abbey of Gloucester, who, speaking of conditions under William Rufus, said that, "Her [England's] whole body is spotted with the leprosy of villany . . . ," making a strong association with decay and sin.[76] John of Salisbury, describing the leprosy of the illegitimate son of Ralph of Vermandois, presents it as a punishment for the sins of the father.[77] Oliver of Paderborn, the chronicler of the Fifth Crusade, writing a century later, is more mystical, when he describes the apostasy of a certain Christian as "a leprosy in his soul," an idea which is characteristic of ecclesiastical interpretation during this period.[78]

As a consequence, Shulamith Shahar argues that the eastern and western parts of Christendom displayed contrasting attitudes toward leprosy. She calls the brothers of Saint Lazarus, "lepers like no others," and points to the sympathy shown by William of Tyre toward the affliction of the young King of Jerusalem, Baldwin IV. The archbishop said that he found it "impossible to refrain from tears while speaking of this great misfortune."[79] The fact was that leprosy was a much more central problem in the society of Latin settlers in the East than it was in the West, despite the thirteenth-century fashion for founding leper houses. Leprosy tends to run in families, since it is often contracted by close physical proximity over a long period of time,[80] and the

[76]Orderic Vitalis, *Ecclesiastical History*, Vol. 4, ed. and tr. Marjorie Chibnall (Oxford, 1973), bk. VIII, pp. 166–167; vol. 5, 1975, bk. X, pp. 286–287.

[77]John of Salisbury, *Historia Pontificalis*, ed. and tr. Marjorie Chibnall (London, 1956), p. 14.

[78]Oliver of Paderborn, *Historia Damiatina*, ed. Hermann Hoogweg, *Die Schriften des Kölner Domscholasters*, in *Bibliothek des Litterarischen Vereins in Stuttgart*, Vol. 202 (Tübingen, 1894), cap. 22, p. 200. Leprosy could be seen as a symbol of sin, and sin cut a man off from the Church, which was what the Christian apostate in Egypt had done to himself. For the context, see Saul N. Brody, *The Disease of the Soul. Leprosy in Medieval Literature* (Ithaca, New York, and London, 1974), esp. pp. 132–146. Comparison can be made with attitudes toward leprosy in contemporary Islam; see Michael W. Dols, "The Leper in Medieval Islamic Society," *Speculum*, 58 (1983), 891–916. In Muslim society the approach seems more practical than moralistic. It would be interesting to know whether the Western settlers in the East had been influenced by Islamic practice.

[79]Shahar, *loc. cit.* William of Tyre's view does, however, reflect a certain amount of special pleading, since he was trying to show that Baldwin IV was a suitable king. Moreover, he felt a personal affection for him, having been his tutor when he was a boy. See Peter W. Edbury and John G. Rowe, *William of Tyre, Historian of the Latin East* (Cambridge, 1988), pp. 61–65.

[80]See *The New Encyclopaedia Britannica, Micropaedia*, Vol. 7, p. 287, and Robert

# XIII

families of Outremer knew very well that this could happen to any of them. However, the contrast between the East and West can be made too sharp. In both areas they might be segregated into special houses or into a particular order, but equally they do appear independent of any institution, taking part in everyday activities and moving about the countryside. The alleged lepers' plot of 1321 would not have been possible even in people's imaginations had not the leper on the roads of France been a common sight.[81] Therefore, despite the papal recognition of the equality of Saint Lazarus with the three leading military orders, Joinville described the master of Saint Lazarus as "a man who held no rank in the host, but who could do as he wished," a situation which led to the disastrous foray near Ramla in 1252, since "he went without speaking to the king."[82] Similar independence by the Templars at about the same time provoked the king into imposing a dramatic and humiliating display of public penitence upon the master. Equally, in the West, favorable interpretations of leprosy were common: the researches of Léon Le Grand on the statutes of hospitals and leper houses in France, published at the beginning of this century, show the leper as "chosen of God" rather than as a Levitical outcast, while Orderic Vitalis could also interpret it as a means provided by God for the purging of past sins.[83] There is, therefore, an ambiguity about attitudes toward lepers which runs through the whole of their history in the Middle Ages: sympathy for the lepers' plight was not exclusive to the East, nor segregation stemming from biblical precept and physical repulsion found only in the West.

---

I. Moore, *The Formation of a Persecuting Society. Power and Deviance in Western Europe, 950–1250* (Oxford, 1987), p. 73.

[81]See Malcolm Barber, "Lepers, Jews and Moslems: The Plot to Overthrow Christendom in 1321," *History*, 66 (1981), 1–17.

[82]Joinville, para. 540, pp. 296–297.

[83]See *Statuts d'Hôtels-Dieu et de Léproseries. Recueil de textes du XII<sup>e</sup> au XIV<sup>e</sup> siècle*, ed. Léon Le Grand (Paris, 1901), pp. xxvi–xxvii; Orderic Vitalis, Vol. 2 (Oxford, 1969), pp. 28–29.

# ADDENDA

No major changes have been made to the articles but, where possible, the opportunity has been taken to correct minor slips and proof-reading errors. Matters of interpretative substance are discussed below. As might be expected, the oldest articles are the ones most in need of revision, particularly in the light of the great growth in crusading studies since the early 1970s.

I. In 1974 Marie-Luise Bulst-Thiele published an impressively comprehensive study of the masters of the Temple, *Sacrae Domus Militiae Templi Hierosolymitani: Untersuchungen zur Geschichte des Templeordens 1118/9-1314*, Göttingen, which contains analyses of the careers of both Hugh of Payns and James of Molay.

My view of these events has, to some extent, changed since this article was written. In particular, the chronology has been modified by the work of Rudolf Hiestand in two important articles: 'Chronologisches zur Geschichte des Königreiches Jerusalem um 1130', *Deutsches Archiv*, 26 (1970), 220-9, and 'Kardinal Matthäus von Albano, das Konzil von Troyes und die Entstehung des Templeordens', *Zeitschrift für Kirchengeschichte*, 99 (1988), 295-325. In the latter he convincingly argues that the Council of Troyes should be placed in 1129. Thus it represents the climax of Hugh of Payns' European tour, rather than the beginning. As Hiestand suggests, D'Albon apparently believed this too, as he dated the donation of Raoul the Fat and his wife made *ante Trecas*, in the presence of five Templars - as *c.* January, 1129. Three of these Templars - Hugh of Payns, Godfrey of St Omer and Payen of Montdidier, are recorded as having attended the Council. My footnote on p.234, n.84, therefore reflects the triumph of conventional wisdom over logical thought, and is certainly wrong.

It is also interesting to note that the other two Templars listed in Raoul's charter are called Ralph and John, and are not the same as the two additional Templars present at Troyes, a circumstance which suggests either that Ralph and John were recruits to the Order acquired during the perambulations of the previous year, or that Hugh brought more than four companions with him from the east in 1127-28. If the latter supposition is correct, it reinforces the view that the Templars in the east numbered considerably more than the nine claimed by William of Tyre in his later account of the Order's origins.

The motivation behind the visit of Hugh of Payns to the West has recently been the subject of a study by Jonathan Phillips, 'Hugh of Payns and the 1129 Damascus Crusade', in *The Military Orders. Fighting for the Faith and Caring for the Sick*, ed. M. Barber, Aldershot, 1994, pp.141-7. While this article does not contradict the points on pp.225-9, it adds considerably to our understanding of the motivations of the principal participants. For the overall context, see my *The New Knighthood. A History of the Order of the Temple*, Cambridge, 1994, chapter 1.


**II.** The circumstances within which Molay was obliged to operate have been the subject of intensive study during the 1980s. Much of this work has emphasised the continuing importance of the crusade to western Christendom and has drawn attention to the effort put into plans for mounting a new expedition to recover the lands lost in 1291 and to the connected issue of the reform of the military orders. My comments on pages 96-7 in particular should now be viewed in the light of this work. Notable contributions to the discussion are Alan J. Forey, 'The Military Orders in the Crusading Proposals of the Late-Thirteenth and Early Fourteenth Centuries', *Traditio*, 36 (1980), 317-45; Christopher J. Tyerman, 'Sed Nihil Fecit? The Last Capetians and the Recovery of the Holy Land', in *War and Government in the Middle Ages*, ed. John Gillingham and James C. Holt, Woodbridge, 1984, pp.170-81; Sylvia Schein, *Fidelis Crucis. The Papacy, the West and the Recovery of the Holy Land 1274-1314*, Oxford, 1991; and Norman Housley, *The Later Crusades. From Lyons to Alcazar, 1274-1580*, Oxford, 1992.

The Cypriot scene has now been authoritatively interpreted by Peter Edbury, *The Kingdom of Cyprus and the Crusades 1191-1374*, Cambridge, 1991. Pages 102-3 should therefore now be seen within the framework of this book.

The interpretation of the bull *Omne datum optimum* given on p.107 is too sweeping. It has been shown by Jonathan Riley-Smith that the Templars continued to accept the jurisdiction of the Patriarch of Jerusalem for some time after this, and that the bull did not immediately transform the juridical position of the Order. See 'The Templars and the Castle of Tortosa in Syria: An Unknown Document Concerning the Acquisition of the Fortress', *English Historical Review*, 84 (1969), 278-88.

3

**III.** The subject of Catharism continues to arouse intense interest among French historians. There is now a sensitive full-length study of Cathar women by Anne Brenon, *Les Femmes Cathares*, Paris, 1992. Her sympathies clearly lie with the Cathars, but this does not prevent her giving a detailed and convincing picture of the role of women, largely based on a careful study of the inquisitorial records. Outside France the Cathars attract relatively little interest, but one exception is the study by F. Abels and E. Harrison, 'The Participation of Women in Languedocian Catharism', *Medieval Studies*, 41, 1979, 215-51.

**IV.** F. Beriac has since looked at this attack on the lepers in a specific region, 'La persécution des lépreux dans la France méridionale en 1321', *Le Moyen Age*, 93 (1987), 203-21.

**VII.** The enigmatic figure of Philip the Fair remains difficult to fathom. It is still unclear whether the pronouncements of his government emanated from the king or from his lawyers and advisers, who had been schooled in the methods of thought favoured by the universities of the late thirteenth century. Two of the most interesting contributors to the debate about his character and motivation are Robert-Henri Bautier, 'Diplomatique et histoire politique: ce que la critique diplomatique nous apprend sur la personnalité de Philippe le Bel', *Revue Historique*, 259 (1978), 3-27, and Elizabeth A. R. Brown, '"The Prince is Father of the King: The Character and Childhood of Philip the Fair of France', *Medieval Studies*, 49 (1987), 282-334, and 'Persona et Gesta: The Image and Deeds of the Thirteenth-Century Capetians. - 3.The Case of Philip the Fair', *Viator*, 19 (1988), 219-46, with bibliography of other recent work on Philip.

**IX.** In addition to the points on p.2, see Gary Dickson, 'The Advent of the *Pastores* (1251)', *Revue Belge de Philologie et d'Histoire*, 66 (1988), 249-67, where he pins down the chronology and geographical origins of the movement more precisely.

**X.** The belief that crusades and crusading went into decline during the thirteenth century has been vigorously challenged in recent crusade historiography. Apart from Housley above, see Elizabeth Siberry, *Criticism* *of Crusading 1095-1274*, Oxford, 1985. From this work has emerged a more nuanced picture. However, enthusiasm for Latin Greece in the thirteenth century does seem to have been largely confined to special interest groups.


**XII.** Regional studies of the Templars would provide more detailed figures for both preceptories and manpower. Another approach is through the information contained in the depositions of the Templars during their trial, as in Anne Gilmour-Bryson, 'Age-Related Data from the Templar Trials', in *Aging and the Aged in Medieval Europe*, ed. Michael M. Sheehan, Toronto, 1990, pp.129-42, and Alan J. Forey, 'Towards a Profile of the Templars in the Early Fourteenth Century', in *The Military Orders. Fighting for the Faith and Caring for the Sick*, pp. 196-204.

# INDEX

3

4

9

V 155
Guillaume de Nangis, chronicler: IX 2,
5–6, 9, 12, 14, 18 n.8, 21 n.40
Guillaume de Niort: III 47
Guillaume de Nogaret, Keeper of the
Seals in France: II 101, 116, 120
Guillaume Normand, leper of Estang:
IV 6–7, 9
Guillaume Pagès, Cathar *perfectus*:
XI 19
Guillaume de Paris, Papal Inquisitor in
France: II 110; VI 215; VII 14
Guillaume Pierre, knight, donor to the
Temple, later Templar: VIII 40
Guillaume de Plaisians, minister of
Philip IV of France: II 109, 113,
116, 118; VII 14–16, 18–23, 25;
VIII 43–4
Guillaume de Puylaurens, chronicler:
III 53; XI 11, 12
Guillaume de Rabat, Cathar believer:
III 54
Guillaume Salamon, Cathar deacon at
Toulouse: III 50
Guillaume de Tudela, chronicler: XI 3,
5, 8, 10, 16
Guillaume-Roger de Mirepoix: III 47
Guillelme, daughter of Bernard Faber de
Caragodas, Cathar *perfecta*: III 55
Guillelme de Tonneins, Cathar *perfecta*:
III 47
Guiot de l'Aubépin, canon of Mâcon:
IV 9
Guiraud Abith, Cathar Bishop of
Carcassone: XI 14–15
Guiraude de Lavaur, Cathar believer:
III 47
Gunther of Pairis, Cistercian chronicler:
VI 207–8
Guy Dauphin, Templar knight: II 110
Guy of Foresta, Master of the Temple in
England: II 93, 96
Guy of Ibelin, titular Count of Jaffa:
II 99
Guy of Payns: I 222
Guy des Vaux-de-Cernay, Bishop of
Carcassonne: III 46
Guy of Vignory: I 221

Hainault: IX 2; X 125
Hama: I 219
Hamerin, Constable of Cyprus: II 102
Hattin, battle of (1187): VI 222 n.51;
X 116; XII 315, 318; XIII 449
Haute-Provence: I 222
Hebron: I 220; XIII 442
Heliazer, *scriptor* of Salamon de Vudas:
V 150
Hélis de Mazerolles, Cathar believer:
III 47, 48, 54
Henri de Mondeville, physician: IV 13,
15
Henri de Sully, Royal Butler: V 161
Henry II, King of Cyprus and
Jerusalem: II 97–8, 102–3
Henry Bolingbroke, Duke of Hereford:
VI 13
Henry I, King of England: I 235
Henry III, King of England: IX 6, 17
n.1; X 123–4
Henry of Hainault, Latin Emperor of
Romania: X 113, 122
Henry Sanglier, Archbishop of Sens:
I 229
heretics, heresy: II 110, 114, 116, 118,
120–21; III 45–58; IV 8, 11, 14,
16–17; V 150, 153; VI 207–8,
213–15, 217; VII 14–26; VIII 35,
44 n.53; IX 9–10, 15, 17; X 114;
XI 1–19; *see also* Cathars
Hervey of Donzi, Count of Nevers: XI 3
Hetoum II, King of Cilician Armenia:
II 98
Hildebert, Archbishop of Tours: I 234
Hilduin of Villemar: I 221
Hilton, Rodney, historian: IX 1–2, 16
Hohenstaufen: IX 12; X 125
Holy Lance: IX 13
Holy Land: I 222; II 94, 99–100,
103–6, 108; V 144, 146, 148,
159–60, 165; VI 208–9; VIII 41,
44; IX 2, 6–7, 12–13; X 113–17,
120–1; X 122, 122; XII 320;
XIII 448
Holy Sepulchre, canons of: I 236
homosexuality: II 110, 120, 122–3
Homs: I 219; II 97
Honorius II, Pope: I 230

12

13

Low Countries: IX 1–2, 16, 23 n.66
Luke, St, Gospel of: V 162; VIII 34;
    XI 12
Lyons: II 108; IV 6, 12; V 160
    Council of (1245): X 123
    Council of (1274): II 92, 94, 105;
        X 118, 121

Mabille de Laurac, Cathar *perfecta*:
    III 47
McNeal, Edgar H., historian: VI 207
Mâcon: IV 6, 9
Macrobius: VII 17
magic: IV 11 n.36, 15–16; IX 11–12, 15
Magna Mahumeria (Kingdom of
    Jerusalem): XIII 444 n.29
Magnou, Elisabeth, historian: VIII 41,
    43
Mahaut d'Artois, trial of: IV 11 n.36
Mairano brothers, of Venice: XII 324
Majorca: II 113
Mamluks: IV 17; XIII 454
Manfred, King of Sicily: X 120, 125
Manfredonia: II 95; XII 325
Manrique, A., historian: I 228
Maraclea: II 98
Marc Rivel, deputy to Jacques Fournier:
    IV 6
Marcellina, Cathar *perfecta*: XI 15
Marches of Treviso and Lombardy,
    chronicle of: X 119
Maria, *domina* of Beirut: XIII 442
Maria, widow of Hugues, Cathar
    believer: III 51
Maria, titular Countess of Jaffa: II 99
Marino Sanudo Torsello: II 104; IX 21
    n.36; X 121, 125; XIII 447 n.43
Mark, St, Gospel of: VII 24
Marmande (Lot-et-Garonne): XI 18
Marmoutier, Abbey of: I 234
'Marmoutier, Abbot of': IV 10
Marquèse, wife of Bertrand de Prouille:
    III 45
Marquèse de Lanta, Cathar *perfecta*:
    III 54
Marquèse de Mirepoix, Cathar believer:
    III 47
Marseilles: I 236; V 146, 158; IX 5;
    X 123; XII 317, 322, 324, 325

n.44, 326
*Viguier* of: IX 5
Martin IV, Pope: X 118
Martin, Abbot of Pairis: VI 208–9
Martino da Canal, chronicler: X 119,
    123, 125
Mary, The Blessed Virgin: VI 223;
    IX 2–4, 6–7, 15
Masada: V 156
Massabrac (Haute-Garonne), family of:
    III 54
Mas-Saintes-Puelles (Aude): III 53
    family of: III 54
'Master of Hungary': *see* Jacob
Masters of Theology at the University of
    Paris: VII 14–15, 18–20, 22;
    VIII 46; IX 10; X 112–13
Mathieu Ermengaud, notary of Lézat:
    V 153
Matilda of England, Empress: I 235
Matthew, St, Gospel of: VII 24
Matthew Paris, chronicler of St Albans:
    II, 107; IV 17; IX 1, 3–8, 10, 12,
    15–16, 17 n.1, 21 n.37, 41, 43 and
    44; X 124–5; XII 314–15; XIII 449
Matthew du Remois, Cardinal-Bishop of
    Albano: I 229–30
Mazères (Ariège): V 152
    leper house: IV 7
Mazerolles, family of: III 47
Meaux, Diocese of: VI 214
medicine: III 49
Meline de Prades, Cathar *perfecta*:
    III 48
Melisende, Queen of Jerusalem:
    XIII 440, 442, 444
Melville, Marion, historian: I 229; II 107
Messina: XII 324, 325
Michael VIII Palaeologus, Byzantine
    Emperor: X 111, 115–16, 118–20,
    122
Miles, Count of Bar-sur-Seine: I 221
*Milicia Dei* (1145), papal bull:
    XII 321–2
military orders: III 53; VIII 38 n.33, 44
    n.53; XII 315–16, 322, 324;
    XIII 452
    union of: II 94–5, 103, 105–7; VIII 43
    n.52

T - #0018 - 230922 - C0 - 224/150/16 [18] - CB - 9780860784760 - Gloss Lamination